THE EUROPEAN UNION

General Editors: Neill Nugent, William E. Paters...

The European Union series provides an authoritative library
from general introductory texts to definitive assessments of
policies and policy processes, and the role of member states.

Books in the series are written by leading scholars in their fields and reflect the most up-to-date research and debate. Particular attention is paid to accessibility and clear presentation for a wide audience of students, practitioners and interested general readers.

The series editors are **Neill Nugent**, Professor of Politics and Jean Monnet Professor of European Integration, Manchester Metropolitan University, and **William E. Paterson**, Founding Director of the Institute of German Studies, University of Birmingham, and Chairman of the German British Forum. Their co-editor until his death in July 1999, **Vincent Wright**, was a Fellow of Nuffield College, Oxford University.

Feedback on the series and book proposals are always welcome and should be sent to Steven Kennedy, Palgrave Macmillan, Houndmills, Basingstoke, Hampshire RG21 6XS, UK, or by e-mail to s.kennedy@palgrave.com

---

General textbooks

Published

Desmond Dinan **Encyclopedia of the European Union**
[Rights: Europe only]
Desmond Dinan **Europe Recast: A History of European Union**
[Rights: Europe only]
Desmond Dinan **Ever Closer Union: An Introduction to European Integration (3rd edn)**
[Rights: Europe only]
Mette Eilstrup Sangiovanni (ed.) **Debates on European Integration: A Reader**
Simon Hix **The Political System of the European Union (2nd edn)**
Paul Magnette **What is the European Union? Nature and Prospects**
John McCormick **Understanding the European Union: A Concise Introduction (4th edn)**
Brent F. Nelsen and Alexander Stubb **The European Union: Readings on the Theory and Practice of European Integration (3rd edn)**
[Rights: Europe only]

Neill Nugent (ed.) **European Union Enlargement**
Neill Nugent **The Government and Politics of the European Union (6th edn)**
[Rights: World excluding USA and dependencies and Canada]
John Peterson and Elizabeth Bomberg **Decision-Making in the European Union**
Ben Rosamond **Theories of European Integration**

Forthcoming

Laurie Buonanno and Neill Nugent **Policies and Policy Processes of the European Union**
David Howarth **The Political Economy of European Integration**
Philippa Sherrington **Understanding European Union Governance**

Series Standing Order (outside North America only)
ISBN 0–333–71695–7 hardback
ISBN 0–333–69352–3 paperback
Full details from www.palgrave.com

Visit Palgrave Macmillan's
EU Resource area at
www.palgrave.com/politics/eu/

The major institutions and actors

Published

Renaud Dehousse **The European Court of Justice**

Justin Greenwood **Interest Representation in the European Union (2nd edn)**

Fiona Hayes-Renshaw and Helen Wallace **The Council of Ministers (2nd edn)**

Simon Hix and Christopher Lord **Political Parties in the European Union**

David Judge and David Earnshaw **The European Parliament (2nd edn)**

Neill Nugent **The European Commission**

Anne Stevens with Handley Stevens **Brussels Bureaucrats? The Administration of the European Union**

Forthcoming

Wolfgang Wessels **The European Council**

The main areas of policy

Published

Michelle Cini and Lee McGowan **Competition Policy in the European Union (2nd edn)**

Wyn Grant **The Common Agricultural Policy**

Martin Holland **The European Union and the Third World**

Jolyon Howorth **Security and Defence Policy in the European Union**

Stephan Keukeleire and Jennifer MacNaughtan **The Foreign Policy of the European Union**

Brigid Laffan **The Finances of the European Union**

Malcolm Levitt and Christopher Lord **The Political Economy of Monetary Union**

Janne Haaland Matláry **Energy Policy in the European Union**

John McCormick **Environmental Policy in the European Union**

John Peterson and Margaret Sharp **Technology Policy in the European Union**

Handley Stevens **Transport Policy in the European Union**

Forthcoming

Michelle Chang **Monetary Integration in the European Union**

Johanna Kantola **Gender and the European Union**

Bart Kerremans, David Allen and Geoffrey Edwards **The External Economic Relations of the European Union**

Jörg Monar **Justice and Home Affairs in the European Union**

John Vogler, Richard Whitman and Charlotte Bretherton **The External Policies of the European Union**

Also planned

Political Union

Social Policy in the European Union

The member states and the Union

Published

Carlos Closa and Paul Heywood **Spain and the European Union**

Alain Guyomarch, Howard Machin and Ella Ritchie **France in the European Union**

Brigid Laffan and Jane O'Mahony **Ireland and the European Union**

Forthcoming

Simon Bulmer and William E. Paterson **Germany and the European Union**

Phil Daniels and Ella Ritchie **Britain and the European Union**

Brigid Laffan **The European Union and its Member States**

Luisa Perrotti **Italy and the European Union**

Baldur Thorhallson **Small States in the European Union**

Issues

Published

Derek Beach **The Dynamics of European Integration: Why and When EU Institutions Matter**

Steven McGuire and Michael Smith **The United States and the European Union**

Forthcoming

Thomas Christiansen and Christine Reh **Constitutionalizing the European Union**

Robert Ladrech **Europeanization and National Politics**

Ireland and the European Union

Brigid Laffan
and
Jane O'Mahony

palgrave
macmillan

First published 2008 by
PALGRAVE MACMILLAN

Palgrave Macmillan in the UK is an imprint of Macmillan Publishers Limited, registered in England, company number 785998, of Houndmills, Basingstoke, Hampshire RG21 6XS.

Palgrave Macmillan in the US is a division of St Martin's Press LLC, 175 Fifth Avenue, New York, NY 10010.

Palgrave Macmillan is the global academic imprint of the above companies and has companies and representatives throughout the world.

Palgrave® and Macmillan® are registered trademarks in the United States, the United Kingdom, Europe and other countries.

ISBN-13: 978—1—4039—4927—1   hardback
ISBN-10: 1—4039—4927—1   hardback
ISBN-13: 978—1—4039—4928—8   paperback
ISBN-10: 1—4039—4928—X   paperback

This book is printed on paper suitable for recycling and made from fully managed and sustained forest sources. Logging, pulping and manufacturing processes are expected to conform to the environmental regulations of the country of origin.

A catalogue record for this book is available from the British Library.

A catalog record for this book is available from the Library of Congress.

10   9   8   7   6   5   4   3   2   1
17   16   15   14   13   12   11   10   09   08

Printed and bound in China

For Joe and Betty O'Mahony

Contents

List of Boxes, Figures and Tables	x
Acknowledgements	xii
Preface	xiii
List of Abbreviations	xv
Glossary of Irish Terms	xviii
Introduction	**1**
1 Becoming a Member State	**6**
Introduction	6
Establishing and consolidating independence	8
Choosing Europe	12
Applying for membership	19
Preparing for membership	22
Negotiating membership	23
Legitimizing membership	26
Conclusions	28
2 Ireland's EU Experience	**30**
1973–86: learning to live within the European system	35
1987–97: the emergence of the Celtic Tiger	42
1998 and beyond: a new Ireland living in the new EU	48
A different relationship	54
3 Managing Europe	**56**
Executive adaptation to EU membership – framing the analysis	57
Managing EU issues in Ireland: origins and development	60
Dissecting the system	62
The Holy Trinity: Departments of Foreign Affairs, the Taoiseach and Finance	64
The inner core and outer circle	67
Horizontal structures	68
The permanent representation	71
Processes	72

Information pathways   73
Executive–parliamentary relations   76
The balance sheet   79

4 **Parties and Parliament**   **81**
Irish political parties and the EU   83
European Parliament elections in Ireland: second-order?   93
Voting on Europe   104

5 **Referendums and Public Opinion**   **105**
EU referendums in Ireland   107
Irish attitudes to European integration   122
The National Forum on Europe   130

6 **Multi-level Governance and Territorial Politics**   **132**
Multi-level governance   132
Territorial organization in Ireland   134
Brussels money   138
Agenda 2000   144
European regulation   147
Over there in Brussels   147
Conclusions   148

7 **The EU and Irish Public Policy**   **151**
Ireland and European economic governance   154
Irish agriculture and the CAP   160
Protecting Ireland's environment?   164
Out on a limb? Ireland and EU Justice and
   Home Affairs policy   170

8 **Irish Foreign Policy in the EU**   **175**
From isolation to interdependence?   178
New horizons – Ireland and European political
   cooperation   180
After 1989 – Ireland's new security choices   184
Towards a common European defence? Ireland's
   ongoing security dilemma   189
Irish foreign policy into the future   195

9 **British–Irish Relations: The European Dimension**   **197**
Introduction   197
Membership of the European Union   198

Managing the conflict   201
EU involvement in Northern Ireland   202
The Good Friday Agreement   213
Conclusions   216

10 **Ireland as a Model?**   **219**
Model I: what not to do   222
Model II: economic catch-up   224
Model III: conflict resolution and development
  cooperation   236
Challenges   237
Conclusions   241

11 **Ireland: A Small State in a Large Union**   **243**
Ireland: a small state in the Union   244
Just how Europeanized?   253
What this 'Union' has meant to Ireland   256
What the Irish experience tells us about the EU   263

Further Reading   265
Bibliography   267
Index   290

List of Boxes, Figures and Tables

Boxes

2.1 Ireland Inc at the helm: Irish EU presidencies   40
2.2 Ireland's contribution to the EU   52
5.1 Dissenting voices in EU referendums   110

Figures

3.1 The Irish core executive   63
3.2 Central committees for the organization of
     cross-cutting EU issues (including *ad hoc* committees) 70
3.3 Number of documents considered by the EU scrutiny
     sub-committee by year   78
3.4 Breakdown of proposals/documents received by
     the EU scrutiny sub-committee from each government
     department during 2006   79
4.1 Turnout in Irish general and EP elections, 1977–2007   97
4.2 Turnout in European Parliament elections   97
4.3 Party share of votes in national and EP elections,
     1977–2007   98
5.1 European referendums in Ireland: Yes, No and
     abstention as proportions of the electorate   114
5.2 Percentages of respondents that feel country has
     (1) benefited from EU membership (Ireland),
     and that (2) EU membership is a good thing
     (Ireland and 25 member states)   124
5.3 Respondents who feel membership of the EU is
     a good thing   125
5.4 Respondents across member states who feel they
     have benefited from EU membership   125
7.1 The EU's policy types   153
7.2 Employment in agriculture, forestry and fishing as
     % of total employment, 1973–2005   162
7.3 Number of open environment infringements,
     EU15 2005   167

11.1   Population of EU27, 2007   245
11.2   EU27 GDP per capita in purchasing power
       standards, 2007   246
11.3   EU27 member states by area   246

Tables

1.1   Key dates: Ireland's road to Europe   17
2.1   Key dates in Ireland's membership of the
       European Economic Community/European Union   34
2.2   Result of Nice I referendum, 7 June 2001   49
3.1   Department of Foreign Affairs staffing   65
3.2   EU committees in the Irish system   69
4.1   Irish MEPs in the 2004–09 European Parliament   94
4.2   Results of EP elections in Ireland, 1979–2004   99
4.3   Comparison of 1989 European Parliament and
       Dáil elections   100
4.4   Comparison of 2004 European Parliament and
       2002 Dáil elections, percentage, shares of the vote   100
5.1   European referendum results, 1972–2008   108
5.2   Results of 2001, 2002 and 2008 referendums   119
5.3   Reasons for voting No in first and second Nice
       referendums   119
5.4   Reasons for voting No in Lisbon referendum   120
5.5   Respondents' attitudes towards Ireland's
       membership of the EU by demographic groupings   126
6.1   Local government organization   135
7.1   EU receipts to Ireland, 1973–2004   161
7.2   Cases before the ECJ, 1998–2006,
       relating to Ireland   167
7.3   Open infringement proceedings against Ireland in
       the field of environment, as of 31 December 2005   168
8.1   Irish army overseas operations, as of 1 October 2007   192
8.2   Irish forces overseas operations in Europe   193
9.1   Results of European elections in Northern Ireland,
       1979–2004   205
9.2   Phases of Interreg   209
9.3   Northern Ireland peace funds   212
9.4   Northern Ireland Assembly elections   216
10.1   The A.T. Kearney *Foreign Affairs* globalization index   220

Acknowledgements

The authors and publishers would like to thank the following for their kind permission to reproduce copyright material: Manchester University Press for Table 2.1; Blackwell Publishing Ltd for Figures 3.1 and 3.2 and Table 3.2; Taylor & Francis for Table 7.2. Tables 5.3, 5.4, 5.5 and 7.3 and Figures 5.3, 5.4, 7.3, 11.1, 11.2 and 11.3 are European Union copyright. Table 7.1 and Figures 3.3 and 3.4 are copyright of the Government of Ireland. Tables 8.1 and 8.2 are copyright of the Defence Forces.

Preface

This volume was written by two political scientists and therefore reflects that disciplinary emphasis. Throughout this volume, it is clear that there is a complex interaction between the political and the economic and between the domestic and the European. Ireland is an interesting study of the experience of one small peripheral state in the European Union. Ireland's engagement with this Union since 1973 stands in marked contrast to its membership of an earlier Union, the Union of Great Britain and Ireland, which lasted until the foundation of the Irish state in 1922. Joining the EU in 1973 reconnected Ireland to its continental European past. This volume was completed as Ireland celebrated the 400th anniversary of the founding of the Irish College in Louvain, the first of 34 Irish Colleges on the European continent. Today, notwithstanding disagreement about Ireland's European experience, the vast majority of Irish people view membership of the EU as a 'good thing'. Joining its original manifestation, the EEC, offered Ireland an external framework that was more benign than 'going it alone'. The restrictions of membership were preferable to formal sovereignty with economic dependency.

This volume was also completed as Ireland faced the aftermath of a referendum on the European Union's Lisbon Treaty (also known as the Reform Treaty) in June 2008. The referendum was defeated by a decisive margin of 53 per cent against and 46 per cent for, with a turnout of 53 per cent of the electorate. Successive governments effectively positioned Ireland as a committed member state and in turn the EU provided Ireland with a strong anchor in a rapidly changing world. The anchor is now loose of its moorings: Ireland's longstanding consensus on the EU is over. This volume traces the story of Ireland's relationship with the European Union and includes initial analysis of the impact of the referendum (see in particular Chapters 5 and 11). The growth of the 'no' vote in the Lisbon Referendum in June 2008 suggests that the EU and the project of European integration is very much contested in Ireland. Whether this reflects the contingencies of the time or is a deeper shift will only become clearer over time.

On a final note, this volume was written over a three-year period from 2005 to 2008. The authors are indebted to the Palgrave

Macmillan editor Steven Kennedy, whose inspired decision to give responsibility for the completion of the manuscript to Jane meant that it was completed in 2008. We wish to acknowledge the insightful comments of Steven Kennedy, Willie Paterson, Clive Church, Brendan Halligan and Paul Gillespie of the *Irish Times*. The views of two anonymous reviewers were also very helpful and we are grateful to them. The work conducted under the EU Fifth Framework Project, *Organizing for Europe*, coordinated from University College Dublin's Dublin European Institute, contributed to this endeavour. The two authors have enjoyed working on the volume and are aware that there are many dimensions of Ireland's experience in the EU that are ripe for further exploration. We are, of course, responsible for all errors, omissions and debatable judgements.

BRIGID LAFFAN
JANE O'MAHONY

Bloomsday, 16 June 2008

List of Abbreviations

ACP	African, Caribbean and Pacific Countries
Afri	Action from Ireland
ALDE	Alliance of Liberals and Democrats for Europe
BEPG	Broad Economic Policy Guidelines
CAP	Common Agricultural Policy
CFSP	Common Foreign and Security Policy
CFP	Common Fisheries Policy
COR	Committee of the Regions
COREPER	Committee of Permanent Representatives
CSF	Community Support Framework
DDR	Democratic Republic of Germany
DFA	Department of Foreign Affairs
DG	Directorate General
DUP	Democratic Unionist Party
EAGGF	European Agriculture Guidance and Guarantee Fund
EC	European Community
ECB	European Central Bank
ECJ	European Court of Justice
ECSC	European Coal and Steel Community
ECU	European Currency Unit
EEC	European Economic Community
EFTA	European Free Trade Association
ELDR	European Liberal, Democratic and Reformist Party
EMS	European Monetary System
EMU	Economic and Monetary Union
EP	European Parliament
EPA	Environmental Protection Agency
EPP-ED	European People's Party and European Democrats
EPC	European Political Cooperation
ERDF	European Regional Development Fund
ESF	European Social Fund
ESRI	Economic and Social Research Institute
EU	European Union

EUL	European United Left
FDI	Foreign direct investment
FDS	Flexible Development State
FUE	Federated Union of Employers
GAA	Gaelic Athletic Association
GATT	General Agreement on Tariffs and Trade
GDP	Gross domestic product
GNI	Gross national income
GNP	Gross national product
ICTU	Irish Congress of Trade Unions
IDA	Industrial Development Authority
ICMSA	Irish Creamery and Milk Suppliers Association
IFA	Irish Farmers Association
IGC	Intergovernmental Conference
IMF	International Monetary Fund
IPA	Institute of Public Administration
IRO	Irish Regions Office
JHA	Justice and Home Affairs
NATO	North Atlantic Treaty Organization
NDP	National Development Plan
NESC	National Social and Economic Council
NRA	National Regulatory Authority
NSS	National Spatial Strategy
ODTR	Office of the Director of Telecommunications Regulation
OECD	Organisation for Economic Co-operation and Development
OEEC	Organization for European Economic Cooperation
OMC	Open Method of Coordination
PANA	Peace and Neutrality Alliance
PES	European Socialist Party
PfP	Partnership for Peace Programme
QMV	Qualified Majority Voting
RDO	Regional Development Organization
REPS	Rural Environmental Protection Scheme
RTC	Regional Technical College
RTE	Radio Telifis Éireann
SDLP	Social Democratic and Labour Party
SEA	Single European Act
SGP	Stability and Growth Pact

TD	Teachta Dála (Member of the Irish lower house of Parliament – Dáil)
TEU	Treaty on European Union (Maastricht Treaty)
UEN	Union for Europe of the Nations
UN	United Nations
UUP	Ulster Unionist Party
WEU	Western European Union
WTO	World Trade Organization

Glossary of Irish Terms

Bunreacht na hÉireann	The Constitution of Ireland
Dáil (full title *Dáil Éireann*)	Lower house of parliament, directly elected
Fianna Fáil	'Soldiers of Destiny'. Largest political party, founded in 1926
Fine Gael	'League of Gaels'. Successor of Cumann na nGaedheal. Currently second largest political party
Oireachtas	Parliament
Seanad (full title *Seanad Éireann*)	Senate. Upper house of Parliament
Sinn Féin	'We ourselves'. At the time of independence a coalition of separatist groups. Currently a nationalist political party
Tánaiste	Deputy Prime Minister
Taoiseach	Prime Minister
Teachta Dála	Member of the Dáil. Abbreviated to TD

Introduction

The purpose of this volume is to examine the relationship between Ireland and the European Union. What difference has participation in European integration made to Ireland? The decision taken in 1961 to seek membership of the European Economic Community (EEC/EC), the original manifestation of the now European Union (EU), formed part of a new national project for Irish political elites begun in the late 1950s – the economic modernization of Ireland. Since accession in 1973, the Irish story of membership has been, on balance, a positive one. Despite such upsets as the Nice and Lisbon Treaty referendums along the way, European Union membership has allowed Ireland to take her economic and political place amongst the nations of Europe.

Given its subject matter, the key analytical concept underpinning this volume is that of *Europeanization*. Having gained widespread currency amongst political scientists since the late 1990s, Europeanization denotes the impact of participation in European integration processes on EU member states themselves. As a framework for research, it has reflected the trend of scholars working on the EU to switch their focus of attention from the European to the national level and revisit the impact of the EU on the domestic. This is in large part due to the increased salience of the EU as a result of over 15 years of continuous treaty reform and task expansion (beginning with the Single European Act). 'Europe' has hit virtually all policy areas, has added new dimensions to the domestic political arena and has also given rise to institutional change at the national level, most notably in national administrations. As a concept, Europeanization is essentially contested, yet as a research agenda Europeanization connects domestic and European politics and is an extremely useful entry-point for greater understanding of the important changes occurring in Irish politics, economy and society as a result of EU membership (Graziano and Vink, 2006, p. 4; Featherstone, 2003, p. 3; McGowan and Murphy, 2003).

1

The most common interpretation of Europeanization is the top-down 'institutionalist' perspective where the EU is seen to impact on the policies, administrative structures and patterns of intermediation of its member states. Within the top-down perspective, a myriad of definitions of Europeanization exist with little agreement on how to define the term. Keatinge (1984b) was one of the first authors to refer to the 'Europeanization of foreign policy' in his study of how Irish foreign policy had been reoriented as a consequence of European Community entry. The most commonly cited definition describes Europeanization as 'an incremental process re-orienting the direction and shape of politics to the degree that EC political and economic dynamics become part of the organisational logic of national politics and policy-making' (Ladrech, 1994, p. 69). Héritier has defined Europeanization as 'the process of influence deriving from European decisions and impacting member states' policies and political and administrative structures' (Héritier *et al.*, 2001, p. 3). Radaelli defines it in broader terms as consisting of

> processes of (a) construction, (b) diffusion and (c) institutionalisation of formal and informal rules, procedures, policy paradigms, styles, 'ways of doing things', and shared beliefs and norms which are first defined and consolidated in the EU policy process and then incorporated into the logic of domestic (national and sub-national) discourse, political structures, and public policies. (Radaelli, 2003)

These definitional examples illustrate the common tendency amongst political scientists to assess the relative degree of Europeanization across three domains or dimensions of change: policy, politics and polity (Bache and Jordan, 2006; Bulmer and Radaelli, 2005; Börzel and Risse, 2003, 2006). In the literature, the EU is found to impact on the nature and content of domestic public policy (policy), the issues, actors and actions of the domestic political process (politics), and the constitutional and institutional architecture of the system (polity).

Yet Europeanization is more than that; it is also a process of structural change, variously affecting actors and institutions, ideas and interests. Europeanization can represent the strengthening of subnational governance within member states as a result of the EU's economic and social cohesion policies. It can 'represent the restructuring of the strategic opportunities available to domestic actors, as

EU commitments, having a differential impact on such actors, may serve as a source of leverage' (Featherstone, 2003, p. 20). Moreover it encompasses the international positioning of the state in the global economy, as membership of the EU is used as a way of managing globalization. Its impact is typically incremental, irregular and uneven over time and between locations, that is national and subnational (Featherstone, 2003). It can also encompass the projection of member state priorities into the EU. This volume adopts this broader perspective of Europeanization.

It must also be acknowledged, however, that Europeanization on its own is not a stand-alone theory. In order to answer *how* European policies, rules and norms affection domestic political systems, Europeanization scholars have employed, either explicitly or implicitly, the broad spectrum of theories which, according to Graziano and Vink (2006, p. 17) fall 'under the umbrella of the so-called 'new institutionalism'. Using the methodology of process-tracing (the systematic description and analysis of empirical evidence), this volume unpacks the historical context of key decisions, political events and policy adaptations and also illuminates the causal mechanisms through which European integration has mattered for the Irish political system. The adoption of a broad institutionalist perspective helps us isolate the key moments or critical junctures in European and national policy and institutional change and the interaction between the two. Where necessary, our investigations are couched within longer-established meta-theoretical frames, for example historical institutionalism and multilevel governance (as we will see in Chapters 3 and 6 for instance).

Before dissecting how the relationship between Ireland and the European Union has led to changes in the politics, polity and policies of the contemporary Ireland, we examine the path taken towards membership of the EU. Chapter 1 examines the rationale behind the choice for Europe by focusing on the key political and official players. It explores the way in which the Irish state elite opted to use membership of the EU as a way to modernize Ireland. The decision to apply for membership intersected with profound changes in Ireland characterized by industrialization, urbanization and social change. This decision was born out of the failure of the 1950s when the Irish economy and society was trapped in stagnation and social conservatism. Ireland was a poor rural country characterized by high levels of emigration, economic dependence on the United Kingdom and reliance on agricultural exports. In 1958 a decision was taken to open the Irish economy to international market forces and move away from high levels of protectionism. Choosing Europe became part and parcel of Ireland's new national project. Chapter 2 provides an overview of how, once a member, Ireland adapted to the demands of membership over time, tracing the impact of the EU on the Irish economy, society and political system across time as Ireland developed and the EU itself experienced deep change.

Chapter 3 explores the impact of the EU on the Irish polity focusing on a key element of Ireland's political system, the core executive of government and administration. Employing an historical institutionalist framework, we map the formal and informal organizational and procedural devices or structures used to manage EU affairs in Ireland, as well as dissecting the key relationships that govern this management process and the role of the domestic agents actively involved in the EU's governance structure. The chapter also explores the development of the capacity for the management of EU affairs in Ireland over time.

Has Irish politics become Europeanized? Every five years, Irish parliamentary politics takes on a European hue as candidates contest European Parliament (EP) elections. European Parliament elections across the EU have been cast as 'second-order elections', where they become either votes of confidence for the incumbent governments or 'markers' for future domestic electoral competitions. It is posited that those who vote in second-order elections tend to vote in a less strategic manner as these elections do not involve the creation of an executive and thus it is perceived that less is at stake. In Chapter 4, we see that Irish EP elections are clearly second-order elections, in terms of both trends in electoral results and important campaign issues. Irish political parties fight European election contests on national issues and voters decide accordingly.

Chapter 5 continues our investigation into the impact of the EU on Ireland's political arena. We examine Irish attitudes to the EU over time as expressed through referendums and public opinion polls. The case of Ireland is unique in the EU because of the constitutional and legal framework within which referendums are conducted. The 1987 Supreme Court judgement has established a very entrenched norm of holding a referendum on all European treaties. In addition, two landmark cases prescribe the conditions for financing referendums and providing balanced information to the public. Pro- and anti-EU actors in Ireland operate within a context whereby political communication on European matters is carefully regulated. The challenge of referendums on European treaties is analysed in this chapter.

Next we excavate the impact of the EU on domestic policy and policy structures. Looking at territorial politics (Chapter 6), economic governance, agriculture, environment, justice and home affairs (Chapter 7) and foreign policy (Chapter 8), we investigate how the EU has had an impact on key national policies. We show how EU priorities and policy agendas can act as new opportunities for domestic change in a positive direction. EU obligations can also pose serious challenges for domestic policy makers as Irish priorities come under pressure. For example, a core feature and value of Irish foreign and security policy is non-membership of military alliances (military neutrality). The recent development of a European security pillar has proved deeply problematic for Ireland during key periods of change.

Chapter 9 reflects on an important dimension of Ireland's EU membership: relations with Ireland's nearest neighbour, Great Britain, in the context of Northern Ireland. EU membership coincided with the outbreak of communal conflict in Northern Ireland in 1969, and the management of this conflict was and remains a major focus of British–Irish relations since then. Membership of the EU helped Ireland overcome the post-colonial legacy and provided a multilateral context for the asymmetrical relationship between these large and small states. Finally, Chapters 10 and 11 explore how EU membership contributed to deep structural change within the Irish economy in a globalized world. As a result of unprecedented economic growth in the 1990s and the success in achieving economic convergence and catch-up, Ireland has been invoked as a model for other states in Europe and more widely. Chapter 10 examines the Irish model of economic development in the EU, how it emerged, what lessons can be learned and the challenges it faces in the future. The concluding chapter, Chapter 11, reviews Ireland's contribution to the EU and what the EU has meant for Ireland.

Chapter 1

Becoming a Member State

Introduction

In January 1972, the Prime Minister Jack Lynch and his foreign minister, Patrick Hillery, left Dublin airport for Brussels to sign Ireland's Treaty of Accession to what were then called the European Communities, now the European Union. Following the signing ceremony on 22 January, Brussels experienced its first Irish 'session' or party with songs and music from members of the Irish delegation, including a well-known ballad from the Irish Prime Minister. Just over fifty years after the signing of the Anglo-Irish Treaty, a treaty that gave the people of 26 of the 32 counties of the island of Ireland the right to establish a state (the Irish Free State) separate from the United Kingdom, an Irish Government had successfully negotiated accession to the European Communities and was about to put the question of membership of the EEC to the Irish people in a referendum. The Communities had profoundly altered the European system of states that Ireland entered in 1922. To be a member state would in turn transform Ireland's external environment, its engagement with the world and the internal dynamic of its economy and society. The Prime Minister and his party were seen off at Dublin airport by the then President, Eamon de Valera. The photograph capturing the departing Prime Minister and the ageing President was hugely symbolic. That *tableau* captured the ties but also the tensions between the Ireland of 1972 and the young Irish state that was founded in 1922. Missing from the photograph was the Prime Minister Sean Lemass, who succeeded Eamon de Valera as Prime Minister in 1959. Lemass provided the decisive political leadership and vision that saw the Irish state and its people abandon the Ireland that de Valera would have had.

Eamon de Valera, one of the leaders of the 1916 rising and founder of the most successful Irish political party, Fianna Fáil, was the most powerful political leader, known as the Chief, in Irish politics following independence. As prime minister from 1932 to 1959, apart from two short periods in opposition, he moulded Irish public policy, the foreign policy of the state and the Irish national image. He fostered a nation and state-building programme that portrayed a highly idealized and romantic vision of Ireland and its role in the world (Lee, 1989; Keogh, 1994; Foster, 2007). In the 1930s in particular, de Valera's idea or ideal of Ireland was that of a rural and preferably Gaelic-speaking society committed to spiritual rather than material values. It was an Ireland that was Catholic and distinct from England. It was an Ireland built on an ancient culture linked to the seats of learning in Europe through the influence of its missionaries. De Valera's state and nation-building programme was predicated on an Ireland that was independent politically, economically and culturally (Foster, 2007). The pillars of his programme were the ending of the partition of the island, the revival of the Gaelic language as the spoken language of the country and the enactment of a new constitution that would make Ireland a republic in all but name. He succeeded only in the latter.

The tone and substance of de Valera's state and nation-building programme echoed that of other newly independent states and state-seeking nationalisms. There was, however, a gap between the symbol of independence and entrenched economic dependence on Britain, between the bucolic images of rural Ireland and mass emigration, and between the aspiration to restore Irish as the vernacular language and its continuing decline. Ireland from the 1920s to the 1950s was an Ireland fearful of economic modernization, urbanization and growth. It was also a state and society fearful for its future. De Valera lacked the economic competence to translate his ideals into a viable Irish society free of emigration and high unemployment (Lee, 1989, pp. 332–40). Ireland was only one of two countries in Europe that experienced population decline in the 1950s; the other was East Germany. The decline in population highlighted by the 1956 Irish Census was the result of an acceleration of emigration in the 1950s; net emigration reached a staggering 197,000 between 1951 and 1956 (Daly, 2006, p. 184).

Jack Lynch's departure to sign the Rome Treaties in 1972 represented the final nail in the coffin of the Ireland that de Valera would have had. Becoming a member state in 1973 was the culmination of a decisive shift in Ireland's domestic and foreign economic policy, a shift that embraced internationalization and economic development. The shift, once embarked on in 1958, was maintained with determined consistency by successive governments until membership was achieved in 1973. Speaking to the Irish electorate on the eve of the 1972 referendum on membership, the Prime Minister said, 'If I were to sum up in one word what the European Community will mean for Ireland I would say "opportunity" ' (quoted in Maher, 1986, p. 349). Put simply, accession to the Union afforded Ireland an opportunity to participate in a multilateral framework that would mediate between Ireland and the wider world, one that involved the United Kingdom but that was not dominated by the UK. This chapter traces the evolution of Ireland's European policy in the period leading to accession and places the decisive 1958 shift in an historical perspective. An overview of the rationale behind Ireland's road to Europe, described as a tortuous path by one of Ireland's chief negotiators, is important because all member states carry with them their distinctive historical experiences into the Union (Maher, 1986). What 'Europe' stands for in domestic discourse and the manner in which Europe resonates or fails to resonate with national aspirations has an important impact on how states and societies experience the Union.

Establishing and consolidating independence

The Irish Free State emerged from a modern state seeking nationalism that developed in the latter half of the nineteenth century (English, 2006). The demands of Irish nationalists ranged from complete independence from Great Britain to Home Rule within the British Commonwealth. Those in favour of secession came to prominence in the aftermath of the 1916 Rising when the execution of the leaders of that rising provoked a shift in public opinion in favour of those seeking independence rather than home rule. The 1918 election resulted in the newly formed Sinn Féin replacing the old Home Rule party as the dominant party in most parts of Ireland, with the notable exception of the north-eastern part of the island where a majority of the population favoured retaining the Union with Great Britain.

What is known as the war of independence, which was fought as a guerrilla campaign between 1919–21, ended with the opening of negotiations between the British Government and the Sinn Féin leaders on the future government of Ireland. The negotiations concluded the Anglo-Irish Treaty of 1921, a treaty that provided the constitutional framework for the Irish Free State that came into being in January 1922 (Laffan, M., 1999).

A number of features of the Treaty had a major impact on the constitutional status and the foreign policy of the young Irish state as it sought to establish its sovereignty and presence in the international system. The salient features were the exclusion from the new state of the six north-eastern counties of the island that remained as part of the United Kingdom, the constitutional status of the new state as a Dominion of the British Commonwealth, and the retention by Great Britain of a military presence in a number of Irish ports. Dominion status limited the external prerogatives of the new state; it was not free to pursue an independent foreign policy, was represented in third countries by British embassies and international treaties were not binding on internal relations between Commonwealth states. Hence, the sovereignty of the Free State was constrained both geographically and constitutionally. The partition of the island resulted in a highly contested border between the two states in Ireland and the presence of a disaffected nationalist catholic minority in Northern Ireland. The Anglo-Irish Treaty proved highly contentious in Sinn Féin; the pro- and anti-treaty forces played out their conflict in highly charged parliamentary debates and later in armed conflict when a bitter civil war raged between those in favour of the treaty and those against. The young Irish state was born with an ambiguous and contested constitutional status and was geographically limited to 26 of the historic counties that made up the island of Ireland.

Not surprisingly securing the internal and external sovereignty of the young state was the first priority of the first Free State Government which was made up of the pro-treaty forces. External sovereignty was consolidated by the opening of Ireland's first legations in the 1920s, membership of the fledgling League of Nations and intensive diplomacy within the Commonwealth to loosen British control over its dominions. Irish government representatives worked assiduously at both bilateral and multilateral levels first to establish and then gradually to strengthen the attributes of sovereign statehood. Over time, Ireland's ambiguous constitutional position (as a British dominion) was successfully exploited to secure the maximum leverage over Ireland's external affairs. These efforts began with multilateral negotiations within the British Commonwealth as Ireland together with other dominions successfully used the Imperial Conferences of 1926 and 1930 to establish their right to an independent foreign policy. The League of Nations provided the new state with the opportunity to establish and develop its international credentials and the legal bona fides of the Irish state in international law (Kennedy, 1996). Engagement with the Commonwealth and the League of Nations heralded a tradition of multilateralism in Irish foreign policy, a tradition that was built on in the period after the Second World War. Ireland was elected to the Council of the League of Nations in 1930 (Fanning, 2002, *Documents on Irish Foreign Policy Vol. III, 1926–32*).

The Fianna Fáil Government that took power in 1932 was committed to continuing a high level of international engagement, particularly in the League of Nations. A liberal nationalist, the Taoiseach and Minister for External Affairs, Eamon de Valera was very active in the League, chairing the Council and speaking on a number of occasions to the League Assembly (Fanning, 2002, *Documents on Irish Foreign Policy, Vol. IV, 1932–36*). De Valera and Fianna Fáil attached great importance to the role of the League of Nations in the 1930s. However, the failure of the League of Nations to secure an international rule of law and the deterioration in great power relations in the latter half of the 1930s brought the instability and dangers of the international system home to small states like Ireland and with it a certain sense of disillusionment. Paradoxically, the outbreak of war in Europe afforded the young Irish state an opportunity to assert its sovereignty by remaining neutral in a war involving the United Kingdom. Neutrality in the war left a lasting legacy on Irish foreign policy, a legacy that continues to influence Ireland's engagement with the evolution of the EU as an international actor.

During the 1930s, a major shift in political power from Cumann na nGaedheal Government to one led by Eamon de Valera and Fianna Fáil brought Anglo-Irish Relations to the fore. De Valera opposed the 1922 Treaty and was determined when he gained power in 1932 to remove the contested features of the Treaty. In power, de Valera unilaterally sought to revise the 1921 Anglo-Irish Treaty by launching what became known as the 'economic war' with Britain and by replacing the contested features of the Treaty with a new constitution in 1937. The British government's policy of appeasement of Germany was mirrored on a much smaller scale by the appeasement of Ireland. Following a difficult period of bilateral conflict a resolution was achieved. This included – rather surprisingly given the wider European context – the handing over to Irish control in 1938 of naval ports originally retained by the British government in the 1921 treaty to provide for the effective defence of the British Isles. The return of the ports was an absolute prerequisite for the successful pursuit of Irish neutrality in the Second World War (Keatinge, 1986; Fisk, 1983).

The comparative success of Irish neutrality over the course of the Second World War, and the way in which the concept of neutrality came to be defined as the very leitmotif of Irish independence and sovereignty, proved to be the enduring legacy of what was known in Ireland as the Emergency. Although wartime neutrality had not been played strictly according to legal definitions of neutrality (Salmon, 1989; Fisk, 1983) it was played very skilfully by de Valera. In the end, however, Ireland's ability to remain out of the war owed more to geopolitical realities than to government policy, and it left Irish negotiators with limited political capital in the postwar period. Ireland's international position was that of a small peripheral and relatively isolated state, and Irish politicians and diplomats grappled with the challenge of positioning Ireland in a changing international environment in the decade after the Second World War. The internationalism of the 1920s and 1930s was dashed by the breakdown of the interstate system and international institutions in the 1930s. It took the Irish state elite well over a decade to come to terms with the liberal international order that was constructed by the USA in the late 1940s. Notwithstanding formal political independence since 1922, the economy remained almost wholly dependent on the performance of one of Europe's least successful economies, Great Britain. Moreover, the political partition of the island was, if anything, more firmly consolidated after the war, in spite of sporadic attempts to make it an international issue.

As the cold war developed in the immediate postwar period, the weakness of the Irish position was brought sharply into focus. Early soundings on Irish membership of the North Atlantic Treaty Organization (NATO) were rebuffed by Dublin when it became clear that the USA would not allow such negotiations to become embroiled in the partition issue (McCabe, 1991). Irish leaders hoped that playing the (Irish) American card would mobilize Washington against London, but this card turned out to be of very limited value when the exigencies of a great power alliance such as that between the USA and Great Britain was at stake. The special relationship between Washington and London proved more salient than the relationship between Washington and Dublin. Non-membership of NATO made Ireland, together with a number of other small European neutrals, outliers in the emerging Trans Atlantic security arrangements, a significant feature of Cold War Europe. Ireland's geographical position on the western periphery of Europe meant that the state and its people were far removed from any direct security threat in the emerging bipolar system. In the postwar period, neutrality was not a 'security' policy; rather it was bound up with identity, values and the projection of a certain idea of Ireland's role in the world.

Choosing Europe

Notwithstanding neutrality, the state made some tentative moves towards engaging with the myriad of multilateral organizations that were emerging in postwar Europe. Ireland was a founding member of the Organization for European Economic Cooperation (OEEC – later to become the OECD) and the Council of Europe in the late 1940s. The OEEC was designed to distribute Marshall Aid and marked the first faint glimmer of economic cooperation among West European states. The Council of Europe, although it failed to deliver its lofty ambition to unify Europe, established the Convention of Human Rights and the Court of Human Rights as a significant extra-national regime for the protection of human rights. Marshall Aid was a harbinger of EU transfers following membership and the Court of Human Rights afforded Irish citizens a judicial arena in which to assert their rights beyond the state. Ireland's membership of the UN was vetoed by the Soviet Union in 1946 which delayed membership until 1955. The delay had more to do with cold war politics than with any particular opposition to Ireland as such. Participation in the UN provided the basis of a peacekeeping role that soon emerged as a keystone of Irish foreign policy, and it also prompted the formation of policies towards the emerging 'third world' countries. In a UN dominated by wealthy industrialized countries and ex-colonial powers, Irish diplomats played a significant and active role in several early UN debates such as those on China, on decolonisation and on nuclear non-proliferation (Skelly, 1997) and thereby established something of a benchmark for independence in what came to be seen as a 'golden age' in Irish foreign policy (Kennedy and Skelly,

2000, p. 34). The Irish Minister for External Relations between 1957 and 1969, Frank Aiken, played a very active role in the UN. Minister Aiken would remain in New York for the duration of the General Assembly every autumn, something that no contemporary Foreign Minister could envisage.

Although Ireland's political foreign policy was dominated by the UN during this period, a major shift occurred in Ireland's foreign economic policy that would lead to a re-orientation of Ireland towards Europe, and developments in economic integration. While Minister Aiken was managing the political dimension of foreign policy and engaging in global politics, others were debating the future of Ireland's domestic economic policy. The outcome of that debate would lead to the national objective of becoming a member state of the European Communities. The quest for the establishment and consolidation of independence and sovereignty would be replaced by the quest for accession to a multilateral regime characterized by a sharing of sovereignty and a federal legal order. Independence would be replaced by the goal of interdependence and indivisible sovereignty by divisible sovereignty. Autarchy and the strict control of foreign ownership of firms in Ireland would be replaced by openness and internationalization. Why did a young state, born from an enduring nationalist struggle, seek to join the European Communities 40 years after the foundation of the state and how did the European Communities resonate with the concerns of Irish nationalism? The answer to these questions lies in the search for a project for Ireland's future at the end of the 1950s. The quest was characterized by soul-searching within the Irish public service, continuous assessment of the position of the UK Government and the responses of the 'Six', transformative policy changes at domestic level and institution-building to put in place the capacity for the state to play a major role in the development of the country. The constraints on Ireland as a small state to influence its external environment become apparent in this period. So too does the capacity of the state elite, both political and administrative, to chart a different future for Ireland.

Within the Irish civil service, a battle was waged in the 1950s about the future direction of economic policy. The battle fought in well-crafted departmental memos and letters between senior administrators was a battle between protectionism and free trade and between economic conservatism and liberalization. At issue was whether or not the Irish State and its people could or would embrace the liberalising postwar political economy fostered by the United

States. Could it make the journey from autarchy to interdependence? Ireland's prevailing deep-seated political and economic conservatism was challenged by the irrefutable evidence that Irish freedom had failed to deliver prosperity and well-being to its people. The reality of de Valera's idealized Ireland was an Ireland of urban and rural poverty, late marriage, high unemployment, emigration and high levels of disease. A seminal volume that explored the 1950s had the evocative title, *Preventing the Future: Why was Ireland so Poor for so Long?* (Garvin, 2004). Ireland was classified as a less-developed country together with Greece, Iceland and Turkey in the 1957 OEEC negotiations on a European-wide free-trade area. For the duration of the talks, these four states were collectively known as the 'peripherals'. There was in the country a palpable sense of failure and concern for the future of the country (Lee, 1989). Ken Whitaker, the secretary of the Finance ministry, argued that

> After 35 years of native government people are asking whether we can achieve an acceptable degree of economic progress. The common talk amongst parents in the towns, as in rural Ireland, is of their children having to emigrate as soon as their education is completed in order to be sure of a reasonable livelihood. (Quoted in Whitaker, 1974, p. 115)

Would Ireland remain forever a 'peripheral' or could it find the institutional and cultural capacity to fundamentally shift the 'policy paradigm' and find an alternative path of economic development? Was the Irish State and Irish political leaders capable of steering Irish society and the Irish economy in a new direction? Was Ireland capable of overcoming its deep-rooted economic dependence on Great Britain, notwithstanding political independence? Choosing Europe was bound up with fundamental choices about the direction of the Irish economy and hence Irish society. Embracing international liberalization and economic growth would carry with it the seeds of deep societal change and challenge.

Within the Irish system of public administration, the ministries' of the Taoiseach (Prime Minister), Finance, External Affairs (later Foreign Affairs), Agriculture and Industry and Commerce attempted to craft an Irish response to the intensive search for new multilateral economic arrangements in Europe. The modernizers favoured a decisive shift in domestic economic policy whereas others were fearful that a shift would undermine access to the UK market. The policy debate revolved around the privileged position of Irish exports (both manufacturing and agricultural) in the UK market and the Irish response to trade liberalization. In addition to the pervasive concern with dependency on the British market was the challenge of abandoning the autarchy of previous decades. Ken Whitaker was the main advocate of economic liberalization in the public service, and throughout the 1950s he decried the policy of sheltering permanently behind tariff barriers and sought to move the economy in the direction of free trade. The Departments of Industry and Commerce and Agriculture remained conservative on external economic policy, more concerned with protecting exports to Britain than exploring how Ireland might escape from dependency. The Department of Agriculture had considerable status within the administrative system because Ireland's future prosperity was seen in pastoral rather than industrial terms. The Department of Industry and Commerce was the champion of the Irish industries that had been set up behind high tariff walls. It was fearful of the consequences of competition and liberalization for all those indigenous companies that had sheltered behind high tariff levels and restrictive ownership regulations (Murphy, 1997, pp. 58–9).

Whitaker was responsible for penning the Grey Book on *Economic Development*, a report published in May 1958 that set out the strategy Ireland should adopt in search of economic modernization. The report strongly advocated the abandonment of protectionism and an acceptance of free trade and economic liberalization. Whitaker and those who supported him offered a diagnosis of Ireland's weak economic performance and a road map for the future. The report was followed by a White Paper entitled a *Programme for Economic Expansion* published in November 1958. The programme required decisive backing from senior politicians to ensure that the 'paradigm shift' occurred. The endorsement and active pursuit of the strategy by the new Fianna Fáil Prime Minister, Sean Lemass, ensured that the policy shift transformed Ireland's relations with Europe and the international political economy. Lemass, who participated in the 1916 Rising, was ideally placed to mediate between Ireland's past and its future. Having been a loyal supporter of de Valera over many decades, he was going to use his short time as prime minister to push, cajole and energize Irish society in a new direction. Using the narratives of traditional Irish nationalism, Lemass, an architect of protectionism in the 1930s, was convinced of the inevitability of economic liberalization and free trade by the end of the 1950s. He spent his term of office as prime minister from 1959 to 1966 tirelessly steering Ireland in the direction of free trade and an open economy. The Control of Manufacturers Act that restricted ownership of Irish companies was abandoned, tariffs were reduced and a range of incentives were put in place to attract foreign capital to Ireland. Lemass was determined that Ireland would have an industrial rather than just a pastoral future.

Having altered the paradigm of domestic economic policy in 1958, the challenge for Ireland was to embed the new policy in the emerging system of economic cooperation and integration in Europe, always mindful of the overwhelming significance of the UK. The failure of the OEEC-sponsored talks on a European-wide free-trade area left Western Europe divided between the 'inner six' that had established the European Economic Communities (EEC) in 1957 and the 'outer seven' that were to establish EFTA in 1960. Ireland found itself outside the two alternative and competing European structures that were promoting differing forms of trade liberalization and economic integration. Prime Minister Lemass identified the dilemma facing Ireland in the following terms:

> There are now two trading blocs in Europe into neither of which this country can enter, accepting the full obligations of membership, without taking what most of us would regard as an undue risk. This country is predominantly agricultural. That fact must determine our thinking and our policy in this respect as in all others. (Sean Lemass, Dáil Debates 1959, Vol. 178, 11 December)

Within the Irish governmental system there were intense discussions between 1959 and 1961 concerning Ireland's approach to European developments. The Secretaries of the key economic departments, Finance, Industry and Commerce, Agriculture and External Affairs met frequently to chart the official view on the rapidly changing European environment. Political responsibility rested with the prime minister who chaired a Cabinet sub-committee on the issue. There was deep-rooted concern in the Irish administration arising from Ireland's relative isolation during this time. The period of reflection ended with Ireland's first application for membership on 31 July 1961, which followed the formal opening of diplomatic relations between Ireland and the European Communities in October 1959. Sean Lemass sold membership of the European Communities as a natural step for the Irish state and its people. The EEC could serve

TABLE 1.1 *Key dates: Ireland's road to Europe*

Date	Event
9 October 1956	Establishment of a Committee of Secretaries of the key economic ministries and External Affairs under the direction of the Taoiseach to examine moves towards further economic integration in Europe.
8 February 1957	Reviewing the report of the Committee of Secretaries, the Irish Government decided that no commitment should be given to joining a proposed free trade area unless adequate safeguards were available to Ireland.
May 1957	Ireland submits a memorandum to the OEEC Working Party outlining the conditions that Ireland would need in order to join a free trade area – a 25-year transition period being the key demand.
May 1958 – paradigm shift	Publication of the Whitaker analysis of the Irish Economy(*Economic Development*) identifying the need for a change in the policy paradigm.
12 November 1958 – paradigm shift	Publication of the White Paper, *Programme for Economic Expansion*, which became the first of a series of economic plans.
November 1958	Breakdown of negotiations on the creation of a free-trade area between the common market and the other OEEC states.
8 July 1959	Report submitted to Government by the Committee of Secretaries on Anglo-Irish trade relations.
13 April 1960	Trade Agreement between UK and Ireland (2 page document).
25 July 1960	Memorandum to Government on the possibility of joining the GATT.
5 July 1961	Presentation by the Irish Government of an *aide mémoire* to the Governments of the Six outlining Ireland's intention to seek membership of the EU in the event of a UK application.
5 July 1961	First White Paper on the EEC laid before the Irish parliament and followed by a debate.
31 July 1961	Ireland applies for membership.
14 July 1961	Acknowledgement from the Council of the Irish letter.
18 January 1962	Meeting with the Council and Commission attended by the Taoiseach, Sean Lemass – no formal date for opening negotiations established.

(Continued)

18

TABLE 1.1 (*Continued*)

Date	Event
7–22 October 1962	The Taoiseach visits the capitals of the Six and the Commission in an effort to made progress on the opening of negotiations.
22 October 1962	Council agrees to open negotiations with Ireland as the Taoiseach begins an official visit to Bonn.
14 January 1963	De Gaulle press conference – veto of UK membership.
May 1963	Discussions with the UK on a bilateral trade agreement.
August 1963 and July 1964	Publication of the second Programme for Economic Expansion in two parts: assumption that Ireland would be a member of EU by 1970.
14 December 1965	Signing of the Anglo-Irish Free Trade Agreement.
December 1967	Ireland accedes to the GATT.
11 May 1967	British, Irish and Danish applications presented to the Union.
April 1967	Publication of White Paper on the European Communities.
16 May 1967	De Gaulle again raises doubts about the UK application.
18 December 1967	Deadlock in the Council of Ministers on enlagement.
28 April 1969	De Gaulle resign as French President.
1–2 December 1969	Hague Summit opens the way for enlargment.
30 June 1970	Formal opening of enlargement negotiations.
21 September 1970	Ministerial meeting of the EU–Irish negotiating team.
18 January 1972	Final negotiations on the Treaty of Accession.
22 January 1972	Signing of the Treaties of Accession in the Palais d'Egmont, Brussels.
23 April 1972	The referendum on membership is carried by 83.1 per cent 'yes'.
1 January 1973	Ireland joins the European Union, 12 years after its initial bid for membership.

Source: Maher (1986).

the dual objective of reducing Ireland's dependence on the British market and of providing a large liberalizing market for Irish products. In essence, the economic modernizers won the battle of ideas and action in the crucial period 1958–61. The desire to become a member state was a logical consequence of the change in the domestic policy paradigm; the EU offered Ireland the advantage of market access for both agricultural and industrial goods. It provided a means of modernizing rural Ireland, on the one hand, and charting Ireland's urban future, on the other (O'Toole, 2003, pp. 20–1). Lemass spent the remainder of his time in office pursuing membership and preparing Ireland for membership.

Applying for membership

The emphasis so far has been on the domestic political and economic changes in Ireland that led to the first application for membership. A small group of change agents argued successfully for a shift in the policy paradigm from protectionism to liberalization, and they argued, cajoled and led those who were fearful of the consequences of such a major shift. The drivers were not just domestic; there was a realisation that the world was moving in a liberalizing direction and that Ireland could not ignore fundamental shifts in the global political economy. Nor could Ireland ignore its economic dependence on the UK. Notwithstanding over thirty five years of independence, the Irish economy was locked into the economy of its nearest neighbour. In 1959, 75 per cent of Irish exports were destined for the UK market and 52 per cent of its imports originated there. Economic dependence meant that the UK attitude to the EEC would have a major bearing on evolving Irish attitudes and strategies.

During 1961, there was considerable discussion and speculation about a possible British decision to apply for membership of the European Communities. This discussion was closely monitored in Dublin, and meetings of ministers and secretaries sought to chart Ireland's course in the event of a British application. By May 1961, it appeared increasingly likely that Britain would apply for membership, and the Irish Government undertook a number of preparatory steps. It sent an *aide mémoire* to the Governments of the Six outlining Ireland's intention to seek membership of the Union in the event of a British application. The umbilical cord linking Irish and

British membership was central to the mémoire. In it the Government asserted that

> The circumstances of Ireland's trade and economic position, however, are such that membership of the Community could not be envisaged except in the context of a decision by the United Kingdom to apply to become a member. (Irish Government, Aide Mémoire, July 1961)

The mémoire was tentative and conditional with regard to Ireland's ability to take on the obligations of membership. There is reference to Ireland's 'present stage of development' and to the need for Community support to achieve the objectives of the Programme for Economic Expansion (Maher, 1986, p. 125). The mémoire was met initially with a reasonably positive response by the Governments of the Six but the conditionality apparent in the text was raised later when Ireland formally applied for membership. (Fitzgerald, 2000, pp. 139–47). Other preparatory measures taken at this time included a commitment to producing a White Paper entitled *European Economic Community*, an assessment of Irish agriculture and industry and the likely impact of membership (Maher, 1986, pp. 124–5). The White Paper was published on 30 June 1961 and debated in the Dáil on 5 July. Discussions among the Six on political union that culminated in what became known as the Bonn Declaration, raised in a more explicit manner the political implications of membership of the Communities for Ireland. The Bonn Declaration was an embryonic attempt to foster foreign policy cooperation among the member states (Maher, 1986, pp. 134–5; Fitzgerald, 2000, pp. 153–4). Ireland's non-membership of NATO was on the agenda.

On 31 July, when Prime Minister Macmillan announced to the UK Government's intention to apply for membership to the House of Commons, the Taoiseach formally wrote a short and terse letter to the President in Office of the Council of Ministers requesting the opening of discussions concerning Ireland's accession to the Communities. This was followed ten days later by the UK application. The response to Ireland's application was less than fulsome. In discussions between a representative of the Dutch Foreign Ministry and the Irish *chargé d'affaires* in the Hague, it became clear that there were serious reservations among the Six concerning the prospect of Irish membership. Those concerns arose from the original *aide mémoire* sent by the Irish Government which identified Ireland as an underdeveloped country needing concessions (Fitzgerald, 2000, pp. 159–60). There were also concerns arising from Irish neutrality and non-membership of NATO. The lacklustre and tentative response to the Irish application was in stark contrast to the official response to the UK, Denmark and Norway. The Council opened negotiations with the UK and Denmark in November 1961 and with Norway in November 1962 even though the Norwegian application dated only from April 1962. During this period, the Irish Government sought to allay fears and concerns about Ireland's suitability for membership. The Taoiseach reiterated on more than one occasion that Ireland would willingly accept the political consequences of membership as those became clearer. A meeting between the Taoiseach and members of the Council of Ministers in January 1962 which was followed by a meeting at senior official level in May 1962 did not succeed in agreement to a date for the formal opening of negotiations with Ireland. Ireland was at the end of the enlargement queue. The meeting in January 1962, noted above, afforded Lemass the opportunity to assert Ireland's European credentials and overcome the unease among the member states concerning Ireland's economic development and commitment to the political goals of membership. Lemass argued that 'Ireland belongs to Europe by history, tradition and sentiment no less than by geography' and 'that the political aims of the Community are aims to which the Irish Government and people are ready to subscribe and in the realisation of which they wish to play an active part' (Sean Lemass, Statement to the Council of Ministers, 18 January 1962).

The absence of a date for the opening of negotiations caused considerable unease in Dublin. The Taoiseach decided to undertake a tour of the capitals of the Six and visit the Commission in October 1962 to press the Irish case. As he began his official visit to the Federal Republic on 22 October, the Council agreed to the opening of negotiations at a date to be specified. Ireland had become a pre-accession state. Preparations for the opening of negotiations continued in Dublin. Moreover, membership of the customs union was anticipated with a unilateral 10 per cent reduction on tariffs in 1963. It was anticipated that negotiations in 1963 would lead to membership by 1 January 1964 (Maher, 1986, p. 161). These hopes were dashed as the depth and extent of De Gaulle's antipathy to UK membership became apparent. De Gaulle's declaration on UK membership in January 1963 led to deadlock in the negotiations and was in effect a 'veto'. It would take the UK, Ireland and Denmark a further ten years to finally accede to the Union. The reactivation of membership applications in 1967 was again met with De Gaulle's implacable opposition to UK membership.

Preparing for membership

Throughout the 1960s, successive governments remained wedded to Ireland's eventual membership of the EEC. The Taoiseach and key domestic ministers established contact with the emerging EC institutions, made official visits to Brussels and continued to prepare Ireland for membership of the Brussels club. Following the breakdown of the enlargement negotiations, the Taoiseach made a commitment to continue 'to prepare and plan for our entry to an enlarged Community, taking every step which will further this objective and avoiding any that might make it more difficult to attain' in the Dáil (Sean Lemass, Dáil Debates, Vol. 199, 30 January 1963). The debate within the civil service and the Government on the question of Europe was mirrored by a debate in the key economic interest groups, the industrialists and trade unions. The National Farmers Association emerged as an early advocate of membership. Lemass actively sought to bring the key economic actors along with the membership drive but would have persisted even without them (Murphy, 1997, pp. 57–68). The shift in Ireland's economic paradigm was led by the political and administrative classes rather than by civil society. The Committee on Industrial Organization established in 1961 began its work of analysing and assessing the implications of free trade for Irish firms in all sectors. It became clear that indigenous industry would face considerable challenges in a free trade environment, particularly in relation to productivity, quality and marketing. The analysis was accurate, but it was unlikely that companies that had grown up behind high tariff barriers in an unsophisticated market could easily adapt to the rigours of free trade regardless of state aids for re-equipment and marketing.

Faced with French intransigence concerning UK membership, Lemass sought to maintain the momentum towards openness, the hallmark of the paradigm shift in 1958. This led, paradoxically, to pursuing a bilateral trade agreement with the United Kingdom. The Irish initiated discussions with the UK on the possible terms of a wider trade agreement. The Irish side stressed that they would make concessions to the UK in relation to market access for industrial goods in return for concessions on agricultural products and some manufactured products in the UK market. It took two and a half years of tough negotiations to reach agreement on the Anglo-Irish Free Trade Area Agreement which was signed in December 1965. The agreement was preceded by a series of unilateral tariff cuts by Ireland in an effort to maintain adjustment pressure on Irish industry. Lemass resigned as Taoiseach in November 1966 and died in 1971 before Ireland had achieved membership of the Community. The urgency and energy with which Lemass pursued membership of the Union, notwithstanding Ireland's level of economic development and ambiguous political position on security, makes him the architect of Ireland's European ambition and Ireland's Schuman. Unlike de Valera, who engaged in idealized visions of his preferred Ireland, Lemass sought to transform the Irish economy. He felt that Irish expectations of well being and material prosperity should be no less than those of other Europeans. It was also clear to him that prosperity would come largely from industrialization rather than agriculture. Sean Lemass was a fervent Irish nationalist, but one who wanted to exercise freedom and sovereignty for the well-being and prosperity of the people (Farrell, 1983). The Ireland he was trying to change was an Ireland in which agriculture was still the most important economic activity and source of employment and a society in which the influence of the Catholic Church was pervasive. Irish society was deeply conservative in terms of its values and mores. The imperative of generating economic activity and jobs would have a transformative impact on Irish society. Membership for Ireland was not about ending centuries of conflict, it was about embedding Ireland in an external environment that would enable it address the challenge of economic modernisation.

Negotiating membership

Following the Hague Summit in 1969 which opened the way for the commencement of accession negotiations with the applicant states, the Irish Government prepared a White Paper entitled *Membership of the European Communities: Implications for Ireland* which was laid before the Houses of Parliament in April 1970. The White Paper was intended as a discussion document setting out the likely consequences of membership of the European Communities for the country and particular sectors of the economy. It covered the constitutional, legal, political and economic implications of membership. The document underlined the fact that membership of the Communities would necessitate a change in the Irish Constitution and hence a referendum. The Government would negotiate the terms of membership but the Irish electorate would have the final say. Without a change to the Irish Constitution there would have been a direct conflict between the provisions of the constitution and the European treaties. Three articles of the Irish Constitution were affected:

> Article 5 which stated that 'Ireland is a sovereign, independent, democratic state';
> Article 6.2 which stated that 'the legislative, executive and judicial powers of the state were exercisable only by or on the authority of the organs of the State' established by the Constitution;
> Article 15.2 which vested the sole and exclusive power of making laws for the State in the Oireachtas (parliament).

The need for a referendum established a pattern that continued after membership. Ireland was from the outset a referendum country.

The chapter on the political implications of membership was particularly tentative because of the evolving nature of the Union and the fact that 'Progress in the political development of the Communities has been very slow up to the present time' according to the White Paper (Irish Government, 1970, p. 6). There was recognition, however, that the goal of the Communities was essentially political and that membership would have consequences for Irish sovereignty. Attention was drawn to the Hague Summit and the emerging discussion on political union among the Foreign Ministers. More importantly, it was argued that 'as the Communities evolve towards their political objectives, those participating in the new Europe thereby created must be prepared to assist, if necessary, in its defence' (Irish Government, 1970, p. 8). No reference was made in the White Paper to Ireland's non-membership of NATO and its traditional foreign policy stance concerning participation in military alliances.

The central focus on the document was on the economic and policy consequences of membership. Concerning the impact of membership on Irish industry, the likelihood of problems for some sectors of industry was alluded to but it was argued that the long-term gains would outweigh the costs. Access to the large EU market, notwithstanding increased competition, was highlighted as a major long-term gain. Access to the larger market would also improve the prospects for Irish agriculture and higher prices for agricultural products would raise farm incomes and increase agricultural production. It would also bring higher prices for consumers. The introduction of VAT and contributions to the budget would alter the fiscal regime and the public finances. The likelihood of Ireland becoming a 'net beneficiary' of the European budget was clearly understood. The document made the case for membership largely in economic terms. It concluded that 'because of its small scale, the domestic market does not of itself afford a sufficient basis for the expansion of the economy at a pace and to an extent that will enable the country to achieve its principle economic objectives, namely full employment, the cessation of involuntary emigration and a standard of living comparable with that of other Western European countries' (Irish Government, 1970, p. 106). Economic catch-up would drive Ireland's European policy for the first twenty years of membership. The White Paper was the subject of debate in the Irish parliament in June and July 1970. Contributions to the debate underlined the support for membership from the government party Fianna Fáil and the main opposition party, Fine Gael. The Labour Party favoured associate membership rather than full membership. They were concerned about the loss of sovereignty, the weak voice that Ireland would have in the Union and the fact that Ireland was ill-equipped for membership (see Dáil Debates, Vol. 247, 23 June 1970).

The formal enlargement negotiations opened with the four applicant states on 30 June 1970. The EU was by then a far more integrated economic unit than it was at the beginning of the 1960s and its ambition had grown following the 1969 Hague Summit which had launched a process of widening and deepening the Union. Those representing the Union drew attention to the importance of the *acquis communautaire* and the role of transitional arrangements in addressing problems of adjustment in the candidate states. The opening phase of the negotiations with Ireland and the other applicants lasted for the second half of 1970. During this period, the Irish delegation set out the issues that were of particular concern to them, notably the length of transitional arrangements, Anglo-Irish trading relations, sensitive Irish industries, dumping, financing the

EU budget, animal and plant health, tariff quotas, and the common fisheries policy (Maher, 1986, pp. 274–91). The negotiations to address each of these issues lasted until 18 January 1972.

Ireland together with the other candidate states agreed a five-year transitional period for both the customs union and agriculture. Ireland was allowed special arrangements with regard to the motor assembly industry, state incentives for economic development, animal and plant health and a number of safeguards against dumping. In addition, the Union agreed to a special protocol relating to Irish economic development as an annex to the Treaty of Accession. The economic development of Ireland became a shared goal of Ireland and the Union. This was a harbinger of the expansion of the Union's role in regional and cohesion policy in the decades ahead. The terms of accession were outlined in a White Paper laid before the Irish Parliament entitled *The Accession of Ireland to the European Communities* (Irish Government, 1972). The White Paper asked if there was an alternative of membership (Irish Government, 1972, pp. 61–6). The official view, strongly worded in the document, was that there was no realistic alternative to becoming a member state. Would the Irish people endorse that choice, a choice that was made as early as 1961?

Legitimizing membership

The referendum to alter the constitution held in April 1972 was characterized by a lively debate on the likely consequences of membership for Ireland (see Keogh, 1990), and the party divide on Europe followed a left–right cleavage. The two centre-right parties, Fianna Fáil, then in Government and the main opposition party, Fine Gael, strongly supported membership. The parliamentary Labour party opposed membership together with a number of small left-wing parties without parliamentary representation. Two umbrella groups on either side of the question were very active during the campaign. The Irish Council of the European Movement (ICEM) was to the fore in promoting the benefits of membership and the Common Market Defence Group put the anti-EEC case. Those supporting membership argued strongly in favour of full membership on the basis of the opportunities it would offer. One of the main pamphlets produced by the ICEM was entitled *Opportunity: Ireland and Europe*. Underpinning the 'yes' case was the impact of British membership of the EEC.

It was argued that if Britain joined, Ireland had no option to but to follow suit or face the prospect of negotiating a trade agreement with the EEC. The arguments were not all defensive. Membership offered opportunities for Irish agriculture, industry and improvements in living standards were envisaged. Membership was a project for Ireland's future. The ICEM pamphlet ended by suggesting that Ireland:

> Could timorously shelter behind policies of protectionism and isolationism, which have in the past singularly failed to solve the basic problems of our community – the emigration of tens of thousands of people every year and the lowest living standards and poorest social services in Western Europe. That is what opting out of the European Community would mean. (ICEM, 1972, pp. 46–7).

In putting the case for membership, the political parties and civil society groups were strongly supported by the Ministry for Foreign Affairs. The ministry published extensive material on the case for membership.

The case against membership was put by the Labour party and the Common Market Study Group (a civil-society organization with members such as Raymond Crotty, Anthony Coughlan and Micheal O Loinsigh). The latter produced a large number of pamphlets on all aspects of membership. The 'no' campaign led by the Labour Party and the Irish Congress of Trade Unions based the core of its argument on the detrimental consequences for peripheral poor economies of joining a common market with more developed economies. Capital and industry would agglomerate in the core and Ireland reduced to a cattle ranch and tourist resort. The potential loss of economic and political sovereignty was highlighted. Ireland should do what 'the Swiss and the Swedes, the Austrians, Spaniards, Finns, Icelanders, Cypriots, and the Portuguese' were doing and retain their sovereignty for economic development. All but two of those states later joined the EU. The referendum resulted in a very high yes vote, 83 per cent with a turnout of 71 per cent. The result can be explained by the support of the two main political parties and the active engagement of a number of significant civil-society organizations, notably the main farming groups. Opposition to membership was too weak to garner sizeable support. Membership of the European Union was the settled will of the Irish people.

Conclusions

Ireland's engagement with the dynamic of integration and its policy preferences following accession were moulded by its historical legacy and the nature of its economy and society. Its small size and relatively recent independence ensured that it was attentive to balances between the large and small states and to questions of voice and representation. Non-membership of military alliances made it an outlier, at least until the accession of the EFTA neutrals, with regard to the Union's evolving cooperation on foreign and security policy. The political implications of membership were secondary to the national project of economic modernization. The importance of agriculture to employment and the economy ensured that Ireland would quickly become an ardent member of the 'CAP supporters club'. Its position as a relatively poor member state moulded its approach to the EU budget and made it a champion of policies designed to promote economic and social cohesion. The vital importance of inward investment to Ireland's economic development would also prove significant. There was a pronounced preference to maintain as much domestic head-room as possible in the areas of social and labour-market regulation. The outbreak of communal conflict in Northern Ireland in 1969 proved a long-term challenge as both British and Irish Governments grappled with the ensuing violence and the consequential bloodshed. What were known as the 'Troubles' cast a shadow over the first 25 years of membership.

Successive Irish Governments would bring to the Union an enthusiasm for membership and an engagement with the development and dynamic of European integration. Notwithstanding Ireland's low level of development, there was a 'goodness of fit' between the EU and Ireland, a far better fit than for the other two new member states, the United Kingdom and Denmark. The electorate had voted overwhelmingly for membership and the main political parties supported it. For Irish politicians and civil servants, membership of the Union offered the prospect of actively contributing to a governance system that was multilateral and not dominated by the United Kingdom. EU institutions offered the prospect of new and interesting jobs for ambitious Irish officials in Brussels and Luxemburg. Irish commission officials would rise to the highest level in that organization. Irish politicians and civil servants would quickly become 'insiders' in the chambers of the Council and its myriad committees, adept at extracting concessions in interminable negotiations. The focus on the United Kingdom for economic and policy templates slowly gave way to a wider interdependence. The deep-rooted concern and anxiety about Ireland's future that characterized the decade after the Second World War was followed by a profound change in domestic policy and an engagement with a changing international environment. The changes were driven by the need for Ireland to find a sustainable path to economic modernization, to lessen its economic dependence on the United Kingdom and to fulfil the promise of political independence. The continuity and change between the period prior to membership and life in the Union was captured by Garret FitzGerald, as Irish Foreign Minister, when he suggested that

> In the past 50 years we evolved as a nation from dependence to independence and over much of the period our objective was to develop and consolidate that independence. We are now committed to a new and open-ended development towards interdependence. (FitzGerald, 1973)

How Ireland and its people fared in the processes and dynamics of engagement with the EU is the subject of this volume. Could Ireland – small, poor and peripheral – make a success of membership or would the critique of the consequences of the EU for poor peripheral states, posited by the Labour Party in the 1972 referendum, prove prescient? Could Ireland embrace Europeanization? Could it become a showcase for EU membership?

Chapter 2

Ireland's EU Experience

Ireland joined the EU on 1 January 1973 following a long period in search of membership. Within months of accession, a general election returned a new Government to power, a coalition between Fine Gael and the Labour party. The Labour party had opposed Ireland's membership in the 1972 referendum but accepted engagement with Europe as the settled will of the Irish people and worked to ensure that Ireland would adapt to membership and take advantage of the opportunities it offered. The appointment of Dr Garret FitzGerald as Foreign Minister in the new coalition Government was significant; FitzGerald was very involved in the Irish Council of the European Movement and knowledgeable about how Brussels worked. A committed Francophile, FitzGerald did much to ensure that, from 1973 onwards, the Irish governmental system prepared adequately for Ireland's first presidency of the Council in 1975. The successful presidency in the latter half of 1975 marked the end of the governmental system's apprenticeship in the EU, but it would take longer for the economy to flourish in the Union.

The impact of EU membership in Ireland was perhaps most quickly felt in the economic sphere, but Irish interaction with and adaptation to the EU had other important consequences in the social and political spheres. While the economic advantages of the common agricultural policy and the common market were uppermost in the minds of both politicians and the electorate when Ireland voted to join the EEC in 1972, membership also helped Ireland mature socially and politically. Membership of the EU helped move the social agenda forward in Ireland, with the granting of further rights to women, and it opened Ireland up to both Europe and the world. As a small state joining the EEC family, Ireland became part of a system of multi-level governance that had an impact on its recognition and presence on the world stage, enabling Ireland to punch well above its weight. It is also possible to argue that membership of the EU was a further step along the road of Irish independence: in moving away from the straitjacket of overwhelming economic dependence on the United Kingdom, Ireland was entering into a new economic and political realm where it would be received as an equal partner, with all the rights this entailed (Coombes, 1983). Paradoxically, the decision to pool sovereignty can be seen as another declaration of Irish independence and sovereignty (Noël, in Hillery 1999, p. 18).

To paint such an overwhelmingly positive picture of Ireland's experience of the EU since 1973 would be misleading. In overall terms, Ireland's economic success and the phenomenon of the Celtic Tiger is a relatively recent development. For the first twenty years of membership at least, the self-perception of Ireland in the EU was of a small, poor, peripheral member. As a net beneficiary of EU funds, successive Irish governments and negotiators sought to maximize receipts of EU funding, be it through the Common Agricultural Policy or the structural and cohesion funds. Ireland was said to be suffering from a 'sponger syndrome', in viewing the EC/EU as a source of additional exchequer funding for a poor member state, Irish politicians and officials possessed a 'begging-bowl mentality' (Matthews, 1983; Lee, 1989; Hussey, 1993). The first ten years of membership were seen to have been unimpressive as the high hopes on accession were dashed by the oil crises and a period of deep recession in Europe (Coombes, 1983). The original mood of celebration was seen to give way 'to something more sober and detached' (Drudy and McAleese, 1984, p. 2), as Irish companies felt the cold-shower effects of competition stemming from the common market (O'Donnell, 2001). Apart from some impact in the social and agricultural spheres; the impact of the EU in Ireland was for the most part disappointing. This situation was to change, however, as events within the EEC itself fed into Irish economic development and consequently its relationship to the EEC/EU. The negotiation and signature of the Single European Act in 1986, with its aim of completing the internal market, alongside the 1988 reform of the structural fund policies, were contributing factors in helping successive Irish governments turn the economy around after the previous years of economic mismanagement. An increasingly open and single European market, alongside moves towards the creation of a single currency and the economic and budgetary discipline needed for this, helped frame Irish economic strategy. Ireland benefited considerably from the increased injection of cash into the EU's regional policy coffers in order to combat the effects of its peripheral status. Alongside the decisions taken at the domestic level, these developments helped consolidate Irish economic recovery and growth.

In the 1990s, some commentators perceived that while Ireland, its government and society were pro-European and *communautaire*, support for the EU and the integration process itself was conditional (Scott, 1994; McAleese, 2000). In the words of former Minister for Europe, Maire Geoghegan Quinn, Ireland was seen to be 'conditionally integrationist': governments agreed to further economic and political integration in return for monetary benefits (quoted in Laffan, 2002, p. 93). In economist Dermot McAleese's view, Irish policy was dominated by the desire to maximize receipts from EC funds, while minimizing the amount of interference in domestic policy (in the application of funds, competition policy and other areas) and seeking derogations on difficult parts. The Irish approach was to ask what Brussels could do for the Irish economy rather than the reverse (McAleese, 2000, p. 103). In the assessment of Pat Cox, former MEP and President of the European Parliament, Ireland needed to develop 'a vision for Europe that is more sophisticated than milking a cow' (quoted in Hussey, 1993, p. 213). As the Irish economy became more successful, Ireland's vision of Europe did change and a number of critiques of Irish membership of the EU emerged. This became evident from the late 1990s and reached its zenith after the rejection of the Nice Treaty in 2001. This period of questioning was followed by a successful second Nice referendum and a re-commitment amongst political elites to Ireland's place at the heart of the EU, while at the same time recognizing that Irish priorities and goals have changed as it has moved from being a net beneficiary to a net contributor to the EU's budget. Even so (and as we will see in more detail in Chapters 4 and 5), dissenting voices are still clearly heard. It is fair to say that Ireland has now entered a new phase in its relationship with the European Union.

This chapter offers a brief survey of Ireland's membership of the EU since accession in 1973. For the purposes of analysis, three key periods of membership suggest themselves: 1973–86, 1987–97, 1998 to the present. We deal with each of these broadly-defined periods in turn. The period of 1973 to 1986 marked Ireland's apprenticeship to the EU system. Internal adjustment to the demands of EU membership took place in an incremental fashion and the great expectations for significant economic benefits were not fulfilled, although membership did have a significant impact on the agricultural sector and played an important role in advancing social rights in Ireland. It was during this period that the tone for Irish engagement in the EU for the next 25 years was set: as a poor member state on the edge of Europe, Ireland's participation in the European integration project was seen in purely intrinsic economic terms. From 1987 to 1997, successive Irish governments did indeed make decision after decision to participate in the great European projects undertaken, such as economic and monetary union (EMU) and the common foreign and security policy (with the special position of neutrality clearly recognized). Such decisions were strongly endorsed by the electorate in a series of referendums. In return, Ireland benefited from considerable financial transfers from Brussels which helped revitalize the Irish economy and played a part in sowing the seeds for the unprecedented economic success that became known as the 'Celtic Tiger'. More importantly, however, Ireland benefited from the further liberalization of EU trade as increasing numbers of foreign firms were attracted to Ireland as an English-speaking EU member state with direct access to the single market. From the mid-1990s onwards Ireland went on to experience a period of unprecedented economic growth, not only by comparison with the country's economic history, but also in global terms (O'Donnell and Moss, 2004, pp. 9–10).

By the late 1990s, signs emerged that Ireland's relationship with the EU was changing. On the one hand, on the eve of the new millennium the Irish coalition government of Fianna Fáil and the Progressive Democrats (1997–2002) found itself at a critical juncture economically in its experience with the EU – Ireland would no longer be a net beneficiary of the EU budget but a net contributor due to Ireland's economic turnaround. Ireland now finds itself as a small prosperous West European state with per capita incomes that have converged with those of other wealthy EU member states (Laffan, 2002). On the other hand, while the continuous process of constitutional evolution undertaken by the EU member states, beginning with the Single European Act in 1986 and the 1993 Treaty on European Union, was supported by the Irish electorate in successive referendums, the need to ratify these and later treaties and their implications for Ireland provoked concern and in some cases outright opposition amongst some Irish political parties and civil society groups. Following the rejection by the electorate of the Nice Treaty in June 2001, such concerns could no longer be easily cast aside. The

TABLE 2.1 Key dates in Ireland's membership of the European Economic Community/European Union

Year	Date	Event
1959	December	Diplomatic relations established with the EEC.
1961	31 July	Ireland's application to join EEC sent to Council.
1963	January	Breakdown of negotiations with UK, Denmark, Ireland and Norway on EEC membership.
1966	January	Irish Government decision to accredit a separate diplomatic mission to the European Communities.
1967	May	Second application for EEC membership.
1970	30 June	Formal opening of accession negotiations.
1972	January	Taoiseach Jack Lynch and Minister for Foreign Affairs P.J. Hillery sign instruments of accession.
1972	May	Referendum on membership (83 per cent in favour, 17 per cent against).
1975	First six months	Ireland holds EC Presidency for the first time.
1979	Second six months	Ireland holds EC Presidency.
1984	First six months	Ireland holds EC Presidency.
1985		Senator Jim Dooge chairs Intergovernmental Committee which led to the negotiation of Single European Act.
1987	May	Ratification of Single European Act (69.9 per cent in favour, 30.1 per cent against).
1990	First six months	Ireland holds EC Presidency.
1992	June	Ratification of Maastricht Treaty (69.1 per cent in favour, 30.9 per cent against).
1996	Second six months	Ireland holds EU Presidency.
1998	May	Ratification of Amsterdam Treaty (61.7 per cent in favour, 38.3 per cent against).
2001	June	Referendum on Nice Treaty (46 per cent in favour, 54 per cent against, failure to ratify treaty).
2002	October	Ratification of Nice Treaty (63 per cent in favour, 37 per cent against).
2004	First six months	Ireland holds EU Presidency and successfully leads completion of negotiations on the EU's Constitutional Treaty.
2008	June	Referendum on Lisbon Treaty (53.4 per cent in favour, 46.6 per cent against, failure to ratify treaty).

Source: O'Mahony, in Collins and Cradden (2004), p. 17.

shock rejection of the first Nice referendum in June 2001 forced the largely pro-European political elites to recognize that they could no longer be complacent with regard to the EU. The Irish 'permissive consensus' on the EU was at an end.

1973–86: learning to live within the European system

The decision to join the EEC, analysed in Chapter 1, was the logical outcome of the economic policies pursued by successive Irish governments since the 1950s, involving as it did a commitment to trade liberalization, the free movement of capital and the attraction of foreign direct investment and enterprises (Matthews, 1983, p. 110). In agriculture came the prospect of higher prices for farmers through the Common Agricultural Policy (CAP) and access to the European market (Sheehy, 1984). Ireland's low level of economic development meant that an important aspect of membership was the desire to develop structural and regional policies at the Community level. It was anticipated that financial resources would be channelled to Ireland and would supplement national resources (Hart and Laffan, 1983, p. 136). Expectations were therefore high on accession, and the Government White Paper on the Treaty of Accession forecast growth of 5 per cent per annum as a result of membership (Matthews, 1983, p. 110).

A number of early studies of the impact of the EEC on Ireland (Coombes, 1983; Drudy and McAleese, 1984; Lee, 1989) highlight a sense of disappointment felt after the first ten years or so of membership. Although membership was viewed in favourable terms overall, the perception existed that the high expectations in the economic arena had not been met. In 1983, Ireland's gross domestic product per head continued to remain less than half the Community average. According to Matthews, 'in looking at the Irish economic performance during the first decade of membership, one is struck by the evidence of lost opportunities . . . Irish industry today is as structurally unsuited to providing the motor for an internationally-trading economy as it was ten years ago' (Matthews, 1983, p. 131). Ireland found it difficult to break out of the constraints of peripherality and the weakness of its industrial base. On the positive side, a diversification of Irish trade did occur with increased trade between Ireland and other EEC partners apart from the UK (Coombes, 1983, p. 4).

Yet Ireland's performance in the EEC in its first ten years of membership was fundamentally affected by the global recession of the 1970s, domestic economic mismanagement and the lack of appetite among EEC members themselves for further integration in particular in regional development policies.

Focusing on narrow economic performance, however, hides a number of benefits evident in the early years of Ireland's experience of EEC membership. For industry, membership was the culmination of a trend towards free trade and the outward-looking economic policies which had begun in the 1950s. The increased economic output evident in the early years of membership was directly attributable to the rise in manufacturing as a result of foreign direct investment from multinational firms. Access to the European market played an important role in making it possible for Ireland to attract these overseas firms (Drudy and McAleese, 1984). The sector with the most substantial and immediate prospect of economic gain from membership was the farming sector (Drudy and McAleese, 1984, p. 5). Historically, before 1973 food prices in Ireland tended to be lower than in the Common Market. As an example, in 1969 the EC guide-price for butter was three times higher than the average export price for Irish butter sold on the world market (McAleese, 2000, p. 85). Consequently there was a high expectation on accession that prices and consequently farm incomes would increase dramatically given the export rate of Irish agricultural products (McAleese, 2000; Sheehy, 1984; Cox and Kearney, 1983). An historic transfer of income did occur between 1970 and 1978 as prices rose by 35 per cent in real terms. Although prices began to fall after 1978, the significant point at this stage is that unlike the period before accession, farm incomes were now financed by Brussels and not Dublin, thus removing a serious burden from the Irish exchequer and taxpayer (McAleese, 2000, pp. 85–7). By the end of the transitional period in 1978, the EEC paid for 70 per cent of Irish public expenditure on agriculture, and this had increased to 88 per cent by 1988 (Daly, 2002, p. 504). Irish agriculture and the farming community were clear beneficiaries from EU membership at this point.

The experience of the farming community was in stark contrast to the experience of the fishing industry in Ireland. The new member states, the UK, Denmark and Ireland, had to accept as part of the *acquis*, the key common fisheries regulation 2141.70 which was passed the day before accession negotiations began in 1970. The legislative act would not have been passed if the four candidate countries, which included Norway, were already in the Union. When in 1976, the Commission published its first proposals on the implementation of a common fisheries policy, Ireland, together with the UK, were strongly opposed to the measures and put forward alternative proposals that proved unsuccessful. In an attempt to protect Irish costal zones and a small and old fishing fleet, the Irish government introduced a regulation 'Sea Fisheries (Conservation and Rational Exploitation) Order 1977'. The regulation imposed restrictions on vessels above a certain size in a large zone off the Irish coast. The regulation had the effect of excluding a large proportion of the French and Dutch fishing fleets that had fished traditionally in Irish waters. An Irish court, when faced with a case involving Dutch trawlers, referred the issue to the European Court of Justice seeking a preliminary ruling on the compatibility of the Irish regulation with European law. The Irish measure was found by the Court to be discriminatory because no comparable obligation was imposed on Irish trawlers (EUR-lex, 1978, Case 88/77). The early years of the common fisheries policy offered Ireland an experience in the difficulty of ensuring that national preferences are reflected in European policy when supported by only one country, in this case the UK. Moreover, it offered an early lesson in the supremacy of European law and the principle of non-discrimination.

Social and political impact

On accession, hopes were high for the creation of a relatively substantial European Regional Development fund, but such hopes were dashed when the size of the fund was determined in 1975 and Irish policy-makers were disappointed by Ireland's eventual allocation of 6 per cent (Hart and Laffan, 1983, p. 138). Nevertheless, Ireland did benefit from the creation of the European Social Fund (ESF) with significant funding going towards vocational training programmes originally offered by the state-run vocational training body AnCo (now FÁS). This funding was particularly welcome at a time when government spending on such schemes was being curtailed and Irish officials adapted quickly to the new funding environment. In Dublin, dossiers were processed in such a way that most Irish applications received finance. Owing to the financial importance of the fund, the beneficiaries were extremely careful to conform to Commission rules; standard operating procedures were fashioned to exploit the opportunities offered by the fund (Laffan, 1991, p. 239).

A small number of Social Fund officials, including the director of the Fund Wolfgang Stabenau, engaged actively with Irish state agencies and helped modernize the approach to vocational training. Young people in particular benefited from the ESF: in 1979, 50,000 people under the age of 25 availed of ESF-backed programmes, representing 70 per cent of the total number trained in Ireland (Hart and Laffan, 1983, p. 149). The importance of the ESF in underpinning vocational training in Ireland continued throughout membership. In the five years to the end of 1995, Ireland received IR£1 billion from the fund, which represented just over one-third of all money spent in Ireland in that period on vocational training and employment programmes. A significantly larger percentage of the labour force in Ireland has benefited from the ESF than in any other member state. By 1993, 18 per cent of women and 13 per cent of men had received ESF assistance in Ireland, while the EU average was 2 per cent (Ó Cinneide, 1993, p. 20).

Membership had a significant impact on social issues in Ireland and in particular women's rights. It is true to say that, from the 1960s onwards, Irish society was experiencing transformational change. Changing patterns of population growth and fertility were evident. For example, in 1926 only 32 per cent of the population lived in towns inhabited by 1,500 or more people, whilst in 1971 the proportion reached 52 per cent as Ireland became more urbanized (Brown, 1985, p. 257). As the old cultural norms of Catholic, rural Ireland were increasingly questioned, the issue of women's rights came to the fore. In 1970 the government commissioned a study on the role of women in Irish society in response to the UN Decade for Women. The report was the first major public document that catalogued the numerous inequities and injustices experienced by women across the whole range of societal life in Ireland, including the level of restrictions on women's employment, inequities in the tax system, inequalities before the law and unequal pay (Laffan, 1991, p. 244). The report galvanized the women's movement highlighting the degree of inequality existing between men and women in Ireland. Accession to the EEC in 1973 coincided with this arrival of women's issues on the domestic political agenda and greatly enhanced the efforts of those in the women's and trade-union movements in pushing for further modernization of Irish society as EC anti-discrimination legislation was progressively introduced domestically. The need to implement the EC's equality directives led to a series of equality laws in Ireland. While such

domestic anti-discrimination legislation would more than likely have
been introduced in the fullness of time, accession to the EC speeded
up this process. According to a report of the Joint Committee on
Secondary Legislation of the European Communities:

> The Community has brought about changes in employment prac-
> tices which might otherwise have taken decades to achieve. Irish
> women have the Community to thank for ... the introduction
> of maternity leave, protection against dismissal on pregnancy and
> greater equality in the social welfare code. After farmers, Irish
> women in employment have probably benefited most from entry
> to the EEC. (Joint Committee Report on Proposals Relating to
> the Equality of Opportunity, 17 October 1984)

Although the Treaty of Rome contained only one article concerning women (former Article 119 which provided for equal pay for
equal work), the Community had developed a number of action
programmes involving a variety of measures to protect and promote
women's rights. The first directive on equal pay for men and women
was adopted in 1975 and became effective in 1976. All discrimination with regard to pay for 'the same work' or 'work of equal
value' within the Community was to be eliminated. In anticipation of this directive, the Irish Oireachtas (Parliament) passed the
Anti-Discrimination Act of 1974, which provided that men and
women should receive equal treatment in regard to remuneration
for similar work. This act would transpose the European directive
into Irish law and provide for full implementation of equal pay by
31 December 1975 in accordance with the European deadline. Yet
as the domestic economic situation deteriorated, the then employers' body, the Federated Union of Employers (FUE) put considerable
pressure on the government to seek a deferral of the implementation of the equal-pay legislation in 1976. Indeed, in December 1975,
the Taoiseach, Liam Cosgrave announced that employers would be
allowed to claim inability to pay and that the Government would
seek a derogation from the Commission for those employers (the
Government itself admitted that it would be unable fulfil its commitment to equal pay in the public sector) (Cassells, 2000, p. 70;
Laffan, 1991, p. 245; Ferriter, 2004, p. 684). Thanks to EEC membership, in the face of such government resistance the trade union
organizations and women's groups were able to lobby the European
Commission in order to ensure that the legislation was not deferred

Box 2.1   Ireland Inc at the helm: Irish EU presidencies

Ireland has held the presidency of the EU six times since its accession in 1973: 1975, 1979, 1984, 1990, 1996 and 2004. During
the last three presidencies in particular, Ireland has been at the
helm of the EU during major periods of constitutional change,
most especially in 2004 when Irish leaders and civil servants successfully negotiated agreement on the EU's Constitutional Treaty.
Irish civil servants have regarded ensuring the success of Irish
Presidencies as a matter of vital national interest (Humphreys,
1997, p. 33) and staffing levels at the EU Permanent Representation in Brussels are always increased significantly during these
periods (staffing levels in the permanent representation reached
160 in 2004 for the sixth presidency). Back at home, an attitude of 'all hands on deck' amongst Dublin-based civil servants
also prevails during Presidencies. Irish EU Presidencies have been
generally regarded very highly by other EU politicians and commentators, and in 1997, in once such judgement of the Irish 1996
presidency Ludlow commented:

> Ireland passed the test with flying colours because they
> observed the two golden rules of any successful presidency.
> Firstly, the presidency is an office of the Union rather than
> a vehicle for the gratification of national ambitions. Sec-
> ondly, efficiency is more highly esteemed than proud posturing
>
> →

and was enforced in its entirety. The Commission, under Irish Commissioner Patrick Hillery, refused the derogation so that the 1974
Act did indeed come into force on 1 January 1976. The effects of
such action were significant; as Peter Cassells, former head of the
Irish Congress of Trade Unions noted:

> this legislation not only transformed the workplace for Irish
> women but also gave a strong underpinning to the demands from
> women's organisations and unions for major changes in the role
> of women in Irish society – changes, which still reverberate with
> us today. (Cassells, 2000, p. 70)

In the late 1970s and 1980s, the equal pay directive was followed
by directives on the equal treatment of men and women as regards
access to employment, vocational training and working conditions,

→

amongst those most immediately affected... The Irish were remarkably efficient and they did not try to impose their own agenda. (Ludlow, 1997, p. 2)

In its sixth Presidency, the Irish core executive was given the extremely difficult challenge of securing agreement on the EU's constitutional treaty. Its success in achieving agreement was acknowledged by European leaders such as French President Jacques Chirac who was quoted as saying: 'my officials have seen many Presidencies. None has equalled this one' (*Irish Times*, 19 June 2004). Chris Patten, EU Commissioner for External Affairs from 1999 to 2004 concurred:

The Irish steered the constitution through the IGC with great skill... As often happens when a smaller member state has the task of presiding over the EU's affairs, the Irish were not encumbered by a host of national preoccupations. There was no Dublin wish list that took priority over Europe's agenda. They also had outstanding officials both in their Brussels team and back home in Dublin. (Patten, 2005, pp. 128–9)

The success of the 2004 Presidency helped rehabilitate negative perceptions of Ireland amongst its European partners following the Nice rejection in 2001.

equality in matters of social security, equal treatment for men and women engaged in self-employed activity and a directive on the protection of self-employed women during pregnancy and maternity.

Politically, membership also opened up Irish political circles to European and world affairs as Ireland came to terms with a new interpretation of the nature of sovereignty among European states (Coombes, 1983, p. 9). Participation in the Community's foreign policy coordination mechanism, European Political Cooperation (EPC), exposed Irish foreign policy-makers to international politics in a new way. EPC required Ireland to take positions on issues outside its traditional range of interests, but it also provided access to the detailed and specialized information collected by its partners (Keatinge, 1991, p. 150). The obligation to speak on behalf of the Community as chair of the EC presidency also enhanced Irish international status, as Ireland held the Presidency in 1975, 1979 and 1984. Ireland quickly gained a reputation for holding successful Presidencies (see Box 2.1). Indeed, as Minister for Foreign Affairs in 1975 and subsequently as Taoiseach in 1984, Garret FitzGerald endeavoured to carve out an active role for Ireland in the integration process. Until the Single European Act, the ambiguous nature of Ireland's neutrality did not cause successive governments concern (apart from the Falklands conflict) and Ireland was able to participate fully in the collective diplomacy of EPC.

In sum, in the early years of membership, the underlying patterns of Irish behaviour within the European Community were set. Ireland was integrationist in broad terms, but conditionally so. The emphasis was invariably on economics, given Ireland's difficult economic situation. At the same time, the Community itself was going through a period of stagnation and inertia. This was to change, however, by the mid-1980s, and Ireland entered into a new phase in its engagement with the Community.

1987–97: the emergence of the Celtic Tiger

The commitment by EU member states in the Single European Act signed in 1986 to complete the European single market by the target date of 1992 was rapidly followed by a much-welcomed increase in funding to poorer member states and regions of the EU. This increased funding under the EU's community support framework programmes (as part of the so-called Delors packages) was widely welcomed in Irish government and economic sources, heralding as it did an important new source of funding in domestic infrastructure at a time when money for such projects was lacking from the exchequer. In addition, it encouraged the government to raise public investment from its low level in the late 1980s and indeed, given the requirement that EU funds be matched domestically, possibly enabled a bigger increase in public investment than would otherwise have occurred (FitzGerald, 2004, p. 22).

From the mid-1990s onwards, Ireland became Europe's economic success story as Ireland greatly outperformed all other OECD economies. A more detailed analysis of the factors contributing to economic catch-up is found in Chapter 10. Irish GNP expanded by 140 per cent between 1987 and 2000, for example, compared to an expansion of 40 per cent in the USA and 35 per cent in the

EU-15 (Barry, Bradley and Hannan, 2001, pp. 537–52). Much debate has focused on the question of whether the 'Celtic tiger' economy resulted from the large amount of financial receipts from the European Union. A number of studies have argued that Ireland's spectacular economic success of the late 1990s with rapid convergence towards the EU average should be seen as a belated convergence, one that would have occurred more gradually over the previous twenty years if more appropriate domestic policies had been pursued (FitzGerald, 2000; Honohan and Walsh, 2003). In particular, the public finance crisis of Ireland in the 1980s was a self-inflicted wound and the serious delays in undertaking the necessary adjustment in the early years of the 1980s made matters worse (FitzGerald, 2004, p. 6). The precise timing of the economic turnaround can be said to be as a result of a number of concurrent developments (FitzGerald, 1998, 2000 and 2004; Bradley, 2002; Honohan and Walsh, 2002, NESC, 2003; O'Donnell, 2000). These included a dramatic increase in foreign direct investment (FDI) inflows, particularly from the USA; the stabilization of the public finances and an associated improvement in competitiveness since 1987; and the development of an Irish labour force with higher educational qualifications (FitzGerald, 1998). The social partnership process, which began in 1987, institutionalized wage bargaining between the government, employers and trade unions and involved an explicit trade-off of tax cuts for wage moderation, thus contributing to a positive economic environment for foreign and indigenous investment.

However, in addition to these factors there is no doubt that the EU's structural funds also had a significant impact on the Irish economy. During the decade from 1989 to 1999, Ireland's receipts from the structural funds averaged about 2.6 per cent of GNP. While the impact of the funds is hard to quantify, statistical estimates suggest that they increased the level of GNP by 2 percentage points (O'Donnell, 2001). Even more importantly, the Economic and Social Research Institute also calculated that the beneficial effect of the European Single Market on the Irish economy was to add as much as 9 per cent to GNP (FitzGerald, 1998). Beneficial European influence also came in the form of: exchange rate stability; low inflation; financial discipline; inward investment; competitive re-orientation; a new regulatory framework in services and utilities; developmental planning, monitoring and evaluation; new standards and agencies for consumer protection and social regulation; and support for policy innovation and experimentation (O'Donnell, 2001).

A new regulatory regime for Ireland

Structural fund reform had an additional benefit for the Irish system of public policy-making as it introduced the need for more long-term and rational planning of the economy and economic development as National Development Plans had to be produced (FitzGerald, 2004; O'Donnell, 2000). In order to satisfy the European Commission and net budgetary contributors that the money was being well spent, evaluation units and auditing procedures were introduced within government departments, enhancing systematized public policy making. Links between multiple levels of governance were also improved, as the government established a set of regional consultative committees and eventually a set of regional authorities in order to oversee implementation of the funds (see Chapter 6). Participation within the Single European Market also changed the nature of the Irish regulatory regime as the establishment of independent regulatory agencies increased. This process had begun with the creation of the Employment Equality Agency in 1977 and the Director of Consumer Affairs in 1978. The Health and Safety Authority was established in 1989, followed by the Pensions Board (1990), the Competition Authority (1992), the Environmental Protection Agency (1992), the Irish Aviation Authority (1994), the Food Safety Authority (1995) and the telecommunications regulator ComReg (1997) amongst others. This marked a major change away from public ownership of public utilities and direct state responsibility for the regulation of such sectors as these agencies became part of a network of European regulatory agencies (O'Donnell, 2000, p. 184).

Participation in EMU in the 1990s also had important consequences for economic governance in Ireland. The decision to take part in economic and monetary union (negotiated as part of the Maastricht Treaty in 1991) represented a significant stage in Ireland's engagement with the EU, involving as it did the commitment to transfer sovereignty on monetary issues to the European level. It was said at the time that the then Fianna Fáil/Labour government under Albert Reynolds acquiesced to EMU in return for the creation of the new cohesion fund (part of Ireland's conditionally integrationist strategy, as it were) (Scott, 1994). Be that as it may, this decision was to have important consequences for Irish economic performance in subsequent years. Signing up to EMU was not Ireland's first foray into European monetary cooperation. Ireland joined the European Monetary System (EMS) of fixed exchange rates on its establishment in 1979, abandoning its 150-year link with sterling in the hope of a more stable, low-inflation regime linked to the German mark (O'Donnell, 2000, p. 188). At the time, this decision was seen as perhaps even more significant than the original decision to join the EEC (Walsh, 1984, p. 170).

Why was the decision taken to participate in the EMS given the strong ties with the British pound? In the White Paper issued in December 1978, one of the reasons advanced in favour of Ireland's membership of the EMS was the belief that 'the discipline involved in a zone of monetary stability acts as a powerful aid in the fight against inflation' (quoted in Walsh, 1984, pp. 175–6). Other reasons given by the then Governor of the Central Bank included showing commitment to a major Community initiative and the expectation that support from the Community would result in the form of a significant transfer of resources (Walsh, 1984, p. 175).

For just over twenty years, Irish monetary policy was conducted within this framework until Ireland joined the new EMU at the beginning of 1999. The 20-year experience of EMS showed that the ideal of complete monetary independence was limited in Ireland (FitzGerald, 2000, p. 1355); given the small size of the economy, with free movement of capital, monetary policy was in effect determined elsewhere. The UK's decision to remain outside the EMS did cause difficulties for the punt in the early 1980s and inflation was high. However, from 1987 until the EMS crisis of 1992–93, participation in the EMS helped foster exchange-rate stability and low inflation rates and meant that Irish policy-makers were predisposed to participation in economic and monetary union. As part of the EMS fallout, the decision to devalue the Irish punt by 10 per cent in 1993 helped re-establish the competitiveness of Irish exports and at the same time put EMU firmly on the Irish agenda. The consequent need to meet the Maastricht criteria for entry to EMU (for example low budget deficit, low inflation and interest rates) provided the parameters for Irish fiscal policy through much of the 1990s and encouraged greater discipline in both public finance and wage bargaining, feeding into the economic turnaround.

Why did Irish policy-makers support joining EMU? Economists are agreed that the decision was taken more on political than on economic grounds (FitzGerald, 2001; Honohan, 2000). The impact of the financial recession in the 1980s and the fluctuations in exchange rates between the Irish pound and British sterling meant that it was risky for financial investors to borrow in Irish pound assets.

Within EMU, lending in Ireland would involve no exchange risk and would not require special study of the prospects for the Irish pound, increasing the attractiveness of capital investment in Ireland. On the flip-side, while not participating and participating in a floating exchange-rate regime would have been possible, no other option was held to be clearly superior (Honohan, 2000, p. 7). One of the key long-term reasons why membership of EMU was considered desirable for Ireland was the expected impact on interest rates and the cost of capital (Baker *et al.*, 1996). When the decision on membership was made in the mid-1990s, there was extensive evidence from 15 years of monetary independence that independence was bought at the cost of much higher interest rates (FitzGerald, 2001, p. 1359). The most significant potential cost for the Irish economy from EMU membership was expected to arise from the increased policy inflexibility in the face of external shock, due to the loss of an important instrument to Europe – monetary policy.

But what of Ireland's experience in EMU? According to Honohan's assessment of Ireland in EMU in 2000, EMU 'has been a straitjacket and exchange rate policy and this has had bite: Ireland has proved to be an EMU outlier, its boom contrasting with more subdued conditions in the zone as a whole' (Honohan, 2000, p. 9). There was indeed a credibility gain with lower interest rates, but the option of raising interest rates was removed as a monetary mechanism by Irish policy-makers to curb rising inflation. The fall in nominal interest rates was reflected in the rise in property prices, fuelling the property price boom and increased construction activity (Honohan, 2000). Economic management became a little more complicated and what has changed for the Irish government are the economic issues that they control. Now the focus of Irish economic policy-makers is on managing the economy through fiscal policy (and this is also where the Commission keeps an eye on Irish spending levels in its budgetary policies as part of the Stability and Growth Pact), as well as domestic wage policies and flexibility in the labour market.

The image of Ireland projected by successive Irish governments in the EU in this period was as a *communautaire*, constructive and fully committed member notwithstanding periodic debate about neutrality. The broad political consensus on Ireland's involvement in the EU meant that little contention existed on European issues in the media or in parliament. The European dimension was not a central subject for the Irish media and public, prompting Maurice Doyle, former Governor of the Central Bank, to liken Irish lack of engagement with EU issues to 'a process akin to sleep-walking' (quoted in Hussey, 1993, p. 215). In both political circles and amongst the public, the consensus that membership was a good thing for Ireland appeared to be widespread. Newly emerging political parties such as the Green Party joined groups such as the Irish Sovereignty Movement and individuals such as economist Raymond Crotty and social policy expert Anthony Coughlan in challenging the consensus, in providing dissenting voices to the perceived orthodox perspective on Irish membership of the EU. Contention in the first instance focused on the issue of security policy and the clash between Ireland's policy of military neutrality and its involvement with moves by other member states to integrate further in the foreign policy sphere.

The electorate, on the other hand, was broadly supportive of membership, with the conviction that membership was of benefit to the country clear in the EU's Eurobarometer surveys. From the mid-1980s onwards, the EU's Eurobarometer surveys consistently showed the high level of approval given by the Irish people to membership of the EU. Yet this positive perception was accompanied by relatively low levels of knowledge about the EU. In a study carried out in 1995, Sinnott discovered that 'there is very considerable room for improvement in levels of knowledge' about the EU. Ireland ranked just above the EU average in knowledge of European affairs, and 59 per cent of Irish respondents to Eurobarometer surveys displayed 'low' or 'very low knowledge' of the EU (Sinnott, 1995, p. 34). Such ignorance is all the more surprising given the events surrounding the ratification of the Single European Act in 1986 and the subsequent political requirement that all changes to EU treaties be ratified by referendum.

At the time of the signature of the SEA in 1986 the Fine Gael/ Labour Government assumed that approval of the Act by the Dáil and Seanad was sufficient for its ratification. The legislative process began on 9 December 1986, and concluded two days later, weeks before the ratification deadline of 31 December 1986. There was little parliamentary debate on the implications of the Act and it received, in the words of one expert, 'only the most perfunctory consideration' (McCutcheon, 1991, p. 215). Yet on the very eve of Ireland's ratification of the SEA, Raymond Crotty, an economist, journalist and long-time critical voice regarding Ireland's membership of the EEC, sought an injunction from the Courts restraining the Government from ratifying the Act due to the provisions of Title III,

European Political Cooperation. Basing its judgements on the provisions in Title III, the Supreme Court held by a three-to-two majority that Title III was inconsistent with the Constitution and the Constitution as it stood did not allow the State to ratify the SEA. The immediate consequence was that a constitutional amendment was required to authorise ratification of the SEA, to the apparent astonishment of members of the political and legal establishments (McCutcheon, 1991, p. 218; Crotty, 1988). The long-term political consequence of the Supreme Court's decision on the SEA was subsequent Governments would seek to ratify European treaties by referendum.

Thus the Maastricht, Amsterdam and Nice treaties were subsequently submitted to the electorate for approval. The 1998 Amsterdam Treaty campaign differed from previous campaigns due to the existence of the Referendum Commission, a body set up to publicize the issues at stake in a fair and unbiased manner. In previous referendum campaigns, governments used public money to finance a campaign in favour of the option they advocated, until this was declared unconstitutional in a judgement delivered by the Supreme Court a week before the 1995 divorce referendum in a case brought by Green Party MEP Patricia McKenna. Although the McKenna challenge was timed to coincide with the divorce referendum, her longstanding opposition to the EU was the motivating factor. The judgement resulted in the establishment of a Referendum Commission in 1998 to disseminate information in advance of the Amsterdam Treaty referendum. The Referendum Acts of 1994 and 1998 contain the regulations and mechanics governing the holding of referendums in Ireland. Yet the existence of such a Commission did little to increase knowledge or understanding of the issues at stake. Turnout at 56.3 per cent was slightly lower than in the Maastricht referendum of 1992, with 61.7 per cent of those who voted voting Yes and 38.3 per cent voting No, until then the highest ever No vote in an EU referendum in Ireland.

1998 and beyond: a new Ireland living in the new EU

> Even before the [Nice] referendum, it had become clear that, just as the European Union itself is changing, so is Ireland's place within it. (Minister for Foreign Affairs Brian Cowen, Dáil Éireann, 11 December 2001)

TABLE 2.2   *Result of Nice I referendum, 7 June 2001*

Electorate	2,867,960	
Total poll	997,826	34.79%
Yes	453,461	46.13%
No	529,478	53.87%
Spoiled votes	14,887	–

Notes: Only two constituencies in the Republic accepted the Nice Treaty – Dun Laoghaire (53.58% Yes) and Dublin South (51.88% Yes). There was little regional variation in the vote, with the lowest No vote recorded in the Rest of Leinster (52.37%) and the highest No vote in Ulster (56.13%).

From the late 1990s onwards the broad consensus on Ireland's place and role within the EU altered perceptibly. From 2000 to 2006 Ireland remained a net beneficiary of the EU budget. As a result of Ireland's economic catch-up and the accession of ten new and poorer member states in 2004, however, for the budgetary period of 2007– 13, Ireland is a net contributor. As Ireland's economic position within the EU changed, so too did perspectives on European integration and the future direction of the EU. Critical voices to the EU grew louder amongst the political classes (in particular the Green Party and Sinn Féin) and increasing levels of opposition to the EU amongst the electorate was evident from those who voted against ratification of the Treaty of Amsterdam in 1998 (38 per cent of those who turned out to vote voted no). The subsequent rejection of the Nice Treaty in June 2001 (Table 2.2) seemed to reinforce the sense of an increasing hostility, or at least scepticism, on the part of the public to the EU. Turnout at 34.79 per cent was the lowest level ever recorded for a European referendum and the referendum was rejected by 54 per cent. The rejection of the Nice Treaty was a major shock to the Irish political class, its partners in Europe and the then candidate states in central and Eastern Europe. Ireland's stable European policy was perceived to be loose of its moorings (Laffan and Falkner, 2004, p. 212). Was this result just a temporary phenomenon, or is it a sign of growing anti-European feeling in Ireland?

Changing attitude of the political elites and the public?

From 2000 to late 2001, uncertainty about Ireland's place in the EU system was perceptible amongst a number of government ministers. Indeed, the reaction of a number of Fianna Fáil ministers, both before and in the aftermath of the Nice I referendum, seemed to suggest that a more questioning attitude to the European Union was emerging in the party. Minister for Finance Charlie McCreevy, Minister for Arts Síle de Valera, Minister of State Eamon Ó Cuiv and Minister of State Willie O'Dea all critiqued the EU in the public arena. This would not have happened when Ireland was a poorer and more dependent member state. Ó Cuiv announced soon after the referendum result that he had voted No, in spite of campaigning for a Yes vote. His engagement with the Commission on the habitats directive contributed to his negative stance on the treaty (Laffan and O'Mahony, 2008). O'Dea is on record as saying that the referendum result 'showed that Irish people are stubborn, and if they want to make a decision, they will. It shows a certain robust independence which I admire' (*Irish Times*, 18 June 2001).

In early 2001, the European Commission criticized and ultimately reprimanded the Fianna Fáil–Progressive Democrat government's December 2000 budget, and Commissioner Pedro Solbes advised Charlie McCreevy to rewrite his budget to take money out of the Irish economy. In response, Minister McCreevy questioned the Commission's and the EU Economic and Finance Ministers' analysis of Ireland's macro-economic policy and their subsequent decision to censure his budgetary policy, given the fact that other member states were more seriously breaching the broad economic guidelines (Gilland, 2004, p. 180). McCreevy later argued that the censure had been a contributing factor to the Nice 1 No vote. During the Gothenburg EU Summit in June 2001, he went on to state:

> Here we had all the political parties, all of the media, both in broadcast and print, all of the organisations – IBEC, ICTU, the IFA and everybody else – yet the plain people of Ireland in their wisdom have decided to vote No. I think that's a very healthy sign. (*Irish Times*, 18 June 2001)

While many politicians and commentators expressed surprise and shock at the referendum result, there were signs of a possible upset even before the results of the referendum were revealed (Sinnott, 2001). In an MRBI poll conducted a week before the referendum vote, 45 per cent of those surveyed indicated that they would vote Yes, 28 per cent would vote No and 27 per cent had no opinion (*Irish Times*, 30 May 2001). This showed a narrowing in the gap between the Yes and No votes over the course of the campaign. Perhaps even more importantly, however, when asked how well they understood what the Treaty was about, 15 per cent felt they had a good understanding of what the Treaty was about, 32 per cent understood some of the issues but not all, 31 per cent were only vaguely aware of the issues involved, 19 per cent did not know what the Treaty was about at all and 2 per cent had no opinion.

The image of Ireland as a 'communautaire' member state took a battering amongst Ireland's European partners. For the first time ever since accession, European reaction following the referendum result was, predictably, negative. Political reaction came from Commission President Romano Prodi and Swedish President of the EU Goran Persson, who stressed that while the EU was ready to take on board the concerns of the Irish electorate, there was no question of treaty re-negotiation; they emphasized that accession negotiations must not be delayed by the vote. The European press reaction was not so muted, with the French daily *Le Monde* referring to Ireland as 'l'enfant terrible', the Italian daily *Corriere della Sera* saying that Ireland was now suffering from the syndrome of the selfish 'full stomach' (O'Mahony, 2004).

So what reasons lay behind the rejection of the Nice Treaty? Was the decision to vote No by such a proportion of the electorate based on the issues contained in the Nice Treaty itself? Were the Irish people against the further enlargement of the European Union to include 10 new countries from Central and Eastern Europe, Malta and Cyprus now that Ireland would be a net contributor to the EU budget? Or did they vote on the basis of ignorance; that is, if you don't know, vote No?

It is fair to say the Irish political elite took a positive result for granted. The government allocated merely three weeks to what was a lacklustre campaign and made half-hearted efforts to explain the issues to the electorate (Laffan and Tonra, 2005, p. 448). The European Commission Representation in Ireland commissioned a survey following the negative result in order to ascertain the reasons behind the No vote. In this research, Sinnott found that turnout had a major bearing on outcome with 53 per cent of those who had voted 'Yes' to Amsterdam abstaining in Nice I. By far the most frequent subjective explanation given for abstention was lack of information and lack of understanding of the issues; 44 per cent of Nice abstainers explained their non-voting in these terms. The predominant characteristic of those surveyed who voted No was a feeling of not being adequately on top of the issues and a tendency to follow the maxim, which had also been prominent in the No campaign in the Amsterdam referendum, 'if you don't know, vote No'. On the basis

Box 2.2   Ireland's contribution to the EU

In viewing EU membership as a source of Ireland's economic prosperity and political standing, it is easy to lose sight of the contribution that Ireland has made towards the EU. In policy terms at least, at first glance, the Irish contribution to the EU appears weak. Big ideas on the future of the EU tend not to emanate from Irish shores. Yet Ireland, in holding its six EU Presidencies and acting as an honest broker, has helped steer the EU through periods of internal change and evolution, be it in 1990 with Charles Haughey's positive stance on German reunification, progress towards the signature of the Treaty of Amsterdam in 1996 (and the championing of the social inclusion agenda) and the successful negotiation of the Constitutional Treaty in 2004. Irish officials and politicians have also been active in Brussels, with a number of top-level officials such as David O'Sullivan and Catherine Day and politicians such as Pat Cox as President of the European Parliament from 2002–04 and John Bruton of Fine Gael as EU Ambassador to the United States. Irish commissioners have been highly regarded and for the most part been given significant portfolios within the Commission:

Commissioner	Appointing Government	Period	Portfolio
Patrick Hillery	FF	1973–76	Social Affairs
Richard Burke	FG-Lab	1977–80	Transport,
		–	Consumer Affairs, Taxation,
		–	Relations with EP

→

of these figures, Garret FitzGerald extrapolated that almost one million people either opposed the treaty or failed to vote because of lack of information/understanding or confusion (*Irish Times*, 5 January 2002; O'Mahony, 2004, p. 27). Hence, the claim that a growing proportion of the population was becoming increasingly anti-European must be viewed carefully – instead a significant proportion of the Irish electorate must be characterized as lacking in knowledge and confused about the nature of the European Union and Ireland's

→			
Michael O'Kennedy	FF	1981–82	President's Delegate, Administration
Richard Burke	FF	1982–84	Greek Renegotiation
Peter Sutherland	FG-Lab	1985–88	Competition
Ray MacSharry	FF	1989–92	CAP
Padraig Flynn	FF	1993–99	Social Affairs
David Byrne	FF-PD	1999–2004	Health and Consumer Protection
Charlie McCreevy	FF-PD	2004–09	Internal Market

As an example of a member state that has demonstrated such economic catch-up and that has taken considerable advantage of its position as an EU member states, Ireland has been seen as a model for the Central and Eastern European member states that joined the EU in 2004 (see Chapter 10). Finally, following the defeat of the EU Constitutional treaty in referendums in France and the Netherlands in 2005, the performance of the National Forum on Europe attracted widespread attention in the EU as a means of overcoming the disconnect between the EU and its citizens).

place within it. The electorate was also receiving mixed cues from the political elite about the EU.

Re-engaging with the EU?

The shock of the Nice rejection served to galvanize the government into action in order to bring about a solution. The government was faced with a difficult task as it had to persuade its partners and the candidate states that the electorate had not rejected enlargement *per se* and at the same time it had to persuade the electorate that it had listened to their concerns. It was clear that the political elite could no longer rely on the electorate's unquestioning support for Ireland's continued participation in moves to further EU integration; the permissive consensus that existed from accession to the late 1990s was over. The government carefully pursued a strategy of creating the domestic conditions that would lead to the holding of a second Nice referendum. In order to ascertain the electorate's views on the EU and Ireland's engagement within it, as well as being seen to respond to the electorate's concerns, the government established a cross-party National Forum on Europe in the autumn of 2001. The Forum consisted of representatives of the political parties from both houses of the Oireachtas and a number of observers from a range of interest and civil-society groups encompassing the diverse range of attitudes now found towards the EU. It met regularly in public, both in Dublin and throughout the country, inviting guest speakers such as ministers, MEPs, national parliamentarians and academics. The forum provided a locus for debate on all aspects of the EU and the Nice Treaty. The government also enhanced parliamentary scrutiny of EU legislation and Ireland's EU policy in July 2002 (see Chapter 3) and the government succeeded in getting other EU member states to accept its declarations on Irish neutrality and a common defence in June 2002. Following re-election in May 2002, the government was in a position to re-run the referendum in October 2002 (Hayward, 2003).

The Nice II referendum was very different to the first, both in its conduct and in its outcome. The result was a strong endorsement of the treaty, with 63 per cent voting Yes, 37 per cent voting No, and with a turnout of 49 per cent. With turnout up by 14 per cent, instead of two of every three electors abstaining, only one in every two abstained. The second campaign was characterized by engaged mobilization on the part of the government parties, the pro-EU opposition parties, business and civil society groups. Yet such an active campaign did not significantly increase levels of knowledge about the EU. In one of the Eurobarometer polls of 2003, a pronounced sense of lack of knowledge of the European Union was still evident in Ireland, with 42 per cent of respondents feeling that they had a poor knowledge of the EU and its policies. The only two member states standing lower were the United Kingdom and Portugal (Eurobarometer 60, 2003; Laffan and Tonra, 2005, p. 449).

A different relationship

Over thirty years on, Ireland is a prosperous member state of the European Union. The Ireland that existed at accession is long gone as the Irish people embraced the vision of Lemass rather than that of de Valera. The complex interaction between events at the domestic and EU levels enabled Ireland to profit from participation in the European integration project. EU membership continues to be perceived as a matter of vital national interest to the electorate, and Irish political elites continue to be committed to full engagement with the EU. But such engagement is not unquestioning. As a net contributor to the EU budget Irish expectations have altered. Politicians and officials negotiating with EU partners are focused on a wider range of issues than the CAP and the structural funds. Gone are the certainties of the first 25 years of membership. This was brought sharply home with the defeat of a second referendum on a European treaty in eight years when the Irish followed the 'no' to Nice with 'no' to Lisbon in June 2008.

Chapter 3

Managing Europe

When Ireland joined the EEC, an additional layer of governance was added to its domestic system of policy-making, posing a challenge to its national political and administrative systems. The national core executive, that is, the Irish government and central administration or bureaucracy, became a dominant carrier of Europeanization, as the system was required to adjust to engagement with the EU's system of collective governance. Public policy-making was no longer to be conducted within the confines of the structures and processes of Irish government as EU policy-making triggered institutional adaptation 'at home' and altered domestic rules (c.f. Laffan and O'Mahony, 2007). Adaptation to this system required more than just a once-off adjustment as the EU policy regime itself expanded and evolved over time. The Irish core executive became the key bridge between the national and the European in the EU's networked system of governance, with members of government and senior civil service officials, the *cadre* or boundary managers, acting as translators of EU policies, norms and practices into the domestic arena and projecting domestic preferences back into the EU arena (Bulmer and Burch, 1998, 2000 and 2001; Featherstone and Radaelli, 2003). Managing this additional layer of governance thus became increasingly important to the Irish core executive. So how does the Irish core executive manage EU business at home and in Brussels? Has the Irish public administration system developed the capacity to act effectively at the EU level? How has the system of domestic management of EU business evolved over time?

This chapter investigates the adaptation and change of the Irish core executive to EU membership from an institutionalist perspective. Focusing on organizational and formal and informal institutional configurations, the chapter examines the demands placed by EU membership on the Irish core executive system and how the system has responded to those demands. Institutionalist concepts such as critical junctures and path dependency are also used to analyse in a dynamic way the changes over time to the core executive. Adaptation to EU business in Ireland was path-dependent and consisted of gradual incremental adjustment. This system of flexible adaptation generally served Ireland well as the EU's policy regime expanded and evolved, but in response to the shock rejection of the Nice Treaty in 2001, significant formalization of the Irish system occurred with the establishment of new processes and rules for managing relations between the core executive and the EU.

Executive adaptation to EU membership – framing the analysis

The study of core executive adaptation to EU membership forms part of the Europeanization literature which focuses on national executives as key 'translator' devices' between the European and the domestic levels of governance (Genschel, 2001, p. 98). The substantive focus of this part of the literature has been on the formal organizational changes that membership has brought and the manner in which national governments respond to engagement with the Union. Historical institutionalism (HI) has been the preferred framework in a number of studies (for example Bulmer and Burch, 1998, 2000, 2001; Harmsen, 1999; Kassim, 2003; and Laffan, 2006). With HI, the focus is on mapping the para-constitutional, organizational and institutional configurations and the coordination processes within domestic systems over time rather than analysing particular institutions in isolation (Pierson, 2000a). While the impact of the EU on member states' politics has been found to be great, the effect on their governmental systems has been far less evident (Bulmer and Burch, 2001, p. 75; Knill, 2001). Managing EU business has not been a source of transformative change in national core executives; adaptation is deeply rooted in national style, and existing structures and operating procedures have been adapted around the edges rather than fundamentally altered by EU membership, as we see is the case in Ireland. Nor have convergent patterns of national adaptation emerged.

The notion of the core executive was developed in research on central government in the UK and includes all those organizations and structures which primarily serve to pull together and integrate central government policies, or act as final arbiters within the executive of conflicts between different elements of the government machine

(Dunleavy and Rhodes, 1990; Rhodes, 2000a and 2000b). The core executive lies at the interface between the political and administrative arenas involving a 'highly institutionalized set of relationships' (Smith, 2000, p. 29). Yet the concept of the core executive does not just capture formal structures – cabinet and ministries – but also the more informal roles, networks and relationships between actors at the heart of government, be it politicians or senior officials. The Irish core executive and system of government has been categorized as a variant of the Westminster model with one important difference – a written constitution (see Gallagher, Laver and Mair, 2001). The key conventions of collective and ministerial responsibility lie at the heart of the Irish Constitution and political authority is invested in the Government, which meets in Cabinet. The Irish core executive consists of the Prime Minister or Taoiseach, the Government, ministries known as departments (corresponding to all main areas of policy) and the civil or administrative service. The 1937 Constitution placed the Taoiseach in a powerful position as head of the government with the authority to hire and fire ministers.

With HI, attention is also paid to the configuration of political order around formal institutions, organizations, norms, rules, roles and practices which frame the conduct and strategies of actors over time (Thelen and Steinmo, 1992, p. 2). In their study of core executive management of EU business in Britain, Bulmer and Burch (1998) divided their organizational field as follows: the formal institutional structure, processes and procedures, codes and guidelines, and the cultural dimension. This was later adapted to focus on four institutional dimensions, notably the systemic, organizational, procedural and regulative (Bulmer and Burch, 2000, p. 50). The analytical framework used here builds on and adapts Bulmer and Burch's institutionalist framework by dividing the institutional field into three levels, analysing not just the structural and process dimension of core executive management, but also the key role of agents.

The *structural component* maps the organizations and structures that form the core executive in Ireland and the key relationships in the management of EU affairs over time. Was EU business absorbed into existing organizations or did it lead to major institutional innovation? The *process component* examines the pathways for EU related information through the Irish domestic system and the codes, rules, guidelines that govern the handling of EU business over time. How is EU business that is cross-cutting in nature coordinated in the Irish system? The third component, the *agents*, examines the role of the individuals who act as the boundary managers or gate-keepers between the domestic and the European. In all member states, there are a number of key political roles held by individuals who have primary responsibility for managing European affairs. An administrative *cadre* (which includes senior civil service officials, the permanent representative) complements the political *cadre* (heads of government and key ministers). Heretofore little has been known about the key attitudes, belief systems and values of such individuals (Wessels, 2003, p. 7).

As well as helping us to identify various institutional configurations, HI also pays attention to institutional evolution and processes of change over time. HI accounts of institutional change point to the 'stickiness' of institutions once established and the importance of path-dependence in institutional development. According to HI, the dynamic of change is path-dependent; once created, institutions (be it structures, processes or roles of agents) may prove difficult and costly to change. Change, when it does occur, for example the decision to alter the system of core executive management, can be either incremental (minor change around the edges) or episodic (Cortell and Peterson, 1999, p. 182). Episodic change can be said to be related to what has been termed 'critical junctures' (Ikenberry, 1988, p. 16), described by Collier and Collier as 'a period of significant change ... which is hypothesised to produce distinct legacies' (Collier and Collier, 1991, p. 29; Capoccia and Keleman, 2007). This episodic and significant change may result from events or processes internal and external to the domestic system. Systemic change at the national level or political events at the national level that have a wide and significant impact may trigger the adoption of new modes of management. At the same time, policy and regime change in the Union, such as through significant treaty reform, may also prompt further development of the domestic capacity for management of EU affairs (Pierson, 2000a, 2000b; Scott, 2001). Taking institutional evolution seriously enables us to track incremental change and path-dependency, as well as to distinguish between internal and external sources of change, in particular enabling us to identify the effects of any critical junctures on the process of institutional development. Adaptation to EU membership is seen as a continuous process punctuated by occasional critical junctures or moments. This chapter analyses Irish adaptation in four ways. First we explore the origins and development of the management of EU issues in Ireland, with the identification of triggers for significant change. We then dissect the structures established to manage the EU–domestic interface. Finally, the formal and informal coordination processes and the role of the agents or *cadre* managing these processes are examined.

Managing EU issues in Ireland: origins and development

From accession in 1973 to the end of the 1990s, Ireland's system for managing EU business was relatively stable. The structures and processes put in place on accession to position Ireland in the EU system appeared to work well over time, and change, when it occurred, was incremental, slow and adaptive in response to developments at the EU level. The expansion of the EU's policy regime to include economic and monetary union, foreign and security policy and justice and home affairs in the Maastricht Treaty brought new domestic actors into the management system and increased the amount of EU business that had to be dealt with. A subtle shift also occurred with the enhancement of the Taoiseach's position as overall guide of Irish EU policy. In 2001, however, a domestic critical juncture occurred with the No vote to the Nice Treaty by the Irish electorate. The negative vote triggered a period of review and evaluation and resulted in significant change in how EU business was and is managed in Ireland.

Ireland's approach to the management of its engagement with the EU was established in the latter half of the 1950s when the decision was taken by Sean Lemass to consider joining the EEC. From the outset, the mapping of Ireland's European policy and the management of EU business was cross-cutting in nature, involving as it did a core of key senior officials from the main government departments. The Taoiseach, senior domestic ministers and a small group of senior civil servants played the key role in charting Ireland's relationship with the system and in negotiating Irish EEC entry. A Committee of Secretaries provided the forum for inter-ministerial discussion on the key issues and the Cabinet agreed the political framework within which the relationship would evolve.

The period between accession in January 1973 and the end of Ireland's first Presidency in December 1975 was Ireland's apprenticeship in the EU system. During this period, the Irish Governmental system put in place structures and processes for managing the relationship with Brussels. In its fundamentals the management system put in place remained unchanged until the late 1980s. Responsibility for day-to-day coordination on EU matters was assigned to the Department of Foreign Affairs (DFA) and the principle of the 'lead department' was firmly established. In this way, individual departments as lead ministries became the domestic interlocutors with the EU and were responsible from the outset for coordinating preparations for Council meetings falling within their remit (Kassim, 2003, p. 98). Overall, there was very little institution building in the form of new structures, rather there was a reliance on the adaptation of existing domestic structures within the broad parameters of collective responsibility and ministerial responsibility. The Irish administration faced the challenge of adapting to the Brussels system with limited human resources. There was a relatively small increase in full-time non-industrial civil servants as a result of EU membership. The preparations for the 1975 Presidency were important for Ireland's adjustment to EU membership as the demands of running a Presidency ensured that departmental responsibility for different policy areas was clearly delineated and management of Council business meant that ministers and officials became familiar with the nuts and bolts of the Union's policy process. Indeed, the experience of the Presidency had an important effect on the psychological environment of national policy-makers: thereafter, the Union became an accepted albeit complicating factor in national decision-making.

The resurgence of integration at the EU level in the late 1980s and beyond prompted change in the Irish system. Beginning with the signature of the Single European Act (SEA), the negotiation of the Delors I multi-annual budgetary package and the signature and ratification of the Maastricht Treaty, the amount of EU business to be dealt with increased dramatically. New domestic players became involved in the EU game. With increased policy making in areas such as environment and internal security, the Departments of Environment and Justice moved from being peripheral actors to key departments involved in managing EU business and cross-cutting issues. The growing importance of the European Council in EU policy-making enhanced the position of the Taoiseach in determining the broad contours of Ireland's EU policy. Under the premiership of Charles Haughey in particular (1987–91), the Taoiseach's office adopted a stronger leadership role and played a key role in negotiating and implementing Ireland's first national development plan using the increased structural funds gained from the Delors I package. The hitherto moribund interdepartmental European Communities

Committee was rejuvenated by the Taoiseach's office under Haughey and chaired by a new Minister of State for European Affairs. A high-level committee of ministers and senior civil servants was also established and serviced by the Taoiseach's office. These committees were never fully formalized, however, and subsequently relied on prime ministerial will for their existence. Finally, the dominance of the executive in the management of EU business weakened the already limited role of parliament in monitoring Irish EU policy and added to the process of de-parliamentarization evident in political systems throughout Europe (Kassim, 2003, p. 91).

The electorate's decision to reject the Nice Treaty in 2001 shook the Irish system for the management of EU business to its core. Until 2001, Ireland managed to portray itself as a constructive player in the Union with a relatively *communautaire* approach in general. The desire to be seen as broadly *communautaire* led governments to go with the emerging EU consensus unless an issue was highly sensitive. The 'no' to Nice and the low turnout in the referendum (34 per cent) of the electorate highlighted the fact that the hitherto benign domestic environment towards the EU would not continue and the Government could no longer take its voters for granted. The rejection of the treaty also led to considerable soul-searching at official and political level of how EU business was managed and how Europe was communicated at national level. Ireland's core executive had reached a critical juncture in its management of EU business and a number of key structural and procedural reforms were set in train as a response (most notably the 'ratcheting-up' of interdepartmental coordination and enhanced Parliamentary scrutiny). These reforms in turn helped contribute to the success of Ireland's Sixth EU Presidency from January to June 2004 and the final negotiation of the EU's Constitutional Treaty under the Irish presidency (Rees, 2005a).

Dissecting the system

The structures of the Irish core executive that deal with EU business include: the ministries, committees and designated units with responsibility for managing EU affairs. Given the reach of EU policies on national policy-making, every department and office in the Irish core executive system is required to deal with the European Union in some way. The extent of interaction and need to manage EU business depends primarily on the degree of Europeanization found in the respective policy domains of each office and department. It is possible to place the Irish core executive system's management of EU business on three distinct gradations based on this measure: the Holy Trinity (the hub of EU management), the inner core and the outer circle.

The salience of the EU in the particular policy area determines the response of the individual departments in setting up structures to deal with the flow of EU business (see Figure 3.1). Three over-arching ministries – the 'Holy Trinity' of Foreign Affairs, Taoiseach and Finance – manage Irish EU policy from a macro perspective and are the central structural nodes through which Ireland's overall EU strategy must pass through at varying stages (Laffan, 2001). At the second

FIGURE 3.1   The Irish core executive

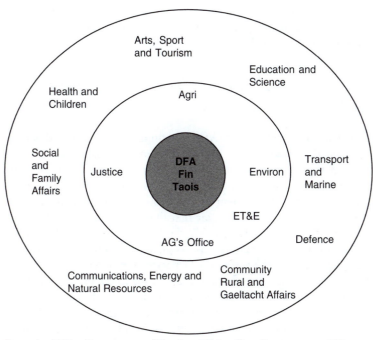

Legend: DFA = Department of Foreign Affairs, Fin = Department of Finance, Taois = Department of the Taoiseach, Justice = Justice, Equality and Law Reform, Environ = Department of Environment, Heritage and Local Government, AG's Office = Attorney General's Office, ET&E = Department of Enterprise, Trade and Employment, Agri = Department of Agriculture, Fisheries and Food.
Source: Laffan and O'Mahony (2007), p. 174.

level, or the inner core, EU policies are central or increasingly central to the work undertaken by the Departments of Agriculture, Justice, Enterprise, Trade & Employment and the Environment. Given its responsibility for the translation of all European law into domestic law, the Office of the Attorney General is also included in this level. As EU competence grew from the 1980s onwards in new policy areas such as environment and internal security and more hands-on involvement in the formulation, coordination and monitoring of new legislation was necessary, some departments (namely Justice and Environment) moved from the outer circle to the inner core. For the departments at the outer circle of core-executive management, coordinating and managing national policy remains the over-arching concern. However, each of these departments, to varying degrees, deal with a certain amount of EU business; in particular as they became involved in the Lisbon agenda, the ten-year strategy to make the EU the most competitive and most dynamic knowledge-based economy in the world.

The Holy Trinity: Departments of Foreign Affairs, the Taoiseach and Finance

The Department of Foreign Affairs assumed the role of lead department on EU matters from the Department of Finance in 1973. Its place at the heart of the Irish core executive is still taken as given, however it now shares its coordinating responsibilities to a greater degree with the Department of the Taoiseach. In September 1973, the DFA issued its main circular that that established how EU business should be handled (CH/177/35). Responsibility for day-to-day coordination on EU matters was assigned to the DFA, which constituted a break with the past as the Department of Finance was the lead department in the period leading up to membership. Membership had a major impact on the structure of the Department of Foreign Affairs and was instrumental in promoting the modernization of the Irish Foreign Service (Keatinge, 1995, p. 2). The department's modernization was characterized by an increase in the number of staff in head office and in Irish missions abroad (see Table 3.1).

Increased resources were accompanied by internal organizational changes with the creation of new divisions, the reorganization of existing ones and increased functional specialization at head office. Those changes were a response to membership; the demands of

TABLE 3.1 *Department of Foreign Affairs staffing*

Year	Total number in DFA	Total number in Economic/EU Division
1967	40	6
1971	51	11
1974	87	31
1979	114	27
1982	130	30
1986	136	29
1988	125	24
1992	123	15
1995	126	19
2000	175	19

Source: State Directories, 1967–2000.

managing a presidency and the widening scope and reach of Irish foreign policy. In the late 1980s, Foreign Affairs, like all government departments, suffered a reduction in staff during the public-sector recruitment embargo. However, concern about the capacity of headquarters to direct the growing diplomatic network and to respond to the demands of strategic policy-making led to a major internal review of its resources and organizational structure in 1999–2000. The *chef de file* or lead unit arrangement was put in place in February 2002 where each unit within the Department has overall responsibility for particular regions or countries of the world.

Within the Irish system, the DFA is the department with an overview of developments in the EU from an institutional and political perspective. In addition, its embassies in the member states can provide information and briefing on the policy positions of the member states. The Irish Representation in Brussels is a pivotal source of intelligence on developments in the EU and has a key function in identifying how and what national preferences can be promoted within the EU and in identifying the trade-offs that might be necessary as negotiations develop. The EU Division coordinates Ireland's approach within the EU. The Political Division is responsible for international political issues and manages Ireland's participation in the EU's common foreign security policy and defence issues. The EU Division and the Irish Representation in Brussels form two central nodes in the management of EU business as they interact with (a) EU institutions, particularly the Council but also the Commission and the Parliament, and (b) government departments both individually and collectively.

The Taoiseach's Department, while small in size compared to other government departments, is central to the conduct of EU business as it serves as the secretariat to the Taoiseach. Its role in the conduct of EU business has been considerably enhanced in recent years to the extent that it is now considered as one of the two 'EU coordinating departments' (Interview Senior Official, Department of An Taoiseach, 26 March 2002). While primary responsibility for the development of Ireland's European policy on specific issues rests with individual Departments, the core role of the Department of the Taoiseach is to provide a strategic direction and focus for this European policy in overall terms. The aim of those in the Department is to work in tandem with the relevant line departments rather than duplicate the work that is already being done. The relatively small size of the Department of the Taoiseach necessitates this approach. The department can be brought into any set of negotiations if they become problematic or in the event of deep-rooted interdepartmental conflict. The tendency is 'to delegate and to co-ordinate as required and not to micro-manage' (Interview with Department of An Taoiseach Official, 12 March 2002).

The Department of Finance's role in EU business increased significantly from the mid-1980s with the single market programme, EU structural and cohesion funds, taxation and EMU to the extent that the Department of Finance could now be said to have an interest in everything European for its role as the controller of the public finances gives it a central role in EU affairs. It is standard practice that EU proposals with financial implications for the Exchequer must be cleared with the Department of Finance before being approved. The Department plays a major role in negotiations on taxation, where the Department of Foreign Affairs' involvement is minimal. The two Divisions centrally involved in EU business are the Budget, Economic and Pensions Division and the Taxation and Financial Services Division. These sections have autonomy and responsibility for policy in respect of issues under their aegis and pull together when going to ECOFIN.

In sum, the roles of the three departments in the core of the system are complementary rather than competitive. The Department of the Taoiseach brings the authority of the prime minister to bear on cross-cutting issues and meetings called by this department will always be taken seriously. Foreign Affairs brings its knowledge of the EU, its negotiating expertise and its knowledge of the attitudes of other member states to the table. These two departments are major players in all of the macro-negotiations and have very close relations on the management of EU business. The Department of Finance is less involved in macro-issues to do with the development of the EU but is central to all aspects of economic governance.

The inner core and outer circle

Although EU business now permeates the work of all sectoral departments in some form, four in particular have key EU responsibilities and form part of the inner core of the core executive in managing EU business from home: Enterprise, Trade and Employment (ET&E), Agriculture, Fisheries and Food, Justice, Equality and Law Reform, and Environment, Heritage and Local Government. Together, these departments account for a sizeable proportion of Ireland's EU business. Given the size of these departments and the salience of their responsibilities, they have a high degree of autonomy in the exercise of their policy responsibilities. They also tend to be involved in macro-negotiations on cross-cutting issues and have well-established units or divisions devoted to EU and international affairs. ET&E and Agriculture have been key players from accession, whereas Justice and Environment have become increasingly involved in EU business from the 1990s onwards. The EU task facing each of these departments differs greatly one from the other. Agriculture is a clearly defined sector with a well-organized and politically significant client group. The Department of Enterprise, Trade and Employment is multi-sectoral with responsibility for a wide range of policy areas such as regulation, trade, social and employment policy, consumer policy, research and certain EU funds.

The Department of Justice, Equality and Law Reform is managing a relatively new but rapidly changing policy domain, which is characterized by complex decision rules, and the UK and Irish opt-out from the Schengen area (with its removal of passport checks at common borders and ancillary measures to facilitate freedom of movement in the EU) and aspects of JHA dealing with police and judicial cooperation in criminal matters. Environment policy in Ireland is increasingly formulated within the European frame and environmental issues are touching other policy areas of government and other departments business, such as sustainable development, which is relevant not only for Environment but also Agriculture and Communications, Energy and Natural Resources. Ireland's implementation record with regard to EU environmental legislation is closely monitored by a plethora of environmental lobby groups and NGOs at national and European level (see Chapter 7).

The Office of the Attorney General is included in the inner core of governmental departments who manage the interface with Brussels for one primary reason – the Office of the Attorney General offers legal advices and legislative drafting required as a result of the State's membership of the EU. Any departmental queries on EU legislation come to this office and this Office drafts every statutory instrument or statute produced in order to transpose EU legislation into domestic law.

Departments in the inner core and outer circle differ in two ways with regard to structures. First, the primary responsibilities of the Departments of the outer circle of the Irish executive continue to lie in the national arena. Even so, such is the reach of the EU, particularly with the development of the open method of coordination as a mode of governance, each of the departments in the outer circle finds itself increasingly obliged to manage EU business to varying degrees. Each of the departments in the outer circle has placed staff in the permanent representation in Brussels. It must also be borne in mind that the EU's competences in policy areas within the remit of these departments is also relatively weak in comparison with policy areas covered by departments in the inner core. Second, departments in the outer circle may or may not have specific divisions or units dedicated to dealing with EU business.

Horizontal structures

In all of the member states, committees at different levels in the hierarchy play a central role in the inter-ministerial or horizontal coordination of EU affairs. They are the main institutional devices for formal horizontal coordination. Until 2001, a key characteristic of the Irish committee system was its institutional fluidity and malleability (see Table 3.2 for a chronology of the different committee devices that have been established in Ireland). The Cabinet is the centre of political decision-making in the Irish system; it processes

TABLE 3.2 *EU committees in the Irish system*

Period	Committee	Chair
Pre-Accession	European Communities Committee	Department of Finance
1973–84	European Communities Committee	Department of Foreign Affairs
1985–87	No meetings of the committee	
1987–90	European Communities Committee	Geoghegan-Quinn (Minister of State)
1988–90	Ministers and Secretaries Group	Haughey (Taoiseach)
1989–90	Ministerial Group on the Presidency	Haughey (Taoiseach)
1992–94	European Communities Committee	Kitt (Minister of State)
1994–97	European Communities Committee	Mitchell (Minister of State)
1994–99	Ministers and Secretaries Group	Bruton/Ahern (Taoiseach)
1994–98	Senior Officials Group	Department of the Taoiseach
1998–99	Expert Technical Group	Ahern (Taoiseach)
1998–to date	Cabinet Sub-Committee	Ahern (Taoiseach)
1998–to date	Senior Officials Group	Department of the Taoiseach
2002–04	Interdepartmental Coordinating Committee on European Union Affairs	Roche (Minister of State)
2004–07	Interdepartmental Coordinating Committee on European Union Affairs	Treacy (Minister of State)
2007–to date	Interdepartmental Coordinating Committee on European Union Affairs	Roche (Minister of State)

Source: Laffan and O'Mahony (2007), p. 179.

EU issues according to the same standard operating procedures and rules that govern the processing of domestic issues. Although under-institutionalized by continental standards, the sub-structure of the Irish Cabinet has been strengthened by the establishment of a series of Cabinet sub-committees, including an EU Committee. It is attended by the key ministers with an EU brief, ministerial advisors, and senior civil servants. In preparation for the 2004 Presidency, this Committee met once every two weeks and was chaired by the Taoiseach.

Following the first Nice referendum defeat, the Irish committee system became embedded in the Irish system with formalization of the interdepartmental coordinating committee (Figure 3.2) (chaired by the Minister of State for European Affairs) in particular. Senior Officials attend the Committee from each Department, as can the

FIGURE 3.2   Central committees for the organization of cross-cutting EU issues (including *ad hoc* committees)

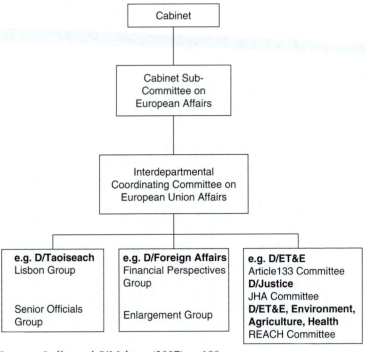

Source: Laffan and O'Mahony (2007), p. 180.

Permanent Representative. As the key driver of coordination across the Irish system and alongside the civil servant-led Senior Officials Group, the Committee is used as an early warning system for potentially problematic issues arising out of EU business, as well as a forum to facilitate strategic thinking across government departments (interview with Senior Official, Department of Foreign Affairs, 1 October 2007). As in the Cabinet Sub-Committee, the practice of holding presentations on relevant issues also takes place within the Committee. Senior officials from government departments attend a number of other, generally *ad hoc*, interdepartmental committees designed to deal with specific cross-cutting issues that arise.

The permanent representation

The Permanent Representation is an integral part of Ireland's management of EU business. It is a microcosm of Ireland's core executive in Brussels and staff maintain very close links with their home departments in Dublin. Traditionally, staff numbers had always been small (in the 1990s Ireland had the second smallest Permanent Representation in the EU). However, a significant increase in staffing occurred in the 1990s when a number of domestic ministries felt the need for a presence in Brussels. By the 2004 presidency, staff numbered more than 160 (including military staff) (Department of Foreign Affairs Presidency Report, 2004). The incremental process of Europeanization is evident in the number of ministries that have a presence in the representation. In 1973, six ministries had staff in Brussels, and a further three ministries joined them in the late 1970s and 1980s. In the 1990s and onwards the Ministries of the Marine (1991), Justice (1995), Health (1996), Attorney General's Office (1999), Defence (2000), Education (2001), Arts Culture and the Gaeltacht (2002) were added to the list. All domestic departments with the exception of the Taoiseach's department are now represented in Brussels. Officials at the representation regard servicing the Council as their core business and the cycle of Council, COREPER and working party business sets the tempo of work in the Representation (Laffan, 2000, p. 289). According to one former ambassador, 'the major job of the Permanent Representative is to ask "is this something we can win" and "what will I advise the Minster?" ' (Interview Senior Official, Department of Foreign Affairs, 7 March 2002). During negotiations, especially those of a sensitive nature, there is continuous and high-level contact between Dublin departments, the DFA and Brussels on the stance Ireland should take.

Processes

In examining processes, we focus on how the structures are animated in reality; that is, how the system lives and the codes, rules and guidelines through which it undertakes business. Ireland's management of EU business is not highly formalized; there is no Bible of European Affairs either for the system as a whole or within individual departments. Unlike the UK system there is no tradition of putting on paper Guidance Notes on substantive policy issues or horizontal procedural issues (Bulmer and Burch, 2000). On accession the DFA did not adopt the role of producing codes, rules and guidelines for the system as a whole; such an approach would have gone against the deep-rooted convention of the dominance of the lead department in the Irish system. Contact between officials was not formalized or paper-driven, with many discussions taking place over the phone (Laffan, 2000, p. 292). Lead departments would inform other departments of relevant negotiations on a need-to-know basis. There was no formal procedure put in place for the production and dissemination of briefing documents, nor was Ireland's performance in implementing EU legislation tracked. However, the need for improved parliamentary scrutiny following the Nice 'No' did lead to the introduction of new rules and guidelines. These are discussed in the section on parliamentary scrutiny.

As mentioned above, the preparation of briefing material is not systematized in the Irish system at all levels in the hierarchy. There is little practice of sending written instructions to the COREPER representatives from Dublin or of holding pre-COREPER meetings in the national capital. Rather, within the Representation, the Permanent Representative and the Deputy establish their own *modus vivendi* with the attachés concerned. Within each department and across the system there are well-established standard operating procedures on how briefing material is prepared for Council meetings. The central features of this are the centrality of departmental and divisional responsibility. The 'lead' department must prepare the brief for its Minister for each Council meeting in their sector and within each department the 'lead' section on a particular agenda item takes responsibility for preparing briefing material for that issue. The EU agenda and timetable dictates the intensity of response needed from

the Irish system while an issue remains within the Council/European
Parliament system. The focus at this stage is on the projection of
Irish preferences into the Brussels arena.

Although there are no formal guidelines about report writing, the
practice of reporting on negotiations does exist within government
departments. The DFA, Agriculture and Justice appear to have the
most comprehensive and systematic approach to report writing and
to the circulation of such reports within the department. In other
departments, individual officers appear to have more autonomy on
report writing yet the circulation of such reports can be somewhat
hit and miss.

Once a law is passed or a programme agreed at the negotiating stage, the focus changes to the reception of the output of EU
decision-making into the national system. The Core Executive must
also ensure the transposition of EC law in the Irish system. Individual Government departments are responsible for implementation.
When Ireland fails to implement or incorrectly transposes EC law, the
DFA receives notice of infringements reasoned opinions and notice
of ECJ proceedings via the Representation in Brussels. It then sends
the relevant documentation to the Attorney General's Office, the
department concerned and the Chief State Solicitor's Office.

Information pathways

Ireland's administrative culture is characterized by considerable
autonomy for individual ministries which could well militate against
the sharing of information. However, the demands of the Brussels
system require a degree of information-sharing. In the Irish system
there are formal pathways for the dissemination of information, and
the EU coordination section in Foreign Affairs is at the centre of the
formal information pathway for pillar-one issues. Commission proposals and related papers are received by the Documentation Centre
and are then distributed to the relevant sections within Foreign
Affairs, other government Departments, and the Oireachtas (Houses
of Parliament). All formal communications from the Commission to
Ireland come to this section via the representation in Brussels. The
DFA clearly adopts a policy of the maximum sharing and distribution
of information. According to a departmental official, 'the over-
riding approach is to get the material out' (Interview Department of
Foreign Affairs Official, 12 March 2002). The approach of domestic
ministries to the sharing and distribution of information depends on

the departmental culture, the sensitivity of the issue and the degree to which a particular department wants to insulate particular issues from system-wide discussion. In the home departments, the most widespread practice is to have one unit responsible for the circulation of information but in some cases there are multiple information points, particularly if a department is responsible for more than one Council formation.

In areas with a tradition of secrecy, such as Justice and Home Affairs (JHA) or financial affairs, the circulation of information can be more limited. Following the attack on the Twin Towers in New York on 11 September 2001, the Department of Justice handled negotiations on the European Arrest Warrant, informing only Foreign Affairs, the Taoiseach's Office and the Office of the Attorney General of the tenor of the negotiations. The Department of Finance can be similarly reticent. Finance handles all issues relating to Ireland's participation in EMU and is careful to inform other departments of developments purely on a need-to-know basis: 'Finance know what they are doing but don't share information' (Interview Department of Foreign Affairs Official, 12 March 2002). Thus although there is considerable sharing of information, there are also pockets of the system where information is harvested and not shared.

Coordination

The coordination ambition depends on the nature of the issue on the Brussels agenda, the phase of the policy process and the national style in managing EU business. A fourfold distinction between routine sectoral policy-making, major policy-shaping decisions within sectors, cross-sectoral issues and the big bargains is apposite. Departments can handle the routine business of dealing with Brussels within clearly defined sectoral areas without engaging in too much interdepartmental consultation and coordination. In addition, the Irish system gives individual departments considerable autonomy within their own sectors even on the major shaping issues provided the wider system is kept informed. On the key national priorities, the Irish system engages in 'selective centralization' (Kassim, 2003). The system will channel political and administrative resources on the big issues, which has occurred on a number of occasions when big issues demanded an interdepartmental coordinated response, for example the 1983 negotiations on the reform of the Common Agricultural

Policy (the super-levy negotiations where quotas were placed on the amount of food/milk etc. farmers could produce in return for financial receipts), the 1996 and 2004 EU Presidencies and the 1999 multi-annual budgetary negotiations (Agenda 2000).

The agents

Participation in the activities of the European Union poses challenges to those who work in national civil services. In order to live with the Brussels system, states need a *cadre* of EU specialists who can combine technical/sectoral expertise with European expertise. Ireland's EU *cadre* can be found in Foreign Affairs, Enterprise, Trade and Employment, Agriculture, Finance and Justice. In all of the other departments, there are significant EU-related posts but these are few in number. Irish civil servants are expected to handle any post that they are placed in and to move to radically different work in the course of their careers. It is thus exceptional in the Irish system that an official would work only on EU matters for their entire career. That said, there are a small number of officials whose careers are largely EU-related in the diplomatic service and in the key EU ministries. These are officials who might have served on high-level EU committees for long periods and because of their EU knowledge become a key resource in the system. Although they constitute an essential resource in the Irish system, the EU *cadre* may not be adequately recognized. One senior official concluded that

> Within the system, there is hardly any incentive to be a 'Brussels insider', in terms of finance or family commitments. There is no one central system to bring this about. People don't want to be pigeonholed in that way... the weighting given in civil service panels to such skills might not be great. (Interview Department of Foreign Affairs Senior Official, 12 February 2002)

There is no specially trained EU *cadre* in the system or no EU-related fast track. Training is *ad hoc* throughout the system, and language training within the Irish system is also weak. Consequently EU expertise is built up on the job.

The manner in which Irish officials do their homework for negotiations in Brussels and conduct negotiations is influenced by a number of factors. Size matters. The relatively small size of central government, coupled with the small size of the country, and the fact that

Irish delegations tend to be smaller than those of other member states all influence perceptions of how the Brussels game should be played. Irish officials have an acute sense of the constraints of size and work on the basis that as a small state Ireland has a limited negotiating margin and should use that margin wisely. Irish officials try to avoid isolation in negotiations and, as one official argued, 'Ireland has fewer guns and not many bullets so it must pick its fights carefully' (Laffan, 2001). The problem-solving approach to negotiations means that Irish officials tend to intervene on specific issues and would have little to say on the broad thrust of policy. Considerable attention is paid to tactics, that is, discerning the negotiating positions of other member states and the working out of trade offs between negotiating camps. Indeed, the Irish have gained a reputation for tactical thinking. In the 2004 intergovernmental conference on the EU's constitutional treaty, former UK Commissioner Chris Patten noted Taoiseach Bertie Ahern's 'tactical wizardry' in the negotiations (Patten, 2005, pp. 128–9). In addition, personalism is a dominant cultural value in Ireland arising from late urbanization and the small size of the country. Civil servants working on EU matters meet frequently in Brussels and Dublin and have an ease of contact. Officials throughout the system can easily identify the necessary contacts in other departments.

There are several well-entrenched norms in the Irish system that influences how EU issues are handled. First, is the norm that Irish delegations should 'sing from the same hymn-sheet' and should not fight interdepartmental battles in Brussels. Delegations would not engage in conflict in front of other delegations. Second, there is a high level of collegiality within the Irish system and a high level of trust between officials from other departments. This is accompanied by an understanding of different departmental perspectives and styles. A high level of trust is particularly prevalent among the EU *cadre*, as officials see themselves fighting for 'Ireland Inc'. Third, is the norm that Ireland should be as *communautaire* as possible within the limits of particular negotiations. As stated above, Irish officials/politicians do not oppose for the sake of opposing.

Executive–parliamentary relations

Until the critical juncture of the first Nice Treaty referendum defeat in June 2001, the relationship between the Oireachtas and the core-executive was weak. Relations between the Oireachtas and the EU had been characterized as a combination of neglect and ignorance (O'Halpin, 1996, p. 124). On accession, a Joint Oireachtas Committee on the Secondary Legislation of the European Communities was established as a 'watchdog committee'. However, its performance was modest, hampered as it was by limited resources and lack of interest by parliamentary deputies and the media in its output. In 1993, it was reconstituted as the Joint Oireachtas Committee on European Affairs and its primary role was to inform deputies and senators of general EU policy developments rather than scrutinize EU legislation as such.

The weakness or perceived absence of parliamentary scrutiny of EU business was highlighted as a serious problem during the 2001 Nice referendum. In response to this, the government developed a new system of enhanced Oireachtas scrutiny of EU affairs codified in the 2002 EU Scrutiny Act. The parliamentary link for the new procedures was to be the EU Scrutiny Sub-Committee of the Joint Oireachtas Committee for European Affairs. In 2007 it became a full Oireachtas Committee. All EU-related documents are deposited in the DFA's EU Coordination Unit and passed on to relevant departments to prepare briefing notes. These briefing notes are then transmitted to the Scrutiny committee to be examined on a two-weekly basis. With the help of policy advisers, the committee identifies EU legislative proposals that are significant enough to merit parliamentary scrutiny by the relevant sectoral or departmental parliamentary committees (see Figure 3.2). For example, of the 552 documents considered by the scrutiny committee in 2006, 18 per cent were deemed to have implications of a significant nature for Ireland and warranting further scrutiny. These proposals were subsequently referred to their relevant sectoral committee (see Figure 3.3). The relevant committee then produces a report on its deliberations, which is laid before the Oireachtas. While the proposals make provision for extensive engagement between the Oireachtas, ministers and officials, a binding scrutiny reserve has not been put in place. Instead, Ministers are honour bound to take the opinion of the relevant committee into account when negotiating in the Council of Ministers. Differences of opinion have been extremely rare, as a high degree of consensus exists between the sectoral committees and departments on issues (Interview Policy adviser to Sub-committee on European Scrutiny, 27 November 2005).

FIGURE 3.3   Number of documents considered by the EU scrutiny
sub-committee by year

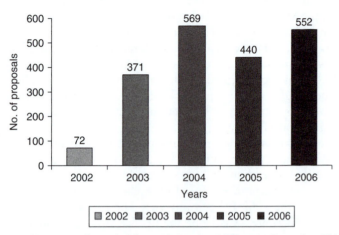

Note: 2002 covers the period from 10 October 2002 to 31 December 2002.
Source: Sub-Committee on EU Scrutiny, *Annual Report*, 2007.

The provisions relating to national parliaments contained in the
Lisbon Treaty, pending ratification, potentially offer a further challenge and opportunity to the Irish *Oireachtas* as a whole in its
scrutinizing role (Fahey, E., 2007). The Treaty gives national parliaments the right to challenge a piece of European legislation they
consider unnecessary; if half of all national parliaments are unhappy
with a Commission proposal, a majority of member states or MEPs
can insist the draft proposal is dropped. However, as in the past, the
role that each national parliament, including the Irish Oireachtas,
plays in this process will depend on how actively it wishes to be
involved (Brady and Barysch, 2007).

Following the original circular on the management of EU business in 1973, the guidelines on Oireachtas scrutiny are the next
most significant formalization of the management of EU business
in Ireland. The need for Government departments to prepare notes
for the Oireachtas committee has ensured that within each department, formal systems were put in place to ensure that such notes
are prepared. The roll-out of the Better Regulation agenda in 2005
with the Government stipulation that regulatory impact assessments
be produced for all European Commission proposals added to the

FIGURE 3.4   Breakdown of proposals/documents received by the EU scrutiny sub-committee from each government department during 2006

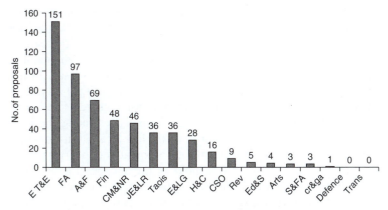

Source: Sub-Committee on EU Scrutiny, *Annual Report*, 2007.

increased formalization of the negotiating process in Ireland (see www.taoiseach.gov.ie/attached_files/RTF%20files/Final%20Version %20Guidelines.rtf – accessed 6 September 2007).

The balance sheet

The Irish approach to the management of EU business has been consistent over time and change when it has occurred has been gradual and incremental. On accession, structures and processes were firmly put in place for managing EU business with the Department of Foreign Affairs as interlocutor between the EU and domestic levels. Key features of this system included strong departmental autonomy, weak processes of interdepartmental coordination and a weakly institutionalized committee system. The Irish officials responsible for managing the EU–domestic interface were small in number, and had a pragmatic, cohesive and collegial style of doing business. These characteristics remained virtually unchanged until the resurgence of EU integration in the late 1980s with the enhancement of the Department of the Taoiseach's coordination role. However, the electorate's rejection of the Nice Treaty in June 2001 was the first considerable shock encountered by the Irish political and administrative system and led to significant systemic change. The critical juncture created by the Nice 'No' led to increased formalization of the structures and processes in place in order to manage EU business.

Nice I was a major domestic shock to the system of core executive management of EU business in Ireland. Until Nice I, Irish ministers and civil servants could engage with the EU system in the past in the context of a broad domestic consensus and within an enabling political environment. Europe was not a contentious issue. In the first Nice referendum the Irish government and political class miscalculated and took this positive support for granted. The No to Nice highlighted the weakness of EU knowledge among the Irish electorate, a degree of disinterest given the low level of turn-out and the emergence of a gap between the government and the Irish people on Europe. One senior official spoke of the 'escape of gases' after Nice (Interview, Senior Official, Department of An Taoiseach, 28 February 2002), which suggested that in place of the previous consensus there were a variety of views about the EU in political parties, the Cabinet and the wider civil society. At the same time, the result brought the core executive's management of EU business sharply into focus with the realization that the system needed to re-engage with the EU. This inevitably led to soul-searching and questioning at political and official levels with talk of 'a need to recharge the batteries on Europe, to go into a new mode and organize accordingly' (Interview, Official, Department of Foreign Affairs, 12 March 2002).

The establishment of the National Forum on Europe (see Chapter 5) helped highlight the issues at stake amongst the electorate in advance of the second Nice referendum and helped contribute to the eventual Yes vote. At the same time, the core executive re-engaged with Europe, with the formalization of EU coordination processes and the improvement of parliamentary–executive relations. These reforms contributed to the successful sixth EU Presidency in the first half of 2004 and fed into the successful conclusion of negotiations on the EU's constitutional treaty. Once again, the Irish core executive was back in gear, showing it to be successful in positioning Ireland in the EU system and in responding to domestic challenges. Post June 2008, senior political and administrative actors must manage the response to the defeat of the Lisbon treaty. This may prove a more significant critical juncture in Ireland's relations with the EU than Nice.

Chapter 4

Parties and Parliament

Hopes were high when the decision was taken to implement direct elections to the European Parliament (EP) in 1978. The EP was to become the only directly elected European body, conferring increased legitimacy on both the parliamentary assembly itself and on the European decision-making process. It was also hoped that elections at the European level would inspire increased debate on European issues at the national level. As in every other member state, direct elections to the EP added a new European dimension to the Irish electoral calendar and introduced Irish political parties to a world of transnational European politics. In European elections Irish political parties are, in theory at least, given the opportunity to put forward their own views on the process of European integration and at the same time engage with the electorate on European issues, thus deepening both their and Ireland's political involvement with the EU. But in reality, have EP elections deepened Irish politicians' and political parties' engagement with the EU? Are European issues salient come national and European election-time?

Irish political parties and the electorate have not made use of the opportunity EP elections offer to express their preferences on the future trajectory of European integration (Ireland is not unusual in this respect). European elections in Ireland have indeed become part of the domestic political process, yet their impact on the Irish political system's engagement with the EU has been marginal. EP elections have not been fought on European issues; they have been primarily national battles, dominated by domestic issues. As such, it has become customary to regard European elections in Ireland as 'second-order' (Moxon-Browne, 2005; Quinlivan and Schön-Quinlivan, 2004; Marsh, 1996; Reif and Schmitt, 1980) in the sense that they tend to be perceived as less important than 'first-order' or national elections, fewer voters turn out to vote and those who do vote tend to use the elections as an opportunity to punish the incumbent government.

The national nature of Irish EP elections is not surprising when one considers the attitudes of the more mainstream of Irish political parties towards the EU. The strong consensus that exists amongst mainstream parties is striking, and Europe is not a salient issue that fundamentally divides these parties. The three largest political parties, Fianna Fáil, Fine Gael and Labour, are all pro-European and have demonstrated broad support for European integration and Ireland's place within that process. Such a consensus has meant that the debate on the EU in Ireland, when it does take place before EP elections, does not tend to overtly question the fundamental value and importance of Ireland's continued relationship with the EU. The focus instead is on what the EU can do for Ireland. In EP election campaigns themselves, lip-service is paid to EU issues. In fact, parties have actually obscured their position on some European issues which might be contentious, thus reducing the salience of EU issues and the level of politicization of EP elections and reinforcing the sense of agreement amongst political parties. At national elections, such unity of opinion is even more in evidence, with European issues attracting little or no attention (Holmes, 2007). Yet some differences between and within parties do exist. Historically, the pro-European consensus of mainstream Irish political parties has been balanced by a more questioning attitude to the EU from parties such as the Green Party and Sinn Féin.

In this chapter we investigate the impact of the EU on party politics in Ireland first by surveying Irish political parties' attitudes to and engagement with the EU through national and European electoral contests and second by examining the conduct of political parties and the behaviour of voters in Irish EP elections. As participants in the European political process, Irish political parties now engage in an additional supranational layer of governance. Irish parties in the EU do not sit together in the EP on the basis of nationality, but in transnational party groupings. Domestically, however, the Irish political system seems to have been well-insulated from the EU: European integration has not emerged as an issue in 'first-order' political contests. Using the second-order election model developed originally by Reif and Schmitt (1980), we examine previous EP elections in Ireland and show that they are indeed perceived by the electorate as less important than national election competitions and perceived on the basis of national and not European issues.

Irish political parties and the EU

In recent years, the gaze of students of party politics has increasingly turned towards the impact of the EU on national party systems and political party behaviour. This body of work endeavours to investigate the possible Europeanization of domestic party politics; that is, the impact of the EU – European elections, European policies, European alliances – on the organization, programmes or strategies of political parties in the domestic arena. Questions investigated include the extent to which membership of the EU has led to a transformation of the party system through the emergence of new political cleavages on the EU and/or the formation of new political parties and the role the EU can and does play in domestic political discourse (cf. Mair, 2006, 2000; Ladrech, 2002; Taggart, 1998; Taggart and Szczerbiak, 2004). Not surprisingly, such investigations point to the imperviousness to change of domestic party systems and the general exclusion of European issues from domestic political discourse (although this does vary between member states). It is true that European party systems have become fragmented since direct elections to the EP in 1979, with new and smaller parties emerging on the scene. Yet while 'Europe' or the issue of European integration has clearly generated new parties domestically in the EU (the most obvious example being the UK Independence Party), on the whole these parties have tended to remain confined to the European arena (for example the Danish June Movement). The prevalence of a cross-left-right pro-EU outlook amongst mainstream political parties has also helped stymie party competition on European issues in domestic electoral campaigns and parliamentary debates and voters have tended not to be targeted in opportunistic strategies, either on pro-or anti-EU lines (Mair, 2001, p. 31; Ladrech, 2002, p. 396; Hix, 2005). Thus the format and the mechanics of European party systems have not been changed perceptibly by membership of the EU.

The impact or limited impact of the EU on the Irish political system therefore reflects European trends. While European integration has appeared as a salient issue in Irish electoral politics in successive referendums on treaty reform (see Chapter 5), its impact on national general election competitions has been minimal. The 2002 general election is a case in point. Held in the aftermath of Ireland's failure to ratify the Nice Treaty, this issue had the potential to be highly salient in the election campaign. Yet 'Europe' was the dog that did not bark (Gilland, 2002a, p. 2). The signal by the outgoing Fianna Fáil–Progressive Democrat government of its intent to hold a second referendum to reverse the result, together with the reluctance of other parties to broach the subject (all parties made minimal reference to the EU in their election manifestos), served to defuse the issue of Europe in the general election (Gilland, 2002a). Nor has European integration generated long-standing internal party conflict and competition (although some divergences of views have appeared from time to time within parties). The consensus amongst the three largest parties of Fianna Fáil, Fine Gael and Labour is reflected in the views of their supporters, for instance (Sinnott, 1995a, 2001, 2002).

Nevertheless, domestic party politics has not been totally shielded from the issue of European integration. In a number of EU member states, increased 'Euroscepticism' has been the corollary of increased integration (particularly since the process of ratification of the Treaty on European Union) (Taggart, 1998, p. 363). Even in the most pro-European of countries Euroscepticism (that is, opposition to the EU as a whole or to certain aspects of European integration) can be found. Euroscepticism is a broad term that encompasses the idea of contingent or qualified opposition, as well as incorporating outright and unqualified opposition to the process of European integration (Taggart, 1998, p. 366). This chapter investigates Euroscepticism amongst Irish political parties by focusing on the hitherto critical attitudes of Sinn Féin and the Green Party towards the European Union.

Attitudes of Irish political parties to the EU – a cosy consensus?

The broad consensus of Irish mainstream political parties towards the EU has been a significant contributing factor to the immunity of the domestic political system from European matters. Fine Gael is perhaps the most strongly identifiable pro-European political party in Ireland. Formed in 1933 by the merger of two small parties with Cumann na nGaedheal (the party which formed Ireland's first governments and lost its majority in 1932), since its inception Fine Gael has never been able to win the majority of votes in a general election. Fine Gael was fully supportive of accession to the

EEC in 1973 and in subsequent European Parliament election and referendum campaigns has always been in favour of further integration, traditionally demonstrating more federalist sensibilities on Europe and a more pragmatic stance on the Irish policy of military neutrality than its main competitor Fianna Fáil. As Minister for Foreign Affairs from 1973–77 and then as Taoiseach from 1982–87, former Fine Gael leader Garret FitzGerald, himself a committed European, was instrumental in developing Ireland's enthusiastic and *communautaire* approach to the EC/EU.

Fianna Fáil, as the largest political party in Ireland since 1932, and the dominant party of government, is also pro-European in its orientation. The party is traditionally supportive of the EU but has had reservations in the past about the directions integration might take. As the party that negotiated the terms of Ireland's accession and as the party in government when all of the EU referendums have been held, it has been successful in dovetailing Irish and Union interests. Yet it cannot be denied that on occasion Fianna Fáil's pro-European credentials have been perceived as less than full. Fianna Fáil has appeared less enthusiastic about the Union when in opposition (Laffan, 1991, p. 198). Under the stewardship of Charles Haughey at the time of the Single European Act negotiations, the party expressed certain doubts about the future trajectory of European integration. In response to the proposal to extend the use of qualified majority voting to the single European market programme, Fianna Fáil attached considerable importance to the 'veto' as a protection of the rights of small countries and was loath to give too much power to the European Parliament because of Ireland's sparse representation (then 15 seats) in this body and was mindful of the importance of Ireland's position of military neutrality in discussions on foreign and security policy cooperation at the European level. On coming to power in March 1987, however, Haughey very swiftly cast aside these doubts and went on to run a very successful Presidency in 1990 at a time of great change in Europe (Keatinge and Marsh, 1990, p. 131). Fianna Fáil's European credentials also took a somewhat of a battering in the run up to and immediate aftermath of the 2001 Nice referendum defeat. Taoiseach Bertie Ahern's swift announcement of a National Forum on Europe and other measures to bring about a second Nice referendum, a strongly fought and successful second referendum campaign where all Ministers were 'on message', and a highly successful EU Presidency in 2004 all served to re-establish Fianna Fáil's firm commitment to the EU.

Conceived by the Irish Trades Union Congress in 1912, the Irish Labour Party has never enjoyed the electoral success of social democratic parties elsewhere in Europe. It achieved its highest ever share of the vote so far in 1992 with 19.3 per cent of first preference votes, and when in power has always been the junior party in coalition governments. The Irish Labour Party opposed accession to the EU in 1973 but accepted the verdict of the electorate and adjusted to the reality of EU membership. While its grassroots remained somewhat hostile, its leaders demonstrated their support. Although Labour was in coalition government with Fine Gael when Ireland signed the Single European Act (SEA) in 1986, it was unable to support the ratification of the Act in the 1987 referendum. A number of leading party members favoured supporting the SEA in the referendum but were faced with a majority of party members who were opposed to the SEA. Its Administrative Council, in a bid to ensure that it did not oppose the constitutional amendment, decided not to adopt an official position – individual members of the party were free to support or oppose the amendment. Since the SEA referendum, however, Labour has always been on the side of those supporting EU referendums, at the same time highlighting its own particular concerns over Irish participation in any European level security and defence initiatives and expressing concern that the free-market emphasis of integration does not overtake the EU's social dimension (Marsh, 1996). In 1999 Labour merged with Democratic Left, a small party to the left of Labour (it first gained Dáil representation in 1981 as the Workers' Party). The Party was the only party to oppose ratification of the SEA. In the sixth European Parliament session (2004–09), former Democratic Left party leader Prionsias de Rossa became Labour's only Member of the European Parliament (MEP).

The final party to form part of the mainstream political consensus on the EU is Progressive Democrats. Formed in 1985 from a split from Fianna Fáil over Northern Ireland and party leadership issues, the Progressive Democrats built a position to the right in Irish politics, advocating a 'new-right' economic agenda and liberal policies on moral issues. As Fianna Fáil's junior partner in a number of coalition governments, the Progressive Democrats have been steadily committed to Irish participation in the European project, expressing particular support for the market liberalizing policies of the EU. Certain members, including former party leaders Mary Harney and Michael McDowell, did on occasion demonstrate reservations about the EU's development in a federalist direction, however.

Euroscepticism in Ireland

Over time, the Green Party and Sinn Féin have provided the most audible voices critical to the EU amongst Irish political parties, at times earning the label of Euroscepticism (Fitzgibbon, 2007; Gilland, 2004). Taggart and Szczerbiak (2004) make the distinction between two types of Euroscepticism: hard and soft. 'Hard' Euroscepticism implies outright rejection of the entire project of European political and economic integration, and opposition to one's country joining or remaining a member of the EU. 'Soft' Euroscepticism, by contrast, involves contingent or qualified opposition to European integration. Soft Eurosceptics may be opposed to measures designed to significantly deepen European political and economic integration (such as EMU) or to particular policy initiatives, and express themselves in terms of opposition to specific extensions of EU competencies. However, 'soft' Euroscepticism is not incompatible with the expression of broad support for the project of European integration. Soft Eurosceptics may also defend or stand up for the 'national interest' in the context of debates about the EU. On the basis of a historical examination of their attitudes towards the EU, the Green Party and Sinn Féin fall in the 'soft' Eurosceptic camp in their opposition to certain aspects of the EU (Gilland, 2000, 2004). Both parties have shifted overtime.

The Irish Green Party first developed as a loose alliance of independent citizen movements in the 1980s, without any substantive policies beyond those relating to the protection of the environment (Mair and Weeks, 2005, p. 139). The Green Party's first Teachta Dála (TD) was elected to the Dáil in 1989. The election of Patricia McKenna and Nuala Ahern as MEPs in 1994 represented a breakthrough for the party and since then the Party has consolidated its position with six TDs entering into coalition government with Fianna Fáil and the Progressive Democrats in June 2007. As elsewhere in Europe, the Irish Greens have carved out a clear ideological left-wing position, reflected in policies which warn of the dangers of corporate-driven globalization and which push for social distribution in economic policy. The Greens' policy towards the EU can be said to be one of critical engagement: they oppose certain elements the current model of European integration but are not anti-European

as such (De Búrca, 2007). While they have always been supportive of
EU action in the environmental realm, and more recently in tackling
climate change, they have been critical of the EU for its emphasis
on neo-liberal free market economics, the inequities inherent in the
CAP, and the EU's democratic deficit.

The Greens opposed the Amsterdam and Nice Treaties, per-
ceiving the treaties as bringing about an unacceptable erosion of
national sovereignty and undermining the principle of a partnership
of equally respected member-states (through the provisions relating
to increased qualified majority voting and the reduction in the number of European Commissioners in an enlarged EU) (Trevor Sargent,
Irish Times, 7 October 2002). As an MEP, Patricia McKenna in particular fought vigorously against any diminution of Irish sovereignty
(Fitzgibbon, 2007). The Greens have also been opposed to any
increase in the militarization of the EU and the concomitant threat
it poses to Irish neutrality. In the past, the Greens have been wary of
Irish participation in an EU common defence: participation in measures such as the establishment of a European Rapid Reaction Force
were seen as an erosion of Ireland's policy of military neutrality. As
part of the Fianna Fáil, Green Party and Progressive Democrat government formed in June 2007, however, senior Green Party leaders
have decisively shifted in favour of the EU. The party was unable
formally to support the Lisbon Treaty in the 2008 referendum as the
leadership failed to get a two-thirds majority approval at a special
party conference. Green ministers, nonetheless, campaigned for a
'yes' to Lisbon. Former Green MEP, Patricia McKenna, was however
a central figure in the 'no' campaign.

Originating from a number of splits from the Sinn Féin movement of the 1920s, the current Sinn Féin party emerged as part
of the conflict in Northern Ireland and prides itself on being the
only all-Ireland political party. Positioning itself to the left of the
Labour Party, Sinn Féin perceives itself as outside the mainstream.
Sinn Féin achieved its electoral breakthrough in the 2002 general
election, increasing its representation from one to five TDs, and
2004 it sent its first representative from the Republic of Ireland,
Mary-Lou McDonald, to the EP. Sinn Féin's opposition to aspects
of European integration has been long-standing, first campaigning
for a No vote in the 1972 referendum campaign (Sinn Féin also
refused to take part in European elections in 1979) (Frampton,
2005). As a protest party Sinn Féin's original outright hostility to
the European project has modified over time: Sinn Féin accepts Irish

membership of the EU but is critical of certain aspects of Irish engagement including the 'unhealthy ... and cosy consensus within the Dáil on EU matters' (McDonald, 2005; Frampton, 2005). Sinn Féin views the EU in intergovernmental terms, and its preference is for the EU to remain a 'partnership of equal states': 'We oppose current attempts to turn the EU into a superstate or a military and economic superpower because we value Irish sovereignty and Irish neutrality' (Sinn Féin, 2004). Sinn Féin opposed ratification of the Amsterdam and Nice treaties and in 2005 announced its opposition to the EU's Constitutional Treaty, criticizing it for laying the legal foundations for a federal Europe, undermining national sovereignty and the equality between states and promoting a policy of substantial militarization (hence undermining Irish neutrality) (www.sinnfe in.ie/gaelic/policies/document/198 – accessed 30 May 2005). Sinn Féin has also called for neutrality to be enshrined in the Irish Constitution (Sinn Féin, 2004). Following a poor general election campaign in 2007, Sinn Féin used the 2008 Lisbon referendum to enhance the profile and positioning of the party in the Republic.

Some further parties, so small that that they have been termed 'micro parties' tend also to be strongly critical of the EU (Gilland, 2002a). These include the Socialist Party, the Socialist Workers' Party, the Workers' Party and the Christian Solidarity Party. The Christian Solidarity Party is primarily concerned with the importance of upholding traditional Catholic values in the EU, including the support of natural life from birth to death. The other parties, on the other hand, share similar views to Sinn Féin with their combination of Marxism/socialism with Irish republicanism.

In his investigation on Euroscepticism across EU member states, Taggart (1998) uncovered a link between the adoption of strong Eurosceptic positions, on the one hand, and the status of a party as a protest or 'outsider' party, on the other. He found that Euroscepticism as an ideological appendage to a more general systemic critique is the most pervasive form of party-based Euroscepticism in Western Europe. Protest parties from either the left or the right may use their position on the EU as one means of differentiating themselves from the established parties: 'the EU issue can then be used as a sort of ideological crowbar that allows protest parties to place some distance between them and the established parties' (Taggart, 1998, pp. 372–82). Hence the opportunity structure offered by the European electoral arena can sometimes enhance the prospects for parties that may be more marginal in domestic politics (Mair, 2001, p. 38).

The transformation in the Green Party stance on the European Union since it entered government does suggest that small party opposition to the EU may be contingent and may change when the spoils of office are on offer. Sinn Féin's opposition to European treaties may peter out if the prospect of office emerges.

Irish membership of transnational EP party groupings

As mentioned above, each Irish political party represented in the EP has forged formal links with European transnational party federations. In anticipation of direct EP elections in 1979, these federations were formed at the European level, reflecting the prevailing political party traditions. The Confederation of Socialist Parties of the EC was the first to be established in 1974 (now the Party of European Socialists, PES), followed by the Federation of Liberal and Democratic Parties of the EC and the European People's Party of Christian democratic parties in 1976. Initially, these transnational party federations were loose political groupings without clear or coherent policy orientation, but in more recent years have established more coherent organizations with central offices and identifiable party lines. Throughout the history of the EP, the two largest groups have been the Christian Democrat European People's Party (EPP) (with the conservative-affiliated European Democrats – EPP-ED) and the Party of European Socialists (PES). Together these two groups constitute on average two-thirds of the composition of the European Parliament. As a member of the Socialist International and the Confederation of European Socialists, the Labour Party's choice of the PES as its political home within the EP was fairly straightforward.

The choice of EP party group membership was not so clear for Fianna Fáil and Fine Gael as the two main conservative or centre-right parties on accession. It was imperative for both parties to join different groups so that electoral competition at domestic level could continue. In what was regarded as an astute move, Fine Gael opted for the Christian Democratic EPP group prior to accession. This gave Fine Gael membership of one of the two mainstream political groupings in the Parliament and subsequently, as Taoisigh, both Garret FitzGerald and John Bruton forged close links with their Christian Democratic colleagues in other member states. As a member of the EPP-ED group, Fine Gael is closely involved the organization of summits of Christian Democratic and Conservative

Party leaders in the run-up to meetings of the European Council. Likewise, Labour as a member of the PES group is involved in similar gatherings. Both groupings have sought to influence the outcome of successive intergovernmental conferences by submitting position papers and lobbying national leaders. Both parties also make use of their transnational party election manifestos when preparing their own manifestos for national EP elections.

Like Fine Gael, Fianna Fáil would be more at home in the Christian Democratic/Conservative group, but Fine Gael's prior membership of this grouping ruled out Fianna Fáil affiliation. Thus the party found itself in a very difficult position with regard to its choice of EP party grouping and for the first six months of the 1979–84 EP term was unaligned. The privileges associated with group status and their unwillingness to join any of the existing groups led the party to join with the French Gaullists to form the European Progressive Democrats, later the European Democratic Alliance. This was a pragmatic alliance for both Fianna Fáil and the French Gaullists as both parties agreed to differ on many policy issues, apart from their strong commitment to the defence of the Common Agricultural Policy. In 1995 the European Democratic Alliance merged with Forza Europa, a group made up exclusively of members of Forza Italia, Italian media tycoon and former Prime Minister Silvio Berlusconi's political party, and renamed itself the Union for Europe Group. For a short while it briefly surpassed the Liberals in size until a number of the Forza Italia members broke away in 1998 and joined the European People's Party group as individual members (Dinan, 2005, p. 272). Following the realignment of French politics in 2002 when most centre-right parties merged into the Union for a Popular Movement, the French Gaullists also joined the EPP-ED group. Now called the Union for Europe of the Nations group (UEN), Fianna Fáil finds itself part of one of the smaller EP political groups.

The UEN is currently comprised of 44 MEPs whose members also include Italy's National Alliance (heir to the far-right Italian Social Movement) and Poland's Law and Justice Party, parties whose attitude towards the EU would traditionally be more questioning than that of Fianna Fáil. In 2004, Minister of State for European Affairs Dick Roche proposed a plan to integrate Fianna Fáil's MEPs into the Liberal Group (ALDE – Alliance of Liberals and Democrats for Europe). At that time, however, the four Fianna Fáil MEPs refused to join ALDE citing differences in policy, particularly its support for reform of the Common Agricultural Policy and personal freedom in moral issues such as abortion (*Irish Times*, 6 June 2006). Following the June 2004 EP election, Fianna Fáil MEP Brian Crowley became co-President of the UEN, giving the party access to a range of benefits including extra speaking time in parliamentary debates, office staff and key positions on committees.

While the Progressive Democrats have not had a representative in the European Parliament since Pat Cox's first term as an MEP (1989–94), they are affiliated with the Liberal group, the third largest group in the parliament, having about half as many members as the Socialists and the Christian Democrats/Conservatives and twice as many as the smaller groups. For a long time the Liberals were officially called the Group of the European Liberal, Democratic and Reformist Party before reinventing themselves after the 2004 elections as the Alliance of Liberals and Democrats for Europe. As an independent MEP, Pat Cox was elected President of the Liberal Democrat Group in 1998 and assumed the presidency of the EP in 2002 for two years. Independent MEP for North-West, Marian Harkin, is a member of this group.

The home for Green Party MEPs Patricia McKenna and Nuala Ahern elected in 1994 was naturally the transnational Green Party alliance with Catalan, Scottish and Welsh nationalists in the Greens/European Free Alliance. The choice of Sinn Féin's political grouping gives a clear indication of how the party views itself as a party of the left, and on election in 2004 new Sinn Féin MEP Mary Lou McDonald joined the heterogeneous group of the 'nonsocialist' Left, that is, the confederal Group of the European United Left/Nordic Green Left. As the fifth largest political grouping in the 2004–09 Parliament, the EUL/NGL is, as its name suggests, a confederal group where each component party is purported to retain its own identity and policies while pooling efforts in pursuit of common political objectives. As with Fianna Fáil's UEN Group, its identity and *raison d'être* is somewhat less clear-cut than that of the PES, EPP/ED and ALDE and is seen as somewhat of a marriage of convenience between environmentalists such as some far-left Scandinavians, French, Italian, Greek and Spanish Communists, and nationalists such as Sinn Féin (Dinan, 2005). Finally, following the 2004 EP election, independent MEP Kathy Sinnott indicated her more critical stance towards the EU with her decision to join the Independence/Democracy group, a party grouping organized along anti-EU lines (the Independence/Democracy group emerged out of the anti-Maastricht movement in the early 1990s and consists of French and Danish Eurosceptic MEPs, such as Philippe De Villiers and Jens Peter Bonde and the anti-EU UK Independence Party).

Given that Irish MEPs currently number 13 out of 785, the impact they can have in EP committees is limited. To date no Irish MEP has held the chair of an important EP Committee (although Fianna Fáil's Sean Ó Neachtain has chaired the EP's delegation for relations with Canada since 2004 and many Irish MEPs have been vice-chairs of important committees). Irish MEPs have sought positions in EP committees that mirror Ireland's interests in the EU, most particularly agriculture, regional development, fisheries, environment, economic and monetary affairs, and employment and social affairs. Some Irish MEPs have also sat on committees that have mirrored their own personal interests, such as Gay Mitchell's membership of the EP's Development Committee and former MEP Mary Bannotti's longstanding membership of the Culture, Youth, Education and the Media Committee (where she was vice-chair from 1989–97).

As we have seen so far, in sum the Irish party system has not been affected substantially by participation in the EU, nor has the European issue led to significant internal splits within parties. Taking three classical dimensions of party activity – electoral, organizational and ideological-programmatic – the influence of Europe is felt only marginally on the third. In national election competitions, it is national and not European cleavages, conflicts and policies which dictate electoral tactics and guide voting behaviour. Apart from joining European party groupings, the impact on party organization has been limited. Finally, from a programmatic level, with the exception of the more nuanced attitudes of the Green Party and Sinn Féin, Irish political parties have wholeheartedly embraced EU membership. It is not surprising therefore, that European Parliament elections themselves have been less politicized than national or first-order elections and contested on the basis of national and not European issues.

European Parliament elections in Ireland: second-order?

Research since the EP was first directly elected in 1979 confirms that European elections are what political scientists call 'second-order' national contests (Reif and Schmitt, 1980; van der Eijk and Franklin, 1996; Marsh, 1998; Schmitt, 2005; Hix and Marsh, 2007).

TABLE 4.1 *Irish MEPs in the 2004–09 European Parliament*

Groups	Description	No. of MEPs	Irish Members	Constituency
EPP-ED	European People's Party and European Democrats	278	Colm Burke (FG)*	South
			Avril Doyle (FG)	East
			Jim Higgins (FG)	North West
			Gay Mitchell (FG)	Dublin
			Mairead McGuinness (FG)	East
PES	Party of European Socialists	217	Prionsias de Rossa (Labour)	Dublin
ALDE	Alliance of Liberals and Democrats for Europe	103	Marian Harkin (Independent)	North West
Greens/EFA	Greens/European Free Alliance	42	None	
EUL/NGL	European United Left/Nordic Green Left	41	Mary Lou McDonald (SF)	Dublin
UEN	Union for Europe of the Nations	44	Liam Aylward (FF)	East
			Brian Crowley (FF)	South
			Sean O Neachtain (FF)	North West
			Eoin Ryan (FF)	Dublin
IND/DEM	Independence/Democracy	24	Kathy Sinnott (Independent)	South
Total number of Members of European Parliament as of 1 January 2007		785		

Notes: *Replaced Simon Coveney in June 2007. In per capita terms, Ireland is generously represented in the EP: each of Ireland's 13 MEPs represent some 225,000 voters whereas their German counterparts represent some 806,000.

According to this approach, second-order elections differ from first-order contests as there is less at stake – such elections do not determine the distribution of power at the national decision-making governmental level. Examples therefore include local, regional and European elections. The second-order nature of European elections has two effects. First, second-order elections are less politicized than first-order elections and as a consequence fewer people turn out to vote. Second, when people do vote they use their vote to send a message to the national government of the day. There is a tendency (particularly pronounced when national elections are a long way off) to punish incumbent governments. National governments (be they composed of large or small parties) tend to do worse in EP elections than they have done in the previous, and will do in the following, first-order election. Finally, because there is less at stake in second-order elections, there is less reason to vote strategically – strategic voting being defined as supporting a party that is closest to their ideal policy preferences, rather than supporting a (usually larger) party that is further from their preferences but has a greater chance of forming government. This phenomenon has been repeatedly referred to as 'voting with the head' rather than 'voting with the heart'. As strategic considerations apparently do not play much of a role in European Parliament elections, this suggests that small parties do relatively better compared to first-order election results (Schmitt, 2005; Hix and Marsh, 2007). Marsh in particular has found that gains are most obvious amongst the very small parties (less than 4 per cent) and the losses most obvious amongst the larger parties – those over 30 per cent (Marsh, 1998, p. 606).

Thus according to the evidence amassed, the role that EP elections can play in contributing to the creation of a European identity among the citizens of the member states is small. But that is not to say that EP elections are without impact. EP elections take place within a wider political context (in the shadow of 'first-order contests') and their results must then be understood in such terms (Hix and Marsh, 2007). EP elections do play a part in the domestic politics of member states as both parties and voters use them (and their results) as signals and portents, which may then affect their subsequent behaviour. For instance, EP elections allow new entrants onto the political scene and may bolster the performance of smaller political parties in subsequent national contests. On the other hand, poor EP election performance may persuade parties that either leaders or party direction need to be overhauled. So are EP elections in Ireland typical second-order elections – do Irish voters perceive them as being less important than general elections and vote differently?

EP elections in Ireland – a national or European contest?

Irish MEPs are elected by the same electoral system as is used in Irish general elections, proportional representation by means of a single transferable vote (PR-STV). The Treaty of Nice reduced the number of Irish MEPs from 15 to 13, with all the constituencies except Dublin being redrawn and renamed. Seats in the East constituency (formerly Leinster) and the South constituency (formerly Munster) were reduced from four to three, while Dublin retained four seats and the North-West three. At first glance (see Figure 4.1) European elections have not attracted voters to the polls as effectively as national elections. Yet, at the same time, turnout in Irish elections has not mirrored the declining turnout in elections across the rest of Europe (see Figure 4.2). The practice of holding other electoral competitions such as local elections and referendums at the same time as European elections has had some impact on levels of voting. The first European elections in 1979 coincided with local elections and Marsh has estimated that these probably helped push turnout up to 63.6 per cent (Marsh, 1996, p. 169). Turnout in 1984 was low (47.6 per cent) in spite of holding a referendum on voting rights for non-citizens on the same day. In 1989 turnout was well over 60 per cent but this was a special occasion as the EP election was held at the same time as a general election. In 1999 and 2004, the European elections were held at the same time as local elections and referendums on local government and citizenship respectively. In 1994, on the only occasion where European elections occupied centre-stage, turnout was low at 44 per cent – considerably below the EU average of 58.6 per cent (see Figure 4.2).

The tendency to hold local elections and referendums at the same time as EP elections can perhaps be seen as a way of encouraging more people to vote. Be that as it may, the danger is that European elections can become completely overshadowed by national contests, as was the case in 1989 with the Dáil election (Keatinge and Marsh, 1990). In 2004, the citizenship referendum was perceived by commentators as sparking more interest and debates in the weeks preceding election day than the EP election (Quinlivan and Schön-Quinlivan, 2004, p. 91). In addition, the multiplicity of new 'faces' in

FIGURE 4.1   Turnout in Irish general and EP elections, 1977–2007

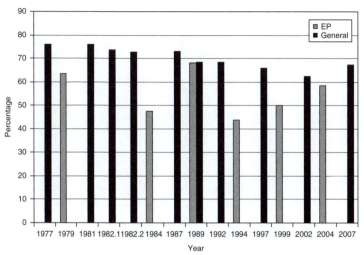

Source: http://electionsiselect.org/results/europe/index.cfm

FIGURE 4.2   Turnout in European Parliament elections

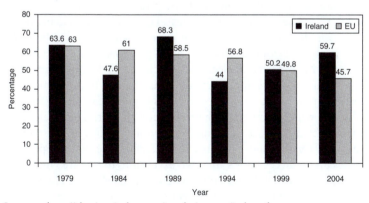

Source: http://electionsiselect.org/results/europe/index.cfm

the European and local elections did lead to some confusion amongst voters in 2004: posters of candidates dangling from lampposts did not always distinguish between the campaigns (Moxon-Browne, 2005, p. 149).

FIGURE 4.3   Party share of votes in national and EP elections, 1977–2007

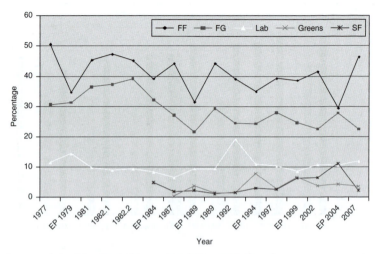

Source: http://electionsiselect.org/results/europe/index.cfm

So what of the propositions that government parties are less successful in second-order elections, and that smaller parties, on average, fare better than larger ones? There is indeed a general tendency for the share of the vote of government parties to be lower than in the previous general election, and this was even the case when the EP and general elections coincided. As the dominant party of government in Ireland, Fianna Fáil has tended to do worse in EP elections than in national elections, as Figure 4.3 shows (see also Table 4.2 which summarize the results for all parties in EP elections from 1979–2004). At the same time, while parties in government tend to do badly (most notably Fianna Fáil), the main opposition parties do not necessarily gain. Two exceptions to this are Fine Gael's performances in 1979 and 2004, where Fine Gael's vote did increase by comparison with the previous general election, thus restoring the parties' flagging performances in the previous general elections (see Tables 4.3 and 4.4). So, while the governing and larger parties tend to do worse, small parties and independents have tended to do better in EP elections. The performance of the Green Party is particular testament to this, gaining at times 5 per cent greater a share of

TABLE 4.2 *Results of EP elections in Ireland, 1979–2004*

	1979		1984		1989		1994		1999		2004	
	% Share of vote	Seats won	% Share of vote	Seats won	% Share of vote	Seats won	% Share of vote	Seats won	% Share of vote	Seats won	% Share of vote	Seats won
FF[a]	34.7	5	39.2	8	31.5	6	35.0	7	38.6	6	29.5	4
FG	33.1	4	32.2	6	21.6	4	24.3	4	24.6	4	27.8	5
Lab	14.5	4	8.4	0	9.5	1	11.0	1	8.7	1	10.6	1
PD					11.9	1	6.5	0				
Greens					3.7	0	7.9	2	6.7	2	4.3	0
Sinn Féin			4.9		2.3		3.0	0	6.3	0	11.1	1
Workers' Party	3.3	0	4.3	0	7.5	1	1.9	0				
DL							3.5	0				
Other[b]	14.4	2	11.0	1	12.0	2	6.9	1	15.0	2	16.7	2
Turnout	63.6[c]		47.6[d]		68.3[e]		44		50.2[f]		59.7[f]	

Notes: [a]FF = Fianna Fáil, FG = Fine Gael, Lab = Labour Party, PD = Progressive Democrats, DL = Democratic Left. [b]For 1979 includes Sinn Féin; seats won by 'Others' include fringe parties and seats won by independent candidates. [c]EP election held together with local election. [d]EP election held together with referendum. [e]EP election held together with general election. [f]EP election held together with local election and referendum.

Sources: Adapted from Holmes (1996); Coakley and Gallagher (2005), p. 469.

TABLE 4.3   *Comparison of 1989 European Parliament and Dáil elections (percentage first preferences gained)*

	EP Election	General Election	Shift
Fianna Fáil	31.5	44.1	−12.6
Fine Gael	21.6	29.3	−7.7
Labour	9.5	9.5	0
Progressive Democrats	11.9	5.5	6.4
Workers' Party	7.6	5.0	2.6
Greens	3.7	1.5	2.2
Others	14.1	5.1	9.0

Source: Marsh (1996), p. 173.

TABLE 4.4   *Comparison of 2004 European Parliament and 2002 Dáil elections, percentage, shares of the vote*

	General Election 2002	EP Election 2004	Shift
Fianna Fáil	41.5	29.5	−12
Fine Gael	22.5	27.8	+5.3
Labour	10.8	10.6	−0.2
Sinn Féin	6.5	11.1	+4.6
Progressive Democrats	4.0	0	Na (−4)
Greens	3.8	4.3	+0.5
Others	11.0	16.8	+5.8

Source: www.ireland.com/focus/election_2002/

first-preference votes in European elections compared with national elections. This was the case most especially in its breakthrough performance in the 1994 EP election when its share of the vote jumped to 7.9 per cent from 1.4 per cent in the previous general election.

The weaker performance of mainstream parties in Irish European elections has on occasion had consequences for the Irish political system. When a party such as Fianna Fáil does not do well in a European election, questions are always asked, often about the leader. The result of the 1979 EP election is a case in point. This election was seen as a mid-term report on the Fianna Fáil government elected in 1977, and it came when the bills were being presented for all the electoral promises which had secured the party its over-whelming victory. Hardening critical opinion on the backbenches, it helped hasten the departure of the then leader, Jack Lynch, and the arrival of the new one, Charles Haughey – although Lynch had been intending to retire in any case and had also presided over defeats in by-elections (Marsh, 1996, p. 183). On the other hand, improved performance can also have positive consequences domestically. The position of John Bruton as leader of Fine Gael was reinforced by the party's strong performance in the 1994 EP election. Bruton had been under considerable pressure as party leader (narrowly surviving an attempt to unseat him in February 1994) and his leadership received a much-needed fillip by retaining its four seats in the EP, increasing its nationwide percentage of the vote and winning almost exactly the same share of first preference votes as it did in the 1992 general election (Moxon-Browne, 1996, p. 130). Stronger performances in EP elections have also served as a springboard for parties such as the Green Party and Sinn Féin in national elections.

Independents also do well at the European level – on average two independent MEPs are elected to represent Irish constituents in Europe at each European election. In the 2004 EP election, independent candidates gained 16.7 per cent of the vote and two MEPs were elected (Table 4.2), Marian Harkin from the North-West and Kathy Sinnott from the South, replacing Dana Rosemary Scallon and Pat Cox respectively.

As we can see from this brief survey, Irish voters tend to behave differently in European elections than in national elections. This phenomenon was never more clearly in evidence than in 1989 when European and national elections were held on the same day. Though almost everyone who voted in the general election also voted in the European election, the difference between the results of the two elections was considerable (Marsh, 1996). The biggest differences concerned Fianna Fáil and Fine Gael, with the Fianna Fáil vote down 12.6 per cent on its general election figure and Fine Gaeil down 7.7 per cent (Table 4.3). There was a substantial swing towards smaller parties, with the Progressive Democrats gaining 6.4 per cent of the vote and other small parties (most specifically the Greens) and independents garnering 11.3 per cent of first preference votes.

Thus we can see that in Ireland, government and larger parties tend to do worse in EP elections than in national elections and smaller parties and independent candidates tend to do better. While levels of turnout are inclined to be lower in EP elections than in general elections, turnout in Ireland does not quite mirror the steady decline in average levels of turnout throughout the EU, attributable in certain respects to the practice of holding other electoral contests simultaneously. Yet looking at European elections in Ireland through the lens of the second-order election model does not wholly complete the picture of Irish electoral choice. Noting in his study of the 1989 election that some of the more striking successes by the smaller parties occurred where they ran high-profile candidates, Marsh has suggested focusing on a more 'candidate'-oriented account of European election behaviour in Ireland (Marsh, 1996, pp. 174–82). It is true that, since 1979, certain characteristics apparent in Irish EP elections can easily be identified and the most obvious is the emphasis placed on personality over policy, evident from the high-profile nature of candidates, be they from political parties or running as independents.

The 'ambassadorial effect'

In Ireland, the party label appears to provide candidates with less electoral help in European elections than it does in national ones (Marsh, 1995, p. 211). Irish voters seem to be inclined to vote more on the basis of personality than party or policy in EP elections, with the result that most of the parties seek high-profile candidates and some go as far as inviting prominent personalities outside the party to join and stand in EP elections. The importance of this 'ambassadorial effect' was perceived from the very first elections in 1979 when Fine Gael research carried out in the run-up to the election indicated that candidates should be 'well-known people... articulate and knowledgeable in European affairs... and not necessarily aligned with a political party' (Sinnott, 1995a, p. 257). The evidence shows that the mainstream political parties in particular have carefully heeded this message and, when it comes to candidate selection, party leaders have often been willing to use their own authority to ensure that high-profile candidates as opposed to party activists are selected, as was the case in 1994 when Dick Spring 'parachuted' TV journalist Orla Guerin into the Dublin constituency to run alongside the lesser-known Bernie Malone. Fianna Fáil in their attempt to woo the liberal and female vote drafted in Olive Braiden, Chair of the Rape Crisis centre in the same 1994 election. Other examples of high-profile candidates include Alan Gillis of the Irish Farmers Association (IFA) (Fine Gael), Paddy Lane also of the IFA (Fianna Fáil), and former TV journalist Mairead McGuinness (Fine Gael).

Interestingly, the Progressive Democrats' inability to attract high-profile candidates led to its failure to field any candidates in the 1999 and 2004 EP elections.

The emphasis on personality is also visible when two or more candidates from the same party run in the same constituency and the campaign becomes overshadowed by intra-party fighting. The competition between Bernie Malone and Orla Guerin for the Labour Party in the 1994 election is a case in point. The competition between the two became particularly bitter with Bernie Malone appearing sometimes to be running against the party machine. This divergence was reflected in voting preferences where only 39 per cent of her running mate's votes transferred to her. The most notorious episode of in-fighting also occurred in the 1994 election between Pat Cox and Desmond O'Malley of the Progressive Democrats. The decision of Pat Cox, a sitting MEP, to resign from the PDs and stand as an Independent in Munster against his former party leader, Des O'Malley, caused considerable controversy not only in Munster, but throughout the country and within the Progressive Democrat party (Moxon-Browne, 1996, pp. 124–7). In the 2004 election, tensions ran high between between Fianna Fáil's Eoin Ryan and Royston Brady in Dublin; Labour's Ivana Bacik and Prionsias De Rossa in the same constituency; Fianna Fáil's Jim McDaid and Sean Ó Neachtain in the North West and Fine Gael's Avril Doyle and Mairead McGuinness who were running neck and neck in the East (Quinlivan and Schön-Quinlivan, 2004, p. 88).

The primacy of personality over party is also manifest in the continued success of independent candidates in Irish EP elections. Independent candidates are generally successful in two constituencies: the North-West and the South. As well as being well-known nationally, independent candidates are usually allied to certain interest groups (for example the farmers, as in the case of T. J. Maher) or particular special interests or causes (such as Sean D. 'Dublin Bay' Loftus in 1979 and 1984 and more recently Marian Harkin (the West) and Kathy Sinnott (disability issues)). Probably the most well-known independent MEP was former Eurovision song contest winner and presidential candidate Dana Rosemary Scallon, elected in 1999 who struck a deep chord with traditional West of Ireland voters. In more recent years, both as independent and party candidates, women have done well in EP elections and the gender imbalance amongst Irish MEPs continues to improve, in marked contrast to Dáil elections. In 1994, four women were successful

(28.7 per cent); in 1999, five women were returned (33.3 per cent); and in 2004, the percentage rose to 38.5 per cent with female candidates taking five of the thirteen seats. More encouragingly, there is a wide geographical dispersion with women being elected in all four constituencies (Quinlivan and Schön-Quinlivan, 2004, p. 92). This is in stark contrast with the proportion of women TDs elected to the Dáil – in 2007, only 12.6 per cent of those elected to the Dáil were women (21 out of 166). The Green party, Labour and Fine Gael have had a tendency to give women a significant share of nominations and have had more success in having women elected. Fianna Fáil, on the other hand, has never succeeded in sending a woman to the European Parliament.

Voting on Europe

As we have seen in this chapter, the impact of European integration on Ireland's political system has been minimal. There is a strong political consensus on European matters amongst the mainstream political parties, and European issues do not feature heavily in national political discourse. Europe is the dog that does not bark come European Parliament election time, as neither politicians nor the electorate perceive it to be salient. It is not surprising, therefore, that European elections have become national battles and Irish voters often use the election as an opportunity to vote on national political issues. When not voting on the basis of national political issues, voters rely on personality over party to determine their electoral choice (Sinnott 1995a, p. 258). Parties have heeded this message and the number of high-profile candidates elected at EP elections is notable. Yet while the European project has not really caused great controversy in Irish electoral contests, it is incorrect to say that Irish politics have been completely immune from EU issues. The politicisation of European integration has occurred in the EU-related referendum campaigns that have taken place since 1972, as we will see in the next chapter.

Chapter 5

Referendums and Public Opinion

'We in Ireland have had recent experience – painful at first, but ultimately very positive – of how vital it is to maintain the connection between the Union and its citizens. Various lessons can be drawn from our two Nice referendums ... there is widespread public uncertainty. People say they want the Union to do more in some areas – but they are also cautious. They accept that change is inevitable and often desirable: but they want it justified, explained, argued about, honestly and clearly. They are not willing to take anyone's word for it.' (Brian Cowen, TD, former Minister for Foreign Affairs, speaking at the European Policy Centre, Brussels, 3 April 2003)

Until the first referendum held on the Treaty of Nice in June 2001, the mainstream Irish political elite's pro-European consensus was reflected in the attitude of the Irish electorate towards the EU – referendums were comfortably passed and Ireland signed up to reforms and initiatives contained in the Single European Act (SEA), the Treaty on European Union (TEU, also called the Maastricht Treaty) and the Amsterdam Treaty. Successive referendum success cemented Ireland's reputation as a 'good European' (see Table 5.1). The positive attitude of the electorate was mirrored by public opinion polls on the EU: a healthy majority of those surveyed declared themselves in favour of membership and appreciated the perceived benefits that membership has brought Ireland. Hence the rejection of the Nice Treaty by the electorate in 2001 was an electric shock to the political system. Following the second successful referendum on Nice in 2002, the rejection of the Lisbon Treaty in 2008 re-opened the debate about Ireland's place in Europe.

In June 2001 the Irish political elite's sense of complacency was obvious: a positive result was simply taken for granted. The pro-Treaty campaign was lacklustre and ambivalent, conducted with limited resources (O'Brennan, 2003; Garry *et al.*, 2005). Little effort was made to explain the issues. Instead politicians resorted to tried and tested platitudes pointing out Ireland's gains from the EU. It was not surprising to discover that the main reason the Irish electorate voted against the treaty was out of ignorance. Voters responded to the anti-Treaty campaigners' catchy slogan of 'if you don't know, vote no' and did precisely that, to the tune of 54 per cent. An effective campaign and a high level of mobilization delivered a 'yes' vote a year later in 2002. However, the lessons of Nice were forgotten when the main political parties ran an ineffective and rushed campaign in 2008, leaving the field open to the extremes of right and left who managed to out-campaign the established parties in Ireland. For the second time in eight years, the Irish electorate rejected a European treaty with a vote of 53.4 per cent.

This chapter is divided into two parts. In the first we survey Ireland's experience of voting in EU-related referendums. Beginning with an analysis of why each reform of the EU's basic law, the Treaty of Rome, must be ratified by the Irish electorate in a referendum, this section reviews the campaigns, protagonists and results of the various referendums from 1987 onwards. In the 1987 and 1992 referendums, a permissive consensus on European matters existed between the Irish political elite and the electorate and both referendums were fought in relatively uncompetitive environments (Kennedy and Sinnott, 2007, p. 63). This changed during the Amsterdam referendum campaign, when Euro-critical voices, marginalized in the key political institutions such as the Oireachtas, fought increasingly vigorous campaigns against EU treaties. In the aftermath of the Nice and Lisbon referendums, the pro-European consensus of the mainstream political elites remains, but their ability to persuade the Irish electorate to follow their lead is weakened. The second part of this chapter focuses on Irish public opinion on the EU and whether the efforts of those to communicate the issues are bearing fruit. The Irish public is currently one of the most pre-disposed towards the EU, recording consistently high levels of overall support in the EU's regular Eurobarometer reports since the late 1980s (Sinnott, 2007). Yet the evidence available in these polls amongst others shows that Irish support for EU integration is somewhat nuanced and low levels of EU knowledge exist. There is strong support for economic integration and a clear recognition of the economic benefits the EU has brought Ireland, but Irish voters are more cautious when it comes to the future enlargement of the EU and a common European security and defence policy.

EU referendums in Ireland

The reason behind the 1972 referendum on accession to the EEC was fairly straightforward: it was necessary in order to correct the conflict the obligations of membership would cause for the Constitution, *Bunreacht na hÉireann*. Under the obligations of EEC membership and alongside the doctrine of supremacy of European law, legislative authority would no longer be solely invested in the Oireachtas and the European Court of Justice would be superior to the state's Supreme Court. Rather than amending each of the affected articles accordingly, the decision was taken to introduce a catch-all amendment (Article 29.4.3) allowing the state to join the EEC. The 1972 referendum was the first and only time Irish political parties divided on a European issue according to the (rather weak) left–right economic cleavage evident in Irish electoral politics (Sinnott, 2002; Gallagher, 2003), with the parties of the centre-right/right, Fianna Fáil and Fine Gael, alongside business leaders and farmers groups, strongly advocating membership of the common market, while parties of the left, primarily the Irish Labour Party and the Workers Party campaigned for a No vote (alongside the civil society group the Common Market Study Group and the Irish Congress of Trade Unions). The mounting of a vigorous campaign by political parties and civil society groups which were clearly divided on the issue, together with wide public discussion of the issues, helped push turnout up (at 70.88 per cent it is the highest level of turnout heretofore recorded in any referendum in Ireland) and the referendum was comfortably carried with 83.1 per cent in favour.

By the time of the signature of the SEA in 1986, the consensus amongst political and legal circles was that parliamentary approval was sufficient in order for Ireland to ratify the new treaty. After a period of delay, the SEA was put before the Dáil on 9 December 1986. However, concern in certain legal and academic circles as to the means used to ratify the SEA was growing, and just before Christmas 1986 development economist and anti-EEC campaigner Raymond Crotty, backed by a larger group, challenged the constitutionality of the bill in the courts. Crotty opposed the SEA on a number of fronts. He and fellow campaigner Anthony Coughlan believed that

TABLE 5.1   *European referendum results, 1972–2008*

Date	Issue	% Yes	% No	Turnout	Spoilt or blank papers
10.5.72	Accession to EEC	83.10	16.90	70.88	0.83
26.5.87	Ratify Single European Act	69.92	30.08	44.09	0.45
18.6.92	Ratify Maastricht Treaty	69.10	30.90	57.30	0.50
22.5.98	Ratify Amsterdam Treaty	61.7	38.3	56.2	2.2
7.6.01	Ratify Nice Treaty (first time)	46.1	53.9	34.8	1.5
20.10.02	Ratify Nice Treaty (second time)	62.9	37.1	48.5	0.4
12.06.08	Ratify Lisbon Treaty	46.6	53.4	53.1	0.38

the SEA went far beyond what the Irish people consented to when they originally approved membership of the EEC in 1972. In a letter he wrote to all members of the Oireachtas, Crotty felt that

> this treaty will adversely affect our sovereignty, our democracy, the character of our government, the constitutional rights of citizens, and the economic and social interests of most members of our community. (Crotty, 1988, p. 104)

On appeal to the Supreme Court in early 1987, Crotty succeeded in stopping the Oireachtas from ratifying the SEA. Basing its judgements on the provisions in Title III of the SEA entitled European Political Cooperation, by a three-to-two majority the Supreme Court held that Title III was inconsistent with the Constitution as it imposed restrictions on the state's right to decide its own foreign policy and in so doing infringed upon Irish sovereignty. Thus the Constitution as it stood did not allow the State to ratify the SEA and required amendment if the SEA was to be ratified. The judgement appeared to take political and legal circles by surprise, and was greeted by some with outright disbelief (Sinnott, 1995a; Gallagher, 1988; see McCutcheon, 1991, for a full discussion of the legal issues involved). The government moved quickly to approve legislation which would enable the Constitution to be amended, setting the stage for another

EU-related referendum in 1987. As in 1972, the decision was taken to confine the 1987 referendum to the specific issue at hand, namely the amendment of the constitution in order to ratify the SEA, rather than introducing an all-encompassing amendment that would make all future referendums unnecessary. This political decision has meant that any ratification of an EC/EU treaty in Ireland is carried out through a referendum.

Voting on Europe: the Single European Act and Maastricht

The SEA set the tone for referendum campaigns to follow. While the Workers Party and Sinn Féin campaigned for a No vote (the Labour Party did not adopt an official position due to internal differences), the main opposition came from groupings outside the party political system, including anti-EU campaigners Anthony Coughlan and Raymond Crotty (see Box 5.1). Those campaigning for a Yes vote argued that Ireland's membership of the EC would be at stake and that damage would be done to the economy and employment if the referendum was defeated. Little effort was made to inform voters fully about the issues. In the end, the campaign was relatively short and the referendum was comfortably carried with an almost 70 per cent Yes vote. Turnout at 44 per cent was more alarming, however, and until that time was the second-lowest-ever turnout in a referendum (Gallagher, 1988, p. 80). The effect of the low turnout was that the Yes vote amounted to only 30.7 per cent of the electorate, compared with 58.4 per cent in 1972.

In some ways, the Maastricht referendum of 1992 could be said to have been merely a re-run of the SEA referendum. The referendum was comfortably carried (with 69.1 per cent voting Yes) and the pro-European consensus amongst mainstream political parties and interest groups such as the trade unions was solidified as both the Labour Party and the Irish Congress of Trade Unions (ICTU) came out in favour, thus marking the first time that Labour had given official support to an initiative towards integration. Yet what is interesting about the Maastricht referendum campaign is not just the emergence of a pro-European consensus amongst political parties (with the exception of the Green Party and Sinn Féin), but also the rise in importance of interest groups and civil-society umbrella groupings in the referendum campaign. In what has since become an enduring characteristic of Irish EU referendums, political parties are not always the main actors. These Euro-critical groupings

Box 5.1   Dissenting voices in EU referendums

A number of civil society groups have actively campaigned in successive Irish referendum campaigns. Appearing first during the 1972 accession referendum campaign, these groups have provided critical voices to Ireland's participation in the EU and have opposed the ratification of successive treaties amending the Treaty of Rome. Usually relying on limited resources, since the 1998 referendum on the Treaty of Amsterdam in particular, they have nevertheless conducted vigorous campaigns in EU referendum contests and have criticized the EU on three main fronts:

- **Successive treaty reforms have undermined Irish sovereignty and the principle of the equality of states in the EU.** Originally a member of the Common Market Defence Campaign (along with Raymond Crotty), Anthony Coughlan of the National Platform EU Research and Information Centre has consistently criticized the EU for 'eroding national independence and democracy of its member states by removing ever more State powers from the national to the supranational level' (Submission to National Forum on Europe, December 2006). Multimillionaire businessman Declan Ganley with his neo-conservative campaigning organization Libertas, campaigned against the Lisbon Treaty in 2008 on related lines, arguing that the treaty was *de facto* a European constitution. Ganley argued that the Lisbon Treaty fundamentally undermined the principle of equality between member states through the reforms to voting procedures in the Council and the loss of an Irish Commissioner, handed over new areas of power to Brussels, enshrined EU law as superior to national law and opened the door to EU interference in domestic taxation and other economic issues.

$\rightarrow$

(often formed on an *ad hoc* basis) play an important role in campaigns. In the Maastricht treaty campaign, these groups included Anthony Coughlan's National Platform for Employment, Democracy and Neutrality (comprising of other groups such as the People First/Meitheal organization and Irish CND). Neutrality, sovereignty and independence, and the threat integration posed to traditional,

→

- **Participation in EU security and defence provisions is incompatible with Ireland's policy of neutrality and the principle of an independent foreign policy.** Coming from the left and espousing anti-war and pacifist values, groups such as the People First/Meitheal (organized by solicitors Joe Noonan and Mary Lenihan), the Peace and Neutrality Alliance (PANA, chaired by Roger Cole, http://ww.pana.ie), Campaign for Nuclear Disarmament and Afri (Action from Ireland, http://www.afri.ie) have campaigned against successive EU treaties on the grounds of the threat they have posed to Irish neutrality. For these groups, any move towards a Common European Defence and any relationship with NATO undermine the primacy of Ireland's relationship with the United Nations. In 2008 these groups were joined by left-wing, anti-globalization groups such as the Peoples' Movement (led by Patricia McKenna) and the People before Profit Alliance amongst others.

- **Ratification of EU Treaties constitutes a threat to Irish Catholic values, such as the importance of family values, the abolition of abortion and the concomitant respect of the right to life.** Abortion as an issue linked to the EU properly emerged during the Maastricht referendum campaign in 1992. Pro-life Catholic groups such as Youth Defence and the Mother and Child campaign feared that the Maastricht Treaty would permit the legalization of abortion. Former MEP Dana Rosemary Scallon also criticized EU treaties from this perspective. During the first and second Nice referendum campaigns, the No to Nice group, led by longstanding conservative campaigner Justin Barrett, himself a former leader of Youth Defence, campaigned against the Nice Treaty on this and other issues. In 2008, Youth Defence re-emerged as *Cóir* (meaning Justice) and opposed the Lisbon treaty on similar grounds.

Catholic values were recurring motifs of the debate. The threat of possible conscription to a common European army was even mooted. The focus of the 1992 campaign was also deflected away from the content of the treaty itself towards issues such as the record financial sum negotiated by the then Taoiseach Albert Reynolds as part of the Delors II structural fund package and the controversial rulings on abortion by the High Court and Supreme Court in the 'X' case, which led to discussions on the treaty becoming embroiled in the issue of the introduction of abortion in Ireland.

During the Maastricht campaign the government also came under fire from treaty opponents for the use of public funding in order to campaign for a Yes vote. Feeling hampered by their limited financial resources, especially in comparison with the resources held by the Yes side, anti-Maastricht groups criticized the decision by the state broadcaster RTE to show a special government television appeal for a Yes vote without allowing equal airtime to the opposition campaign. Their criticism of biased media coverage was to have important consequences.

The changing conduct of referendums in Ireland

The Amsterdam referendum differed from previous EU referendums in one important respect: it was the first EU referendum held in the aftermath of the McKenna and Coughlan judgements. In the run up to the divorce referendum in 1995, Green party MEP Patricia McKenna questioned the constitutionality of the use of public money by the government to campaign for a Yes vote. Such funding was declared unconstitutional as the Supreme Court ruled that the government was not entitled to use public money to put forward only one side of the case, since not all citizens would support one side. Thus, for each referendum since 1995, the government of the day has established a Referendum Commission whose function is to inform the public about the issues and arguments in non-biased manner. The Commission is composed of non-political figures, and usually headed by either a former or current member of the judiciary nominated by the Chief Justice, alongside the Ombudsman, the Comptroller and Auditor General and other senior civil servants. One month before the Amsterdam referendum in 1998, in response to a request for judicial review by Anthony Coughlan, the High Court found that the failure by state public broadcasting service RTE to allocate equal time for uncontested broadcasts by the Yes and No sides in the 1995 divorce referendum had resulted in inequality amounting to 'unconstitutional unfairness'. The implication of this judgement was that in subsequent referendums, equal airtime must be allotted to parties and groups advocating a Yes and No respectively, in a given campaign. Taken together, both judgements considerably altered the way EU referendums were to be conducted in the future, redressing the balance between the Yes and No sides.

The party-political pro-European consensus continued in the 1998 referendum with the leaders of the government coalition parties Fianna Fáil and the Progressive Democrats joining forces with Fine Gael, Labour and Democratic Left to host a press conference in which they jointly urged a Yes vote based on the economic and political benefits active EU membership would bring. Rejecting the treaty would hurt Ireland's position in the EU (Minister for Foreign Affairs David Andrews quoted in *Irish Times*, 19 May 1998). Much of the debate during the campaign focused on the issue of neutrality with protagonists in favour of the treaty asserting that the treaty had no negative implications for neutrality. The Peace and Neutrality Alliance (PANA) chaired by Roger Cole opposed the treaty on the grounds of the threat it posed to Irish neutrality and much of the discussion during the campaign focused on Ireland's participation in NATO's Partnership for Peace framework.

While again the referendum was comfortably carried with a 61.7 per cent Yes vote, the No vote of just over 38 per cent was the largest vote against EU integration hitherto recorded. With a turnout of 56.2 per cent, the proportion of the electorate rejecting further integration reached a high of 21 per cent, with 45 per cent of the electorate choosing to abstain (see Figure 5.1). The Referendum Commission's approach of making a public call for arguments from individuals, interest groups or parties, and then putting these together in leaflets, newspaper advertisements and television and radio broadcasts was widely criticized leading as it did to erroneous arguments being presented as facts. Deputy Prime Minister Mary Harney questioned the usefulness of such a procedure declaring 'it is unsatisfactory that such spurious arguments have to be put forward in the interests of balance' (*Irish Times*, 25 May 1998). The material disseminated by the Commission was also criticized for its turgid and confusing nature, turning off voters rather than enlightening them (Gallagher, 2003; Mansergh, 1999). The ineffectiveness of the Commission in informing voters of the issues at stake was highlighted even more when the results of an exit poll were published in May 1998. Asked 'why did you vote no against the Amsterdam Treaty', those polled cited a perceived lack of information as the main reason (Gilland, 1999, p. 435).

Ireland's honeymoon with the EU at an end

The rejection of the Nice treaty by Irish voters in June 2001 (hereafter called Nice 1) prompted many commentators to conclude that

FIGURE 5.1   European referendums in Ireland: Yes, No and abstention as proportions of the electorate

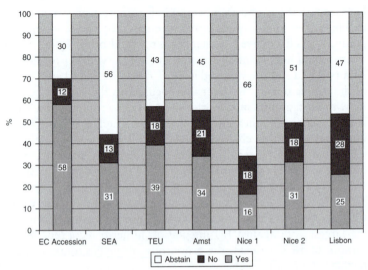

Source: http://www.ireland.com/focus/thelisbontreaty/analysis/graphics/#result (accessed 19 June 2008).

Ireland's honeymoon with the EU had come to an end. Instead of being a 'model' pupil, Ireland had become the problem child of the EU family (O'Brennan, 2003). While many politicians and commentators expressed shock at the negative result, in hindsight there were signs of a possible upset even before the results of the referendum were revealed, as opinion polls conducted before the vote pointed to the possibility that the treaty might be rejected. This was accompanied by low levels of knowledge of the Treaty.

As before, protagonists in favour ranged from the main political parties (excluding the Green Party and Sinn Féin), the European Movement, ICTU, the Irish Business and Employers' Confederation, the Irish Farmers Association, the Chambers of Commerce of Ireland, and the Irish Bishops' Conference. They argued that the Treaty of Nice was about an historic enlargement of the EU from 15 to 25 which would also be in Ireland's best interests, given the access it would bring to an enlarged single market. Political parties were reluctant to spend money campaigning and the message put forward to the voters was unclear and inconsistent. Media interest in the campaign was low and the discussion on the Treaty was diluted by the fact that two other referendums on the International Criminal Court and the death penalty were held on the same day (Hayward, 2002). In contrast, No campaigners – including the Greens, Sinn Féin, the National Platform, the 'No to Nice' group (including anti-abortion campaigner Justin Barrett), the Peace and Neutrality Alliance and Afri – ran highly visible and committed campaigns capitalizing on voter doubt and ignorance ('if you don't know, vote no').

Turnout at 34.7 per cent was the lowest level ever recorded for a European integration referendum. The high level of abstention had a considerable impact on the result – more than half of those who had voted 'yes' in the Amsterdam referendum chose to abstain in 2001 (see Figure 5.1). A European Commission survey conducted found that amongst abstainers 'lack of understanding/lack of information' was the single most cited reason not to vote (44 per cent as compared with 25 per cent in a survey following the Amsterdam referendum) (Sinnott, 2001; Gilland, 2002).

It became clear in the aftermath of the rejection that a second referendum (hereafter called Nice 2) would be held. The government had a three-pronged strategy to address the issues emerging from the defeat and neutralize them in advance of the second referendum. A National Forum on Europe was set up to communicate the issues to the wider public; national parliamentary scrutiny on EU matters was enhanced (thus addressing the domestic 'democratic deficit') and the government secured two declarations at the June 2002 Seville European Council recognizing Irish neutrality.

The Nice 2 campaign was an altogether different affair from that of Nice 1. PANA, the National Platform and the No to Nice group spearheaded the No campaign, alongside the Green Party and Sinn Féin. On the yes-side, a re-engaged political elite was joined by a number of strongly committed civil society groups organized under the umbrella group 'Irish Alliance for Europe'. The main opposition parties emphasized the importance of voting on the actual issue at stake and not using the referendum as an opportunity to punish the incumbent government. In response to widespread criticism for its performance during Nice 1, the Referendum Commission's role was changed in Nice 2 to simply make the electorate aware that a referendum was being held and to familiarize it with the issues at stake.

Nice 2, held on 18 October 2002, had a turnout of 49.5 per cent and produced a 63 to 37 per cent majority in favour of ratification of the treaty. However, just over 50 per cent of the electorate abstained from voting. There was an improvement in communication in the mass media and in interpersonal discussion of the issues and a substantial increase in people's sense that they could understand the issues at stake (by 25 per cent overall). The Yes campaigners did succeed in tempting those more positively disposed to the EU and to its enlargement who had not voted in the first referendum back out to vote. Yet the evidence also showed that there were limits to the communication process in that the specific measures taken by the government with a view to the second referendum generated, at best, only moderate levels of awareness among the public (Sinnott, 2003). There was little spillover from an understanding of the issues raised by the Treaty of Nice to a more general understanding of the institutions of the Union and how they work. This lack of engagement with EU issues was to have important consequences when the Irish electorate failed to ratify the Treaty of Lisbon ('Plan B' to the failed Constitutional Treaty rejected by the French and the Dutch electorates) on 12 June 2008.

The rejection of the Constitutional Treaty was particularly poignant for Taoiseach Bertie Ahern in the context of his efforts in securing agreement amongst all member states during Ireland's 2004 EU Presidency. The amending treaty of Lisbon signed in December 2007 set out various incremental reforms to EU decision making procedures, as well as enhancing democracy through increased involvement of national parliaments in EU policy making and the citizens' initiative, a strengthening of the EU's ability to project itself on the world stage and the EU's capacity to deal with climate change and energy security. It also became clear that Ireland would be the only member state to ratify the treaty by referendum.

There were early indications that ratification would be a challenge. In a poll conducted in November 2007, only 25 per cent of those surveyed said they would vote Yes to the new Treaty, while 13 per cent intended to vote No and 62 per cent said they didn't know or had no opinion (TNS/MRBI *Irish Times* Poll, 5 November 2007). In addition, from the beginning of 2008 Ahern came under increased scrutiny due to his exposure to a judicial enquiry into planning matters. Amidst growing public disquiet, Ahern was distracted from the business of government due to his need to respond to ongoing revelations at the tribunal. Confusion also existed as to when the referendum itself would be held as Ahern procrastinated in naming a date, eventually plumping for a date in June. Between the shock announcement of his intention to resign in early April 2008 and the appointment of Brian Cowen as Taoiseach on 8 May 2008, a political vacuum emerged which was filled by effectively organized No campaigners. Cowen said that passing Lisbon was his first priority, but he had barely four weeks in which to campaign.

Once again the Treaty had the support of all mainstream political parties, including the parliamentary Green Party. Sinn Féin was the only party in the Dáil to campaign against Lisbon. Coming from the margins of the political spectrum, Lisbon witnessed an explosion of groups advocating a No vote (see Box 5.1). They gained a strong foothold from very early on, also benefiting from the rules of the referendum game as dictated by the McKenna and Coughlan judgements. Declan Ganley's Libertas ran a high profile campaign, making effective use of internet platforms (all No groups made very effective use of the internet) and gaining support from businessman Ulick McEvaddy (who claimed that the treaty was unintelligible drivel) (*Irish Times*, 2 May 2008). For the first time in a referendum campaign, a No group had a significant amount of money to spend on their campaign, as anecdotal estimates of the Libertas spend ranged from €1.3 to €1.8 million.

The No campaigners' strategy was to cherry-pick elements of the treaty and attack them, instilling fear into the minds of an electorate already showing high levels of ignorance of the Treaty (Referendum Commission, 2008). Libertas focused on the issue of tax harmonization and also drew on populist sentiment arguing that the Treaty was undemocratic. The People's Movement and Joe Higgins's Socialist party argued that the Treaty was a step in the direction of a more 'Corporate Europe'. Sinn Féin focused on claims of loss of influence, sovereignty and neutrality, arguing that the Treaty was a bad deal for Europe and that the government could renegotiate a better deal. Catholic fundamentalist group Cóir, going against the official position of the Irish Bishops, argued that the Charter of Fundamental Rights (annexed to the Treaty and given legal status) would force Ireland to legalize abortion, gay marriage, prostitution and euthanasia. All of these claims were factually erroneous. Cóir also tapped into the 'anti-establishment, anti-authority and anti-politician' mood in the country (*Irish Times*, 7 June 2008) through their use of provocative posters such as 'Don't be bullied, Vote No'. Fears for the economic future of the country also played a role.

The Yes campaigners in contrast failed to construct a narrative on the Treaty, exhorting voters to trust them and vote 'Yes'. Given the early foothold gained by the No campaign, they spent their time attempting to counter 'No' arguments and misinformation. The performance of the Referendum Commission was also questioned as, in a press conference called to bring clarity to the debate,

Chairman Mr Justice Iarfhlaith O'Neill was embarrassed when he could not explain one provision of the Treaty when asked by a journalist. In-fighting amongst mainstream political parties also undermined the Yes campaign, as did the threat by sectional interests such as the farmers' organizations, most notably the IFA, to withhold their support for the Treaty unless a commitment was given by the government to veto ongoing WTO talks if the ultimate deal undermined Irish farmers' interests. The split in the trade union movement was also damaging to the Yes campaign. The result of a TNS/MRBI poll a week before the referendum showing that 30 per cent of the electorate intended to vote Yes, 35 per cent would vote No and 35 per cent had yet to decide, intensified the efforts of yes campaigners as it indicated that the referendum clearly could be lost. On 12 June 2008, 53.1 per cent of the electorate turned out to vote decisively against the Treaty. Significantly, the proportion of the electorate that voted No increased from 18 per cent in Nice 1 to 28 per cent (see Figure 5.1). Lisbon was approved in only ten of the country's 43 constituencies, half of those constituencies in the Dublin area.

Voting behaviour at EU referendums

So who actually votes in Irish EU referendums and why? Such information is patchy and we are reliant on the opinion polls and surveys conducted in the immediate aftermath of referendums in order to answer these questions. Surveys carried out on behalf of the European Commission's office in Ireland provide the most extensive information on the determinants of voting. In his early analysis of the SEA referendum, Sinnott found that farmers were more likely to vote Yes (because of CAP reform), whereas those from working-class areas were more likely to vote no (Sinnott, 1995a, pp. 232–3). At Maastricht men were also slightly more likely to support the Treaty than women. For supporters of the Treaty, the most important attitudinal factor influencing their vote was economic, including employment and financial aid for Ireland. Opponents expressed reservations about the implications of the TEU for Irish neutrality, moral and women's issues/rights. As mentioned above, nearly half the electorate admitted to having been ill-informed on the day of the referendum (Holmes, 1993, p. 109). At Amsterdam, such lack of knowledge was also the most significant reason behind their vote for those who voted No. In an RTE exit poll, 36 per cent of those who voted No did so because of lack of sufficient information.

TABLE 5.2 *Results of 2001, 2002 and 2008 referendums*

Result of Referendums	Nice 1 7 June 2001	Nice 2 19 October 2002	Lisbon 12 June 2008
Electorate	2,867,960	2,924,172	3,051,278
Total poll	34.79%	49.47%	53.1%
Yes	46.13%	62.89%	46.6%
No	53.57%	37.11%	53.4%

TABLE 5.3 *Reasons for voting No in first and second Nice referendums*

	Nice 1	Nice 2
Lack of information	39	14
Loss of sovereignty/independence	16	8
Neutrality and military issues	12	17
Bad idea in general	7	25
Influence of political party, politician, TV debate	6	5
Would create refugee problems	3	11
Abortion issue	1	1
Advice of family or friends	1	2
Anti-government/anti-politician		10
Refuse to change vote		5
Other	2	14
Don't know	13	2

Source: Taken from Sinnott (2003), p. 43.

In Nice 1, 39 per cent of those who voted No did so because they did not feel adequately on top of the issues (see Table 5.3). The most important attitudinal determinant seems to have been a general dissatisfaction with EU policy-making processes rather than concern about specific issues. In addition, women were more likely to vote No than men. The predominant characteristic of those who voted Yes was a general belief in European integration or in Irish membership of the EU and in the desirability of enlargement. A lack of information/understanding of issues was the largest factor in abstention (44 per cent), and the probability of abstention was also increased by being young. On the other hand, the probability of abstention was reduced by having a lower middle-class occupation. At Nice 2, however, the greatest reason for voting No was the belief that it was a 'bad idea in general' (25 per cent), whilst the issue of neutrality rose by 5 per cent to 17 per cent as a cause for a No vote. As in Nice 1, the largest reason given for abstention was lack of understanding but this was significantly reduced from 44 to 26 per cent (see Table 5.3).

At Nice 2, the greatest reason for voting No was the belief that it was a 'bad idea in general' (25 per cent), whilst the issue of neutrality rose by 5 per cent to 17 per cent as a cause for a No vote. As in Nice 1, the largest reason given for abstention was lack of understanding/lack of information but this was significantly reduced from 44 per cent to 26 per cent (see Table 5.3). The second most important reason for abstention was that people simply were not interested or bothered (32 per cent). Sinnott found that turnout was boosted by enthusiasm for European integration and by having an allegiance to one or other of the political parties. There was a tendency for Fianna Fáil, Fine Gael and Progressive Democrat

TABLE 5.4   *Reasons for voting No in Lisbon referendum*

	Lisbon
Lack of information	22
To protect Irish identity	12
To safeguard neutrality in security and defence matters	6
Lack of trust in politicians	6
Loss of right to have a Commissioner in every Commission	6
To protect Irish tax system	6
Against the idea of a unified Europe	5
To protest against government's policies	4
To avoid that the EU speaks with one voice on global issues	4
Because larger member states decide on EU matters	4
To protect the influence of small states	3
Abortion, gay marriage, euthanasia	2
To avoid an influx of immigrants	1
The EU does not need any fixing, it works fine	1
Other	14
Don't know	3

Source: Flash Eurobarometer 245 (2008). % of reasons mentioned.
Base: those who participated in survey and voted 'no' in the referendum.

supporters to support ratification whereas Labour Party supporters, taking all other factors into account, tended to oppose ratification. All other things being equal, women were more likely to vote than men. In terms of attitudes towards integration, a general feeling of enthusiasm for European integration and EU enlargement boosted a Yes vote, whereas No-voters held the view that too many issues are decided on by the EU and were dissatisfied with the way EU policies are made, and the feeling that Ireland should do all it can to strengthen its neutrality.

At the time of writing, the Flash Eurobarometer report published in the immediate aftermath of the referendum defeat provided an initial picture as to why Lisbon was rejected. Over half of those who abstained said this was due to a lack of understanding of the issues (young people being more likely to abstain). For Yes voters, the prime motivation was the feeling that the Treaty was in Ireland's best interest. No voters, in contrast, evinced a diverse range of reasons to explain their vote (see Table 5.4), illustrating the 'multidimensional character of the explanations' (Flash Eurobarometer 245, 2008). Top of the list was lack of knowledge of the Treaty followed by a desire to keep Ireland's power and identity. Concerns regarding the loss of a permanent Irish Commissioner may be reflected in this reason. Young voters voted No by a margin of two to one. Women and those not working were more likely to vote No, whereas only 45 per cent of retired people voted against Lisbon. The main supporters of the Yes vote were found in the higher socio-economic groups. Party loyalty did not persuade voters to back the Yes campaign, with Labour, and Green Party supporters more likely to vote No. By contrast, a huge majority of Sinn Féin supporters followed their party's line. A large majority of those polled (68 per cent) felt that the No campaign was the more convincing one. Significantly, 42 per cent of No voters were of the opinion that the referendum was not important for Ireland's future position in the EU, compared to only 5 per cent of the Yes voters. In addition, 76 per cent of No voters believed that a No vote would allow the Irish government to renegotiate 'exceptions' within the Treaty. A strong majority of both camps said they supported Ireland's membership of the EU.

Voting on the issues or putting the boot in?

Political scientists are divided on the reasons why voters vote the way they do in EU referendums (Binzer Hobolt, 2003; Svensson,

2002; Franklin, van der Eijk and Marsh, 1995). Some focus on individuals' values and beliefs, and argue that voting behaviour in EU referendums reflects people's underlying broad attitudes towards Europe – it is voters' general views on Europe that influences how they vote (Svensson, 2002). Others argue that EU referendums work very much like second-order European Parliament elections – their determining factor is support for or opposition to the party or parties in government at the time of the referendum (Franklin *et al.*, 1995).

Analysing the Nice 1 and 2 referendum results and the survey data emanating from these votes, Garry, Marsh and Sinnott investigated whether these two referendums were decided by Irish voters' attitudes to Europe or by their attitude to the incumbent Fianna Fáil/Progressive Democrat coalition government (Garry *et al.*, 2005). Using issue-voting variables and government-satisfaction variables derived from the datasets from the European Commission's two surveys following the Nice 1 and 2 referendums, they ran a number of logistical regressions testing different voting models only to find that while there is some evidence of second-order effects, issues were stronger predictors of vote choice: 'both referendums on the Nice Treaty were closer to being processes of deliberation on EU issues than to being plebiscites on the incumbent government' (Garry *et al.*, 2005, p. 215). On the basis of their analyses, Garry *et al.* came to the conclusion that the more vigorous a European referendum campaign, the greater the effect of the key substantive issues relating to the referendum will be – in the case of Nice 2 attitudes to EU enlargement – and the less the effect of second-order considerations. The implication of this analysis is that if governments want attitudes towards EU issues to determine the outcome of EU referendums, they must campaign strongly and effectively.

Irish attitudes to European integration

Since 1973, the European Commission has commissioned Europe-wide public opinion polls every six months, conducted by private polling agencies in each member state and involving a sample of approximately 1,000 interviewees in each country. These Euro-barometer surveys consequently provide a very large dataset for the study of Irish attitudes towards European integration since accession. The level of support for European integration in Ireland, as in other member-states, varies according to the question asked (Sinnott, 2003), but at first glance Irish attitudes to integration look extremely positive in the surveys. Since the early 1980s, support for the EU changed dramatically in Ireland, rising from lower levels of support in the early 1980s to very high levels, well above the EU average (Sinnott, 2007).

Irish support for the EU is even higher in response (on average more than 10 per cent) to the second most frequently asked question in Eurobarometer surveys – whether a country has benefited from EU membership (Figure 5.2). And in 2007, 86 per cent of those surveyed felt that Ireland has benefited from EU membership, the highest in the EU (compared with an EU average of 59 per cent (Figure 5.4). Seven per cent of Irish people believed that Ireland has not benefited from being a member of the EU, in contrast with 36 per cent of Germans, 44 per cent of British and 46 per cent of Cypriots (Table 5.5).

On other measures of attitude, however, the picture is a little different and enthusiasm for European integration in Ireland appears at a lower level. Faced with a hypothetical situation whereby the EU would be scrapped (the dissolution question), in 2004 54 per cent of Irish respondents said they would be sorry, whereas 43 per cent felt they would be either indifferent or did not know what to think, giving the impression that enthusiasm for the EU is not deep-seated. Coming from levels of almost 60 per cent in the early 1990s, enthusiasm for the EU dropped to just over 40 per cent in the spring of 2001. In response to a question posed in 2007 of how the Irish view the EU, while 69 per cent of respondents had a very or fairly positive image of the Union, just 21 per cent of respondents had a very positive image. For 48 per cent the image was only fairly positive, suggesting that the bulk of support for the EU in Ireland is not unqualified (Eurobarometer 68). Irish enthusiasm for certain aspects of integration, for example further political integration, is also more measured.

Determinants of public support

Research into public opinion on the EU shows that with regard to individual level characteristics, 'utilitarian theory is the strongest and most robust predictor of support for European integration' across EU member states (Gabel, 1998, p. 352). The utilitarian perspective posits that those who benefit more in an economic sense from European integration should be more supportive of the process than those who do not. Those who are more educated, of the professional/managerial classes, more likely to have travelled, and have benefited from trade liberalization are more likely to perceive the

FIGURE 5.2   Percentages of respondents that feel country has (1) benefited from EU membership (Ireland), and that (2) EU membership is a good thing (Ireland and 25 member states)

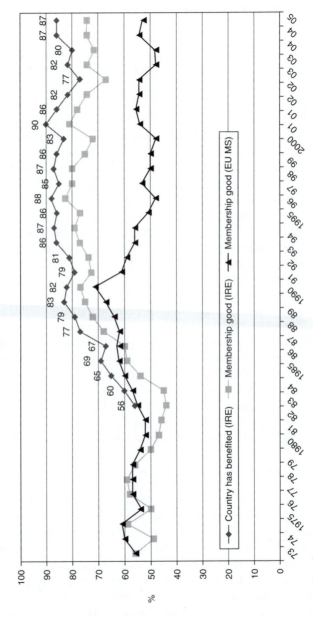

Source: Eurobarometer, various.

FIGURE 5.3   Respondents who feel membership of the EU is a good thing

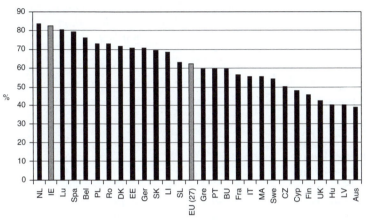

Source: Eurobarometer 67 (2007).

FIGURE 5.4   Respondents across member states who feel they have benefited from EU membership

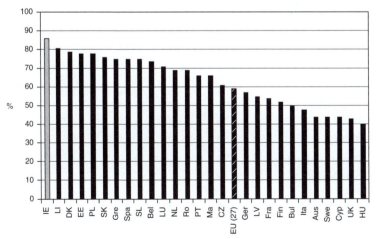

Source: Eurobarometer 67 (2007).

TABLE 5.5 *Respondents' attitudes towards Ireland's membership of the EU by demographic groupings*

	A good thing	A bad thing	Neither good nor bad	Don't know	No. of cases
Total	73	6	16	5	1,109
Male	75	7	16	3	498
Female	72	5	16	7	
Age					
15–24 years	74	4	16	5	209
25–34 years	72	7	17	5	186
35–44 years	77	4	16	4	201
45–54 years	73	7	17	3	157
55–64 years	69	11	18	3	114
65+	74	5	12	9	142
Education					
Low	55	12	22	12	137
Middle	74	5	18	3	538
High	83	6	9	3	194
Currently studying	78	3	11	8	118
Current occupation					
Self-employed	69	6	22	3	72
Managers	81	5	11	2	133
Other White Collars	74	3	22	2	107
Manual Workers	69	8	19	4	233
House person	71	6	16	8	205
Unemployed	70	13	13	4	23
Retired	76	8	11	6	120
Student	78	3	11	8	118
Rural area/village	70	6	19	6	379
Small/Middle sized town	79	7	9	5	175
Large Town	74	5	17	4	426
Dublin	72	5	18	5	290
Rest of Leinster	69	6	18	6	253
Munster	79	8	10	3	283
Connaught/Ulster	73	3	19	5	182

Source: Eurobarometer 64.2, Autumn 2005, Ireland.

benefits European integration brings and hence support European integration. In Ireland, survey evidence shows that individuals in higher occupational categories and more highly educated are more favourable towards European integration than those in lower categories and with lower levels of education (Kennedy and Sinnott, 2007; see also Table 5.5). Farmers, surprisingly, are relatively sceptical (they were relatively pro-European in the 1980s but their support declined in the 1990s, most likely reflecting their opposition to reform of the Common Agricultural Policy). Students and young people are relatively supportive of integration, while the retired, unemployed and house-persons are relatively sceptical. Catholicism is the most pro-European religion (see McLaren, 2002; Hix, 2005; Gabel, 2001). Irish public opinion corresponds with this pattern. While the differences are slight (Table 5.5), men tend to be more positively disposed to the EU than women in Ireland, those aged between 55 and 64 are less likely to support the EU than other age groups, manual workers and those living in rural areas are slightly less predisposed than others. Interestingly, research has also shown that there is support for the hypothesis that those Irish who identify exclusively with the Irish nation (in terms of expressing their identity) are more likely than those with at least some sense of feeling European to think that Ireland's membership of the EU is 'a bad thing' (Kennedy and Sinnott, 2007, p. 72).

Attitudes towards the issues

As mentioned above, the tendency towards a strong positive opinion of the EU is not evident across all measures of Irish public opinion on the EU, attitudes towards future developments such as political union being the most notable exception. When asked what the EU means to them personally, Irish respondents are more likely to refer to the economic aspects of the EU, such as freedom of movement, the euro and economic prosperity (Eurobarometer 57, Spring 2002). While attitudes to security and defence matters in general are more likely to be positive than negative, a large percentage of Irish people are unsure about these issues (as evinced by numbers of respondents who are reluctant to offer an opinion). In the 2005 Eurobarometer report, support for moves towards a European political union is more measured in Ireland than in other member states (Ireland ranked 20th out of 25 in terms of support, higher only than Denmark, Sweden, Austria, Finland and the UK) with 51 per cent of respondents for, 15 per cent against, 33 per cent saying they did not know. In answer to the question of whether there should be one common foreign policy among the member states of the EU towards other countries, 61 per cent of Irish respondents declared themselves to be in favour (Eurobarometer 63, September 2005), in comparison with an EU average of 67 per cent. Irish people are also more likely on average to express reservations regarding the adoption of a strongly supranational approach to defence (in 2002, only 34 per cent of respondents declared themselves happy to see defence and security policy issues jointly decided within the EU – compared with 51 per cent in the Union as a whole).

Unsurprisingly given the economic nature of the Irish public opinion support for the EU, attitudes towards the euro are much more positive. When asked to evaluate the performance of the euro four years after it was introduced, 84 per cent of Irish respondents (the highest in the EU) felt the euro caused no difficulty at all, compared with an EU average of 53 per cent. Eighty-eight per cent felt that the euro has added to the increase of prices, and 90 per cent believed that it has become an international currency like the dollar or the yen. And as to whether the euro engendered feelings of 'Europeanness' amongst the Irish public, 38 per cent said that they felt a little more European, 2 per cent a little less and 59 per cent felt that nothing had changed (Flash Eurobarometer 175, November 2005).

But what of attitudes towards enlargement? Comparatively, Ireland's level of support for further EU enlargement is low with 18 of the 26 other member states showing higher levels of support. In Eurobarometer 67 (2007), 42 per cent of Irish people said they were in favour of future enlargement, while 38 per cent said they were against it. Ireland's level of support was towards the bottom of the table with the UK 0(41 per cent), Germany (34 per cent), France (32 per cent) and Luxembourg (25 per cent) amongst the six countries with lower levels of support. The remoteness of key European developments from large sections of the Irish public was also evident in the fact that 46 per cent of Irish people had no view on the impact of the 2004 enlargement of the EU.

Knowledge of the EU amongst the Irish public

In his 1995 study of levels of knowledge of the EU, Sinnott discovered that the positive perceptions of EU membership in Ireland were accompanied by relatively low levels of knowledge regarding the EU (Ireland ranked sixth overall in actual levels of knowledge of how the

EU functions). In analysing the results of the 1993 Eurobarometer, Sinnott also drew attention to the positive relation between higher levels of knowledge of European affairs and a favourable attitude towards the EU. He observed that a generally favourable attitude to European integration went from 36 per cent among those with very low levels of knowledge, to 76 per cent among those with very high levels (Sinnott, 1995b, p. 16). Low levels of knowledge are closely associated with social class and education. Being either a skilled or unskilled manual worker had a substantial negative effect on the level of knowledge of European affairs, as did low levels of education. Holding all other effects constant, Sinnott also found gender and age also mattered: men were better informed about European affairs than women, and being over 65 was more likely to mean being less informed and less supportive.

The evidence also appears to show that levels of knowledge of the EU have not increased dramatically in Ireland since Sinnott's original research. Knowledge of the EU can be measured subjectively (that is by looking at the respondent's own assessment of his or her knowledge of the EU, its policies and institutions) or objectively, that is by means of a battery of factual questions that seek to measure how much respondents actually know about the EU. Focusing on the subjective measure, Irish respondents currently place themselves amongst the four countries with the most widespread sense of lack of knowledge of the European Union and its policies (alongside the UK, Portugal and Spain). In spite of a second and more visible Nice referendum campaign where great efforts were made to communicate Europe, 47 per cent of those respondents polled in the Eurobarometer of early Spring 2003 felt that their level of knowledge of the EU was low. In terms of actual knowledge, Eurobarometer 64.2 (2005) posed a number of true or false questions in order to gauge people's knowledge of the EU. Using these true or false items, researchers constructed a scale measuring people's knowledge of the EU; those who are 'informed' about the EU are those who answer at least three questions correctly. A fifth of Irish people were 'informed' (19 per cent) but just 3 per cent provided the correct answers to the four questions. The vast majority of Irish respondents were 'uninformed' about the EU, answering two or fewer questions correctly (81 per cent) and a fifth of Irish people did not answer any question correctly (20 per cent). As in the 1990s, those Irish people who tend to be 'uninformed' are 55 years of age or older (as well as people aged 25–34 years), have low levels of education, are manual workers and live in rural areas and small towns. They also continue to be less likely to see EU membership as a good thing.

The results of Eurobarometer 67 (Spring 2007) pointed to a slight improvement in levels of knowledge in Ireland, compared with previous reports. The survey also pointed to a low level of political engagement on the part of the Irish populace. From a survey conducted in the midst of a general election campaign, only 10 per cent of Irish respondents said they discuss political matters frequently when they meet up with friends, 48 per cent of respondents said they discuss matters occasionally, whilst 41 per cent said they never discuss such matters. The proportion of respondents who said they never discuss political matters with friends was substantially higher than the EU rate of 28 per cent. This low level of political discussion, coupled with low levels of knowledge on the EU, makes the challenge of communicating Europe in EU referendums all the greater.

The National Forum on Europe

The shock of the Nice 1 result galvanized the political elites into action, and for the first time concerted efforts were made to 'communicate' Europe in Ireland. The most obvious demonstration of this was the setting up and continued running of the National Forum on Europe, modelled on the New Ireland Forum and its successor the Forum for Peace and Reconciliation (in Northern Ireland). Originally a Labour Party idea, the Forum's first brief was to inform the public of the issues surrounding the Nice Treaty. Based in Dublin Castle and chaired by independent Northern Ireland Senator Maurice Hayes, the Forum consists of nominees from all political parties in the Oireachtas, MEPs, independent TDs and Senators, with the addition of a Special Observer Pillar which includes representatives from other registered political parties, including those from Northern Ireland, the Social Partners, interested elements of civil society, and other groups active in European Affairs. No time limit was set for its duration. The Forum has held plenary sessions inviting keynote speakers from Ireland and Europe to come and debate with issues with Forum participants. In the winter period 2001–02 the Forum moved out of Dublin Castle and held a series of 'listening sessions' in six regional centres and in Dublin suburban locations, and calls for submissions on the Nice Treaty and other issues were invited (Brown, 2005). Following the success of the Nice 2 referendum, the Forum's work moved towards publicising the issues surrounding the Constitutional Treaty and targeting those in society who would not normally be exposed to EU issues through conferences and competitions, for example school children and women's groups (National Forum on Europe, 2006). Following the rejection of the Constitutional Treaty in France and the Netherlands in 2005, the Forum expanded its brief to debate wider issues relating to the EU such as globalization, human rights, enlargement, agriculture, the European social model and development.

National Forum on Europe survey results assessing its own impact have been seen to be encouraging (National Forum on Europe, 2005, p. 37); levels of awareness of the Forum amongst the public rose from 24 per cent in March 2002 to 38 per cent in May 2005. Media coverage of the Forum itself, however, has been disappointingly patchy, reflecting the inadequacy of the reporting of European issues amongst the Irish media outside of referendum campaigns and European Parliament elections. While the Forum may perhaps have enhanced the range and scope of elite debate on EU issues, its impact on the levels of citizen knowledge has been more limited (O'Brennan, 2004). Even so, the performance of the Forum has not gone unnoticed both inside and outside Ireland. In its 2005 White Paper (Plan D for Democracy), the European Commission referred to the Forum as a model for the organization of domestic debates on the EU (COM(2005)464).

Further innovations in the communication of Europe have also been undertaken. Examples include the devotion of a full day of parliamentary debate to EU matters by the Oireachtas, (10 May 2006), inviting Agriculture Commissioner Mariann Fischer Boel to address the Dáil (the first keynote address by a European commissioner) and debating questions submitted by the public online. The Department of Foreign Affairs also revitalised its 'Communicating Europe' initiative, which provides grants to organizations and individuals for the development of EU-themed projects aimed at increasing awareness of the EU.

The governmental initiatives to enhance knowledge about and interest in the European Union have had a very limited impact on the Irish public. What is clear is that while the Irish electorate may be positively predisposed towards membership of the EU, reservations regarding the future trajectory of integration do exist and there is no longer a consensus on Europe in Ireland. The localism and personalism of Ireland's political culture militates against meaningful and sustained public debate on Ireland's relations with the EU. The old narrative based on modernization has no resonance in post-Celtic tiger Ireland. It has not been replaced with a new narrative.

Chapter 6

Multi-level Governance and Territorial Politics

Membership of the European Union has myriad effects on governance in the member states, including territorial organization and politics. The Union by adding an additional layer of governance takes policy-making beyond the domestic. The laws and policies of the Union penetrate core executives and are taken into the policy processes at national and sub-national levels, and EU policies are designed to trigger institutional, process and policy change in the member states. The impact of the EU on territorial politics is classified as one of the five 'faces' of Europeanization by Olsen (2002). Attention to the multileveled character of the EU accelerated in the 1980s arising from the growth of European regional policy and scholarly research on the dynamics of this policy area. Multilevel governance was developed into a theoretical account of the European Union in opposition to state centric and intergovernmental accounts (Marks and Hooghe, 2001). This chapter explores the interaction and intersection between EU policies and processes and territorial governance and politics in Ireland.

Multi-level governance

Scholars working from a multileveled governance approach make a number of strong claims concerning the dynamic of integration and the impact on the EU on territorial politics and organization. First, they highlight the emergence of overlapping competencies across levels of government and governance rather than a neat delineation of competence. From this perspective, national governments no longer monopolize public policy. Second, engagement in the processes of multilevel governance involves a significant loss of control for individual national governments. Third, sub-national actors are no longer nested exclusively within the member states; they operate in the domestic and EU arenas and have direct access to the supranational actors, particularly the Commission (Marks *et al.*, 1996; Marks and Hooghe, 2001). The central proposition of the multileveled governance literature is that domestic core executives share power with actors both at the supranational and sub-national levels. The message is one of breaking the state mould and of state sovereignty in retreat (*ibid.*). From this perspective we would antici-pate a reduction in the gatekeeping capacity of national governments, the sharing of policy competence across different levels of govern-ment and the mobilization of sub-national actors in the Brussels arena.

Scholarly interest in multilevel governance emerged at the same time as a growing political interest in and advocacy of a 'Europe of Regions'. Across the European Union, the idea of a Regional Europe formed part of the political discourse on European integra-tion from the early 1980s onwards. According to this narrative, the nation-state was being undermined from above by European integra-tion and from below as a consequence of the growing significance of the regional tier of government. There were a variety of reasons for the growing political interest in regionalism. A number of states in Europe were in the throes of significant internal constitutional change and others were engaged in reform of central, regional and local government. The growing salience of European integration led to calls, from Europe's powerful regions, for the formalization of a regional voice in the EU. The iterative process of treaty change since the Single European Act provided regions within states a 'win-dow of opportunity' to press for an enhancement of their say over domestic European policies and the institutional structure of the Union. Beginning with the powerful German Länder, Europe's sub-national authorities were drawn into the Brussels arena underpinned by the growing mobilization of regional actors in the EU. Increas-ingly European policies and laws began to penetrate the domestic systems of public policy-making arising from the growing regulatory reach of the Union and the development of the Union's budgetary instruments, notably, regional and environmental policies. European regionalism as an idea and ideal became part of the discourse of Euro-pean integration. The European Commission became a powerful advocate of a Europe of the Regions. Ireland is an interesting test case of the multilevel governance perspective on European integration because Ireland joined the EU in 1973 as one of Europe's most cen-tralized states. In order to assess the impact of the EU and European regionalism on territorial politics in Ireland, we begin with a brief overview of the key characteristics of sub-national government in Ireland.

Territorial organization in Ireland

Ireland's system of central and local government owes much to the legacy of an older state, the United Kingdom of Great Britain and Ireland. The island of Ireland was one of the four constituent nations of that kingdom. This lasted until 1921 when 26 of the 32 counties on the island of Ireland became an independent state within the British Commonwealth. The Irish Free State, as it was known, was replaced by a Republic in 1949 when the state left the Commonwealth. The structure of territorial politics and local government was based on the inherited British model and for many decades was legally based on the 1898 Local Government Ireland Act, which pre-dated the foundation of the state. This Act established the *county* as the basic division of local government and local democracy, a division that has persisted. The success and popularity of Gaelic games under the auspices of the Gaelic Athletic Association (GAA) serve to embed the county as a major marker of identity and local pride; the annual championships in both Gaelic football and hurling are major national events. Strong county identification coupled with a strong national identity left little room for the emergence of significant regional identities. Apart from the counties, the major cities were designated as county boroughs or corporations. A number of other designated units, notably, urban district councils, town commissioners, and borough corporations, were also established. The multiplicity of territorial divisions, at various levels of aggregation, lasted until the introduction of a new nomenclature in 2001, when the territorial units were re-named as city councils, borough councils and town councils in the Local Government Act 2001. County councils retained their former title (see Table 6.1).

Following the establishment of the state, Irish local government lost a number of its functions and was subordinated to the dynamics of national politics and a highly centralized administration in Dublin. The legacy of a civil war and widespread corruption meant that local government was vulnerable to the centralizing ethos of the young state, and the focus of development in Ireland was national development rather than regional development. The functions of Irish local

TABLE 6.1 *Local government organization*

Before the 2001 Act	Local government Act 2001
County Borough Corporations	City Councils
Borough Corporations	Borough Councils
Urban District Councils	Town Councils
Town Commissioners	Town Councils
County Councils	County Councils

government were much more restricted than usually found in continental Europe, and more restricted even than the United Kingdom where local authorities have a major role in education, police and social welfare. The core functions of Irish local government are:

- Housing
- Road transport and safety
- Water supply and sewerage
- Local economic development and planning
- Environmental protection
- Recreation and amenities
- Agriculture, education, health and welfare

Local authorities exercise a limited role in a number of these areas, and it should be noted that many of these areas have an important EU dimension. A commitment in the 1977 election to abolish rates on private houses deprived Irish local government of an important element of their revenue-raising capacity and made them very dependent on central government for funding.

As part of the local government reform in the 1920s, a distinctive management system was put in place. Each local authority was made the responsibility of a professional county manager, in charge of the 'executive' functions of the authority. Elected councillors had 'reserve' powers, notably in relation to finance, legislation and planning. The county managers are very powerful 'notables' in their local authority areas. A survey on local power found that 73 per cent of respondents regarded county managers as the second most influential person in their area, just one percentage point behind a government minister (Coyle and Sinnott, 1992, p. 92). The balance of power between the county managers and the elected councillors is biased towards the former because of their professional and salaried status in contrast to the part-time local councillors. That said, the county managers are subject to considerable scrutiny by the elected councillors and must report to them on all major issues in public. A provision in the 2001 Act to have a full-time elected chair of each council was repealed in 2003 without ever being implemented.

Reform of Irish local government emerged on the political agenda in the early 1970s and again in the 1990s. A Government White Paper entitled *Local Government Reorganization* dating from 1971, and an accompanying report on staffing and management, had little effect. A series of reports beginning in 1985 placed local government reform back on the political agenda. The desire for reform stemmed from the dual impulse of improving the delivery of public services and enhancing local democracy. The most significant of these reviews was the Barrington Report produced by an Advisory Committee on Local Government Reorganization and Reform. Tom Barrington, founder of the Institute of Public Administration (IPA), who chaired the committee, was a life-long advocate of decentralization and local democracy. The Committee made a large number of recommendations, some of which were echoed in later reports that culminated in the *Better Local Government* process that was embedded in a series of Local Government Acts, 1991, 1993, 1994, 1997 and 2001. The process of reform accelerated in the mid-1990s with a series of further reforms designed to enhance local democracy and the quality of services. This culminated in the consolidation of local government law in the Local Government Act, 2001. The reforms gave constitutional recognition to local government for the first time and provided for local elections every five years. Prior to this, it was not uncommon for the Government to delay or fail to hold local elections; in fact local elections were postponed on 15 occasions since 1923. Such delays were met with widespread indifference by the electorate which highlighted the absence of a vibrant culture of local democracy in Ireland. Notwithstanding important changes in the 1990s, the reform of local government remains thwarted on the key question of local finances. It is argued that

> Local government finance is the litmus test for central government commitment to local government. Since domestic rates were abolished in 1977, successive governments have failed to address resulting shortfalls. (Callanan and Keogan, 2003, p. 96)

Without substantial fiscal capacity, Irish local government remains significantly weaker than its counterparts in Europe.

The limited role of Irish local government is underpinned by an ambiguous attitude towards local democracy. Local government reform was not a salient political issue for the Irish electorate and local councillors have been 'characterised as a kind of standing army of supporters for the main political parties' (Kenny, 2003, p. 103). There is a paradox at the heart of territorial politics in Ireland arising from a distinctive combination of localism and centralization. Although localism is one of the most pervasive characteristics of Irish political culture, Ireland has relatively weak local government and an unelected regional tier. Irish parliamentarians (TDs) are almost all natives of the constituencies they represent, and most tend to live in their constituencies. A very high proportion of national politicians continued to serve on their local authorities while in the national parliament, engaged in extensive constituency work, and made representations on behalf of their constituents to the central state. In 2002, 138 of the 226 members of the Oireachtas (parliament) were members of local councils. There were several unsuccessful attempts to ban the dual mandate so as to loosen the impact of national politicians in the local authorities, and finally the Local Government Act (2003) introduced a ban but included a concession to national parliamentarians by making provision for continued access to local authority information and documentation for them (Kenny, 2003, p. 114). Localism, clientelism and brokerage are central to the political culture. Bringing the concerns of specific areas or citizens to Dublin occupies an inordinate amount of the time and energy of parliamentarians. Ireland entered the EU in 1973 as a highly centralized state, with limited local government, underdeveloped local democracy, and a strongly local political culture.

Relatively weak local government was coupled in Ireland by non-existent regional government. From the 1950s onwards, when Ireland opted for export-led economic growth, national economic development took precedence over regional divergence within the state. The Irish state developed an extensive range of national institutions, most notably the Industrial Development Authority (IDA) to foster industrialization, attract international capital and create employment. In the 1960s, economic divergence emerged as a political issue as it became clear that there was a significant divergence between an affluent South-East, particularly Dublin, and a poorer West/North-West area (Brunt, 1988, p. 56). While nine planning regions were designated in 1963 under the Local Government (Planning and Development) Act, it was not until the publication of the Buchanan Report in 1969 that a regional strategy for development was outlined, proposing as it did a hierarchy of urban centres and growth poles. This novel attempt at a spatial growth strategy became the subject of considerable contention as Ireland's small towns and villages reacted against the 'growth centres'. The pervasive localism identified above ensured that the Buchanan Report would not be implemented. In response, the Government set up non-statutory Regional Development Organizations (RDOs) in each of nine physical planning regions. In addition to the RDOs there were a series of regional bodies dealing with fisheries, health and tourism, all with different spatial configurations. The complexity of the meso-level of government in Ireland was further complicated by the lack of congruence between the various state agencies at the sub-national level. Ireland was not fertile ground for multi-level governance, mobilization and European regionalism. Notwithstanding this, European policy and laws disturbed central–local relations in Ireland and had some significant effects on Irish governance. The impact was driven by the EU budget, notably structural funds, European regulation and a limited mobilization of sub-state actors in the Brussels area.

Brussels money

Expectation of resource transfers from the European budget was one of the fundamental motivations for Ireland's membership of the European Union. Until Ireland achieved economic catch-up by the end of the 1990s, Irish politicians and officials adopted a very active approach to European finances and receipts from Brussels. An active and committed approach ensured that Ireland consistently achieved the highest per capita transfers from the European budget until enlargement to the countries of East Central Europe in 2004. In conformity with the centralized nature of the state, central government dominated the EU budgetary process and controlled access to EU finances. The powerful Ministry for Finance maintained central control over the European Regional Development Fund (ERDF) and ensured that local authorities did not have direct access to the regional fund. Likewise, the Agriculture Ministry controlled receipts from the CAP and the Labour Ministry receipts from the Social Fund. The EU budget was a matter of 'high politics', the preserve of ministers and mandarins in central government. Local officials and elected representatives were discouraged from direct links with Brussels. The fact that the entire country was designated as one region for structural fund purposes underpinned Dublin control, particularly Finance Ministry control, over financial flows and European largesse.

Delors I and Delors II

The reform of the structural funds in 1987/88 posed a considerable challenge to the Irish management of the funds. A European Parliament report in 1987 led by John Hume, the SDLP MEP from Northern Ireland, was critical of the management of the structural funds in Ireland, particularly the absence of a local or regional dimension. The report recommended the setting up of nine regional authorities in Ireland. To coincide with the EP debate on this report, the Dublin Government announced a decision to adopt a programme approach to structural funding and further announced three pilot regional programmes in selected areas. This served to fuel local and regional rivalry and was regarded as an *ad hoc*, largely symbolic response to the fundamental reforms emanating from Brussels. The Single European Act embedded the values of cohesion and solidarity in a treaty framework, and this was followed by the Delors I package that greatly increased the funding available for cohesion purposes and introduced important new features to the grant-awarding process. These features included:

- concentration of EU funding in areas of greatest need;
- a shift from project to programme funding;
- a shift to multi-annual funding;
- an emphasis on additionality and conditionality of funding;
- a pronounced emphasis on partnership between different levels of government and between state and civil society (Laffan 1997).

Two elements of the reform, partnership and programming, were likely to have the greatest impact on territorial organization and on central–local relations within the member states. The commitment to double the flow of funding to the cohesion states, including Ireland, by 1993 acted as a powerful incentive for central governments in the poorer countries to adapt to the new governance processes and principles. Because Ireland was designated as a single region, it was required to submit a National Development Plan (NDP) to Brussels covering the period 1989–92. The then Prime Minister, Charles Haughey, accorded top priority to the NDP and chaired a high-level committee consisting of key ministers and the secretaries of the main government departments which met on a weekly basis, usually on a Sunday morning in his home, until the plan was finalized. The extent of political engagement by the Prime Minister in preparing the first Delors plan underlines the vital nature of EU financial flows to Ireland at this time. Ireland's economic performance during the 1980s was one of the weakest among the member states, characterized by high inflation, high unemployment and large budget deficits. The Delors Plan was regarded as an opportunity to invest in economic development which might in the longer term lead to convergence or 'catch-up' with the richer states in the Union.

Because of the conflict arising from the ill-judged 1987 announcement about programmes, the government opted to divide the country into seven regions which were asked to prepare a regional plan for submission to the Finance Ministry. A two-tiered structure was established to prepare the regional plans: a *working group* consisting of the professional managers in local government, regional representatives of government departments, state agencies and a representative from the Commission and an *advisory group* consisting of elected local representatives and representatives of civil society. The working groups carried the main responsibility for drafting the regional plans whereas the advisory groups were designed to legitimize the exercise. The speed with which the NDP had to be prepared militated against a 'bottom-up' approach. The high-level committee and the Finance ministry took all of the most important decisions concerning allocation. Notwithstanding the regional consultative process, the government opted for a sectoral approach rather than a spatial approach to the first NDP, that consisted of eight sectoral programmes. Central government re-affirmed its gatekeeping role in relation to Europe and European monies. The then Prime Minister defended the approach as follows:

> There is no question but that the requirements of efficiency, effectiveness, and expediency all demand that the National Development Plan and its operational programmes be implemented through the structures, which already exist, with which everyone is familiar and which have evolved to meet the particular circumstances and population structures of this country. (Haughey, 1989, p. 5)

The Department of Finance had central control over the implementation and monitoring of the NDP. It chaired the Community Support Framework Monitoring Committee and the sectoral committees were chaired by the lead ministry. Regional Review Committees meeting every two months provided the sub-national input into the implementation of the first plan. The then Regional Affairs Commissioner, Bruce Millan, expressed his regret at the cosmetic nature of regional involvement in the NDP. The Commission's desire for partnership and enhanced regional engagement, on the one hand, and its desire for effective management of the funds, on the other, were evident in the Irish case. Because of a competent central government and system of public administration, Ireland was the most successful of the Objective One regions in drawing down structural funding during the life of the NDP.

The first programming period was a period of learning for Irish central government and sub-state actors as they came to terms with the new governance structures and governance instruments associated with the structural funds. The establishment of regional review committees was a very pragmatic response to the need to engage with local actors. The consultation process in this period was largely symbolic as the regions were artificial constructs with no staffing, regional data nor financial clout. Moreover, the committees were large and unwieldy bodies consisting of Dublin-based officials and local representatives. The local actors lacked a regional vision and tended to promote the interests of smaller territorial entities within the broader region. Put simply, the local trumped the regional. The membership of the regional review committees regarded the meetings as information gather for a rather than agenda-setting. Those involved did not have the knowledge nor skills to challenge the Dublin-based civil servants or representatives of the powerful state agencies.

The significant injection of European money into the Irish public policy process in the period 1989 to 1992 did, however, mobilize an extensive range of actors all seeking a slice of the Brussels pie or seeking to have an impact on the use of this funding stream. During the drafting of the programme, employers, trade unions and the farming groups paid considerable attention to the distribution of the monies. Subsequently, during the life of the plan, environmental groups engaged critically with the implementation of the plan and sought to monitor its environmental impact.

In many areas there were clashes between those who welcomed development and those who were concerned about its impact on local areas. The Community Workers Co-operative (CWC), a national platform for the voluntary sector, began to monitor the NDP with a particular focus on the impact of the funds on social inequalities. The CWC placed considerable emphasis on area-based partnerships and local development. The western half of the country also began a campaign highlighting the uneven development of the country and argued for balanced regional development. The mobilization of local actors and the emergence of strong community groups are analysed below.

The key features of the 1988–92 programming period survived the reform of the structural funds that accompanied the Treaty on European Union (TEU) and the second financial package known as the Delors II package which was to last from 1993 to 1999. A 1992 report on the first programming period confirmed the importance of the structural funds to Ireland. It was estimated that the CSF would contribute towards higher growth in Ireland (2.6 per cent by 2000). Ireland welcomed the Delors II plan and the Irish government was determined to secure maximum receipts from the new pot of Brussels money. The Prime Minister came back to Dublin from the Edinburgh European Council and announced that Ireland would receive six billion Ecu during the next programming period. This figure was exaggerated, and Ireland's allocated share was 4.5 billion Ecu. The approach to extracting the maximum from the EU budget was captured in an account of the negotiations with the Commission in 1992 (Finlay, 1992). A change of government in November 1992 added a coalition dimension to the new programming period. The new government consisted of Fianna Fáil (centre-right) and Labour (centre-left) with a Fianna Fáil Finance Minister and a Minister for State (junior minister) from the Labour Party with specific responsibility for the National Development Plan. The consultative process was more extensive than for the first NDP. The Minister of State visited all of the Regional Review Committees to get their input into the plan. Technical assistance funding enabled the regions to employ consultants to assist them with their regional plans, which improved the quality of regional data and the regional submissions. That said, the regions found it very difficult to establish priorities in their submissions. The second national development plan was again driven by sectoral concerns with one notable addition, a chapter on local development. This was the first time that the NDP adopted a spatial dimension, albeit a highly restricted one. The seven regions that accompanied the first national development plan were replaced by eight regions (NUTS III in EU parlance) as a consequence of a recommendation of the Barrington Report (1992) discussed above. The eight authorities consisted of elected local councillors from the county and city councils in the regions. The authorities were established on a statutory basis and were given the responsibility to promote the coordination of public services in their region and to advice on the implementation on the NDP. Each authority was required to establish an EU Operational Committee to assist it in the discharge of its EU-related responsibilities. The regional authorities were not given any executive powers unlike their counterparts in other parts of Europe (Callanan, 2003, p. 435).

The emergence of local development in NDPII was the result of local mobilization and the search for local economic development and regeneration. Ireland's high levels of unemployment in the 1980s and early 1990s led to a provision of local groups both in urban and rural areas searching for ways of promoting economic activity and development. Community initiatives such as LEADER (see below) and EC Global Grants for Local Development provided the community groups with access to financial resources for local development. The two coalition parties had differing preferences concerning local development; Fianna Fáil favoured the establishment of County Enterprise Boards in each local authority area, whereas the Labour Party favoured area-based partnerships. Both models were deployed during this programming period.

EU funding provided the incentive and critical support for the emergence of local-community-based initiatives. The poor economic performance of the 1980s led to a profusion of community groups in urban and rural Ireland in search of ways of responding to structural unemployment and economic deprivation. The Government responded to local activism with the chapter on Local Development that formed part of the 1994–99 National Development Plan. The origins of the emerging local initiatives can be found in pilot programmes such as the LEADER programme in rural areas and European global grants for local development. The LEADER programme was introduced as a pilot programme in 1992 in 16 rural areas in the country. The pilot programme was followed by a series of multi-annual LEADER programmes that involved local action groups in development activities within their own areas. EU agri-environmental and rural development policies have had a major impact on evolving concepts of rural community and rural Ireland (Tovey, 2007, p. 287), and local communities have mobilized around the opportunities offered by these policies. In urban areas, area-based partnerships developed as an attempt by the central state to develop at local level the social partnership arrangements of the national level. Championed by the Prime Minister's Department, the partnerships were established by the Government in 1991. The partnerships involved local level arrangements involving the state agencies and the community and voluntary sector actively engaging at local level to overcome the problems of long-term unemployment and social deprivation by developing local-area action plans. Up to 1999, the area-based partnerships were part-funded by the EU budget. There was tension in many parts of the country between the local authorities and the area-based development initiatives emerging from the community and voluntary sector. The local authorities' role in enterprise development was relatively restricted until the establishment of City/County Enterprise Boards in 1993. The purpose of the County Enterprise Boards was to encourage and part-finance local initiatives in job-creation. The boards consisted of a chairperson and 13 members drawn from elected local representatives, the social partners and the state agencies. An OECD report was highly complimentary about the area-based partnerships, which were described as 'democratic experimentalism', given their innovative character (Sabel, 1996). The profusion of local bodies and the lack of a structured relationship between the emerging partnerships and the formal system of local government were identified as problems in a number of reports in the mid-1990s.

Agenda 2000

High levels of economic growth throughout the 1990s brought one of the primary goals of Ireland's European policy to fruition, namely, economic catch-up with the richer European states. Inevitably this altered Ireland's position in relation to the European budget and structural funding. As the second Delors plan was implemented during the 1990s, it was clear that Ireland as a whole would lose its Objective One status because it would have breached the 75 per cent average EU per capita incomes. The Finance Ministry, long practiced in the politics of grantsmanship in the Union, began to develop an approach based on the division of the country into two regions, one region that would not qualify for Objective One status and a second that would. The Government applied to Eurostat to have the country divided into two NUTS II regions, the Border, Midlands and Western Region (BMW) and the Southern and Eastern Region (S&E). In its submission, the Government included two counties, Kerry and Clare, under pressure from a number of independent deputies in the parliament. Eurostat did not accept the inclusion of the two additional counties but did agree to two NUTS II regions, and Regional Assemblies were established in 1999. The members of the Regional Assemblies are drawn from the elected members of the constituent city or county councils, and must also be members of the Regional Authorities. The establishment of the two regions had the benefit from a national perspective of ensuring that the BMW region retained Objective One status whereas the Objective One status of the S&E region was phased out by 2005.

Having managed to get agreement to the two regions, the Government was obliged to design a more spatially oriented national development plan for the 1999–2006 period. The NDP had five main operational programmes:

- Environment and Social Infrastructure
- Employment and Human Resources
- Productive Sector
- BMW Region
- S&E Region

For the first time in a national development plan, the Government agreed to two regional operational programmes. The programmes anticipated expenditure of €4.9 million in the BMW region and €5.3 million in the S&E region. Whereas the focus in three sectoral programmes was on national priorities, the regional programmes were designed to deliver local infrastructure, local enterprise development, agriculture and rural development and targeted initiatives aimed at social inclusion. Balanced regional development was highlighted as one of the key horizontal objectives of the NDP. It offered an important opportunity to the regions to establish their capacity and potential in the eyes of central government and administration. During the life of the NDP, the Government agreed a National Spatial Strategy (NSS) designed to deliver balanced growth and to overcome the over-dominance and overdevelopment of Dublin. A key focus of the NSS was the development of a number of gateways.

The NDP was reviewed in 2003 which provided an opportunity to evaluate the performance of the regions in implementing the region specific operational programme. The overall performance fell short of expectations. In both the BMW and the S&E there was a significant under-spend by 2003. In the S&E region, the under-spend represented 37 per cent of anticipated expenditure or €830 million. Agriculture and rural development fared particularly badly as 37 per cent of the anticipated expenditure did not happen. In the BMW region, eight measures were under 25 per cent of expected expenditure by 2003. There were a number of factors identified as contributing to the challenges to the Regional Assemblies and the regional operational programmes. First, there were a number of important policy and institutional changes that unsettled the policy environment. The publication of the National Spatial Strategy in November 2002, while welcomed, altered the policy frame in an important way. Its implementation required embedding it in the practices and policies of a large number of Government departments, state agencies, regional and local authorities. Second, responsibility for local development was moved to a newly created department for Community, Rural and Gaeltacht Affairs. Third, there was an absence of NUTS III data which made it difficult to plan at the regional level. Fourth, it was argued during the mid-term review that management was underresourced and that the monitoring committees were unwieldy making it difficult for local and regional actors to engage and influence developments in their areas. One study found that 'even those within the process as members of the committees can feel underinformed or confused as to the functions of the bodies and the running of the various programmes and projects (Hayward, 2006, p. 14).

In the discussions of the financial perspective 2007–13, Ireland found itself in the unprecedented position of facing a fundamental change in its budgetary position. Continuing high levels of economic growth lifted Ireland above not just the 75 per cent average of per capita incomes, but to the levels found in richer Europe. Ireland was about to be transformed from a significant net beneficiary to a net contributor to the European budget. The key question was what would survive of the impact of the EU on policies and practices that were facilitated by EU requirements and instruments in the new budgetary environment.

European regulation

The growing regulatory capacity of the Union placed considerable demands on the public administrations of the member states, including local government. The transposition of EU regulations is the responsibility of the central state, but local authorities have a crucial role in implementation on the ground. EU regulations 'hit home' at the local level. Environmental directives have considerable impact at the sub-state level, with Directives on waste, landfill, environmental impact assessment and the water framework having major implications for the functional responsibilities of the local authorities (Callanan, 2003, pp. 408–9). Other regulatory laws in relation to public procurement and social standards also impact on the local authorities as public bodies and large employers. It is anticipated that as 'Ireland moves from being a net beneficiary to being a net contributor to the EU's budget, it is likely that the implications (in many cases very costly implications) of EU legislation for local authorities will receive greater scrutiny' (Callanan, 2003, p. 408).

Over there in Brussels

The growth of regional and local representation in the Brussels arena was a marked characteristic of governance in the Union from the late 1980s onwards. This was driven by the increased salience of the Union and its growing impact on sub-national units, particularly in states with strong regions. Regional representations, once viewed with some suspicion by the member-state permanent representations in Brussels because of fears that they would engage in para-diplomacy, have become part of the landscape of EU policy-making. Irish regions and local authorities were not among the first to seek representation in Brussels. One part of the country did, however, see a presence in Brussels as a means of raising regional issues and pressurising the Irish government to take the needs of their part of the country more seriously. A strong cross-community organization emerged in the western part of Ireland in the 1980s that led to the establishment of the first local representation in Brussels in 1992. Six local authorities in the west opened an office and have since been joined by Údaras na Gaeltachta and the Western Regional Authority (www.nasc.ie), and a number of other local authorities maintained a Brussels office for a number of years, notably Dublin, but discontinued that because of its cost. The Ministry with responsibility for local and regional government initiated the establishment of an Irish Regions Office (IRO) in 2000 to give direct Brussels access to the Regional Authorities and to facilitate members of the Committee of the Regions (COR). Central Government was concerned that Ireland was missing out on access and opportunities to influence the Commission and other EU bodies because of the weakness of its regional representation. The IRO is essentially used by a small number of local councillors when they are in Brussels for COR meetings, and by officials from the regional and local authorities. It does not represent a significant addition to the Irish presence in Brussels; nor can it compare to the heavy presence of regions from member states with strong regional governmental structures.

Conclusions

From 1975 onwards with the establishment of the European Regional Development Fund (ERDF), cohesion policy and financial transfers were 'high politics' in Ireland. As a consequence, negotiations on the European budget and the successive financial perspectives were the preserve of a small group of politicians led by the Prime Minister and a restricted group of senior civil servants. Once the volume of financial flows to Ireland were established, the Cabinet, the Finance Ministry and the most powerful home departments were central to the development of the National Development Plans. The primacy of a sectoral perspective in Irish public administration coupled by the high level of centralization reinforced the prerogatives of the core executive. The Commission's promotion of partnership as one of the guiding principles of cohesion policy led the Irish Government to establish a regional review committees during the first national development plan from 1989–92. The institutional device was designed to satisfy the Commission but was purely cosmetic. Preparations for the second plan (1993–99) were somewhat different; eight regional authorities were established and put on a statutory basis, and were asked to prepare plans that were fed into the national programming process. This did not lead to area-specific operational programmes although the possibilities of local development were acknowledged in a separate chapter on local development. This owed much to the emergence of local community groups as active actors in local development. Community initiatives, notably LEADER, provided both a financial incentive and model for this. Hence although the EU did not lead to the transformation of territorial organization and centre–local relations in Ireland, it distributed territorial politics and loosened the grip of central government. Consultation, partnership and local development found a place in governance structures. Local rather than regional players emerged in the Irish system of public policy.

The establishment of the BMW and S&E regions in 1999 did not represent a major change in the policies and practices of Irish governance. Rather it was a highly instrumental response to the changing economic status of Ireland in the Union. The establishment of two NUTS II regions was classical grantsmanship that enabled Ireland to remain a net beneficiary of the EU budget until 2006. The weak capacity of the two regions was evident during the 2000–06 programming period. It is rightly argued that 'Regional authorities and regional assemblies have been established largely as a result of EU necessities rather than as part of a government commitment to regionalisation' (Callanan, 2003, p. 444). The development of a National Spatial Strategy in 2002 in response to that of the EU may mean that the spatial will join the sectoral as one of the organizing principles of Irish government and governance. The impact of EU cohesion policy on governance in Ireland has manifested itself in policy style and practice rather than in the field of territorial organization and politics. The deep effects are felt in multi-annual programming, cross-sectoral policy-making, goal-setting and evaluation rather than multilevel governance. Contrary to the expectations of the multilevel governance literature, Irish central government remains the most powerful strategic actor in cohesion and development policy. This suited the Commission, because although it was committed to partnership and to the engagement of sub-state actors, it was also driven by technocratic impulse of sound financial management and capacity to spend European monies. The Irish central state had no difficulty in ensuring that Ireland maximized its take from the EU budget and maximized its spend of allocated monies. There was no problem with absorption. Irish local government slowly gained a foothold in EU affairs through the structural funds, the implementation of European law and a growing responsibility for local economic and enterprise development. Local authorities become more knowledgeable about European affairs following the establishment of a dedicated information service by the Institute of Public Administration in 1992. Local authorities needed to enhance their capacity to deal with Europe because of their responsibility for the implementation of significant European directives. Community activism underlined by area-based partnerships was strengthened by the availability of EU funding and the Commission emphasis on partnership. The fundamental power relationship between the centre and the local or regional will not change without local taxation, a domestic issue.

Chapter 7

The EU and Irish Public Policy

How does Europe hit home in terms of its impact on Irish public policy? EU policies and legislation have influenced Irish policy norms and goals, the types of policy instruments used and even, on occasion, the style of domestic policy-making. They have widened the political and discursive context of policy-makers by bringing new ideas and policy norms into the domestic arena. The need to adopt EU legislation has also influenced both the constellation and behaviour of policy-makers and societal actors who have adapted to the new opportunity structure European integration offers (McGowan and Murphy, 2003). Yet, by its very nature, the impact of the EU on Irish public policy is differential. In some areas, such as agriculture, monetary or competition policy, the EU has fundamentally shaped the direction, content and pace of policy development, often exercising exclusive competence. In this context, the EU's policy repertoire becomes the domestic policy repertoire (Mair 2006). In other policy domains such as the environment, competence is shared between the national and the European as domestic priorities are pursued alongside European-level goals. Yet again in policy areas such as health and education, national authorities keep firm control on developments; any European-level move is carefully circumscribed and at most complements action at the national level.

So the question is this: what national public policies are affected by EU membership and to what degree? The effect of the EU on Irish public policy is, in essence, predetermined by the degree of authority with which the EU can act in certain policy domains. Policies related to economic integration form the core of what the EU does. These policies do not involve high levels of expenditure but instead encourage economic liberalization so as to increase economic efficiency and performance within the EU. Economic integration at the supranational European level thereby aims to increase European economic growth and prosperity. This is achieved through the creation and regulation of the European single market: through the removal of barriers to trade (liberalization), through the creation of European-level rules and regulations, through the encouragement of competition amongst firms and through the decision to create a single currency. This is known as 'market-building' (Sbragia, 2003; Héritier, 1999) and the cost of policy implementation is not borne by the EU institutions. Market-building policies include: competition policy, commercial (trade) policy and the macro-economic management framework of economic and monetary union (EMU). Other market-related policies, termed as 'market-correcting', attempt to mitigate the consequences of market forces unleashed by this economic liberalization. These policies try to either compensate the costs the building of markets imposes on certain disadvantaged groups or limit inequality across the board. Market-correcting policies can involve the transfer of resources through the EU budget from one social group or member state to another and also include policies in which Community funds are allocated within sectors (thus distribution and redistribution), such as the Common Agricultural Policy, socioeconomic and regional cohesion policies, and research and development policies. In all these 'market-related' areas, the EU tends to 'co-govern': national governments and the European Parliament often act as co-legislators with the European Commission playing an initiating or agenda-setting role. Once decisions have been taken at the European level, national authorities are then obliged to implement these policies, with the European Commission and Court of Justice acting as arbiters and ensuring the legal authority of the Union.

Since the Treaty of Maastricht in particular, a number of policies have evolved that are not related to the market but are instead seen as 'polity-building'. These policies seek to extend and protect the economic, political and social rights of the citizens of EU member states, as well as endeavouring to ensure that the EU acts as a single voice on the world stage. They include: cooperation in the field of justice and home affairs, common asylum and immigration policies, police and judicial cooperation, trade policies, external economic relations, the Common Foreign and Security Policy, and defence cooperation (Hix, 2005). Decision-making in these areas is firmly intergovernmental with a central role reserved for the EU's Council of Ministers and supranational institutions such as the Commission and the European Parliament more at the sidelines. In contrast to the EU's regulatory policies, these policies are much weaker in scope, content, structure and efficacy.

Using the EU policy typology as outlined above (see also Figure 7.1), this chapter reviews how a selection of policy areas in Ireland have been affected by EU membership. These include economic management through the EU's macro-economic governance structures, competition and liberalization policies (for example telecommunications), agriculture and environmental policy and finally, justice and home affairs policy. Since the mid-1980s, the completion of the single European market, moves towards economic and monetary union, the introduction of economic policy coordination structures (the Stability and Growth Pact and Broad Economic Policy Guidelines) and the espousal of the Lisbon Agenda have become significant frames of Irish economic governance. Turning to agriculture, since the 1970s Irish agricultural policy has been for the most part driven by the Brussels agenda and more specifically the evolution of the EU's Common Agricultural Policy (CAP). In the early years of membership, the focus of Irish policy-makers and farmers on increasing agricultural production was clearly motivated by the perceived need to maximize CAP price subsidies and thereby raise farm income levels. With ongoing CAP reform since the mid-1980s, Irish agricultural policy subsequently became a reaction to agricultural and trade policy developments at the EU and global levels. For its part, the fabric of Irish environmental policy has been fundamentally affected by the policy priorities championed at the European level; Irish environmental policy reflects European environmental norms, policy styles and legislation. Finally, we consider Irish participation in the EU's justice and home affairs policy (JHA).

FIGURE 7.1   The EU's policy types

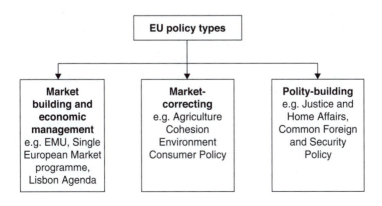

Here Ireland finds itself in a more challenging position and part of a small group of member states who selectively participate in European activity in this policy domain. The exigencies of sustaining and managing a common travel area with the UK (particularly in the context of the former conflict in Northern Ireland) has meant that Irish participation in JHA has been on a case-by-case basis, officially opting out of the Schengen common travel area and with the right to opt in to aspects of the EU's activities in visa, immigration and asylum policies.

Ireland and European economic governance

The significance of participation in EMU for the Irish economy and macroeconomic management has been far-reaching, and the decision to join EMU placed Ireland at the heart of the evolving European macroeconomic (particularly monetary policy) framework. Through EMU, the EU imposed tight requirements on public spending with the obligation to conform to the EU's externally set criteria of low and convergent inflation and interest rates, a budget deficit of 3 per cent of GDP or less, public debt levels of 60 per cent or less, and a stable exchange rate. In the 1990s, Irish economic policy became dominated by the objective of qualifying for membership of EMU in 1999 and the need to meet the Maastricht convergence criteria. In so doing the requirement to reduce inflation and contain the public deficit helped contribute to rapid growth. In May 1998 Ireland was the only member state deemed to have fully met the criteria to participate in the third and final stage of EMU. The most important consequence of participation in EMU for the Irish government (and the governments of other members of the Eurozone) concerns control over economic issues: the only significant macroeconomic policy that remains under government control is taxation. The authority for monetary policy, in particular the setting of interest rates, has decisively moved to the independent European Central Bank in its Frankfurt headquarters.

Once the decision to begin the euro stage of EMU on 1 January 1999 was made, the management of the Irish economy was to be undertaken within the context of the EU's economic policy coordination structures of the Stability and Growth Pact (SGP) and the Broad Economic Policy Guidelines (BEPG). While subsequently subject to much controversy, the SGP agreed in June 1998 set in place the 'excessive debt procedure' which ensures that member states adhere to the spirit of the Maastricht convergence criteria. Stemming from an original German initiative, the excessive debt procedure would be enforced by the Council of Ministers (on the basis of a Commission recommendation) when a member state is found to be running a deficit on public expenditure over revenue of over 3 per cent of GDP in any one year (the revised SGP allowed for some flexibility on this). If a member state is in serious breach of protocol, the Commission can recommend that the Council take action against it (that is levy fines). For its part, the BEPG formed part of the EU's efforts to coordinate economic policy amongst member states from the onset of EMU. Since 1997, and as part of efforts to survey and coordinate economic policies between member states, the BEPGs are jointly agreed by EU finance ministers and provide country-specific and concrete guidelines to member states regarding their budgetary and structural policies. Other processes that also apply in this broad area include the European Employment Strategy (the Luxemburg Process), macro-economic dialogue involving the social partners in the context of the European employment pact (the Cologne process) and the open method of coordination established by the Lisbon European Council in 2000 (the Lisbon process).

Irish ministers and officials are now obliged to participate in this new macroeconomic governance framework and for the most part Ireland has fallen within the guidelines of both the SGP and BEPG. However, in 2001, charged with ignoring repeated warnings that his budgetary policy was inconsistent with the broad economic guidelines, the then Finance Minister Charlie McCreevy provoked a reprimand from the Commission and EU Finance ministers for his overly-expansionist budget of December 2001, which, through sharp cuts in taxation and public spending increases threatened to overheat the Irish economy (*Irish Times*, 25 January 2001).

Participation in the Lisbon process with its championing of the open method of coordination has also had an impact on Irish economic governance, albeit a relatively limited one. At the Lisbon European Council summit in 2000, the EU heads of government and state pledged to make the European Union the most competitive and dynamic knowledge-based economy in the world, capable of sustainable economic growth with more and better jobs and greater social cohesion by 2010. This goal was to be achieved by an extensive reform programme, including the establishment of an effective internal market, boosting research and development and improving education and social inclusion. Its implementation was to take place not on the basis of legislation and sanctions (the so-called Community method), but through a policy methodology known as the Open Method of Coordination (OMC) which involves the setting of commonly agreed targets and a process of benchmarking among member states. Under the Irish 2004 Presidency, a mid-term review of progress was initiated. The results across the EU were generally recognized to have been disappointing and in early 2005, the Lisbon Agenda was relaunched as a partnership for Growth and Employment, with a streamlining and simplification of the overall process. Each member state would produce a three-year National Reform Programme, setting out its national priorities and commitments to improve economic growth and create further employment. While participation in the Lisbon process led to interdepartmental coordination of the relevant issues amongst the Irish core executive, the overall impact of the Lisbon agenda on Ireland has been seen to be indirect. Much of the agenda has been placed in the framework of the social partnership process, and while the Lisbon priorities are consistent with Irish national economic and social goals and priorities, they are not the driving force behind the development of most relevant policies. According to O'Donnell and Moss, 'many of these policies had already been identified at national level and implemented through national level development processes such as the social partnership process' (O'Donnell and Moss, 2004).

The Irish economy in EMU

Until now, Ireland's macroeconomic performance in EMU has been successful and Ireland has generally adhered to the original Maastricht convergence criteria (Traitstaru-Siedschlag, 2007). The Irish economy has evidenced great growth since the adoption of the single currency; and average annual GDP growth in Ireland has been the highest in the euro-area: 6.6 per cent over the period 1999–2006, 4.6 per cent above the EU average. Simultaneously, however, this economic growth has been accompanied by some less positive effects. Nominal wages have grown faster than the euro area average by 3.4 per cent and in 2006 average annual unit labour costs grew faster than the euro area average by 1.7 per cent (MacCoille and McCoy, 2002; Traitstaru-Siedschlag, 2007). A significant positive wage growth differential exists *vis-à-vis* other Eurozone countries. In addition, Irish consumer prices have risen by a cumulative 25 per cent since the start of EMU to mid-2004, well in excess of all other EMU participants (Bergin, FitzGerald and McCoy, 2004). Inflation has also been high. Initially the euro depreciated and Irish prices peaked at inflation of 7 per cent in November 2000, but since then the euro gradually appreciated and Irish inflation has moderated somewhat (to approximately 5 per cent on average). Excessive wage inflation since the start of EMU, together with higher than average inflation and a decline in manufacturing exports, has undermined Irish competitiveness (Honohan and Leddin, 2006).

The Irish housing market has also been affected by participation in the single currency project. One of the most well-known facts relating to the Irish economy in recent times has been the dramatic increase in house prices – the highest in the OECD since the mid-1990s. Participation in EMU contributed to this property boom in an unintended way. At a time when the Irish economy was already doing extremely well, the low interest rates that came with EMU reduced the cost of borrowing for households. Lower interest rates, together with an increased stock of dwellings and the loosening of borrowing conditions by banks led strong housing construction to become a significant driver of Irish economic growth, in particular sustaining growth in the aftermath of the global downturn in the early 2000s (Bergin, FitzGerald and McCoy, 2004; Cech, 2006).

While participation in EMU has heretofore been to Ireland's benefit, the future does bring a number of challenges: (1) the restoration of competitiveness, (2) the risks to macroeconomic and financial stability from the downturn in the housing market and (3) adjustment to the slowdown in the United States. As a small, open, trade-dependent economy, perhaps the biggest danger to the Irish economic performance lies in the possibility of a sustained downturn in the USA (alongside the UK, still one of Ireland's main trading partners) and a significant depreciation of the US dollar *vis-à-vis* the euro. According to the Irish economic think-tank, the Economic and Social Research Institute: 'the resilience of the Irish economy under EMU will be fully tested by a downturn' (Traistaru-Siedschlag, 2007, p. 90).

Market liberalization: the impact of EU rules on Irish markets

The EU's central policy activity is regulation rather than distribution or redistribution and regulation particularly of the market. With the doctrine of the supremacy of Community law firmly established in the early 1960s, the EU has become a prominent source of regulation for its constituent states. A key impact has been on the domestic institutional structures: national markets have been opened to competition, at least in terms of formal rules. The EU has contributed to the ending of legal monopolies hitherto at the heart of state control, including telecommunications, energy and in some countries the railways. It has also spearheaded the introduction of independent regulatory authorities, strongly discouraged state aid to national firms, encouraged a level playing field amongst firms through opening up public procurement and has acted as an indirect spur for privatisation of key industries. The impact of European regulation varies from sector to sector, however. In certain sectors there has been little regulation, in others European measures have replicated what has already been introduced at the national level. In addition, European rules, while initially accepted, may have not been fully internalized in practice with considerable room for national choices. In Ireland, the telecoms sector is an example of a sector that has been challenged by EU membership but where problems of market liberalization remain.

Historically in Ireland (as elsewhere in Europe), the gas, electricity and telecommunications industries operated as public-sector monopolies. State-ownership was viewed as a way of ensuring these industries were operated in the public interest. It was only since the late 1980s that these industries have undergone major changes as EU directives required member states to open up their national markets to competitors from other member states. The process of telecommunications liberalization began gradually in the EU, starting with the liberalization of telecommunications equipment in 1988 and value-added telecommunications services in 1990. In March 1996, EU member states agreed to full liberalization of public voice telephony services and networks by 1 January 1998, and this decision was to have profound implications for the Irish telecommunications market. In the original negotiations, the Irish government sought and received a partial derogation to the introduction of full competition (relating to voice telephony services) in order to give Telecom Éireann enough time to enable it to make the structural changes necessary for it to compete in a competitive market. However, in response to newspaper reports that a major industrial project with Microsoft had been lost because of the inadequacies of the Irish telecommunications network, the Minister for Public Enterprise,

Mary O'Rourke, announced that the remaining derogations were being waived and that full competition in voice telephony would commence on 1 December 1998 (Massey, 1999, 2000).

In spite of pressure from the EU, Irish telecoms liberalization proceeded very slowly, with former state monopoly, Eircom, continuing as a significant market player. A policy bias was also perceived toward producer interests rather than consumer interests, although this is now changing (Fingleton, 2000, p. 74; OECD, 2001, p. 16). The 1991 Competition Act (and subsequently amended in 1996) created a Competition Authority, gave it the power to enforce competition legislation and provided for criminal penalties in the form of fines for firms breaching the legislation. At the same time, the Office of the Director of Telecommunications Regulation (the ODTR) was set up to enforce competition in the telecommunications sector, yet as with the Competition Authority its powers of enforcement were weak – it could punish telecom operators in breach of competition rules by fining them €3,000 or it could withdraw their licence, punishing consumers in the process (Fingleton, 2000, p. 74). As the EU's telecoms regulatory regime was streamlined, member states were required to set up National Regulatory Authorities (NRA) which would facilitate competition in the sector by enabling market entry through a general authorization to provide networks and services and by regulating access to networks so as to develop effective choice for consumers both business and residential. In Ireland's case the Communications Regulation Act 2002 replaced the ODTR with the Commission for Communications Regulation (ComReg). Once again, the commitment to ensure full competition in the field was somewhat lacking: ComReg's enforcement powers were unchanged from those of the ODTR. The European Commission repeatedly highlighted the limited enforcement powers of the Irish NRA and its associated impact on ensuring a level playing field, prompting the Irish government to put forward new primary legislation beefing up ComReg's powers of enforcement (European Commission, 2004, 2006). At the same time, the EU has proven unable to break up Eircom's significant market power, with the Commission signalling its concern with the high prices Irish customers pay, as well as inadequate investment by the fixed incumbent (Eircom) in the broadband network. Firms competing against Eircom in the voice telephony market have been charged high prices to access and rent the local loop, that is the copper-wire circuits from the incumbent Eircom's local switch/exchange facility to the customer's premises that are necessary in order to make calls. Thus, while the EU has prompted the liberalization of the telecommunications sector in Ireland, and the regulatory reforms have been put in place, progress on full and open competition in the sector has been slow.

Irish agriculture and the CAP

The EU's Common Agricultural Policy has been the main financial and ideological influence on Irish agriculture since the early 1970s (Crowley, 2003). The CAP as originally instigated had five key aims: to increase agricultural productivity; to ensure a fair standard of living for the farming community; to stabilize markets; to guarantee regular food supplies; and to ensure reasonable prices for consumers (Article 39 Treaty of Rome). The intervention system rolled out as part of the CAP in 1968 guaranteed markets for unlimited output of agricultural produce at relatively high prices (considerably higher than Irish agricultural prices) through the European Guarantee and Guidance Fund. Thus expectations were high on 1 January 1973 as Irish farmers would benefit from participation in this system of market intervention and support. Added to this, Irish farmers would no longer be dependent on UK markets where Irish exports were sold at cheaper world prices. The absence of quota restrictions on exports to the Community and the system of price supports ensured that there would be no effective barriers to the export or disposal of the increased production of sectors covered by the CAP. Similarly, the burden of responsibility for subsidising farmers would shift from the national exchequer to the Community budget.

Agricultural statistics over the last thirty years demonstrate exactly how much Ireland has benefited in monetary terms from CAP participation. In 2003 alone, the EU, through the guarantee payments and guidance receipts from the CAP, contributed €1.9 billion to Ireland's total public expenditure on agriculture of €2.8 billion. On average agriculture subsidies account for two-thirds of Irish EU receipts since 1973 (see Table 7.1). For the years 1979–86, net CAP transfers amounted to an average of 7 per cent of Irish GNP (Conway, 1991, p. 58).

Export markets for Irish agricultural products also diversified as Ireland became less dependent on the UK market. In 2003, 75 per cent of the total Irish agri-food exports were sold in EU15

TABLE 7.1   *EU receipts to Ireland, 1973–2004*

Year	Agriculture receipts(€m)	Total EU receipts (€m)	Agriculture receipts as % total EU receipts
1973	47.1	47.1	100
1979	527	671.8	78.4
1983	641.7	924.0	69.4
1989	1,320.7	1,644.7	80.3
1993	1,787.5	2,850.9	62.6
1999	1,829.3	2,678.9	68.2
2004	1,891.6	2,601.2	72.7
Total 1973–2004	37,481.7	53,317.3	70.3

Source: Compendium of Irish Agricultural Statistics, 2005.

markets (although the UK is still the main destination for these goods – approximately 47 per cent).

Accession coincided with agriculture's ongoing decline in importance to the Irish economy; in overall terms, its contribution to the economy is now relatively small (approximately 2 per cent of Irish GDP). Similarly, its share of the workforce has also contracted. In 1971 roughly 25 per cent of the total workforce in Ireland was employed in the agricultural, fisheries and forestry sector, but by 2005 this figure had reduced to only 5 per cent (Figure 7.2). Participation in the CAP has helped Irish farmers modernize and has kept some of them on the land, but not all. Traditional structural problems with Irish agriculture have remained: the Department of Agriculture and Food's 2006 *Agrivision 2015 Action Plan* highlighted the ongoing need to consolidate farm holdings and restructure the dairy and beef-processing industries (Department of Agriculture, 2006).

In policy-making terms, participation in the CAP fundamentally altered the process of domestic agriculture policy formulation. Before EC membership agriculture ministers had a difficult task of negotiating with farmers' organizations and with cabinet colleagues over national supports to Irish farmers. Demands from the farm lobby had to be addressed alongside competing demands from other sectors and interests, and were set within the constraints of

FIGURE 7.2   Employment in agriculture, forestry and fishing as % of total employment, 1973–2005

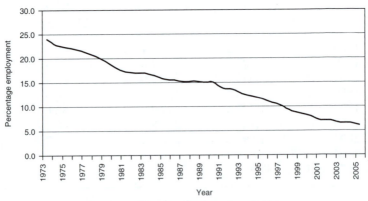

Source: Compendium of Irish Agricultural Statistics, 2005.

the national budget. Under the CAP, farmers' subsidies would be financed by the EC and major policy decisions would be taken in Brussels, although the Department of Agriculture had some discretion over the implementation of the subsidy schemes domestically (Daly, 2002, p. 505).

Department of Agriculture officials were also responsible for implementing subsidy schemes domestically and became the CAP intervention agent in Ireland: officials became responsible for buying and storing produce for intervention. Management and monitoring of this system was a heavy administrative burden for officials who were charged with ensuring that the intervention system was above board and that all claims for European support schemes complied with EC regulations. Between 1973 and 1992 over two million tonnes of beef alone were bought into intervention at a cost of over IR£4 billion. Substantial irregularities in the system were uncovered during the Beef Tribunal Inquiry under Mr Justice Hamilton between 1991 and 1993, where he found that fraud and malpractice had taken place under various EC schemes. This led to a strengthening of internal auditing procedures within the Department itself and the strengthening of the Department's Intervention Unit.

From the mid-1980s onwards, the CAP system of intervention and price guarantee came under considerable pressure for reform both internally and internationally. The increase in EC agricultural output from this time far outstripped demand for agricultural produce and led to the accumulation of stocks and dumping on international markets. A consequence of this was the escalating budget costs of purchasing surplus production for intervention storage and of financing export refunds. At this time the CAP accounted for more than 70 per cent of the EC budget (Matthews, 2005).

While a number of half-hearted reforms had been introduced in the 1980s, the changes introduced by Irish Agriculture Commissioner Ray MacSharry in 1993 on the back of the GATT's Uruguay Round marked the first real reform of the CAP, significantly reducing support prices and extending supply control measures (for example the introduction of 'set-aside' for cereals and oilseeds). EU enlargement provided the trigger for a further round of reform, agreed in March 1999 as part of the negotiations on the Agenda 2000 agreement to prepare the EU for expansion to the East. The Agenda 2000 reforms focused on further reductions in support prices and farmers were compensated through increased direct payments, taking up more of the CAP budget. By 2002, direct payments accounted for up to 70 per cent of farm income in Ireland (Matthews, 2005, p. 222). Ongoing pressure on the EU's budget (at this time CAP spending accounted for over 45 per cent of the EU's budget) led to the Mid-Term Review of the CAP in June 2003, which introduced a single farm payment to each farmer based on the level of assistance received by each farm in the reference period 2000–02. This decoupling of payment from production was accompanied by a growing emphasis on rural development policies and agri-environmental measures such as the Rural Environmental Protection Scheme (REPS). First introduced in 1994, through REPS farmers were offered a fixed annual payment per hectare for periods of up to five years in return for complying with certain environmental standards. The Mid-Term Review explicitly linked participation in such schemes with ongoing CAP funding: current and future direct payments to farmers are predicated on farmers following good farming practice, in line with EU environmental regulations. Failure to 'cross comply' with these measures would affect future CAP funding.

Irish ministers' priority in the ongoing reform negotiations has always been to safeguard the benefits already gained by Irish farmers and to ensure the best possible level of support and protection of Ireland's production base into the future, negotiating transition periods and compensatory measures for the income losses resulting from reduced intervention prices particularly in the arable and beef sectors (Daly, 2002, pp. 514–21). Ministers and officials have proven to be adept negotiators in EU-level agricultural talks, learning the import-ance of forming alliances with other like-minded member states on agricultural issues, such as France. As official policy actors they have also been heavily targeted by the Irish farming lobby, most notably the two largest lobby groups, the Irish Farmers Association (IFA) and the Irish Creamery and Milk Suppliers Association (ICMSA).

As a national interest group, the IFA spends nearly half its income from farmers every year on its European lobbying efforts and exer-cises an influence on core executive policy-makers far greater than its size would suggest (Murphy, 2005). In targeting all actors involved in the implementation of EU environmental legislation at all levels of governance, the farming organizations have well-developed lobbying mechanisms, demonstrating an astuteness in plugging into the polit-ical system (see Collins, 1993; Adshead, 1996; Taylor and Murphy, 2002; Murphy, 2005). In addition, the current structure of elec-toral constituencies, together with the nature of the electoral system (PR STV) means that Irish politicians are reluctant to ignore the views of farmers (Laver, 2005). Farmers' groups have also gained an important foothold in domestic macro-economic policy-making with their inclusion in the successive social partnership agreements, start-ing with the 1987 Programme for National Government. As well as participating in official policy networks, the IFA is not averse to using confrontational tactics in its efforts to highlight farmers' concerns, such as bringing flocks of sheep into the Department of Agriculture to protest at the low price of lamb, and the descent of tractors on Dublin when protesting against declining farmers' incomes (Murphy, 2005, p. 367).

Overall, the impact of the EU on Irish agricultural policy has been great. The CAP forms the overarching structure within which Irish agricultural policy is played out and Irish agriculture officials and farmers groups have become adept at playing the multi-level EU game.

Protecting Ireland's environment?

A number of academics and practitioners have stated that the development of Irish environmental law and policy has been funda-mentally influenced by membership of the EU (Connaughton, 2005;

Flynn, 2003, p. 138; Taylor, 2001; EPA, 2000, p. 187; McGowan, 1999). Indeed, according to former leader of the Irish Green Party, Trevor Sargent TD: 'very little in Ireland has happened with regard to the environment that wasn't due to the EU. The only yardstick for measuring legislation is EU legislation' (Interview, 1 July 2003). In the 1970s and 1980s, the Irish environmental regulation regime was one of the weaker, less developed European policy regimes where successive governments simply 'added on' new elements to the remit of local authorities (charged with the responsibility for the implementation of environmental legislation) on an *ad hoc* and incremental basis, rather than constructing a coherent programme of environmental regulation (Taylor, 2001). Lack of resources meant that local authorities were unable to enforce implementation of the small body of environmental measures effectively. However, from the late 1980s onwards the growing body of EU environmental legislation, pushed forward by 'greener' member states such as West Germany, Denmark and the Netherlands, had a discernible impact as new environmental controls were introduced in order to comply with the ever-increasing range EU directives. From this point on, the fundamental objectives of Irish environmental policies were determined from Brussels, while the mechanisms through which these objectives were to be reached were determined nationally.

At the same time, the establishment of Irish branches of international environmental groups such as Greenpeace, as well as the proliferation of locally-based indigenous groups, helped promote an increased awareness of environmental issues at home (Coyle, 1994; Mullally and Quinlivan, 2004). Environmentalists also had their first electoral success with the election of the first Green Party member of the Dáil, Roger Garland, in Dublin in 1989. All parties across the political spectrum from this point onwards recognized that there was a need to bring some kind of order to the environmental regulation regime in Ireland and the establishment of the Environmental Protection Agency (EPA) was the most obvious result of this (see Taylor, 2001). The establishment of the EPA in 1993 represented a key change in the Irish environmental regime. The EPA introduced integrated pollution control (IPC) licensing for industrial operations (reflecting a European Directive of the same name). Operators would be obliged to obtain environmental licences for their practices, which would be assessed by the EPA. The underlying ethos was to eliminate or minimize the risk of harm to the environment by preventing the emission of potentially polluting substances wherever practical or minimizing such emissions where not practicable. This ethos was reinforced by the BATNEEC principle championed at the EU level – 'best available technology not entailing excessive cost'. Technology adopted must be best at preventing pollution, and available in the sense that it is procurable by the operator of the activity concerned. From the outset of its existence, the role of the EPA as environmental regulator and monitor was hamstrung by its weak powers in the planning system. Local governments were similarly criticized for their poor performance in curbing environmental degradation.

The Irish environmental policy regime since then has been characterized as a whole as purely reactive to legislative and policy agendas set by the EU (Flynn, 2007, p. 85). Irish environmental policy-makers do not attempt to set the agenda at the EU level; indeed, according to Börzel in her 2002 survey of pace-setters, fence-sitters and foot-draggers in the agenda-setting of EU environmental policy, Ireland was in the foot-dragging camp when it came to shaping or uploading policy to the EU level. Foot-draggers were defined as 'industrial latecomers whose regulatory structures are less developed than those of the firstcomers. They are reluctant to accept more stringent measures and hardly ever advance proposals of their own' (Börzel, 2002, p. 203). Difficulties also exist when it comes to downloading EU environmental legislation – in spite of transformative change on paper, Ireland's record of environmental implementation has been mixed at best (Flynn, 2007; Taylor, 2001).

Previous studies have pointed to a solid performance by the Irish authorities in the implementation of EU legislation overall (Laffan *et al.*, 1988; Falkner *et al.*, 2005). Delays, when they have occurred, have been generated by policy conflict, the tendency for governments to engage widely in consultation with affected parties and bureaucratic blockages in the system, most notably due to the small size of the Irish bureaucracy. In his assessment of Irish environmental policy in 1999, however, McGowan commented that Ireland had been one of the least active members of the EU in terms of bringing forth, implementing and enforcing EU environmental legislation and belonged to the laggard camp alongside Greece, Spain and the UK (McGowan, 1999, p. 164). Figure 7.3 supports such a conclusion, with Ireland coming third in 2005 (and for the second year in a row) with the total number of open infringement cases relating to the environment. Indeed, one-quarter of infringement cases taken against Ireland in the ECJ relate to environmental issues (see Table 7.2). According to Flynn, Ireland's implementation record has considerably worsened since the mid-1990s and cases of

FIGURE 7.3   Number of open environment infringements, EUI5 2005

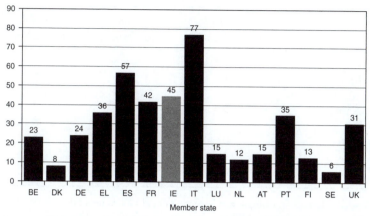

Source: European Commission Seventh Environmental Implementation Report, September 2006.

TABLE 7.2   *Cases before the ECJ, 1998–2006, relating to Ireland*

Policy sector	No. of cases before ECJ	Percentage
Environment and Consumers	10	25
Internal Market	10	25
Transport	7	17
Social Policy	4	10
Agriculture	3	7
Approximation of Laws	3	7
Fisheries	2	5
Taxation	1	2
Laws Governing Institutions	1	2
Total	41	100

Source: O'Mahony (2007).

non-compliance are becoming more serious (Flynn, 2007, p. 145). Of course, this must be placed in the context of a new emphasis by the European Commission on addressing environmental infringements across the board. Even so, such was new Green Party Minister for the Environment John Gormley's concern regarding Ireland's environmental implementation record that one of his first acts as

TABLE 7.3 *Open infringement proceedings against Ireland in the field of environment, as of 31 December 2005*

	Non-communication	Non-conformity	Bad application
Air	1	0	2
Impact Assessment	1	1	7
Nature	0	2	9
Waste	2	0	6
Water	0	3	6
Others	4	1	0
Total	8	7	30

Source: European Commission Seventh Annual Environmental Implementation Report, 2006.

minister was to head to Brussels in July 2007 to meet with Environment Commissioner Stavros Dimas to ask how Ireland should deal with ongoing EU infringement proceedings (*Irish Times*, 14 July 2007).

However, in terms of meeting transposition deadlines and producing domestic legislation that is in conformity with EU legislation, Ireland is much more in the 'middle of the class' with an average transposition rate of 98.8 per cent (Commission Annual Implementation Reports, 2003 and 2005). The majority of open infringement proceedings against Ireland in the field of the environment by the end of 2005 were deemed cases of bad application, that is, where through action or inaction, Ireland had failed to comply with EU environmental law requirements other than the requirements to adopt and communicate correct implementing legislation (see Table 7.3).

Compliance problems have been evident with regard to a number of waste, water and nature conservation directives. The Irish authorities, and specifically the Department of Environment, Heritage and Local Government (DEHLG) have come under pressure from the Commission with regard to waste, provoking widespread criticism for overreliance on landfill, historically low levels of recycling of both municipal and industrial waste (this is now changing), rising public opposition to the location of new landfill sites and waste incinerators and increased instances of illegal dumping. At an institutional level, the Office of Environmental Enforcement (as part of the EPA) was set up in 2003 to combat unauthorized waste activities. The move towards incineration as a means of waste disposal (as the next step up in the EU's waste hierarchy) continues to generate huge controversy with strong locally-based campaign groups successfully using the planning process to put a stop to any proposed waste incineration plants (Mullally and Quinlivan, 2004, p. 120).

Another source of tension has been the effect of environmental regulation on the activities of the Irish farming community. The explicit linking of agricultural support to enhanced environmental practice through cross-compliance has had major consequences for both agriculture and environmental policy-making in Ireland. Environmental groups have pointed to the detrimental effects intensive farming methods have had on the environment, destroying bird and animal habitats and polluting water sources. In response, Irish farmers have repeatedly stressed their opposition to any measures that threaten the maximization of their earning potential and their autonomy as both economic actors and guardians of the rural landscape. They have made full use of their lobbying resources and institutional foothold in the social partnership process to push forward their interests. In contrast, indigenous environmental interest groups have less resources and access to the domestic political system (at the time of writing they are excluded from the social partnership process for instance) (Flynn, 2007, p. 15). On the other hand, they have proved adept in accessing the EU level, 'going through Brussels' and making use of the Commission's complaints procedures. In fact, in 2002 alone, complaints from Irish environmental NGOs and concerned citizens accounted for 10 per cent of complaints submitted to the Commission for non-implementation of EU environmental directives (Flynn, 2003, p. 139).

Faced with the need to implement these important EU directives and the imminent threat of EU fines, the Irish authorities have had no option but to secure compliance through painstaking consultation and negotiation with the farmers' organizations in particular (see Laffan and O'Mahony, 2004, 2008; O'Mahony, 2007). The process of compliance with EU environmental directives thus becomes lengthy and often infused with controversy, and the tortuous journey undertaken to implement the 1991 Nitrates Directive is a case in point. The Nitrates Directive aims to prevent pollution of surface waters and groundwater caused by nitrates (eutrophication) from agricultural sources (chemical fertilisers and livestock manure). In Ireland, almost half the eutrophication on Irish rivers is due to agricultural sources (EPA, 2005, p. 123). Member States were required to carry out monitoring of surface waters and groundwater to identify nitrate-polluted waters and to designate as nitrate-vulnerable zones those areas of their territory draining to polluted water by December 1993. In nitrate-vulnerable zones a set of measures (action programmes) must be introduced to reduce and prevent water pollution from agricultural sources. By 2001, Ireland had still not transposed the directive into domestic law. Faced with vocal opposition from farmers organizations, in particular the IFA, successive Irish Environment Ministers found it very difficult to produce national regulations and a national action programme implementing the directive that would satisfy the farmers. Opposition to the directive led the farmers' organizations to walk out of the 2006 social partnership negotiations on the successor plan to *Sustaining Progress*. At the same time, following a negative judgement in the ECJ in March 2004 (Case C-396/01), the Commission opened further infringement procedures condemning Ireland for failing to designate zones vulnerable to nitrate pollution and to adopt a nitrate action programme that satisfied the conditions set down in the directive.

Since EU accession, therefore, the Irish environmental policy regime has been modernized. It is no longer *ad hoc* and clearly reflects EU policy priorities. Indeed, the EU has had a strong effect as a 'disseminator' of norms and policy ideas within the Irish environmental policy regime (Flynn, 2003, p. 139). However, the building of an environmental regulatory framework has not been without difficulty, and the regulatory framework constructed is lacking in overall coherence (Taylor, 2001). In the past, policy has been formulated and negotiated without adequate consultation; with the result that implementation has become politicized and adversarial. The institutional structures established to deal with policy are highly centralized and access to the policy process is weighted in favour of agricultural and business interests, to the detriment of voluntary indigenous environmental organizations. In the past, economic development has also tended to take priority over stringent environmental protection.

Out on a limb? Ireland and EU Justice and Home Affairs policy

Although the Treaty of Rome included as one of its objectives the free movement of persons within the Community, it did not deal with the crossing of borders, immigration or visa policy. Freedom of movement was viewed in purely economic terms and concerned only workers. The growing importance of problems such as cross-border organized crime, drug trafficking, illegal immigration and international terrorism in the 1970s and early 1980s prompted member-state governments to increase *ad hoc* cooperation and consultation in this field. From 1984 onwards Ministers for Justice and Home Affairs (JHA) held regular six-monthly meetings to discuss these issues. While the focus of the SEA negotiations was primarily on completing the internal market, with the free movement of workers, goods, services and capital, the introduction of compensatory measures such as the strengthening of external border controls and the definition of European asylum and immigration policies was also discussed. Parallel to the SEA negotiations, an *avant garde* of France, Germany and the Benelux countries agreed in the Luxembourg town of Schengen in 1985 to abolish border controls at external borders and to harmonize arrangements relating to visas, asylum and police and judicial cooperation. The Schengen Convention was in some sense a governance laboratory and gave rise to talk of variable geometry and flexible integration in the EU, whereby not all member states would integrate at the same speed or to the same degree.

The 1993 Maastricht Treaty represented a critical juncture in the Europeanization of justice and home affairs policies, introducing a third pillar to the EU which covered nine areas of common interest in the field of JHA. Unlike policies in the first or Community pillar, as with the Common Foreign and Security policy, decision-making in this realm was firmly intergovernmental with unanimous voting in the Council and Community institutions playing a very limited role. Motivated by widespread dissatisfaction with the working of the intergovernmental procedures, decision-making in JHA was substantially reformed with the 1998 Amsterdam Treaty. Amsterdam brought certain areas within the Community legal order (the first pillar), namely policy on visas, asylum, immigration and other policies connected with the free movement of persons, thereby representing a shift towards supranationalism. Police and judicial cooperation in criminal matters remained in the intergovernmental third pillar of the European Union. The Schengen *acquis* was also incorporated into the EC and EU Treaties.

Subsequent reforms in the Nice Treaty and as part of the Tampere and Hague agendas have established and endeavoured to consolidate the EU's area of freedom, security and justice, giving rise to a veritable growth industry in JHA legislation. Measures in JHA now incorporate asylum policy, the crossing of external borders, immigration, combating international fraud, judicial cooperation in civil and criminal matters, and customs and police cooperation. Europol, the European Police Office was also launched. The EU Commission's directorate general on Justice and Home Affairs was expanded considerably and a new institutional structure of working group committees evolved. The EU's JHA Council now meets over nine times a year (almost as much as the agriculture and general affairs councils) – a further indication of the Europeanization of this policy field. In spite of such advances on paper, however, JHA as a policy domain suffers from a number of pathologies which serve to undermine its coherence and efficacy. The transfer of provisions relating to the free movement of persons and external borders to the Community pillar, alongside the phenomenon of variable geometry whereby member states have opted in and out of certain provisions, have had a complicating effect on an area of law that is already not wholly coherent. The special position of Ireland, the UK and Denmark within this policy area has contributed to this overall weakness.

Irish participation in the EU's area of freedom, security and justice belies the image of Ireland as a communautaire member state. In contrast to Ireland's position in the original *avant garde* of member states to adopt the single currency, Ireland's position in the EU's JHA is much more detached and conditional in nature. In Ireland, EU cooperation in border-control matters is viewed through the prism of Ireland's common travel area with the United Kingdom, and police and judicial cooperation in criminal matters is widely seen to be a threat to Ireland's common-law legal tradition. As a result, successive governments have tended to adopt a conservative approach to JHA issues in EU negotiations. Indeed, the special nature of Ireland's involvement is enshrined in a complex series of opt-outs contained in protocols attached to the Treaty of Amsterdam, including opting out of the Schengen *acquis*, and to elements of the 2007 Lisbon Treaty relating to police and judicial cooperation in criminal matters.

While the majority of member states at the Amsterdam treaty negotiations wanted to 'transfer' immigration, asylum and civil cooperation to the first pillar, Ireland, the UK and Denmark explicitly did not. The original Irish decision not to participate in the Schengen area was predicated upon the British decision not to participate and the desire to maintain the 'Common Travel Area' between the two countries. At the time, the costs of participation in the

Schengen system were seen to outweigh the advantages of the common travel area with the UK (given the situation in Northern Ireland and in light of the fact that in the mid-1990s, 70 per cent of all journeys leaving the Republic of Ireland had the UK as their destination (Handoll, 1995, p. 134)). At Amsterdam, a protocol agreed regarding border controls entitled Ireland and the UK to maintain the common travel area in force between them and to check individuals coming from other member states. This protocol specifically exempted Ireland and the UK from any EC legislation requiring the abolition of border controls, overlapping with their general exemption from Title IV of the EC Treaty (dealing with visa, immigration and asylum policy). However, under another protocol Ireland and the UK secured a right to 'opt in' to visa, immigration and asylum measures based on Title IV. The opting-in procedure works as follows: within a period of three months of receiving an initial proposal for a Title IV act, the relevant authorities may choose to inform the Council that they wish to participate in negotiations. The Council would then try to agree to the proposal with their participation. If, however, having originally decided to opt out of negotiations on a proposal, they later decide to join in after its adoption; they can also opt in, again by the same method. At home, the Irish government must also obtain Dáil approval if the decision is made to opt in.

In practice, the Irish and British governments have both chosen to opt in to all civil cooperation measures and almost all measures on asylum and irregular migration. However, they have opted in to only a few measures on visas, border controls, or legal migration (Peers, 2006, p. 56). Both member states participate in almost all of the criminal law and policing provisions of Schengen, as well as the provisions on the control of irregular migration. They also participate in the elements of the Schengen Information System database that relate to policing and judicial cooperation. Yet they do not participate in any of the rules relating to visas, border controls and freedom to travel. In the final negotiations for the Lisbon Treaty in October 2007, the Irish government, together with the UK, negotiated the right to opt out (with the right to opt in) of EU provisions relating to police and judicial cooperation in criminal matters (which following the ratification of the Treaty, would be subject to decision-making by qualified majority voting in the Council of Ministers). Until the Lisbon Treaty, Ireland and the UK remained full participants in these matters, which were part of the third intergovernmental pillar. As with matters relating to immigration and border control, in practice, the Irish and UK governments will have 90 days to tell their EU colleagues if they wish to participate in police and judicial cooperation measures. Indeed, even if they do opt in, an additional safeguard exists – the so-called 'emergency brake' which allows any member state to halt discussions on a JHA measure that is deemed a threat to its national legal system and if necessary to opt out.

What are the consequences of this special and somewhat detached relationship for Ireland? Moves towards further integration in the field of internal security and the harmonization of EU member states' legal systems are viewed with extreme caution by Irish ministers and civil servants. Commission proposals such as the establishment of a judicial training network and a European public prosecutor are seen to pose problems for Irish policy-makers, given the nature of the Irish judiciary and common-law legal system. The decision to opt out of certain JHA provisions has also decreased Irish influence within the JHA Council. Unless the decision is explicitly taken to opt in to discussions on a proposal during negotiations (and parliamentary approval must be reached for this), Irish positions are not taken into account: 'the comments we make on proposals on which we opt out of are not recorded by the Council ... it is a significant loss of influence' (interview with Senior Official in the Department of Justice, Equality and Law Reform, 8 May 2002). The decision not to opt in to Schengen and to opt out of EU judicial cooperation in criminal matters confirmed Ireland's conditional support of EU efforts in the field of JHA. Paradoxically, such a decision means that Ireland may be excluded from new initiatives to fight organized crime, an issue that attracts great attention in domestic public discourse.

Chapter 8

Irish Foreign Policy in the EU

'Ireland's accession to the European Community was probably the most important and far-reaching development in our foreign policy since independence.' (Padraic MacKernan, Former Secretary General of the Department of Foreign Affairs, 1984, p. 177)

It would be fair to say that Irish politicians and diplomats did not envisage any great impact of the EEC on Irish foreign policy at the time of accession (White Paper, 1972; Keatinge, 1978). This was not entirely surprising. In the late 1960s, the competence of the Community in the field of foreign policy, that is, the 'high politics' of diplomacy, defence and security was almost non-existent. Yet the EEC had clear aspirations to develop as a political actor and by the late 1970s a mechanism for foreign policy coordination at the European level, European Political Cooperation (EPC) had been developed and used. EPC consisted of a series of mechanisms through which the national foreign policies of member states could be more closely coordinated. As a process, however, EPC did not involve legally binding obligations and foreign policy was defined in a restricted way (Keatinge, 1984b, p. 45). Over the course of the next 30 years EPC was to evolve into a common European framework of foreign, security and defence policy coordination and integration starting with the Maastricht Treaty's Common Foreign and Security Policy (CFSP). As EPC evolved towards this more ambitious CFSP, Ireland's tradition position on foreign and security policy issues (that is, military neutrality) came under increased scrutiny. The story since then is one of the reconciliation of competing and conflicting interests as successive Irish governments and the electorate have been faced with the need to adapt to this new foreign policy environment.

The challenge facing Irish policy-makers from the early 1990s onwards was how to reconcile the desire to meet the competing demands for a deeper European security and defence identity in the post-Cold War era with a wish to safeguard Ireland's status as militarily neutral or non-aligned. In a sense, a large part of the story of Irish participation in the EU's foreign and security policy mechanisms has been that of a balancing act engaged by Irish policy makers to pull together these two competing dynamics.

This chapter explores the impact of the EU on Irish foreign policy from accession in 1973. Participation in the EU's foreign and security policy mechanisms has had considerable impact on the context, content and conduct of Ireland's external relations with the wider world. Indeed, the story since 1973 is to a large degree one of Europeanization as Ireland's foreign and security policy is now conducted through the EU's foreign, security and defence institutional and policy frameworks (Tonra, 2000, 2001, 2002, 2006; Keatinge, 1991, 1998). This chapter adopts a phased approach, interweaving the evolution of Irish foreign policy with foreign and security policy developments at the European level. In terms of scope, up to 1973 Irish foreign policy was narrowly defined and dominated by two external contexts – bilateral relations with the United Kingdom in the context of the consolidation of independence, and membership of first the League of Nations and subsequently the United Nations (UN). Since accession, the reach and ambition of Irish foreign policy has broadened considerably as the number of foreign policy issues Irish governments and diplomats deal with has grown exponentially. Irish foreign policy is now also conducted within a new multilateral and multi-actor context and adaptation of Irish foreign policy structures and processes to this new setting has been ongoing. At home, the Department of Foreign Affairs is no longer the single purveyor of Irish foreign policy; the Department of Defence is increasingly involved, as are the Houses of the Oireachtas and the Foreign Affairs and European parliamentary committees.

Some policy activists have protested that the EU system has constrained Irish policy options and that a principled, independent foreign policy voice that can make a positive contribution to the international system is being lost (Tonra, 2001, p. 224). Ireland's stance of military neutrality is seen as a touchstone of a global and progressive Irish foreign policy in this context and moves by the EU to carve out a common European defence policy are seen as eroding Ireland's policy of military neutrality (Gormley, 2003, 1998; Peace and Neutrality Alliance, 2006). By contrast, Irish foreign policy actors themselves have concluded that Irish foreign policy has been empowered by its participation within the EU system – membership has provided a new platform for Irish foreign policy, one where a small state on the periphery of Europe is often able to punch above its weight on world issues (cf. Tonra, 1999, 2001, 2006). From this perspective, the European dimension is seen to 'permeate every field of Irish foreign policy, representing "the central framework within which we pursue our foreign policy objectives" (Government White Paper, 1996, p. 8; Tonra, 1999, p. 7).

In more recent years, the primacy of the EU at the heart of Irish foreign policy is undergoing a subtle shift. For the moment at least, the conflict between the desire to play a constructive role in the development of Europe's common foreign and security policy and the traditional attachment to military neutrality appears to have been reconciled. Following the 1999 Helsinki European Council's commitment to establish a 60,000 strong rapid-reaction force, deployable within 60 days and the institutional reforms contained within the Treaty of Nice (namely the setting up of a Political and Security Committee and a Military Committee), the EU's foreign, security and defence policy structures and processes have bedded down. At home, Irish foreign and defence ministers have reached a resolution on neutral Ireland's place within this new security and defence architecture, first by joining the NATO Partnership for Peace programme in late 1999 and secondly by committing Irish troops to the Nordic battle group of the European Rapid Reaction Force in 2007. Irish room for manoeuvre and participation in such multilateral security structures is carefully circumscribed within what is termed the 'triple-lock' mechanism. Participation in any European battle group on an international mission requires a cabinet decision, the approval of the Dáil, and a UN mandate in the form of a Security Council resolution.

Thus it is possible to argue that Irish foreign and security policy within the EU framework has reached a new equilibrium. In addition, following on from the economic success of the Celtic Tiger and in the context of Ireland's new found prosperity and national confidence, the focus of domestic foreign policy actors is shifting away from Europe and towards the identification of new national foreign policy priorities, such as Irish relations with South-East Asia (in the context of economic relations) and with the developing world. While the EU remains the key framework for Irish foreign policy, there is a sense that the absolute priority of Europe over all else in foreign policy matters has faded as Irish policy-makers are carving out new foreign policy priorities and renewing old ones (Tonra, 2006, p. 206).

From isolation to interdependence?

The 'Europeanized' picture of Irish foreign policy portrayed above is in sharp contrast to the immediate aftermath of state independence in the 1920s when the importance of Ireland's external relations was not always recognized. In the early years of independence, it is claimed that Ireland retreated into isolationism and 'the practitioners of diplomacy seemed to be content to take a restricted view of the content of Irish foreign policy' (Keatinge, 1978, p. 2). Until the state joined the EEC in 1973, the main focus of Irish foreign policy efforts was the consolidation of the state's independence from Britain and the establishment of Ireland's international status first within the League of Nations and subsequently within the UN (see also Chapter 1). The decision to remain neutral during the Second World War can also be seen as part of the process of asserting Irish independence from Britain and the exercise of sovereignty. From the final days of the First World War, those who pushed for Irish neutrality did so in the context of Ireland's struggle for independence. The British declaration of war against Germany in September 1939 provided the opportunity for neutrality to move from the status of a political value to concrete state policy. As a policy, the state's neutrality was based on a legal status imposing specific rules of behaviour. Even so, the Irish government showed a certain amount of strategic consideration for Britain during the war including the exchange of information and intelligence (Keatinge, 1984a, p. 17; O'Halpin, 2002). From this point onwards, neutrality became not just a description of the state's external security policy, but part of the internal discourse on national identity as its popularity amongst the populace was firmly entrenched (Keatinge, 1998, p. 33). Indeed the policy of neutrality, while un-codified in the Constitution or in any domestic law, became *the* touchstone of Irish security policy, gaining almost mythic status as a political value (see Government White Paper on Foreign Policy, 1996, p. 51; Keatinge, 1984a; Salmon, 1989; MacGinty, 1995; O'Halpin, 2002; Devine, 2006).

Membership of international organizations, that is the League of Nations and the UN, served to widen the horizons of Irish foreign policy-makers and demonstrated Irish attachment as a small state in the world system to the principle of maintaining international order through the medium of international organizations and law. Indeed, the Irish Constitution of 1937 affirms Ireland's adherence to the principle of the pacific settlement of international disputes by international arbitration or judicial determination' and declares that 'Ireland accepts the generally recognised principles of international law as its rule of conduct in its relations with other states' (Bunreacht na hÉireann, 1937, Article 29). This assertion of the importance of international cooperation is a common characteristic shared by small states that rely on such international fora to ensure their voices are heard by larger and more powerful states (Ingebritsen *et al.*, 2006).

Until EEC accession, the UN was the most important international and multilateral forum through which Irish foreign policy priorities and actions were expressed. The period 1957 to 1961 in particular was seen to represent a 'golden age' of Irish diplomacy as the UN became the forum for the presentation of an Irish foreign policy that advocated disarmament, supported moves for a nuclear non-proliferation treaty, participated in UN peacekeeping missions and voted for de-colonization motions and against South African apartheid in the General Assembly. Minister for External Affairs Frank Aiken's annual speech in the UN General Assembly was taken extremely seriously as a key statement of Irish foreign policy priorities. For the first time, Irish troops participated in UN peacekeeping missions in the Congo (now Zaire), Cyprus and the Lebanon and were seen as extremely effective in carrying out their duties (Dorr, 1996). Irish participation in UN peacekeeping became a source of national pride and part of Irish national identification.

Minister for External Affairs Frank Aiken's preoccupation with the UN meant that once the decision was taken to apply for EEC membership in the early 1960s, Taoiseach Sean Lemass became Ireland's *de facto* Minister for Europe. In this sense, the term 'foreign policy' was almost exclusively attached to the Ireland's participation in the UN. EEC membership was presented not as a diplomatic alignment with Europe but as a complex technical adjustment and as such was handled by Lemass and the Ministers for Finance and Industry and Commerce amongst others. Aiken himself showed very little interest in 'Europe', 'arguing that EEC membership was a constitutional issue and therefore not primarily his business' (Keatinge, 1978, p. 2). Indeed, according to former diplomat Noel Dorr, 'it is probably fair to say that Aiken was more than dubious about the decision to apply for EEC membership and did not wish to be associated with it' (Dorr, 1996, p. 50). The marginalization of the Department of External Affairs from the EEC application process ended with the retirement of Aiken.

In the cold war era at least, neutrality served to set Ireland apart from the UK (thus helping define Ireland as an independent nation) and within the UN contributed to the self-image of Ireland as a progressive and anti-colonial state (what Tonra (2006) refers to as the global citizen narrative of Irish foreign policy). Yet at the time of Ireland's first attempt to join the EEC, Taoiseach Sean Lemass was careful to publicly indicate that Irish neutrality would not be an obstacle to EEC membership. Neutrality in this sense was limited, ultimately negotiable and consisted in practical terms of non-membership of military alliances. In 1962, adopting a more pragmatic and flexible stance, he claimed that Ireland was not neutral in its ideological commitment, and did not belong to NATO because of a complex quarrel with one of its neighbours. Indeed, in an interview to the *New York Times* on 18 July 1962, Lemass went further with his statement that

> we recognise that a military commitment will be an inevitable consequence of our joining the Common Market and ultimately we would be prepared to yield even the technical label of neutrality. We are prepared to go into this integrated Europe without any reservation as to how far this will take us in the field of foreign policy and defence. (Quoted in Keatinge, 1984a, p. 26)

Similarly, after 1969 new Minister for External Affairs Patrick Hillery, echoed this view stating that: 'while Ireland remained neutral during World War II we have never adopted a permanent policy of neutrality in the doctrinaire or ideological sense' (Interview to the Irish Press, 2 December 1970, quoted in Keatinge, 1978, p. 94). Even so, domestically, Lynch and Hillery were careful to rule out membership of NATO and to reiterate that there were no defence commitments in the Rome Treaties.

New horizons – Ireland and European political cooperation

On accession, Ireland became part of the nascent European framework for the coordination of foreign policy – European Political Cooperation. The new procedure of EPC, begun in 1970, was essentially a commitment by member states that the Community would seek to coordinate member state foreign policies on external issues as far as possible. EPC itself grew out of the relaunch of European integration at the Hague Summit meeting of 1969, hot on the heels of French President Charles De Gaulle's departure from office and the European scene. As an entirely intergovernmental process, strictly outside the Treaty of Rome, EPC consisted of quarterly meetings of foreign ministers and was managed by senior diplomats of all EEC member states. The Commission was firmly excluded from this process, particularly in its early years. Decisions on each issue under discussion were to be unanimous and unless all member states agreed, a common position was impossible. A secure telex link, *Coreu*, was managed by the Dutch foreign ministry and provided direct communications between members and joint reporting from EPC embassies in third countries. The institutionalization of the European Council in 1974 served to strengthen the intergovernmental nature of EPC as it gave Heads of State and Government and the six-monthly EC Presidency an overarching role in the coordination of EPC.

For the first time EPC provided a common framework for multilateral diplomacy at the European level. Given its institutional nature, however, EPC gave rise to criticism for its weak, reactive and declaratory nature in the face of international crises such as the Arab–Israeli War of October 1973, the Islamic revolution in Iran and the Soviet invasion of Afghanistan of 1979. The EC's impotence led to steps to strengthen it in the London Report of 1981. A small EPC secretariat was established to aid the Presidency and the Commission was brought into the process with the right to prior consultation. Security and defence matters were firmly excluded from the process, however, as defence ministries remained entirely outside EPC. The primacy of NATO as the venue for European cooperation in this sphere continued as nine European defence ministries and armed forces (with the exception of Spain, France and Ireland) worked together within NATO's integrated military command. Throughout this period until its codification in Treaty form as Title III of the 1987 Single European Act, EPC in this sense was not seen as a threat to Irish neutrality given its firm intergovernmental nature, its understanding and allowance of different national positions and its clear exclusion of security and defence issues. In this way, successive governments were able to welcome developments in the European foreign policy framework irrespective of Ireland's stance of military neutrality.

The Irish presidency of 1975 marked the first time that a small and peripheral country took the helm of EPC. As the official mediator of the Euro–Arab dialogue, Irish ministers and officials found themselves speaking on behalf of the EC on an issue about which Ireland previously had no clear policy. Within EPC, the Middle East was to become a key area of Irish foreign policy in the 1970s, in part motivated by Ireland's reliance on oil supplies from this region and 'also as a result of an historically-rooted sympathy for the plight of the Palestinians as a dispossessed people' (Keatinge, 1991, p. 155). Participation in the UN peacekeeping operation in southern Lebanon, as well as an activist stance adopted in the UN's General Assembly during Ireland's second EC Presidency in 1979, helped contribute to the framing of the 1980 Venice Declaration when the EC acknowledged 'the right to existence and to security of all States in the region, including Israel, and justice for all the peoples, which implies the recognition of the legitimate rights of the Palestinian people' (European Council Venice Declaration, 1980).

The other persistent issue within EPC during the 1970s and 1980s was that of South Africa. Divergent positions within the EC contributed to the EC's weak position on South African apartheid during this period. With an energetic anti-apartheid lobby at home and cross-party support against apartheid since the 1960s, Ireland found itself at the more activist end of the spectrum as far as coming up with a common European stance on South Africa was concerned. Yet Ireland's position as a small state within EPC meant that it was unable to persuade its European partners to move beyond instigating economic sanctions. This weak position was similarly evident in the UN's General Assembly.

From 1973, the EC became the primary medium through which Ireland coordinated its policies towards the developing world; before this time, Ireland's contribution to the developing world was felt more in human rather than financial terms. In contrast to a low official aid contribution of just 0.1 per cent of GNP, 'in 1971 it was estimated that about 6,000 Irish individuals (be they religious or lay) were working in more than 60 developing countries' (Keatinge, 1978, p. 183). In 1969, Minister for External Affairs Patrick Hillery acknowledged the deficiencies of government policy in this respect and promised a review. An official Bilateral Aid Programme was established in 1973 and the EC became the main external medium through which government financial assistance was channelled as the government accepted the Community decision to achieve UN targets for development aid and pledged to increase aid by 0.05 per cent of GNP per annum. While small in overall terms and in relation to other members' contributions, on average 40 per cent of Ireland's total Overseas Development Aid budget was channelled through the EC (Holmes *et al.*, 1993, p. 124). As Minister for Foreign Affairs and President of the Council of Ministers under Ireland's first EC Presidency, Garret FitzGerald played a key role in securing agreement on the 1975 Lomé Convention, the EU's first international trade and aid agreement between the African, Caribbean and Pacific (ACP) countries and the EU. Irish ministers continued to be supportive of developing countries concerns in the subsequent rounds of the Lomé negotiations and worked to bringing the negotiations to a successful conclusion.

Neutrality within EPC proved unproblematic so long as EPC stayed away from military matters. The only time that Irish neutrality emerged as a potentially contentious issue during this early period in the evolution of the EU's foreign and security policy was during the Falklands Island crisis of 1982. At an early stage in the crisis, Ireland joined in the economic sanctions against Argentina, as agreed in EPC and implemented under a regulation under Article 113 of the EEC Treaty. Participation in sanctions of this nature had hitherto not been felt to be in contravention of Irish neutrality, in contrast with other European neutrals. Yet on the eve of the British campaign, the Irish Government (under Charles Haughey as Taoiseach) declared that in the context of armed conflict, support for sanctions was incompatible with military neutrality and Ireland subsequently opted out of the common action (Keatinge, 1991, p. 162). Withdrawal of support primarily served to damage Irish relations with the UK; apart from this deterioration in relations, neutrality appeared to have emerged unscathed from its first real test in the EU context. Squaring Ireland's neutrality as a policy with the EC's foreign policy framework was unproblematic at this time given the fact that it was widely felt that any move towards a political union within the EC was far off in the distant future (Keatinge, 1984a, p. 85).

Participation in EPC also impacted on the management of Irish foreign policy as it served to strengthen the Department of Foreign Affairs within the domestic system. The Department's position as gatekeeper between the European and the national directly contributed to its expansion and reorganisation in the early years of membership. As the new domestic manager of EPC, the Department was confronted with new foreign policy issues and geographical areas and was obliged to produce new policies to address these matters (Holmes *et al.*, 1993, p. 122). By the end of the 1980s, the conduct of Irish foreign policy had changed dramatically as Irish diplomats found themselves part and parcel of an extensive network, involving thousands of diplomats in the foreign ministries of the member states, in their embassies outside the EC and in missions to international organisations. Diplomatic working practices were transformed as diplomats dealt with some 9,000 *Coreu* telegrams a year by 1989. Desk officers in the Department of Foreign Affairs dealt directly with their opposite numbers in working groups, by telephone and through *Coreu*. The sheer scope and wealth of information had a great impact on the 'cognitive reach' of Irish foreign policy (Tonra, 2001, p. 229). Stewardship of EC presidencies and participation in the rolling 'troika' (consisting of representatives of the previous presidency and the next in line as well as the current holder) consolidated this important coordination role as Irish representatives became *de facto* convenors and coordinators of EPC. Taking size into account, however, the ability of Irish foreign policymakers to assert their influence in the Community and within EPC was limited and they relied heavily on their well-honed diplomatic skills (Holmes *et al.*, 1993, p. 122).

After 1989 – Ireland's new security choices

The collapse of communism in Central and Eastern Europe in 1989, the subsequent dismantling of the Soviet regime bringing to the Cold War to an end and the collapse of the former Yugoslavia was to ultimately transform the context within which Irish foreign policy operated. The impact of these events forced foreign and security policy up the European agenda to become part of the 1990 intergovernmental conference (ostensibly convened on economic and monetary union). Against the geopolitical backdrop of a changing world order, a new conceptualization of the notion of security emerged. Security was no longer seen primarily in military terms as the defence of territorial boundaries, but became a larger and broader concept with an emphasis on the military aspects of crisis management. The EU's rejuvenation of the hitherto moribund Western European Union (WEU) and NATO's move into crisis management and peacemaking activities reflected this change. Europe's security choices dominated the context and content of Irish foreign policy in this period and were to seriously challenge Ireland's preferred national security and defence policy, raising domestic opposition to membership for foreign policy reasons and forcing successive governments to make policy choices they might not otherwise have had to face (Tonra, 2001, p. 227).

The eventual package that appeared as the Common Foreign and Security Policy in the Treaty on European Union represented a compromise between the Atlanticists (in Britain, the Netherlands and Portugal) who resisted any substantial weakening of NATO's European framework for defence and security matters and the Europeanists (in France, Belgium and Italy) who wished for a more concrete European competence in such matters through the reactivation of the WEU. As the second pillar of the new European Union, the CFSP superseded EPC and had five main objectives:

- to safeguard the common values and fundamental interests of the Union;
- to strengthen the security of the Union;
- to preserve peace and strengthen international security;
- to promote international cooperation; and
- to develop democracy and the rule of law, including human rights.

The CFSP is strictly intergovernmental, its objectives to be pursued by systematic cooperation amongst member states through joint actions and common positions. According to the Treaty, the common foreign and security policy 'shall include all questions relating to the security of the Union, including the eventual framing of a common defence policy which might lead to a common defence' (Article J.4). This agreement referred to the WEU as an integral part of the development of the EU and requested the WEU to elaborate and implement decisions and actions with defence implications on behalf of the EU. Concurrently, the WEU Council in June 1992 adopted the 'Petersberg Declaration' which included a summing-up of the so-called Petersberg tasks – humanitarian and rescue tasks, peacekeeping tasks and tasks of combat forces in crisis management, including peace-making. At the time of the signature of the TEU, Ireland was not associated with the WEU in any way.

That Ireland's place was to be at the heart of the EU's CFSP was not questioned by the then government. Former Taoiseach Albert Reynolds acknowledged that 'an effective common policy of the Twelve is a better platform from which to address international issues, than a fragmented array of policies reflecting contrasting analyses or conflicting articulations of interests' (quoted in

MacGinty, 1995, p. 136). Yet alongside the desire to be part of the new European security architecture, at home governments had to grapple with an increasingly vocal opposition of a number of the smaller political parties (for example the Green Party and Sinn Féin) and interest groups such as the Peace and Neutrality Alliance (PANA) and Action for Ireland (Afri) who expressed serious reservations about EU foreign and security policy initiatives and their implications for Ireland's policy of military neutrality. For these groups, the mere contemplation of Irish participation in the new European security architecture (most especially regarding any links with the North Atlantic Treaty Organization) undermined Ireland's principled and independent foreign policy and Ireland's cherished relationship with the United Nations. During the referendum debate on the Maastricht Treaty, the question of Irish participation in this new foreign policy framework was somewhat overshadowed by domestic concentration on the success in garnering unprecedented regional development funding and such dissenting voices were not always heard. When foreign and security policy was discussed, it was in the context of a suggestion by certain campaigners against the treaty that conscription into a European army could follow approval of the Treaty (John Gormley, writing in *The Irish Times*, 25 May 1998). The Irish decision to accept WEU observer status in November 1992, following on from the successful domestic ratification also did not give rise to significant publicity. All this was to change, however, following the signature of the Treaty of Amsterdam in 1997 with its move to incorporate the WEU into the EU's institutional structure, its adoption of the Petersberg tasks and the recognition that in order for the EU to carry out Petersberg task missions, NATO's collective assets and capabilities would have to be used.

The roots of the Treaty of Amsterdam lay in a revision clause inserted into the Maastricht Treaty where member states committed to return to the issues of security and defence policy by 1996. The Amsterdam negotiations were conducted within the context of the lessons learned from the Yugoslav conflict, a key learning process for European governments. West Europeans had looked to the US for leadership in the crisis, whereas the US administration in turn had indicated its desire for Western European states to take more responsibility for crises of this kind in the European backyard. The weakness of the WEU in providing structures and logistics to enable the EU to undertake crisis-management tasks and European reliance on NATO structures was widely recognized. The announcement in

December 1995 by the French of their formal return to parts of NATO's integrated structure reinforced this common perception.

In order to facilitate the coordination of common EU positions and to give the EU a foreign policy face, the Treaty of Amsterdam introduced the role of the High Representative for the CFSP (who would also be Secretary General of the Council). The High Representative (Mr or Ms CFSP) would assist the Council in CFSP matters by contributing to the formulation, preparation and implementation of decisions. As a general rule, decision-making was to remain unanimous, but the Treaty did introduce the mechanism of constructive abstention, whereby a member state's abstention to a decision would not block the adoption of the decision by other member states. The Treaty also allowed for the creation of a policy planning and early-warning unit, under the authority of the High Representative in the Council, to assist in producing advanced research and data on foreign policy matters. Divisions between member states over the status of the WEU (echoing earlier cleavages on defence matters) led to the following compromise: the European Council could 'avail itself' of WEU action, with the possibility of a merger of the EU and WEU, should the European Council so decide (Article J.7.1). The position of states such as Ireland was explicitly recognized with the proviso that 'the policy of the Union ... shall not prejudice the specific character of the security and defence policies of certain member states'. The Petersberg tasks were also incorporated into the Treaty with responsibility again given to the WEU to elaborate and implement decisions and actions of the Union with defence implications.

With the Treaty of Amsterdam, the thorny question of Irish participation in European peacekeeping activities could no longer be swept under the carpet. Traditionally, peacekeeping missions were restricted under Irish law to duties of a police character, but the 1993 Defence Act dropped this restriction to facilitate an Irish contribution to the UN operation in Somalia (UNOSOM). It also made it possible for Irish troops to participate in UN-mandated but NATO-led operations in Bosnia (SFOR) and Kosovo (Tonra, 2002, p. 27; Keatinge, 1998). In a new departure, for the first time Irish troops (more specifically a military police company) were placed under NATO command (Doherty, 2000, p. 70). This was explicit recognition of the UN's new practice of sub-contracting its peacekeeping out to regional organizations such as NATO. For its part, within its new partnership for peace programme NATO set up a planning and review process through which EU/WEU Petersberg missions could be planned. Launched at the NATO Brussels summit in January 1994, Partnership for Peace (PfP) is a voluntary programme of practical bilateral cooperation between individual partner countries and NATO, tailored to individual needs and jointly implemented at the level and pace chosen by each participant. It is operationally restricted to three agreed mission areas: peace-support operations, humanitarian aid, and search and rescue.

The possibility of Irish participation, no matter how limited, in NATO's PfP triggered intense opposition from domestic groups who also actively campaigned against the Treaty of Amsterdam on the basis of such developments. Political parties such as the Green Party and Sinn Féin and civil society organizations such as PANA and Afri warned against the 'militarization of the EU'. Green MEP Patricia McKenna and Green parliamentarians Trevor Sargent and John Gormley argued at the time of the 1998 referendum that the Treaty of Amsterdam would drag Ireland into a militarized Europe which would compromise Irish neutrality and non-nuclear status (*The Irish Times*, 24 April 1998). Opponents to the foreign and security policy provisions of the Amsterdam Treaty placed primordial importance on the UN as the primary guarantor of world peace. This political opposition was to a certain extent reflected in the cautious public opinion on a common European defence. Irish voters' traditionally high support for European integration was tempered by doubts of the idea of the EU developing a defence capability (Rees, 2005b). In an earlier 1993 Eurobarometer survey for instance, on the question of whether 'the EC member states should work towards a common defence policy', Irish support at 55.2 per cent was well behind the EC average of 76.6 per cent (MacGinty, 1995, p. 140).

Two consequences sprung from the politicization of the security debate in Ireland. In the first instance, from the Amsterdam Treaty negotiations onwards, Irish governments have tended to strike a cautious attitude towards the development of the CFSP, its decision-making procedures and its moves towards the development of any significant defence capacity at the EU level (Tonra, 2000). Domestically, this politicization was also accompanied by the beginnings of a democratization of the Irish foreign policy process (Keatinge, 1998; Tonra, 2006) as debate on Irish foreign policy opened up beyond the confines of diplomatic practitioners and a select number of politicians in the mid-1990s. The publication of the first-ever White Paper on Foreign policy in 1996, instigated by the then Labour

Minister for Foreign Affairs, Dick Spring, was the most obvious manifestation of this democratization. The White Paper itself was drafted following a long process of public consultation and new parliamentary committees focusing on foreign and European affairs were also established.

While it mapped out Irish foreign policy objectives and options, the 1996 White Paper took no firm decision on Irish participation in the new European security architecture following on from the Treaty of Amsterdam. The government did choose to limit Irish participation in the WEU (ruling out a contribution to crisis-management operations) but did not rule out the possibility of contributing in some way to enforcement actions within the terms of a UN mandate, even where the UN itself was not the operational framework. The White Paper also threw open the debate on participation in NATO's Partnership for Peace (PfP) process (Keatinge, 1997). This debate was to rage on until late 1999 and beyond.

Towards a common European defence? Ireland's ongoing security dilemma

The impact of the late twentieth-century Kosovo conflict was a key element in the moves by EU member states to instigate a European Security and Defence Policy (ESDP). The desire for a rapid-reaction force, that is a force that European allies would be able to mobilize in an emergency, sprang from European dependence, yet again, on US transport, communications and other logistics during the Kosovo conflict which developed in late 1998. The European reliance on US and NATO capabilities meant that the principle of a European pillar within the Atlantic Alliance and the need for an autonomous European defence capability became more widely accepted, with the UK in particular heavily promoting European defence integration. At the Saint Malo Franco-British summit in December 1998, UK Prime Minister Tony Blair and French President Jacques Chirac called for an autonomous European defence capability, backed up by credible military forces within the EU framework and including meetings of defence ministers. Within the context of such events and the further Europeanization of NATO, Ireland's non-participation in NATO's PfP became increasingly problematic. From a military perspective, joining PfP was seen to be of benefit to the Irish armed forces, giving them an opportunity to play a role in the development of and training for new peacekeeping methods and practices in Europe (Ishizuka, 1999, p. 194; O'Halpin, 2002).

Following prolonged domestic debate, Ireland eventually joined PfP in December 1999. Initially, when in opposition, Fianna Fail had been very much against any participation in the PfP programme, its leader Bertie Ahern reflecting the fear that moves towards a common European defence and membership of PfP would lead to membership of NATO and the erosion of Irish neutrality:

> It is the thin end of the wedge which will be justified for all sorts of practical reasons and to increase our alleged influence, whereas in reality we will have no influence on alliance thinking as junior or second-class partners ... Will we have British troops back in the Curragh, the French in Bantry Bay, the Germans on Banna Strand, the Spanish in Kinsale and the Americans in Lough Foyle? ... Our view is that any decisions involving a closer association with NATO or the WEU would represent a substantial change in defence policy, and would have long term if not immediate implications for our policy on neutrality. Any such proposals must be put to the people in a referendum before a decision is taken. (Bertie Ahern, speech in Dáil Éireann, 28 March 1996, pp. 1316–23)

When in government, however, Ahern and new Minister for Foreign Affairs David Andrews gradually shifted to a more positive attitude towards PfP, realising that fears for the abrogation of Irish neutrality were unfounded, especially given the fact that the EU's other neutral or non-aligned member states had already joined PfP. In spite of opposition from peace groups, the Green Party, Sinn Féin and PANA, increasing numbers amongst the political elite cautiously favoured participation in the process. In December 1999, the Fianna Fáil-Progressive Democrat government abandoned the idea of a referendum on PfP and Ireland finally joined the programme.

From CFSP to ESDP

A year on from the Saint Malo declaration, the European Council at its Helsinki summit adopted detailed proposals aimed at developing the Union's military and non-military crisis-management capability as part of a strengthened common European policy on security and defence (ESDP). These proposals formed part of the EU's Head-line Goal to create, by 2003, a military capacity in the form of a rapid-reaction force of up to 60,000 troops that could be deployed within 60 days. The European Council also decided to set up the necessary political and military bodies to manage the ESDP. These bodies included:

- the Political and Security Committee (also known by its French acronym COPS) which exercises political control and strategic direction over EU crisis management operations;
- the European Union Military Committee (EUMC); and
- European Military Staff (EUMS).

Interim versions of these bodies began to operate in early 2000 and later were legally incorporated into the Treaty of Nice. The proposal to establish an EU Military Committee was ultimately accepted by Ireland, in spite of original heavy resistance. The EU also moved into peace keeping and crisis management operations for the first time. Irish troops have been involved in these initiatives right from the very beginning taking part in the EU's first ESDP Mission, the EU Police Mission EUFOR which took over from the UN's stabilization force in Bosnia Herzegovina in 2004 (see Tables 8.1 and 8.2). In light of these developments, the Department of Defence and the Irish defence forces emerged with a much stronger European focus and senior defence and military staff participate fully in the range of new institutional structures based in Brussels. How were these moves reconciled with public support for neutrality?

The desire on the part of Irish elites to participate in the new Euro-pean security dynamic was not reflected in public opinion across the board, and domestic opposition to such moves came to the fore again during the first Nice referendum campaign and its aftermath when the reforms institutionalizing the ESDP gave rise to domestic fears of a common European army and a fatal attack on Irish neu-trality (see Chapter 5). In order ensure acceptance of the Treaty of Nice in the second referendum and to alleviate these fears, some sort of political declaration safeguarding Irish military neutrality was deemed necessary by the Government. Taoiseach Bertie Ahern negotiated what became known as the Seville Declaration at the European Council summit of June 2002. The Declaration repre-sented an additional recognition of Irish neutrality and consolidated the concept of the triple lock, that is, the necessity for Dáil and

192

TABLE 8.1 *Irish army overseas operations, as of 1 October 2007.*

Operation	Duration	Type	Commitment
EUFOR (Bosnia-Herzegovina) (previously SFOR May 1997)	December 2004–to date	EU-led crisis management	40
KFOR (Kosovo)	August 1999–to date	NATO PfP-led Peace Support Operation (from 1 August 2007 Irish Brigadier General Gerry Hegarty was placed in command of the multinational taskforce)	276
ISAF (Afghanistan)	December 2001–to date	NATO PfP-led Peace Support Operation	7
MINURSO (Western (Spanish) Sahara)	September 1991–to date	UN-led Peacekeeping Operation (Observer)	3
MONUC (Congo Observation Mission)	June 2001–to date	UN-led Peacekeeping Operation (Observer)	3
UNIFIL (Lebanon)	May 1978–2001; 2006–to date	UN-led Peacekeeping Operation (Troops)	167
UNMIK (Interim Administration Mission – Kosovo)	July 1999–to date	UN-led Peacekeeping Operation (Observer)	4
UNOCI (Côte d'Ivoire)	June 2004–to date	UN-led Peacekeeping Operation (Observer)	2
UNTSO (Truce Supervision – Syria, Jordan, Lebanon and Israel)	December 1958–to date	UN-led Peacekeeping Operation (Observer)	14

Source: www.military.ie/overseas/ops/index.htm

TABLE 8.2   *Irish forces overseas operations in Europe*

Mission	Dates
EUFOR	December 2004–to date
KFOR	August 1999–to date
Operation Concordia/FYROM	March 2003–December 2003
UNFICYP (Cyprus)	March 1964–May 2005
UNHCR (Y)	December 1992–March 1993
UNMIK	July 1999–to date
UNMLO/UNPROFOR (Yugoslavia)	January 1992–January 1996
UNMOP (Prevlaka Penninsula – Yugoslavia)	February 1996–December 1999
UNPREDEP (Albania – FYROM)	February 1996–February 1999
UNTAES (Eastern Slavonia – Croatia)	February 1996–January 1998

Source: www.military.ie/overseas/ops/index.htm#europe

cabinet approval alongside UN Security Council authorisation for any Irish participation in European overseas operations.

By early 2004, it became clear that progress in establishing the rapid-reaction force was moving very slowly. Again following a Franco-British initiative in December 2004, the General Affairs and External Relations Council adopted a new Headline Goal of 2010 which reiterated the goals of the original 1999 declaration. In the Headline Goal 2010, the EU set itself the objective of being able to 'respond with rapid and decisive action applying for a fully coherent approach to the whole spectrum of crisis management operations covered by the TEU'. A key element of the Headline Goal is the capability to deploy forces at high readiness, the so-called Battlegroups.

These developments had profound implications for Irish defence forces. At the start of 2005, Minister for Defence Willie O'Dea initially ruled out early Irish participation, arguing that the rapid deployment of Irish military forces overseas within 10 days would be impossible in the context of the triple lock. In addition, as Ireland would be unlikely to be able to form a single battle group, if Irish troops were to participate they would need to join with other states.

However, the 1954 Defence Act did not allow the training of Irish troops overseas (Rees, 2006, p. 159). Following positive noises from the rest of the cabinet, the Minister established an interdepartmental group to consider the issues which reported in November 2005. At the end of the group's deliberations, a delegation consisting of representatives from the Departments of Defence, Foreign Affairs and the Defence Forces met with Swedish representatives in March 2006 to discuss possible participation by the Defence Forces in the Nordic Battlegroup, instigated by Sweden and joined by Finland, Estonia and Norway. The Interdepartmental Group recommended some changes to the existing legislation in light of the need for increased interoperability between the Irish defence forces and these Nordic forces, as well as the possibility of overseas training with these partner forces. While the triple lock would stand, the Defence Amendment Act of 2006 would allow Irish troops to engage in overseas training and participation in individual battlegroup missions would be decided through the mechanisms of the triple lock, on a case by case basis:

> There is no conflict between Ireland's participation in regional arrangements including EU Battlegroups and our traditional policy of support for the UN. Participation in any EU operation remains a national sovereign decision, and our policy on the 'Triple Lock' will not be compromised by participating in Battlegroups. (Minister for Defence Willie O'Dea, Address to the IEA Conference on EU Battlegroups, University of Limerick, 28 April 2006)

This commitment endeavoured to assuage the fears of those who felt Irish neutrality was under threat. In the summer of 2007, the Irish government went to offer a contingent of up to 100 members of the Defence Forces to the Nordic Battle Group comprising of specialists in bomb disposal and protection detail. This contribution was met in the context of the overall ceiling of 850 personnel serving overseas at any one time as set out in the 2000 White Paper on Defence.

The content of the 2004 Constitutional Treaty and the Lisbon Treaty illustrate how the emergent European security architecture has also reached equilibrium. The 2007 Lisbon Treaty repeats the Constitutional Treaty's commitment to provide the Union with an operational capacity drawing on civil and military assets of member states, and allows for the creation of a new High Representative who would be at the same time a member of the Council and the European Commission. The Constitutional Treaty's mutual solidarity pledge was also repeated within the Lisbon Treaty, but with the caveat that it would 'not prejudice the specific character of the security and defence policies of certain member states'. Throughout the original constitutional treaty negotiations, Ireland's position on foreign and security matters was close to that of Austria, Sweden and Finland, and this is unlikely to change. According to Rees, all states supported the creation of an EU Foreign Minister, the maintenance of unanimity as the mode of decision-making and extending initiatives under the Petersberg tasks, but were more cautious about enhanced defence cooperation (with the exception of Sweden). All were similarly opposed to a mutual defence guarantee (Rees, 2005, p. 61). While the setting up of a European Defence Agency may have rung alarm bells in the minds of the protectors of neutrality, its existence was not dependent on the ratification of the Lisbon Treaty as it was already established under a Joint Action of the Council of Ministers in July 2004 with Ireland as one of its 26 participants (only Denmark is not involved). The agency is ascribed four functions: (1) developing the EU's defence capabilities; (2) promoting defence research and technology; (3) promoting armaments cooperation; and (4) creating a competitive European defence equipment market. Decisions with regard to the agency are taken on a strictly unanimous basis.

Irish foreign policy into the future

That the EU's CFSP (together with its new ESDP) forms the overarching framework of Irish foreign policy is without doubt; the evolution of the EU's foreign and security policy capacity has significantly broadened the context and content of Irish foreign policy. The conduct of Irish foreign policy has similarly been Europeanized. Indeed, in the words of one Irish diplomat 'where ever there is any new foreign policy initiative in the making, the first reflex is European' (quoted in Tonra, 2001, p. 43). In turn, the bedding-down of European security structures (as evinced most recently in the aborted 2004 Constitutional Treaty and its successor Lisbon Treaty) has been accompanied by the domestic resolution of the issue of Irish participation in EU-led crisis-management operations. The Irish government is now committed to active engagement in the development of the EU's role in conflict prevention, but Ireland's contribution to

European-led military operations is likely to remain limited, given human and budgetary constraints. In relative terms, Irish defence expenditure at 0.7 per cent of GDP is amongst the lowest in Europe, relatively lower than in some other neutral or military non-aligned states such as Sweden and Finland and is not likely to increase in the future (White Paper on Defence, 2000). The more positive attitude of the political elite towards participation in supporting European crisis-management operations is tempered by the ongoing attachment to the principle of military neutrality amongst the public and constrained by the triple-lock mechanism (Rees, 2005b, p. 67). The Irish approach towards security and defence developments at the EU level will continue to be a cautious one.

Active participation in the EU's CFSP may indeed have reduced Ireland's autonomy in foreign policy, but this has occurred in exchange for increased prestige and weight for a small, peripheral state at the edge of Europe. The story of Irish foreign policy is not simply the story of constantly accommodating European developments, however. Irish foreign policy has begun to slowly move beyond its long-time European focus as new priorities and goals emerge. The importance of Northern Ireland as a focus of Irish foreign policy-makers is ever present, with the suspension of the Northern Ireland assembly in October 2002 reinforcing the importance of implementing the Good Friday agreement in full. In turn, valuable expertise gained by Irish foreign policy practitioners in helping to bring the Northern Ireland peace process to a successful conclusion has prompted initiatives such as the Department of Foreign Affairs' new conflict-resolution unit. Ireland's continued attachment to and dynamic role in the United Nations' reform process was reflected in the decision by former Secretary General Kofi Annan's decision in April 2005 to appoint Minister for Foreign Affairs Dermot Ahern as his special envoy to Europe to be 'his eyes and ears' on UN structural reform. Finally, Ireland's active engagement in CFSP has been accompanied by a renewed national focus on development cooperation and Ireland's overseas economic interests such as the renewed Government Asia strategy. The 2007 White Paper on Irish Aid heralded a significant increase in Irish overseas development aid and an expansion in Irish activity in least developed countries independent of the EU.

Chapter 9

British–Irish Relations: The European Dimension

Introduction

On 15 May 2007, the then Irish Prime Minister, Bertie Ahern addressed the Joint Houses of Parliament at Westminster, the first Irish Prime Minister to do so since the foundation of the Irish state in 1922. It was an occasion charged with symbolism given the contentious historical relationship between the two islands to the north-west of the European continent. The islands are governed by two sovereign states, the United Kingdom and the Republic of Ireland. The UK is internally divided, with three devolved authorities Scotland, Wales and Northern Ireland. England, the largest and most populous entity within the UK, is not governed by a devolved authority. The relationship between state and nationhood and between the different nations inhabiting these two islands is highly complex and remains contested, albeit largely by peaceful means. Both states joined the then European Communities, now the EU, on 1 January 1973. For Ireland, the UK decision to accede to the EU was of major significance, and given the level of economic dependency on the UK, Ireland was left with little choice but to seek membership. The dependency this signalled was, however, counterbalanced by the opportunity membership offered Ireland to break free and hence to enhance Ireland's real sovereignty.

The decision to join the Union represented the most significant foreign-policy decision taken by either state in the postwar period. It implied a major shift in the approach of the UK towards its external environment and its role in the world. Having twice rejected engagement with the evolving Communities in the 1950s, the UK lodged its first application for membership in 1961. By sheer coincidence, the outbreak of communal conflict in Northern Ireland coincided with the decision by the EU to open accession negotiations with Britain, Ireland, Norway and Denmark in 1968–69. Neither Britain nor the Republic of Ireland was principally concerned with the potential impact of EU membership on the conflict in Northern Ireland when they sought and secured EU membership; both states were driven primarily by domestic and international considerations. EU membership altered the context of relations between successive British and Irish Governments, impinged on relations between the two communities in Northern Ireland and had an impact on strategies for conflict management. There was and remains a significant 'European' dimension to relations between the two islands.

The objective of this chapter is to analyse the dynamic of change in the relationship between these islands in the context of the European Union. Joint membership of the European Union transformed relations between the two states and assisted them in their continuing search for ways of managing and resolving communal conflict in Northern Ireland. Although American diplomacy was central to the path-breaking Good Friday Agreement (1998), the agreement itself owes much to the changing context of statehood in Europe. This chapter explores the 'European' dimension of relations between the United Kingdom and Ireland and then proceeds to analyse the 'European' dimension of conflict resolution and management in Northern Ireland.

Membership of the European Union

Historically, Ireland's search for independence, identity, security, unity and prosperity, the key concerns of Irish nationalism and Irish foreign policy, were for long mediated by what Keatinge called the 'British Isles sub-system', a sub-system characterized by dominance, dependence and 'unequal sovereigns' (Keatinge, 1978, p. 228; Keatinge, 1986). Irish state-seeking nationalism was constructed in the cauldron of the relationship with England and English/British power in Ireland. Joint membership of the EU altered the context of British/Irish relations in a radical manner by providing the Irish economy, polity and society with a highly-institutionalized and rule-bound context within which it could adapt to economic and political internationalization. The importance of joint membership of the EU in altering the relationship was captured by Bertie Ahern at Westminster when he said 'Our joint membership has served as a vital catalyst for the building of a deeper relationship between our two islands'

(Ahern, 2007). The EU system offered a far more benign external environment for small states, including Ireland, than traditional balance of power systems or empire. EU membership enhanced the presence of the Irish state in the European and global arenas and the European market gave the Irish economy the opportunity to diversify and expand beyond the UK. It provided an escape to Irish agriculture from the cheap food policies of the UK, and represented a continental European home for Ireland and engagement with a non-imperial polity that enabled Ireland to move from dominance and dependence to interdependence. The close, contradictory and contested relationship became embedded in a dynamic less claustrophobic environment. The long-term significance of Europe for Ireland was presciently captured by Thomas Kettle, an Economics Professor and poet killed at the battle of the Somme, when he said in 1910 that 'My only counsel to Ireland is that in order to become deeply Irish, she must become European'. Kettle was quoted by the Irish Prime Minister, Jack Lynch, in January 1972 at the signing of Ireland's Treaty of Accession in Brussels.

The formal equality of the British and Irish states in the EU moderated and tamed the asymmetrical relationship between the two countries. Both states became part of an evolving regional polity. In the Union

> the patron–client pattern was dissolved; in the new circumstance British ministers and diplomats could see their Irish counterparts as clever partners in Europe. Without this transformation it is almost impossible to see how Dublin-London relations could have been transformed as they were between the mid-seventies and the mid-eighties. (Kennedy, 1994, p. 177)

The EU offered the Republic an escape from excessive economic dependence on Britain, clearly apparent in the changing geographical pattern of Irish exports. In 1971, the UK market absorbed 61 per cent of Irish exports; the proportion had fallen to 25 per cent by 1998 (McAleese, 2000). Although material considerations played a pivotal role in Ireland's decision to apply for membership, the EU was also a powerful symbol of Ireland's place in the European order as an independent small state with a seat at the table. The significance of this was seen as early as 1975 during Ireland's first Presidency of the Council of Ministers. The European Union became central to the state's official identity, as highlighted by the 1996 Government

White Paper on Foreign Policy, which concluded that

> Irish people increasingly see the European Union not simply as an organisation to which Ireland belongs, but as an integral part of our future. We see ourselves increasingly as Europeans. (Government of Ireland, 1996, p. 59)

Such a statement would be inconceivable in a British, Danish or Swedish White Paper on foreign policy.

EU membership was a project for Ireland's future which also vindicated one of Ireland's strongest traditions, nationalism. Ireland's engagement with Europe was part of a 'very deep longing for an alliance, a friendship that was non-imperial and psychologically satisfying, combined with a culturally determined wish to be self-sufficient and to be true to no one but one's collective self' (Garvin, 2000, p. 37). As was clear in chapter 1, membership of the EU was intimately linked to the national project of modernization. Sharing sovereignty in the EU provided successive Irish governments with a wider range of strategic policy choices than would have been possible if Ireland remained locked into an uneven and dependent relationship with the UK. Within two years of membership, when Britain engaged in a re-negotiation of its terms of membership in 1975, the then Irish Government decided that even if the UK withdrew following the 1975 referendum, Ireland would remain in the Union. Given the history of dependence, this was a remarkable transformation within two years of membership. This was followed by the decision in 1978 to join the EMS without Britain and to join the euro in the first wave. In both these instances, the Irish Government was prepared to adopt a European policy, which had the potential to drive a wedge between the two parts of the island.

The contrasting experiences of the UK and Ireland as members of the EU enabled Ireland to portray itself as an English-speaking but committed European state, an attractive location for foreign direct investment (FDI). It was able to profile itself as a state committed to European integration because there was a very good fit between the EU's policy portfolio and Ireland's interests. There were no major conflicts between Ireland and the Union. This is in stark contrast to the experience of the UK. From the outset, there were battles about the common agricultural policy, the EU budget and European foreign policy. British public opinion has remained sceptical about the benefits of European integration in contrast to attitudes in

Ireland. The United Kingdom found itself opposing the more federal-ist political projects propounded by France and Germany. It remains an outlier in relation to the Euro and cooperation in Justice and Home Affairs. UK reservations about cooperation in the field of jus-tice and law limited the policy options open to Ireland. Given the common travel area with the UK, Ireland was unwilling to join the Schengen system in the absence of the UK. Notwithstanding differ-ences on a number of European policies and on the institutional development of the Union, both states also have shared interests in the Union. Both states are in the liberal rather than protectionist camp in relation to international trade, both are protective of the domestic fiscal regimes and both oppose excessive EU regulation.

Managing the conflict

Membership of the European Union did more than alter the con-text of British–Irish relations. It provided British and Irish ministers and officials with a forum for continuing and intimate contact across a range of public policy issues. EU meetings, particularly European Councils, provided British and Irish Prime Ministers with an informal arena to discuss Northern Ireland at the margins of EU deliberations. Bilateral meetings during European Council sum-mits became such a common occurrence that officials on both sides prepared for them as a matter of routine. In addition to the business content of such meetings, they provided an important opportunity for relationship-building between the heads of govern-ment and senior officials. Informal contact meant that there was never a complete breakdown in communications even when Anglo–Irish relations were at a low ebb. The momentous Milan European Council in 1985 opened the way not only for the Single European Act (SEA), but also the Anglo–Irish Agreement (FitzGerald, 1991, p. 551). Both Governments sought to keep the question of Northern Ireland separate from their relationship in the Union. The Irish Gov-ernment was never tempted to try to raise the issue in the context of European Political Cooperation and devoted far greater diplomatic resources in getting the US actively involved in conflict resolution. The EU was, however, regarded as means of internationalizing the question of Northern Ireland. In addition, given that Northern Ireland was part of the EU as a region of the United Kingdom, European institutions were external parties to the conflict and gradually developed an interest in and a policy approach to the problems of Northern Ireland. EU institutions, particularly the Commission, became very interested in Northern Ireland.

EU involvement in Northern Ireland

During the referendum on EU membership in 1972, there was a naive belief in the Republic that joint membership of the Union would spirit the border away and that European integration would foster Irish unity by stealth. In an integrating Europe, the border would gradually decline in economic and political salience. A 'borderless Europe' implied a 'borderless' Ireland. Such expectations, although understandable, were based on the assumption that the EU was considerably more integrated than in fact it was, and that its development was leading to the creation of a European state. It ignored the imbalance in the Union between its impressive economic power and a much weaker degree of political integration. The disintegration of Europe's traditional nation-states is a continuing theme in discussions of European regionalism. Proponents of a 'Europe of the Regions' saw such a project as offering the prospect of transcending the British and Irish states and thereby providing a lasting solution to the Northern Ireland conflict in a frontier-free Europe (Kearney, 1988). Although regionalism is a growing phenomenon in Europe over the last 20 years, it is unlikely to transcend the traditional nation states as each regionalism is highly contingent on the constitutional and political environment within which it evolves (Laffan, O'Donnell and Smith, 1999, p. 21). Rather than a 'Europe of the Regions', there is an emerging EU polity with regions. Post-Agreement Northern Ireland finds itself in a Europe of growing regional activism and multi-levelled governance.

Some scholarly assessments of the EU role in Northern Ireland have tended to downplay the Union's role and to conclude that the EU was essentially a 'bystander' that had not weakened the conditions of communal conflict (Ruane and Todd, 1996; Teague, 1996). Others argue that it altered relations between the two states and the two communities involved in the conflict (Bew and Meehan, 1994; Hainsworth, 1981; O'Cleirecáin, 1983). The development of an EU dimension can be analysed under four main headings: the EU as a political arena, EU policies and reports on Northern Ireland, the EU as a model of negotiated governance and the EU in Northern Ireland.

The EU as a political arena

The EU was not just an external party to Northern Ireland but an additional arena of politics above the UK and Irish states; Northern Ireland was part of this evolving and increasingly complex layer of politics and economics. Like all of Europe's regions and states, Northern Ireland had interests to represent and public goods to secure in the EU, and as in all political systems voice and representation mattered. Formally, Northern Ireland was represented in the Union's policy process by London-based ministers and civil servants. The UK system for managing EU business was based on the dominance of the 'lead ministry' with highly centralized mechanisms of coordination emanating from the Cabinet Office. This system favoured sectoral ministries rather than the three territorial ministries as they did not have the status as lead ministries in any field. The representation of Northern Irish, Scottish or Welsh interests in the EU Council of Ministers had to pass through the processes of UK preference and interest formation before they reached the table in Brussels, and it has been argued that the UK system did not adequately represent the specific regional interests of the component parts of the UK. Specifically in relation to Northern Ireland, farming and community interests have felt poorly represented by the UK, and Northern Ireland faced the additional problem of not having ministers in the British Cabinet who could argue for its interests in Cabinet debates (Bew and Meehan, 1994).

Concern with the underrepresentation of Northern Ireland in Brussels led to the opening of the Northern Ireland Centre in Europe in 1991. The Office was modelled on the growing number of regional offices found in Brussels, and was a public/private partnership involving the Chamber of Commerce, local authorities, employers, trade unions and voluntary groups. Crucially, it received cross-party support. Both by its activities in Brussels and in Northern Ireland, the Centre provided an example of the way in which the EU experience allowed for the establishment of common ground where the various parties and sectors in society work together to define and pursue a common agenda for Northern Ireland in relation to EU policies. The Centre established a working group involving the key Chief Executives of the Councils and Northern Ireland's members of the Committee of the Regions. One of its projects, the Concordia project, was designed to develop an active social partnership. In November 1998, it organised a four-day working visit for members of the new Northern Ireland Assembly to Brussels. Such developments would be regarded as routine and mundane in most political systems, but were path-breaking in Northern Ireland. The fact that the visit took place at all was regarded by the participants as the beginning of normal politics. The EU agenda and the need to respond to the development of EU policies provided political space and political opportunities for cross-community cooperative and collaborative work. The question of representation in Brussels was re-opened in the context of the evolving constitutional changes in the United Kingdom and to the implementation of the Good Friday Agreement. In 2001, the Office of the First Minister and Deputy First Minister established an office in Brussels which superseded the Northern Ireland Office in Brussels. The office works together with the representative offices of the other devolved authorities in Scotland and Wales.

The absence of direct ministerial representation in Brussels meant that Northern Ireland's three MEPs played a pivotal political role in links to Brussels and in projecting Northern Ireland in Europe. European Parliament (EP) elections provided an electoral contest every five years and an arena within which to conduct party politics. From the first direct elections in 1979 until 2004, Northern Ireland was represented in the European Parliament by two of the giants of Northern Ireland politics, John Hume of the Social, Democratic and Labour Party (SDLP) and Ian Paisley of the Democratic Unionist Party (DUP). The Ulster Unionist Party (UUP) was represented by John Taylor (1979–1984) followed by Jim Nicholson who remains in the Parliament. Ian Paisley was replaced by Jim Allister and the SDLP lost John Hume's seat to Bairbre de Brún of Sinn Féin in 2004 (see Table 9.1). Northern Ireland MEPs collaborate in the European Parliament on policy issues of relevance to Northern Ireland while at the same time differing in their attitudes towards the EU and the role of the EU in Northern Ireland. During the negotiations on the Community Initiatives for 1994–99, considerable work was undertaken in relation to the eligibility of Belfast and Derry for this programme. The creation of the Peace and Reconciliation fund emerged from a Task Force established by Jacques Delors on the prompting of Northern Ireland's three MEPs at the time. Their assistants in the European Parliament worked closely with the Commission on the design of the programme. Given the importance of the agricultural agenda to Northern Ireland, each of the four main parties – UUP, SDLP,

TABLE 9.1 *Results of European elections in Northern Ireland, 1979–2004 (share of the vote in percentages)*

Year	DUP	UUP	Other U	Alliance	Others	SDLP	SF
2004	32	17	0	0	9	16	26
1999	28	18	5	2	0	28	17
1994	29	24	2	4	3	29	9
1989	30	22	5	5	3	25	9
1984	34	21	3	5	2	22	13
1979	30	22	7	7	9	25	

Note: DUP = Democratic Unionist Party; UUP = Ulster Unionist Party; Other U = Other Unionists; SDLP = Social Democratic and Labour Party; SF = Sinn Fein.
Source: www.europarl.europa.eu/elections2004/elections.html.

Sinn Féin and DUP – pay particular attention to this policy area. Cooperation on policy issues cannot, however, disguise divergence on the EU and its role in Northern Ireland.

Party attitudes towards Europe and an EU role in conflict resolution divide along communal lines. Nationalist opinion is generally supportive of European integration, whereas Unionist opinion is far more sceptical. Unionist opinion is in line with British attitudes, whereas nationalist opinion is in line with opinion in the Republic of Ireland, albeit at a somewhat lower level of support (Reinhardt, 1996, p. 10). Among the political parties, the SDLP and the Alliance Party are the most pro-European, and the pro-European stance of the former was largely moulded by John Hume who was personally very engaged by the model of the European Union. When accepting his Nobel Prize for peace, he said:

> In my own work for peace I was very strongly inspired by my European experience. I always tell this story – and I do so because it is so simple yet so profound and so applicable to conflict resolution anywhere in the world. On my first visit to Strasbourg in 1979, as a member of the European Parliament, I went for a walk across the bridge from Strasbourg to Kehl. Strasbourg is in France, Kehl is in Germany. They are very close. I stopped in the middle of the bridge and I meditated. There is Germany. There is France. (10 December 1998, cain.ulst.ac.uk/events/peace/ docs/ nobeljh.htm)

Hume played the European card with considerable skill and used his membership of the EP's Socialist Grouping to garner support for his analysis of the conflict and its resolution. In the EP, Hume successfully appropriated the European agenda and put it to use to promote his analysis of Northern Ireland. The SDLP went furthest in its support for an active EU role in the governance of Northern Ireland. In 1992, the SDLP proposed that the EU Commission should nominate one member of a six-member Commission which would govern Northern Ireland. The proposal found little support from the other political parties, the British Government and the Commission itself (Bew and Meehan, 1994).

Sinn Féin has gradually altered its traditional deep Euro-scepticism and has become engaged with European politics and the European Union. As mentioned in Chapter 4, Sinn Féin opposed Ireland's membership in the 1972 referendum and maintained a robust ideological opposition to the EU up to the early 1990s. The EU was perceived and portrayed as a capitalist club driven by market forces, a power block of the large states, a threat to Irish neutrality and sovereignty (Frampton, 2005, pp. 235–44). Failure to capture a seat in the European Parliament and the support for EU membership among the Irish electorate led to an internal reappraisal of Sinn Féin's attitude to the EU. It remains deeply suspicious of the market dynamic of European integration and not unexpectedly prone to nationalist rhetoric in relation to the dynamic of integration. It defines its approach as 'critical but constructive engagement' designed to reform the EU (Frampton, 2005, 250). The party made a major breakthrough in the 2004 European elections, winning a seat both in the republic and in Northern Ireland. The contradictions in Sinn Féin policy are starkly underlined by their attitude to the euro; having campaigned against the euro in the Maastricht referendum in the Republic, they support its introduction as the currency in Northern Ireland.

Partly because of John Hume's success in the European Parliament, the Unionist parties were defensive about an EU dimension and intergovernmental in their approach to European integration. The UUP favours intergovernmental cooperation among Europe's nation states, but would not support radical federalization which might undermine the United Kingdom and its position in it. The UUP may have developed a more nuanced and less oppositional approach to the EU had it not been for the strident anti-European analysis introduced to the party by Enoch Powell, the right-wing British Conservative Party parliamentarian, famous for his opposition to Commonwealth immigration to Britain and who moved to Northern Ireland and was an Ulster Unionist Member of Parliament from 1974 until 1987. Its large farming supporters benefit from the Common Agricultural Policy. The DUP is fundamentally opposed to the EU, seeing Brussels as part of a wider Roman Catholic plot to control the continent. Both Unionist parties have opposed the political involvement of the EU in Northern Ireland while accepting functional cooperation and European money, if it can be ring-fenced.

EU policies/reports

The EU's role in Northern Ireland evolved on the basis of European policy regimes and functional competence in agriculture, market integration and regional policy; the latter is one of the most visible of the EU's policies in Northern Ireland. The development of a European regional policy was strengthened by the establishment of the European Regional Development Fund (ERDF) in 1975. The Commission from the outset favoured a role for EU regional policy in alleviating obstacles to the economic development of border areas; the Commission wanted to transform Europe's borders from barriers into bridges, and cross-border cooperation formed a central part of the policy in this domain. The Irish Government supported Commission preferences and argued that the non-quota section of the European Regional Development Fund should be used to finance cross-border projects. Once the possibility of such projects was included in the regulations, the EU had a policy instrument to promote such projects in the context of the Irish border, but their development was slow, tortuous and contested.

Attention to the Irish border began with a series of low-key reports outlining the economic problems of the border region and strategies for its development. In the late 1970s, the Londonderry/Donegal Communications Study and the Erne Catchment Area Study were co-financed by the Commission, in addition to a number of programmes for tourism, small business and handicrafts. This was followed by a report on Irish Border Areas by the Economic and Social Committee (ESC) in 1983 which recommended a strengthening of cross-border initiatives and the use of EU budgetary mechanisms to finance such initiatives. In addition to cross-border projects, the Commission recognized Northern Ireland as a region deserving of special treatment (Objective One status) in the context of its regional policy. It ranked, together with the Republic, as a priority area for structural fund monies. In the late 1970s and early 1980s, financial transfers became a critical and enduring feature of the Union's policy towards Northern Ireland. The significance of budgetary instruments owed much to the fact that the Union had a sound treaty basis for involvement in the economic domain and had the carrot of financial transfers to influence the preference and behaviour of local actors.

The visibility and salience of EU policies was enhanced by the reform of the structural funds, analysed in Chapter 6, and their increased financial resources after 1988. The new regulations required the development of an integrated plan covering all sectors which was then submitted to the Commission, which in turn agreed a Community Support Framework (CSF), a package of financial aid over a number of years. The Commission favoured what it called a partnership model for the development of such plans, which implied that there was extensive consultation by government of political parties and societal groups in the establishment of priorities and programmes. Because of the increase in financial resources and the manner of their delivery, the distribution of the funds became politicized with more and more groups seeking involvement in the programming process. Because of the weakness of the political process in Northern Ireland, the civil service and particularly the Department of Finance and Personnel (DFP) dominated the process at the outset. The department came under pressure from the political parties and the Commission to strengthen the consultative process.

A key feature of the reformed fund was a Community Initiative entitled INTERREG which was specifically designed to promote cross-border cooperation and integration. This provided an opportunity to upgrade the relatively low-key cooperation which had been built up during the 1980s. In practice, funding from INTERREG I went to separate projects on either side of the border. The next programming period, 1993–99 required a review of the mechanism for cross-border cooperation, and both the national plan submitted by the Republic to Brussels and the Single Programming Document (SPD) submitted by the authorities in Northern Ireland contained a chapter on cross-border cooperation which identified five priority areas. What is known as the common chapter contained no new initiatives nor were there proposals for enhanced cooperation between

TABLE 9.2 *Phases of Interreg*

INTERREG	Phase	Period	Funding Secured
	I	1991–93	55 million ECUs
	II	1994–99	157 million ECUs
	IIIa	2000–06	182 million euro
	IV	2007–13	At preparatory stage

Source: www.seupb.org.

the two administrations (Kennedy, 1996, p. 61). The experience of implementing the INTERREG II programme did, however, lead to cross-border mobilization in the border region as local politicians and voluntary groups sought to improve cooperation. Three cross-border networks – the North West Cross Border Group, the East Border Committee and the Irish Central Border Area Network – evolved from the 'bottom-up' with a new approach to cross-border cooperation. The networks were determined to develop cross-border cooperation beyond the formal networks establishment by civil servants, and used the new institutions to press their case for an enhanced role in the implementation of INTEREG III and IV (see Table 9.2)

Once EU policies began to impinge on Northern Ireland as a region, it was inevitable that attention would be drawn to the internal conflicts within Ireland. Whereas the Commission and the Council of Ministers restricted their involvement to functional cooperation within the ambit of EU policy regimes, the European Parliament became increasingly involved in debating the political dimensions of the conflict. Between 1981 and 1984, growing attention was paid to political conditions within Northern Ireland by the European Parliament, and, for example, the Maze hunger strike was debated in 1981 and the use of plastic bullets condemned in 1982. This was followed by a major report issued in March 1984, known as the Haagerup Report after the Danish MEP who was the main rapporteur, on the situation in Northern Ireland. The commissioning of a report on Northern Ireland by the Political Affairs Committee of the Parliament was extremely controversial because it raised questions about the blurring of the boundary between what could be considered as the internal affairs of a member state and the competence of the Union. The British Government was extremely unhappy about the report, and the Prime Minister instructed the Conservative MEPs to try to block the commissioning of the report. Unionist politicians were also implacably opposed to the intervention of the EP in the political and constitutional affairs of Northern Ireland.

The resolution which accompanied the report set out the role that the EU should play in relation to Northern Ireland, in addition to views about the perceived role of other actors. The report strongly endorsed an Anglo–Irish framework for the resolution of the conflict as it was replete with references to the need for 'the closest possible co-operation between the United Kingdom and Irish Governments' and 'for expanding and enlarging their mutual co-operation' (Haagerup, 1984, p. 9). Concerning the EU itself, the report highlighted the role of EU expenditure and called on the Commission and the Council of Ministers to develop an integrated plan for the development of Northern Ireland. This was very much in line with what the EU was already doing, notably with respect to the Integrated Programme for Belfast. The political importance of the report should not be underestimated in that it emphasized the importance of Anglo–Irish relations and recognized the interest of the Republic in Northern Ireland. It has been argued that 'the real significance of Haagerup was that it showed the extent to which an essentially nationalist analysis of the problem was being accepted by external neutrals, as was the idea that progress towards a solution lay in the broader Anglo–Irish context' (Kennedy, 1994, p. 179). Since Haagerup, the EU has supported and endorsed all political agreements between Britain and Ireland. The Commission responded to the Anglo–Irish Agreement by creating a Northern Ireland committee in its services which was followed by an EU donation to the Ireland Fund in 1989. Following the ceasefires in 1994, the Commission established a Commission Task Force which designed the Peace and Reconciliation Fund (1995–99), approved by the Essen European Council at the end of 1994. The Berlin European Council in March 1999 agreed to the continuation of the Peace Fund into the subsequent financing period (2000–06).

The EU as a model

The European Union, established as a peace project in the context of Cold War Europe, offered a model of interstate relations that rested on cooperation, interdependence, mutual understanding and civic statehood. Its founding ideology was based on reconciliation and the transformation of neighbours into partners in a collective project. John Hume appropriated the rhetoric of European integration arguing constantly that if conflict on the scale of two world wars could be resolved through dialogue, then so could the conflict in Northern Ireland. In addition to the rhetoric of integration, participation in the EU offered alternative models of politics and political order. First, the iterative and intensive EU Treaty negotiations, with no final settlement in prospect, underlined the adequacy of partial agreement. Second, the investment in the EU in building institutions drew attention to the importance of institutional innovation in promoting collective action and in socializing political actors into new procedures and norms of policy-making. Third, the emphasis in the Union on problem-solving pragmatic politics was a useful antidote to the zero-sum bargaining of politics in Northern Ireland. Fourth, the sharing of sovereignty in the EU highlighted the divisibility of sovereignty in contemporary Europe. The language and style of politics in the EU – partnership, problem-solving, experimentation, innovation, unending negotiations – offered a way of doing things which characterizes the implementation and operation of the Agreement as it becomes a living settlement. The institutions of the Good Friday Agreement outlined below echo a number of the institutional and procedural features of the EU. The d'Hondt system used for the allocation of political offices according to the share of seats in the European Parliament is used for the allocation of ministerial office to the parties in the Northern Ireland Assembly; and the North–South Ministerial Council which meets in plenary and in different sectoral formations is not unlike the Council of Ministers, and meetings of the British and Irish heads of government resemble the European Council.

The EU in Northern Ireland

Membership of the European Union brought Commissioners, their officials and EP groups to Northern Ireland. A number of high-ranking Commission officials, notably Carlo Trojan, former Secretary General of the Commission, was personally very committed to Northern Ireland. The Commission officials who sat on programme-monitoring committees brought with them their experience of different administrative and political systems and could be regarded as neutral in terms of the division between the communities and the two parts of the island. Many Commission officials were active as 'policy entrepreneurs' suggesting new approaches and financing research on future policy strategies. It was a Commission official who persuaded the three cross-border groups that they needed to think of a border strategy that went beyond projects for their bit of the border. With the growing salience of the EU, more and more groups within Northern Ireland became active in transnational projects and in Brussels-based lobbying groups. Knowledge and interest in the EU is expanding beyond the narrow confines of the mandarins in the civil service. The preparation of the Single Programming Document for structural fund finance provided opportunities for the identification of areas of common interest. The Peace and Reconciliation Fund (1995–99) led to the establishment of new mechanisms of cooperation which enabled people to see the potential for cooperation when the dynamic was changed. It was an important validation and endorsement of the ceasefires and created political space for new developments. It forced politicians and wider civil-society groups to take on the responsibility of resource allocation. The Fund was administered by the Northern Ireland Partnership Board which consists of the political parties, the voluntary and community sector, and the social partners. The Board managed the programme which was largely administered by 26 District Partnerships. At local level, there were funding mechanisms which push the political parties towards agreement on resource allocation which in turn promotes effective working mechanisms. Clearly, the performance of the partnerships was patchy and there continues to be tension between the politicians and wider civil-society groups. The Commission regarded the delivery mechanisms and the inclusive nature of the process as a model for mainstream EU funding (Wulf-Mathies, 1998). The Peace Fund was continued following the initial experimental period; a second tranche of finance was made available for the period 2000–06; and the third peace fund runs from 2007 to 2013 (see Table 9.3).

TABLE 9.3   *Northern Ireland peace funds*

Peace I	1995–99	€500 million
Peace II	2000–04 + extension to 2006	€704 million
Peace III	2007–13	€200 million

Source: www.seupb.org.

The Good Friday Agreement

The constitutional settlement embodied in the Good Friday Agree-ment represented a complex set of institutional and political arrangements within Northern Ireland, between North and South and between Britain and Ireland. Important landmarks in the lead-up to the Agreement were the Anglo–Irish Agreement (1985), the Downing Street Declaration (1993) and the Framework Document (1995). The Anglo–Irish Agreement had little EU content other than a reference to the determination of both governments to develop close cooperation as partners in the EU. The 1995 Framework Docu-ment contained a much stronger reference to the EU, and referred to 'an agreed approach for the whole island in respect of the challenges and opportunities of the European Union', to the implementation of EU programmes 'on a cross-border or island wide basis' and to 'joint submissions' to the EU (Paragraph 26, Framework Document, 1995). The Good Friday Agreement itself is replete with references to the European dimension.

Strand one

This strand consisted of an elected Assembly and an Executive Authority headed by a First Minister and Deputy Minister. The duties of the latter consist in part of coordinating the work of the Executive and managing the external relationships of the administration. The December 1998 agreement on the Executive established 11 depart-ments, all of which have a European dimension. Responsibility for European matters was allocated to the Office of the First Minister and Deputy Minister, which coordinates the European briefs of the other departments and has developed relations with a range of EU players. Seamus Mallon, of the SDLP, the first Deputy Minister, appointed two former senior European Commission officials as advi-sors suggesting that the SDLP intended to have a large input into the development of European policy. The UUP had no corresponding expertise at the outset.

Prior to the formation of the Executive, the Department of Finance and Personnel (DFP) had the central coordinating role within the Northern Irish administration. It remains the lead player in developing and negotiating the Community Support Framework and Community Initiatives with the Commission. Because of direct rule,

civil servants in Northern Ireland have had far less political direction in policy development than is the norm in a democratic system
of government. The representation of Northern Ireland's interests
in Europe had to be renegotiated with London, and the model for
Northern Ireland followed the mechanisms that were negotiated
with Edinburgh and Cardiff. Whitehall was determined to maintain overall control of the UK's European policy but had to agree
standard operating procedures with the devolved administrations.
Depending on the political complexion of these administrations, the
relationship on EU affairs may be cooperative or conflictual. The
experience in other countries, notably Germany, Belgium and Spain,
suggests that there might be tensions about EU business.

Strand two

There were a number of references to EU matters in strand two.
First, the North–South Ministerial Council has a remit to consider
the European Union dimension of relevant matters, including the
implementation of EU policies and programmes under consideration
in the EU. Arrangements must be put in place to ensure that the views
of the Council are taken into account and represented appropriately
at relevant EU meetings (Agreement, Strand 2, Paragraph 17). This
was deliberately ambiguous and offered the prospect that the views
of the Council on EU matters may simply be noted by the relevant
channels, or it could mean that, at some future date, members of the
Council might participate in Irish delegations to the Council and its
working parties. If this were to develop, it would have significant
consequences for Ireland's management of EU policy in the long
term. To date, EU business has not impinged that much on the work
of the North–South Ministerial Council, apart from its treatment of
EU-funded programmes.

The second EU dimension in strand two related to the implementation bodies proposed in the Agreement. In the December 1998
agreement on implementation bodies, it was agreed to establish a
body for Special EU Programmes known as SEUPB. The body was
given responsibility for the existing cross-border programmes, the
development of the Community Initiatives in the next programming
period and their implementation. An implementation body on EU
programmes was high on the SDLP's shopping list and was agreed
by the UUP, albeit with reservations.

Cross-border cooperation to date has had a modest impact on co-operation and integration in border regions, and there are three models for the development of cross-border initiatives:

• parallel or back-to-back implementation;
• joint planning but separate implementation; and
• joint planning and implementation.

The implementation of these initiatives were largely characterized by the first model with an attempt to move to model two in the 1994–99 programming period. The implementation body on Special EU Programmes was clearly designed to move the process to the third model with joint planning and implementation.

The Special EU Programmes Body (SEUPB) was established under an Agreement between the Government of Ireland and the Government of Great Britain and Northern Ireland in March 1999 and came into effect on the 2 December 1999. It is directly accountable to the North/South Ministerial Council which in turn is accountable to the Oireachtas and the Northern Ireland Assembly. Its work was hampered in the early period by the suspension of the Executive, but in the latter half of 2000 it began the slow process of establishing itself in the institutional landscape of Northern Ireland the Republic. In its first year of operation its chief executive and his deputy resigned leading to considerable instability in the organization. The SEUPB found itself at the confluence of a number of different changes – regionalization in the Republic, changes in the EU guidelines on cross-border cooperation, the evolution of the new institutions and 'bottom-up' mobilization in the border region (Laffan and Payne, 2001).

Strand three

The EU dimension to strand three manifested itself in the agreement that EU matters were suitable for discussion by the British–Irish Council. Moreover, the stipulation that two or more members were free to develop bilateral or multilateral arrangements encouraged the development of political and policy links between Dublin, Cardiff and Edinburgh, and will act as an additional spur to the Ireland–Wales INTERREG programme. The development of multiple relations between the component parts of the two islands might, over time, lead to 'these islands' emerging as a sub-system in the

TABLE 9.4   *Northern Ireland Assembly elections*

	DUP	UUP	Alliance	Others	SDLP	Sinn Féin
Seats won (2007)	36	18	7	3	16	28
Vote share (2007)	30.1%	14.9%	5.2%	8.0%	15.2%	26.2%
Seats won (2003)	30	27	6	3	18	24
Vote share (2003)	25.6%	22.7%	3.7%	7.5%	17.0%	23.5%

EU, not unlike the Benelux, Franco-German relations and Nordic Cooperation. Enlargement to the East and the addition of many more states will in any case promote the growth of more sub-system groupings in the EU.

The implementation of the Agreement proved tortuous. Following a short suspension in the immediate aftermath of the establishment of the new institutions, a long-term suspension began in October 2002 because of serious differences on a number of issues among the parties in Northern Ireland. The suspension was not ended until May 2007 when a new Assembly was elected and the Good Friday institutions were re-established (Table 9.4). During this time, a major shift in the electoral fortunes of the key parties occurred. The two centrist parties lost out to the DUP on the Unionist side and Sinn Féin on the nationalist side, and Ian Paisley of the DUP was elected as First Minister and Martin McGuinness of Finn Féin was elected as Deputy First Minister. Once the institutions within Northern Ireland were established, meetings under strands two and three of the agreement took place.

Conclusions

This chapter has analysed the dynamic role that joint membership of the European Union has played in the changing relations between Britain and Ireland and North and South. In the period since then, the Irish state and its political elite continued to grapple with the dilemmas of British–Irish relations and the continuing conflict in Northern Ireland. The Good Friday Agreement concluded in April

1998 and subsequent legislation went a long way towards providing a constitutional settlement for conflict management if not conflict resolution, in Northern Ireland. Its achievement showed just how far British–Irish relations had evolved and developed since the trauma of 1968/69. Tony Blair's address to the Oireachtas in November 1998 and Bertie Ahern's speech at Westminster in May 2007 symbolized just how much the relationship had changed since both states joined the EU in 1973.

The outbreak of communal conflict in Northern Ireland coincided with accession negotiations to the EU and subsequent membership. Without the embeddedness of both states in the wider system of European integration and without the model of politics offered by the EU, it is unlikely that both states and other political actors could have found the political capacity and the institutional models to craft the Good Friday Agreement. The EU made an essential contribution to the changing relations between Britain and Ireland and to conflict management in Northern Ireland.

Constitutional change within Great Britain – the devolution project – has brought Britain's constitution into the main stream of contemporary European governance. Adshead and Bache (2000) distinguish between regionalization – 'the process leading to enhanced governing capacity at the regional level' – on the one hand, and regionalism – 'bottom-up movements seeking to strengthen regional governance in order to develop or support their own political, cultural and/or economic autonomy within the wider state system', on the other hand. At its most basic, *regionalization* might simply be the territorial division of state for administrative purposes, where the boundaries of these territories have no defining historical or cultural characteristic. *Regionalism*, in contrast, is a process driven by local aspirations, and a sense of regional identity. Prior to devolution, Britain was the last remaining large European state that had not experimented with devolution, regionalization and regionalism.

The institutions established by the Good Friday Agreement involving as they do two sovereign states in addition to sub-state entities is different in kind to the other processes of change on the archipelago. It is also different in kind to the structures and processes of cross-border cooperation found on other European borders. On Europe's settled and uncontested borders, cross-border cooperation, if institutionalized, is animated by local and regional actors without the involvement of the central state. The institutions of the Good Friday Agreement, particularly in the North–South and

East–West context, accord a significant role to the governments. In addition, however, the Agreement allows for the development of institutional nodes and networks on the Irish border and in an all-island context provided that the implementation bodies succeed in embedding themselves in the wider frame of governance. The British Irish Council also has the potential to enhance the breath and depth of sub-state policies between Dublin, Edinburgh and Cardiff. Membership of the EU, constitutional change within Great Britain and between Ireland and the United Kingdom pushed territorial politics in the direction of multi-levelled governance, although not what might be described as European regionalism if by that is meant a hollowing-out of the power of the central state. The exercise of state sovereignty has been transformed but not transcended by membership of the EU. The same might be said of the change processes on the two islands of Ireland and Britain.

Chapter 10

Ireland as a Model?

As Ireland strove for economic development and modernization during the postwar period, it often looked to other European states for inspiration about policy or institutional design, and the Nordic states and the Netherlands were frequently invoked as models, the source of ideas and as ideals that Ireland should seek to emulate. Now that Ireland succeeded in achieving economic convergence and catch-up, it in turn is invoked as a model for other states in Europe and more widely. The transformation in Ireland's status may be grasped symbolically by the changing image of Ireland portrayed on the cover of *The Economist*. The 1988 country report on Ireland depicted a mother with a young child on her lap begging on the streets of Dublin with the caption *Poorest of the rich*. This association of Ireland with poverty was replaced in 1997 by one in which the cover depicted the Republic in a map of Europe as *Europe's shining light*. That transformation was not anticipated. A report by the National Economic and Social Council (NESC) in 1981 on Ireland's socio-economic position within the EEC concluded that 'At the national level Ireland is the poorest and least developed of the nine Member States. At the regional level the two most disadvantaged areas are Ireland and the Mezzogiorno' (NESC, 1981, p. 65). The report argued that it was highly unlikely that Ireland would attain continental European living standards over the subsequent decades; there was nothing in Ireland's experience of membership to suggest that 'catch-up' might happen. Just before economic take-off in 1992, a group of Irish academics published a volume whose title was framed as a question, *Is Ireland a Third World Country?* (Caherty *et al.*, 1992). Yet by June 2005, Thomas Friedman, writing for the *New York Times*, opened his article with the line 'Here's something you probably didn't know: Ireland today is the richest country in the European Union after Luxembourg' (*New York Times*, 29 June 2005), and *Le Monde* portrayed Ireland as 'le meilleur élève de l'économie européenne' in January 2006 (*Le Monde*, 24 January 2006). The Irish were not used

219

to receiving plaudits of this kind; in the 1970s and 1980s the annual reviews of the Irish economy at the OECD had been sombre affairs as Finance Ministry officials attempted to account for Ireland's dismal economic performance.

More rapidly than could have been anticipated or imagined, the small island on Europe's western seaboard was transformed from laggard to leader, from 'basket-case' economy to model in less than a decade. Since 2000, the journal *Foreign Affairs* has published an annual Globalization Index measured on the basis of 12 variables organized into four broad categories, namely, economic integration, personal contact, technological connectivity, and political engagement. In 2001 and 2002, Ireland was ranked as the most globalized country in the world. By 2006, it had fallen to fourth place, still extraordinarily high, a position that was based on a ranking of fourth on the economic dimension, second in terms of personal contacts, seventh in the ranking on political engagement and fourteenth under the rubric of technological connectivity. In the 2006 index, Ireland was the most open of all of the European economies (see Table 10.1).

The 'Celtic Tiger' phenomenon invoked considerable interest outside Ireland from Governments, ministries, media, research organizations and academics. Traditionally interest in Ireland and things Irish was triggered by the nineteenth-century emergence of modern Irish nationalism, the battle to found an independent state and the Gaelic revival of language and literature. Ireland's claims to distinctiveness were cultural and literary rather than economic and

TABLE 10.1   *The A.T. Kearney* Foreign Affairs *globalization index*

	Economic	Personal contact	Technological connectivity	Political engagement	2006 overall rank	2005 overall rank
Ireland	4	2	14	7	4	2
Denmark	8	8	5	6	5	7

Notes: Economic: trade and FDI, Personal contact: telephone, travel, remittances and personal transfers, Technological connectivity: internet users, internet hosts, secure servers, Political engagement: international organizations, UN peacekeeping, treaties, government transfers.
Source: The Global Top 20, *Foreign Affairs*, A.T. Kearney, 2006, www.atkearney.com/shared_res/pdf/Globalization-Index_FP_Nov-Dec-06_S.pdf.

material. Yeats, Joyce and Beckett were and remain internationally celebrated, but what made Ireland interesting, however, in the last decade of the twentieth century and the first decade of the twenty-first was the performance of the Irish economy. Ryan Air, Europe's leading low-cost air carrier, and Riverdance a touring company of Irish dancers and musicians, have joined older emblems of things Irish. The political, cultural and social consequences of the Irish experience of globalization are the subjects of a growing academic literature (Foster, 2007; Inglis, 2008; O'Sullivan, 2007; O'Toole, 2003). What are the ingredients that contributed to Ireland's economic performance? What lessons, if any, can be learnt and emulated? Was there an Irish model of economic development?

Countries as diverse as New Zealand, Canada, Singapore and Trinidad and Tobago interrogated the Irish experience to draw lessons for their own economic development. Typical of this genre was a volume entitled *Foreign Investment, Development, and Globalization: Can Costa Rica become Ireland?* (Paus, 2005). Interest in Ireland extended to states within the USA as a long line of delegations made their way to Dublin to explore the Celtic Tiger phenomenon; states as diverse as Michigan, Georgia and West Virginia became interested in different dimensions of Ireland's economic performance. Notwithstanding the extraordinary divergence in terms of size, Chinese official visitors to Ireland displayed a pronounced interest in Ireland's system of social partnership and regional development (*Business World*, 31 October 2006). Alongside the global interest in Ireland, the new EU member states in East Central Europe exhibited the most sustained interest. Just before the accession of the 10 new member states in May 2004, *The Economist* suggested that 'For anyone talking to politicians from the new member states will know the refrain: "We want to be like Ireland"' (*The Economist*, 17 April, 2004). The Irish Government offered extensive pre-accession assistance and training to officials from the candidate states. The Irish Foreign Minister, Brian Cowen, speaking to the Joint Oireachtas European Affairs Committee in 2004 said that 'many of the new member states and candidate countries see Ireland as a model, and they are particularly interested in learning from our experiences' (Joint Oireachtas European Affairs Committee Debate, 6 July 2004).

Why should this be so? There are two compelling reasons. First, Ireland is to date the only poor state that has actually converged with the richer parts of Europe. Although Spain, Portugal and Greece have experienced high growth rates and are converging, they have not yet caught up. Second, the Irish economic boom occurred after the collapse of communism as the states in East Central Europe were undergoing the transition from command economies to the market. As they looked at Western Europe, the Celtic Tiger appeared to have succeeded in managing economic liberalization. In addition, links between Ireland and the new member states have been under-pinned by the extent of migration from the new member states to Ireland after membership in May 2004. An open labour market and extensive job opportunities deepened the ties between the former communist states and Ireland.

In exploring just what kind of model Ireland provides in this era of globalization, three dimensions are analysed. First, from the perspective of the first decade of the twenty-first century, it is understandable that the focus is on Ireland's economic transformation but the failure to catch-up in the 1970s and 1980s is also worthy of examination. It took Irish policy-makers, trade unionists and business leaders a long and tortuous period to learn to live with internationalization. Irish society experienced considerable strain in the first half of the 1980s when it was confronted with economic dislocation and contestation about abortion and divorce. Indeed, Ireland's experience in the 1970s and 1980s provide important lessons on how not to handle internationalization. Second, Ireland's distinctive balance between labour-market flexibility, social partnership and foreign investment is worthy of exploration. And, third, the Good Friday Agreement although designed as a model of conflict-management in Northern Ireland and on the island of Ireland may provide lessons on the constitutional and political dynamics that mediate communal conflict.

Model I: what not to do

The fact that by the end of the 1990s, Ireland was perceived and widely touted as a success story of the European Union and for European integration should not obscure the weak performance of the Irish economy in the late 1970s and 1980s. The core–periphery critique of the EU offered by the Labour party in the 1972 referendum resonated with the performance of the Irish economy in the decade following membership, when thousands of jobs were lost in traditional industry and company closures were commonplace. Ireland experienced nothing less than a profound economic, political and social crisis in that period. Three rapid elections in 1981–82, a number of highly contentious referendums on social and moral issues and a prolonged depression served to undermine confidence in Ireland's ability to prosper in the evolving European political economy. Ireland's approach to managing the liberalization associated with EU membership and the dynamic of integration was severely tested. During the 1980s, Ireland's economic performance was worse than that of the other member states of the Union on most dimensions, and by 1987 the debt/GNP ratio amounted to 150 per cent and budget deficits were more than 8 per cent of GDP. The long-term solvency of the state was at issue and fears of the arrival of the IMF to impose solutions were part of the day-to-day discussion among Finance Ministry officials at this time.

The OECD country report of 1987–88 provides stark reading. In that report, the rise of unemployment from 6 per cent to 19 per cent was underlined as was the deterioration in the public finances noted above. Emigration, so long a characteristic of Irish experience, re-emerged as young qualified Irish people sought prosperity elsewhere. Living standards and investment were on a downward trajectory and were coupled with rising taxation as the government struggled to bring the fiscal crisis under control. Notwithstanding tough policies, Ireland's efforts at stabilization in the 1980s failed (Dornbusch, 1989, p. 173). Electoral pressures in the early 1980s served to reinforce a damaging public policy and public finance mix, and government instability fuelled a vicious circle of poor economic and public finance performance that in turn generated damaging social outcomes.

Analysis of failure rather than success was the dominant narrative in academic and popular writings on Ireland during this period. Fintan O'Toole, a leading public intellectual, captured the spirit of the time in a volume entitled *Black Hole, Green Card; The Disappearance of Ireland* (1994). The causes of Ireland's failure were traced to the legacy of colonialism and emigration, dependency, political structures, Catholicism, and even the character of the Irish themselves (Inglis, 1998; O'Hearn, 1989; Garvin, 1992; Crotty, 1986; and Lee, 1989). Joe Lee's 1989 volume *Ireland 1912–1985* was relentlessly pessimistic. He laid considerable emphasis on the prevalence of a 'possessor ethic' rather than a 'performer ethic' in Ireland, and concluded that 'It is difficult to avoid the conclusion that Irish economic performance has been the least impressive in Western Europe, perhaps in all of Europe, in the twentieth century (Lee, 1989, p. 521). Garvin writing in 1992 asked if Ireland had the cultural and institutional capacity to overcome the crisis.

By 1987, the intensity of the Irish crisis prompted in-depth analysis of the different dimensions of the problem and a conceptualization of what was required to break out of the vicious circle of the 1980s. The National Economic and Social Council, an advisory body to government consisting of the key economic players, senior public officials and a number of independent members provided the key forum for the diagnosis of the patient and the therapy that was required. The NESC Secretariat produced a report on a *Strategy for Development* which provided the policy framework for a new social pact involving the key economic actors and the Government, entitled *Programme for National Recovery* (1987). The political underpinning was provided by the new Fianna Fáil Government that took office in June 1987 and the strategy was supported by the main opposition party, Fine Gael. A national consensus emerged in an effort to address the pervasive economic and social malaise. In 1989, the NESC produced a major analysis of Ireland's experience of European integration and membership of the EU (NESC, 1989). A key message from the NESC analysis was the importance of constructing a domestic policy framework that went with the grain of the international political economy. The important lesson from the Irish experience of the 1980s was that globalization and Europeanization made domestic policies and the behaviour of domestic economic actors more, not less, significant (Laffan and O'Donnell, 1998). Poor domestic policy-making contributed significantly to Ireland's failure to catch up in the 1980s (Barry, 2003, p. 8), and a continuation of poor public finances, rent-seeking and the short-term behaviour of the 1980s would militate against Ireland's prospects of catch-up and future prosperity. Understanding the constraints on a small open economy was a key lesson of this period. The analysis and subsequent actions enabled Ireland to break out of the vicious circle and create the conditions for a virtuous circle that promoted economic recovery and growth in the 1990s.

Model II: economic catch-up

The broad facts of the transformation of the Irish economy are well-known. From 1993 to 2001, very high rates of growth (8 to

10 per cent) enabled Ireland to catch up with its richer European neighbours, and, thereafter, Irish incomes began to outpace those of the core. In 1986, Ireland's GDP per capita was 65.9 per cent of the EU average. This had risen to 122 per cent by 2002. High growth rates were accompanied by a dramatic reduction in the level of unemployment from 17 per cent to less than 4 per cent and a marked expansion in the numbers at work in Ireland. Young people, women, returning migrants and later non-Irish emigrants flooded into the Irish labour market. The numbers at work increased more than 50 per cent (Barry, 2003, p. 10). Fiscal consolidation and buoyant tax receipts transformed the debt/GDP ratio from 150 per cent in 1987 to 26 per cent in 2006. In 1990, the Government established a debt-management agency outside the Finance Ministry as part of its strategy to bring the national debt under control.

Analysts of the Irish experience from the late 1980s onwards agree in broad outline on the ingredients of Ireland's success, but differ in the salience they accord to any one factor. For the purposes of this exploration of the Irish model, a distinction is drawn between internal and external factors, and within that a further distinction between long-term and more proximate factors is identified. Rather than privileging any one factor, the argument here is that the Irish experience in the 1990s was a fusion of a number of factors that, when combined, served to produce the economic miracle. While there is general agreement on the factors that contributed to the Irish boom, there are deep differences on its consequences and on the weight attached to the different factors (Allen, 2000, 2007; Kirby, 2002; O'Hearn, 1998; Smith, 2002, 2006; O'Riain, 2000; Fahey *et al.*, 2007). It is also clear that there was a complex interaction between domestic, European, US and global factors.

Internal factors: long-term

Four long-term domestic factors contributed to the economic transformation. These were the consistency of Ireland's industrial policy and strategy from the end of the 1950s onwards, sustained investment in education that began in the 1960s, the dominance of English as the spoken language, and the severity of the shakeout of indigenous companies in the 1970s and 1980s. The decision at the end of the 1950s to pursue export-led economic growth and to create the domestic conditions favourable to foreign direct investment was pursued by successive governments from that time onwards. A sophisticated institutional infrastructure in the public service designed to attract investment was put in place, complemented by favourable taxation policies and incentives for industrial development. The continuity of policy, the openness to foreign capital and the absence of any serious political contestation around the core of the strategy is related in some measure to the centrist nature of Irish politics. The political spectrum in Ireland is relatively narrow and the relative weakness of the left in electoral terms is a feature of Irish electoral history. The Irish Labour Party always lagged behind the two centrist parties, Fianna Fáil and Fine Gael, in electoral performance, and the dominance of these two large 'catch-all parties' brought politics to the centre. When in power parties of the left never contested the key features of Ireland's development strategy.

Investing in education was an important feature of this strategy. In the mid-1960s, the Irish Government engaged in an in-depth analysis of the Irish educational system with the assistance of the OECD. This led to the publication of a path-breaking report *Investment in Education* in 1965 which showed that over half of Irish children left education at or before the age of 13 (Barry, 2005, p. 9). The report provided the rationale for a major investment in secondary and tertiary education and the development of new vocationally and technologically oriented colleges, the Regional Technical Colleges (RTCs). From the mid-1960s onwards there was a dramatic increase in the numbers of young people staying in secondary school and entering the changing and expanding tertiary system. The introduction of free secondary education accompanied by subsidized school transport, widened educational access and provided a pipeline of students for higher education (Clancy, 1996). In 1965 there were 21,000 students in higher education when the OECD report was published, but when the 2005 OECD report on Ireland's System of Higher Education was published that number had grown to 137,000 (Higher Education Authority, 2005). The technological character of the RTCs, renamed Institutes of Technology (ITs), and the expansion of science and engineering in the universities ensured that Ireland was educating more science and engineering graduates than other European countries (Barry, 2005, p. 8). Financial flows from the European Social Fund (ESF) to the then vocational training agency (ANCO) and the RTCs following EU membership in 1973 had a major impact on the financing of education and vocational training. Investment in education across the three levels persisted even in the 1980s, notwithstanding the pressure on public finances. Priority was placed on increasing the number of graduates in electronics and software as these were seen as sectors of future growth. In 1984, however, in the case of one of Ireland's universities, all graduates in electronic engineering emigrated as there were no jobs for them in Ireland (Flinter, 2005). The 'brain drain' was costly to the Irish public purse, but it was those graduates who returned in the 1980s with extensive international experience that fuelled the boom of the 1990s. The quality and character of the Irish education system was an important attraction to multinational companies as they decided on the European location of their plants. The fact that the products of that educational system spoke English was also an attraction to US investors in particular.

From the time Ireland opted for an outward-looking develop-ment strategy, the economy began to change in a dramatic manner. The openness of the economy increased; exports increased from 38 per cent of the GDP in 1972 to 67 per cent in 1989, and the his-torical dependence on the UK market declined (O'Donnell, 1998, p. 6). The shift in the destination of exports was accompanied by a significant change in the composition of Ireland's trade. Tradi-tional industries such as food, drink and tobacco were overtaken by chemicals and engineering products (*ibid.*), and foreign-owned export-oriented industries prospered whereas those industries depen-dent on the domestic market declined. So, too, did industries such as textiles, food products, motor vehicles and parts, and footwear (*ibid.*). In fact large sectors of the traditional manufacturing base were wiped out in the 1980s. The extent of the adjustment meant, however, that those that survived were ready to take advantage of the opportunities of the developing EU internal market. The severity of the recession in the 1980s meant that Irish companies had weath-ered the worst of the adjustment pressures imposed by the opening of the economy.

Internal factors: proximate

The depth of the crisis facing Ireland in 1986/87 created the condi-tions for a re-assessment of where Ireland was going and facilitated the search for ways out of the crisis. The search for ideas began in the National Economic and Social Council (NESC) which produced a compelling analysis and the case for change, their report *Strategy for Development* concluding that the lack of economic growth was the central problem that in turn contributed to chronic unemployment and the crisis in public finances. The social partners began to accept the parameters of a new agreement and this was nurtured by the Taoiseach, Charles Haughey and his department. Talks involving the state, trade unions and employers' organizations began in October 1987, and concluded with a three-year agreement entitled *Programme for National Recovery* (PNR), the first of seven agreements. The key bargain at the heart of the PNR was wage restraint on the part of the trade unions in return for tax reductions and a number of other social provisions. Tax cuts rather than wage increases have accounted for about a third of the growth of take-home pay since the partnership process began (Barry, 2003, p. 13). The Irish system of social partnership was not modelled on North European neo-corporatism; rather, in the shadow of the crisis, a process of analysis, problem-solving and consensus-building evolved that took roots in the Irish system of public policy. According to one assessment, 'social partnership and the integrated approach have been part of the culture of the new Ireland. This innovative form of governance underlies the Irish turnaround' (House and McGrath, 2004, p. 29).

The system is characterized by a number of core features that have evolved in a flexible manner though a continuous process of deliberation and bargaining. The first characteristic is the *strategic* nature of the deliberations among the partners (House and McGrath, 2004). Prior to each partnership deal, the NESC evaluates the experience of the previous agreement, analyses the overall public policy and political economy dynamics, and sets out the broad parameters that should inform the agreement. This process facilitates the emergence of a shared understanding among the economic actors and the representatives of the state of key challenges and priorities (O'Donnell, 1998, p. 19). Part of that understanding, from the outset, was the importance of a shared policy framework that facilitated Irish competitiveness and prosperity in a globalized and interdependent economy. That understanding also focused on the domestic supply-side policies that were the responsibility of the Irish state (*ibid.*, p. 15). It is suggested by one of the key participants in promoting inward investment, that 'Without that shared understanding and trust, the commitment necessary to gain broad public support to deal with the difficulties that would have to be encountered and managed could not have been garnered' (Flinter, 2005).

The second characteristic of the partnership model was its *inclusive* or *encompassing* nature; it was inclusive in the range of economic and societal actors that were drawn into the process over successive agreements. Beginning with the trade unions and employers' organizations, it expanded to involve the farmers, and a wide range of civil-society organizations representing those who were excluded or poorly engaged in economic and social life. It was inclusive and encompassing also in the range of public policies that came within the remit of its deliberations (O'Donnell, 1996, p. 19).

The third characteristic of the Irish model of social partnership was the manner in which it became *institutionalized* within the system of public policy-making. The preparations for each successive agreement follow a pattern of well-established processes, beginning with the NESC analysis, and then followed by an iterative process of negotiations. A Central Review Committee (CRC) was established to monitor the implementation of the agreement in 1987 and that has become part of successive agreements. The NESC through its analytical role in the partnership process has interrogated the processes and mechanisms of social partnership so that the participants have a highly developed sense of what they are trying to achieve. The key to agreement on seven successive programmes since 1987 rests heavily on the problem-solving approach adopted by the participants, which in turn is heavily dependent on shared understandings of the challenges facing the Irish economy and society. Hence the different preferences and interests of the participants are contained in a manner that allows for trade-offs and 'win–win' outcomes for the social partners. The government and state therefore play a central role in the partnership process; they provide the arena for negotiations and the legitimacy of office to the process. In addition, the Government has resources in terms of public finance to lubricate the process. The partnership process has been characterized by considerable consensus in public policy circles in Ireland although a number of liberal economists have continued to highlight potential problems with the process and outcomes (O'Donnell, 1998, p. 15). House and McGrath (2004) suggest that the Irish system of social partnership can 'serve as a model, with appropriate modification tailor-made to each case, for other jurisdictions hoping to emulate Ireland's success'.

A key feature of Irish industrial policy from 1960 onwards was a taxation and fiscal regime that was attractive to foreign direct investment. A zero rate for corporation tax on exports was decided in 1960, that subsequently increased to 10 per cent. This became a highly contested issue in the EU and among Ireland's partner countries, and very difficult and conflictual set of negotiations between

Ireland and the EU took place in the 1990s concerning Ireland's rate of corporation tax. The Commission found that the 10 per cent rate as it applied only to foreign companies was discriminatory and hence had to be re-negotiated. Following extensive negotiations between the Commission and Ireland, agreement was reached on a level of 12.5 per cent for all companies, which meant a significant reduction in the rate of corporate tax for non-foreign companies. The low rate of corporation tax provided an increasingly large tax take for the Irish exchequer through the 1990s as the corporate sector expanded. Between 1990 and 1998, revenues from corporation tax grew by over 350 per cent in Ireland (Murphy, 2000, p. 21). In 1997 the Government proceeded to reduce the level of capital gains tax from 40 per cent to 20 per cent – a massive reduction. This was a signal that wealth-creation in Ireland would be rewarded, and it also contributed to enhancing the entrepreneurial potential of the society. Ireland has therefore become a low taxation economy from the beginning of the 1990s.

A crucial factor in the Irish economic miracle was the buoyant nature of the Irish labour market in the 1990s; there was a supply of skilled flexible workers to take up the opportunities offered by economic growth. The workforce grew by a half as young people, the unemployed, women and returning emigrants were available for the jobs that were being created in the Irish economy. The Irish birthrate was high by European standards in the 1970s, and the products of the baby boom were emerging from the Irish educational system in the 1990s, just as job opportunities were expanding. The participation rate of women in the labour force has been very low by European standards in Ireland, but as job opportunities opened up, women opted to participate actively in the labour market and female participation increased from 1987 to 2001. Ireland's high rate of unemployment in the 1980s and the early years of the 1990s meant that there was a pool of people waiting for improved work opportunities and, once the economy took off, long-term unemployment was reduced progressively. Finally, the labour force benefited from the returning emigrants who returned to Ireland in the 1990s, bringing with them the skills and experience they had garnered overseas. The expansion of jobs and those working had the added benefit of greatly reducing the dependency ratios in Ireland. According to a former Prime Minister, Garrett FitzGerald, Ireland's ability to catch up 'during the Celtic Tiger years owed everything to a happy timing coincidence between the period of peak demand by foreign industry for Irish labour in Ireland and a parallel peak in the availability of Irish labour' (FitzGerald, 2007, p. 16).

External factors: long-term

Membership of the European Union in 1973 was a necessary but not sufficient condition for economic catch-up. Accession consolidated the industrial policy and economic strategy embarked on from 1958 onwards, and embedded Ireland in an integrating market that gave its producers access to the growing European market. That market was also crucial to the US multinationals that opted to locate in Ireland in the 1970s. Membership led to diversification from the UK as the primary export market, and the common agricultural policy led to significant transfers from the European budget from the outset as farm output and incomes grew. From 1979 onwards, membership of the EMS, a decision that broke the link between the Irish pound and sterling brought the Irish economy within the influence zone of the Bundesbank and its preference for sound public finances. During the 1980s, this decision contributed to squeezing inflation out of the Irish economy but at the expense of high unemployment. The experience of the 1980s prepared Ireland for participation in the single currency, unlike its UK neighbour. The Irish state elite adopted a *communautaire* approach to membership of the EU and adapted to membership with less difficulty than either the UK or Denmark, the other two states.

External factors: proximate

When the single market project was launched in the mid-1980s there was considerable disquiet in Ireland concerning the prospects of Irish companies when faced with the liberalizing European market. Economic performance at that time did not augur well for Ireland's ability to benefit from the 1992 process. However, contrary to expectations, the process of liberalization benefited Europe's peripheral and poorer states. A key feature was the liberalization of public procurement as part of the single market project, which meant that the larger EU countries could not use public procurement as a means of influencing the location decisions of foreign companies (Barry, 2003, p. 15). This had operated to Ireland's disadvantage previously (MacSharry and White, 2000). Two other consequences of the single market worked to Ireland's advantage in this period.

First, the single market and fears of Fortress Europe led to a major expansion of US investment in Europe in this period. Ireland's industrial strategy was designed to attract mobile foreign investment, and an expanding volume of FDI provided a winning environment for Ireland's highly sophisticated infrastructure for attracting overseas investment. Second, agreement to the Single European Act, the constitutional framework for the internal market, necessitated a side-payment to Europe's poorer regions. The side-payment came in the form of a doubling of the resources in the EU budget for the structural funds by 1992, and a doubling of the transfers from those funds to the cohesion countries, including Ireland, by 1993.

Ireland for a variety of reasons proved highly attractive to US FDI in the period following 1989. US investment doubled in Europe but quadrupled in Ireland. The decision by Intel to locate a major chip-manufacturing plant in Ireland in 1989 was a harbinger of the expansion of US capital in Ireland, and Intel was joined by Dell, Microsoft, Boston Scientific and a host of other high-tech companies. The impact of FDI may be gleaned from the expansion of employment in foreign-owned firms from 92,000 in 1995 to 129,000 in 2004 (Flinter, 2005). In 1997, despite its small size, Ireland ranked fifth in the world as a destination for US investment (Murphy, 2000, p. 15). Why did Ireland benefit disproportionally from American investment? Low corporate tax, a buoyant labour market and skilled workers all played their part. Murphy argues that 'Ireland with its low corporate tax rates, its young English-speaking and increasingly computer-literate workforce, along with its full participation in Europe through the Single European Market and the European Monetary Union, was ideally positioned to act as a pontoon linking the US high-tech companies to the European Union' (Murphy, 2000, p. 16). The role of the Industrial Development Authority (IDA) was crucial in managing to attract such a large proportion of mobile US investment. According to a long-term participant in attracting investment, Ireland 'had to rewrite the rules of the game and needed to manage the process of securing inward investment as a business process and not only as an economic development process' (Flinter, 2005). It sought first-mover advantage or opportunities that were not being identified elsewhere. Hence, Ireland identified the significance of software companies in the 1980s, call centres and financial services in the 1990s, and bio-pharmaceuticals in the first decade of the twenty-first century. It benefited from the demonstration effect as companies followed others in their sectors into Ireland, particularly in the engineering, computer, pharmaceutical and chemical sectors (Barry, 2003, p. 15). US investment created high-quality jobs and generally increased the managerial competence of the business sector.

The surge in investment coincided with the significant expansion of structural funds for the poorer European states. The Delors I plan launched in Ireland in 1989 was designed to double the funding flowing into Ireland and the other cohesion countries. The increase in aid allocations from 1989 onwards was a major priority of the Irish government, who closely monitored and sought to influence the regulations governing the funds and created a high-level group chaired by the Taoiseach to prepare Ireland's first national development plan. The structural funds held out the prospect of investment in the long-term future of the economy following the need to stabilize public finances. It reversed the trend of disinvestment by the state in the economy. Moreover, key features of the governance of the funds served to alter the processes of Irish public policy. Multi-annual planning and budgeting was new to the Irish system and provided a necessary long-term strategic impetus to planning. The emergence of monitoring committees for the plan as a whole and its sectoral components, in addition to the need for continuous evaluation, added a much needed deliberative element to Irish public policy. Gradually the significance of monitoring and evaluating public investment took root, and the presence of Commission officials on the monitoring committees added new perspectives to the domestic system. Commission officials, with long-term experience of Ireland, were able to contribute a critical voice concerning the use of EU monies, and the emphasis placed by the Commission on regional and local development supported the emergence of a stronger spatial dimension to Irish development.

In the decade from 1989 to 1999, European aid amounted to approximately 3 per cent of GDP per annum, a very significant transfer to Ireland (Barry, 2003, p. 13). The financial flows from the structural funds facilitated significant investment in the country's physical infrastructure, notably roads, telecommunications, public transport and ports. In addition, Ireland used structural-fund monies to invest in people through training and education. Economists argue that the direct effects of European aid were modest but that the indirect effects were significant. The change in public policy identified above was one of those indirect effects. Funding for R&D, human capital and primary infrastructure reinforced Ireland's policy of attracting foreign direct investment.

Boston or Berlin?

There is considerable debate and contestation about the relative weight of European and US influences on the Irish economy and society (Allen, 2007, pp. 236–7; Foster, 2007, pp. 32–3). Ireland embraced globalization, but just what kind of globalization? A speech by the leader of the Progressive Democrats and then Minister for Entreprise, Trade and Development, Mary Harney, in July 2000 prompted a debate in Ireland about its relationship with the EU and the character of its engagement with the global political economy. Minister Harney in her speech was critical of the regulatory zeal of the EU and there was a palpable unease about the prospect that 'key economic decisions being taken in Brussels' and the possibility that Ireland would be subject to excessive regulation (Harney, 2000). The speech to the American Bar Association emphasized Ireland's attractiveness to corporate America in the following manner:

> What really makes Ireland attractive to corporate America is the kind of economy we have created here. When Americans come here they find a country that believes in the incentive power of low taxation. They find a country that believes in economic liberalisation. They find a country that believes in essential regulation but not over-regulation. On looking further afield in Europe, they find also not every European country believes in all of these things. (Harney, 2000)

The Minister ended her speech with a phrase that has become part of the discourse on contemporary Ireland; she claimed that 'Geographically we are closer to Berlin than Boston. Spiritually we are probably a lot closer to Boston than Berlin (Harney, 2000). The Minister was placing Ireland firmly in the Anglo-Saxon, neo-liberal, capitalist camp. A Marxist account concurs with the Minister; Allen claims that Ireland 'boldly embraced a neo-liberal project – even while receiving handouts from a social Europe' (Allen, 2007, p. 243). Undoubtedly the Irish political economy has strong liberal underpinnings. The objective of creating a winning environment for foreign investment has made successive Irish governments very pro-business.

Neo-liberalism is not just American; the European project in the 1980s took a neo-liberal turn with the single market project which sought to reinvigorate the European economy. There are also other features of the Irish approach that suggest a more nuanced interpretation of the Irish political economy is apposite. The role of the state in Ireland's development does not conform to the Anglo-Saxon minimalist-state model. The Irish state was and continues to be very important in moulding the environment within which business operates. Intense openness and engagement with globalization has not 'hollowed-out' the Irish state. A crucial lesson for Ireland in learning to live with globalization was that domestic policies and institutions mattered. The Irish state has been characterized as a flexible development state (FDS) in contrast to the bureaucratic development states (BDS) of Asia (O Riain, 2000, p. 163). According to O Riain, the FDS is defined precisely by its ability to create and animate post-Fordist networks of production and innovation and international networks of capital, and to link them together in ways that promote local and national development (O Riain, 2000, p. 165). The Irish state has created a robust network of institutions designed to promote business development. One of those with responsibility for moulding the business environment, Dan Flinter, has argued that 'Ireland – through its development agencies, its financial institutions, legal and other support organizations such as engineering design – has developed a significant collective competence in selling to and servicing the needs of international investors' (Flinter, 2005). The system of social partnership, outlined above, is another important part of Ireland's political economy that brings Ireland closer to Berlin than Boston. The state plays a central role in the partnership process.

Ireland's experience of EU membership is best characterized not as a choice between Berlin or Boston, but as one where both European and American influences are apparent in the transformation of the economy. The European contribution was as a regulatory framework, a source of structural funding and most importantly the single market. The US contribution was the volume of investment, the quality of the companies that located in Ireland, the jobs that were created as a result of US investment and the overall improvement in the technical and managerial competence of the Irish corporate sector. Rather than choosing between Boston or Berlin, Ireland positioned itself in a manner that enabled it to straddle both. Domestically, key actors learnt the hard lessons of internationalization in the 1980s and created a consensus around how to manage an increasingly globalized world. Consistency of a number of key policies married to flexibility and adaptability to the changing dynamics of the global economy enabled Ireland to navigate its external environment in the 1990s and the first decade of the twenty-first century. The limitations of and the threats to the sustainability of the Irish model are discussed below, but prior to that discussion the potential for Ireland to project itself as a model of conflict resolution is explored.

Model III: conflict resolution and development cooperation

The Hague Summit in 1969 which opened the way for the first enlargement of the Union coincided with the reawakening of communal conflict in Northern Ireland between the minority nationalist catholic community and the majority protestant loyalist community. The latter had exercised predominant power in the Northern Irish state and there was extensive discrimination against the nationalist community in relation to jobs, housing and electoral boundaries. What began as a civil-rights movement quickly descended into violence which left 3,700 dead by the time various ceasefires were agreed. Within both communities there was an array of paramilitary organizations willing to use force for political ends. Relations between the nationalist community and the British Army, sent to Northern Ireland to protect the nationalist areas, were quickly transformed into a bloody battle between the Army and the Provisional IRA; the British and Irish Governments were confronted with a violent conflict on the island of Ireland. Sustained efforts to find a framework for the management of the conflict culminated in the Good Friday Agreement in 1998.

The Agreement represented a remarkable constitutional settlement for the island of Ireland. The conscious design of these new institutions, by the political parties in Northern Ireland and the two sovereign governments, resulted in an agreed constitutional template. The template, with its three interlocking strands, was complex, elaborate and ambiguous; the strands made provision for power-sharing within Northern Ireland, a North–South dimension involving the power-sharing executive and the Irish state, and an East–West dimension between Britain and Ireland. The solemnity of the agreement was underlined by the fact that it was the subject of a referendum in Northern Ireland and the Republic, the outcome of which endowed the agreement with a high degree of popular legitimacy. Transforming that popular mandate into a new set of 'living institutions' was a major challenge for those who were committed to the peaceful management of conflict in a divided society. Unresolved issues ensured that the power-sharing executive and the other institutions did not become embedded in the political landscape for almost a decade, and it was not until May 2007 that the power-sharing executive with Ian Paisley as First Minister and Martin McGuinness as Deputy First Minister was re-established after numerous aborted attempts.

Although Northern Ireland is not yet a post-conflict society, the prospects for enduring peace are reasonably good at the end of the first decade of the twenty-first century. The tortuous process of crafting a constitutional settlement brought the British and Irish Governments into sustained contact at the very highest levels of government, and transformed that relationship into one of close cooperation. Both Governments moved quickly following the re-establishment of the power-sharing executive to project Northern Ireland as a model of conflict resolution. In June 2007, Peter Hain, the former Secretary of State for Northern Ireland in the Blair Government, delivered a lecture entitled 'Peace in Northern Ireland: A Model to Resolve Conflicts' in Chatham House. In July 2007, the Irish Foreign Minister, Dermot Ahern, announced the establishment of a conflict resolution unit in the Irish Foreign Ministry with an annual budget of €25 million to promote solutions to conflicts in troubled parts of the world. The programme is part of a larger Irish effort to greatly enhance the volume and reach of its development cooperation efforts, and the Government has pledged to quadruple Ireland's aid budget by 2012. A more prosperous Ireland is seeking to project itself in global politics in a manner that is reminiscent of its active role in the United Nations in the latter half of the 1950s and the first half of the 1960s. The EU continues to provide the framework for Irish foreign policy, but one that is complemented by the projection of a distinctive Irish role based on Ireland's experience of conflict-resolution, recent economic prosperity and tradition of peacekeeping.

Challenges

There are numerous pathways to economic development. Unlike Ireland, the small Nordic states notably Denmark, Sweden and Finland focused on developing the capacity and quality of their indigenous companies, extensive investment in R&D and a strong welfare system. The risks associated with the Irish strategy are an overreliance on foreign investment and on a limited number of high-technology companies. In the first decade of the twenty-first century, the economy also developed a vulnerability to an overreliance on the construction industry for jobs and growth. With the 2004 arrival in the EU of 10 new member states, many of whom have emulated Ireland's industrial strategy and low-taxation profile, the competition for foreign investment has intensified. The performance of Ireland's indigenous sector is a cause for concern, and, moreover, high growth rates and a buoyant labour market ended Ireland's status as a low-cost economy. As a result Ireland has fallen in the competitiveness league (Honohan and Leddin, 2006); the 2003 OECD report on Ireland began its summary of Ireland's economic performance with the words, 'The era of the tiger is over' (OECD, 2003). Is the Irish model sustainable and how can it adapt to the increasing competition in the world economy?

The difference in the performance of the foreign-owned sector and Irish companies was a marked feature of Ireland's experience of the EU from the outset. Public policy proved far more effective in attracting foreign investment than in building the indigenous sector. In 1994, Enterprise Ireland was established with the remit of engaging actively with Irish companies in an effort to internationalize them, and in the 1990s the performance of Irish companies improved with the emergence of significant international Irish companies in paper, consumer goods, food ingredients, low-cost airlines and software for example. Building Irish firms is not a substitute for foreign investment, but is a necessary complement to offset Ireland's vulnerability to mobile capital. Forfás (2007) places considerable emphasis on outward direct investment by indigenous Irish enterprises as outward direct investment begins to exceed inward investment. The need for Ireland to move up the value-added chain in the search for competitive advantage has become the new mantra of Irish public policy. A major foresight exercise conducted at the end of the 1990s led to the establishment of a new institution, Science Foundation Ireland (SFI), that has transformed the landscape of research in the Irish university sector; the SFI remit is to invest in research in information technology and biotechnology. Competitive bids for internationally peer-reviewed funding altered the research culture and the scale of research in the universities. SFI was followed by a commitment in the Strategy for Science, Technology and Innovation (SSTI) to double the number of doctoral students in Irish universities by 2013 and to establish an internationally competitive fourth level in the university sector. Investment in education that began in the 1960s with the secondary level is again seen as central to the future prosperity of the country.

There is considerable debate and contestation concerning the social and societal consequences of the Irish boom. Foster distinguishes between the 'Boosters' and the 'Bedrudgers' (Foster, 2007, pp. 8–13). The former tend to be optimistic about the effects of the 'Celtic tiger' and Ireland's future, whereas the latter place considerable emphasis on its social costs. There are a number of scholars who support the argument that 'far from being a model of successful development under the conditions of globalization, Ireland is a warning of the social costs of economic development' (Kirby, 2002, p. 206; Allen, 2000; O'Toole, 2003). Those adopting a Marxist or dependency theory perspective seriously question the social outcomes of the Celtic Tiger era (Allen, 2000; O'Hearn, 1998, 2003), and there is a widespread concern that the good economy has not translated into a good society (Fahey *et al.*, 2007). Some scholars argue that the Irish boom has been accompanied by a rise in inequality within Irish society and the increased marginalization of those at the lower end of the income spectrum and those who do not participate in the labour market (Allen, 2000; Kirby *et al.*, 2006). The ESRI, the Research Institute responsible for the most extensive quantitative social science research in Ireland, assessed the available evidence in 2007 (Fahey *et al.*, 2007). The conclusions here suggest that real incomes and living standards improved for all cohorts of Irish society including those at the lower end of the spectrum (Nolan and Maitre, 2007, p. 39). However, income gaps widened during the boom, particularly between the old and those in employment, and between those at the top and bottom of the income distribution (*ibid.*, p. 41). The fruits of the Celtic Tiger may have been harvested disproportionately by the high income earners, but all of the population has benefited to some extent with significant reductions in poverty (Fahey *et al.*, 2007). Ireland continues, however, to be characterized by significant public-service deficits.

The NESC also engaged in extensive analysis of Ireland's developmental welfare state and identified the need for further development of welfare provision for different cohorts of the population across the life-cycle. Within Irish society there are those who continue to face multiple disadvantage and who are unable to live fully integrated lives. There are vulnerable individuals and groups whose autonomy is limited by the ability of the welfare system to meet their needs. The continuing high levels of benefit dependency among those of working age (19 per cent) is an acute challenge. The steady rise in participation rates in the senior cycle in Ireland's schools which started in the 1980s has levelled out since the mid-1990s. Almost 20 per cent of young people do not complete the senior cycle of second-level education, and this group are ill-prepared to participate fully in a more competitive and knowledge-driven economy which in turn limits their active participation in society. This group are particularly vulnerable in the labour market because of the arrival of a sizable educated workforce from Central Europe. Those in work also require better services, for example childcare, if they are to maintain a presence in the workplace and have an adequate family life. A dense network of development institutions and a set of effective public policies contributed significantly to Ireland's economic transformation, but the infrastructure of the social state must now catch up with the economic state.

The demand for labour arising from economic growth led to the transformation of Ireland from a country with a long history of mass emigration to a country of immigration from the mid-1990s onwards. Moreover, Ireland became a destination for a proportion of the asylum-seekers and refugees arriving in Europe. A white, homogenous and mono-cultural society was transformed into a society with a multiplicity of nationalities, languages and cultures (Loyal, 2007, pp. 32–47). The spatial location of the immigrant population is heavily concentrated in the larger cities, particularly Dublin, with some areas of the city characterized by an immigrant population of 25 per cent. Although most of the immigrants live in the cities, they have sought and found work throughout the state, even in the smallest towns. The workplace in Ireland has become multinational and multilingual. The trend intensified following the 1 May 2004 enlargement when Ireland together with the UK and Sweden opened its labour market to the citizens of the new member states. The 2002 Census showed that 10 per cent of the population in Ireland consisted of those born outside Ireland, a figure that had risen to 14 per cent in the 2006 Census, a 53 per cent increase in the immigrant population in that period. The 2006 census records 419,733 non-Irish living in Ireland, of whom 66 per cent come from EU member states (www.cso.ie/census/Census2006Results.htm). The transformational character of the relatively recent switch from emigration to immigration is the most significant impact of Europeanization and internationalization on Irish society (Loyal, 2007; Inglis, 2008). The opening of Irish society to a diversity of peoples coincided with the politicization of immigration in many European countries and the rise of the Right in some of them. The academic and political debates on multiculturalism, interculturalism, assimilation and integration have a resonance in Ireland. However, most immigrants to Ireland are white and from a Catholic or Christian background (Fahey *et al.*, 2007, p. 28).

The challenges facing Irish society are not just those of social cohesion and the integration of immigrants; the growth of the past decade has posed complex and difficult challenges of sustainable development and planning. The challenge of reconciling growth with environmental sustainability has produced some dramatic conflicts in recent years, such as the development of rural housing, house-price inflation and affordability, the location of waste facilities and incinerators, urban growth (particularly the growth of Dublin), regional development and regional differences. A failure to adequately manage the spatial and environmental consequences of economic growth presents problems in terms of sustaining economic development and quality of life.

Conclusions

This chapter identifies three ways in which Ireland might be thought of as a model, what not to do, economic catch-up, and as a model of conflict resolution. The first model demonstrates how difficult it was for Ireland to flourish in the European Union in the early years of membership. Farming did well and as a consequence the economy benefited in the latter half of the 1970s, notwithstanding the recession induced by the oil crisis. The second oil crisis in 1979 coincided with a period of political turbulence, social strife, weak public finances and economic crisis. This was also a period when the EU lost direction and there was little consensus among the member states. The second model identifies the complex factors that contributed to the economic boom and the role of the EU in that phenomenon. The single-market project, even more than structural funds, provided a framework for the economic resurgence. Without the market, Ireland would not have attracted American investment on the scale that it did. Domestic factors were also important, notably, taxation, labour supply and education. The third model, conflict resolution, relates to the communal conflict in Northern Ireland and the tortuous search for a political and institutional framework that could manage that conflict. The Good Friday Agreement (1998) and the re-establishment of the Good Friday institutions in May 2007 provided that framework. The Irish Government now wants to project the Irish experience internationally and actively wants to engage in conflict resolution in the world's trouble spots. In order to do so, it must have Ireland anchored securely in the European Union. The rejection of the Lisbon Treaty brings Ireland into 'unchartered waters' in the European Union (Cowen, 2008). Unless the EU and Ireland reach a modus operandi on the Treaty, Ireland may find itself in a second tier or outer rim of the European Union, something that was always seen as against Ireland's essential interests.

Chapter 11

Ireland: A Small State in a Large Union

'Let us be absolutely clear, our current economic prosperity, our current standing in the world, the rapid technological, economic and social change that Ireland has undergone over the last thirty years, stems directly from our absolute engagement with Europe ... They are due to our willingness to be active players, not bystanders, in the development of the EU.' (Bertie Ahern, TD, Speech to Institute of European Affairs, 10 September 2002)

This statement by an Irish Prime Minister, 30 years after accession, gives an insight into the official narrative of Ireland's engagement with the European Union; the EU is seen as pivotal to the Irish experience and Irish fortunes. This chapter seeks to explore the validity of this strong claim by identifying how Ireland as a small state has engaged with the development of the EU, followed by an exploration of just how Europeanized Ireland is, and what the EU has meant for Ireland.

Ireland spent the first 50 years of independence asserting its sovereignty and state identity. In the 1920s this had a pronounced international flavour as it established diplomatic missions, joined the League of Nations and worked with other members of the Commonwealth to loosen the ties that limited the international autonomy of Commonwealth states. The focus in the 1930s was on Anglo–Irish relations as Fianna Fáil sought to dismantle those aspects of the Anglo–Irish Treaty that tied Ireland to the United Kingdom. Relations were acrimonious until agreement was reached in 1938. The 1940s were the Emergency as neutral Ireland avoided the destruction of the war across Europe. In the postwar period, Ireland joined the emerging European institutions, notably the Council of Europe and the Organization of European Economic Cooperation (OEEC), but was a peripheral small state with an economy out of step with the liberal agenda of the United States. Membership of the United Nations in 1955 signalled a period of growing engagement with the international system.

Problems in the domestic economy and the shadow of pervasive emigration led to a profound re-assessment of the dominant policy paradigm and a shift in the orientation of the Irish economy from autarchy to free trade. Ireland's first application for membership followed from this domestic shift. The national project of economic modernization was bound up with European integration. The period between 1957 and 1961 was characterized by considerable debate among Ireland's senior civil servants and a small number of senior politicians concerning Ireland's response to developments in Europe. EFTA, EEC membership or association were all canvassed in the shadow of the evolving UK approach to Europe, and there was a pervasive feeling of vulnerability and acknowledgement of dependence on the UK in the Irish debate. Following membership in 1973, the focus on economic catch-up moulded Ireland's approach to membership, and catch-up was achieved in the 1990s following a sustained period of economic growth.

Ireland: a small state in the Union

When Ireland and Denmark joined the EU in 1973, it brought to five the number of small states in the Union. Since then, the Union has expanded to 27 states and a distinct feature of successive enlargements was the growing number of small state members of the Union. Particularly since the EFTA enlargement of the mid-1990s, the number of small states grew to such an extent that a tension developed between large and small states in the Union about voice and representation in EU institutions. Ireland, as with other small states, has been caught up in the dilemma of 'size' in relation to institutional reform. There is a growing scholarly interest in small states in international relations (Ingebritsen *et al.*, 2006) and in the European Union (Archer and Nugent, 2006). How do small states manage the fact that they have fewer power resources available to them than larger states? Does size matter and in what way? Analysts of power relations and the positioning of small states in the international system suggest that in exploring size, it is important to address the perceptual dimension of size and not just the traditional variables of territory, population, wealth and military resources (Thorhallsson,

FIGURE 11.1   Population of EU27, 2007

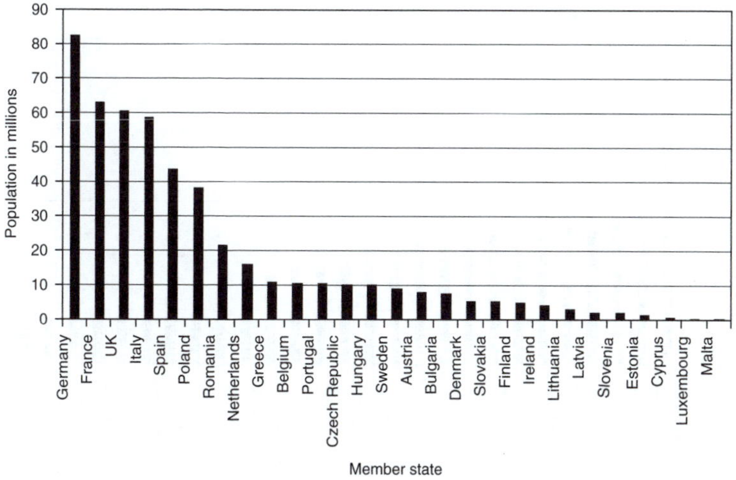

Member state

Source: Eurostat.

2006). Ireland is a small state in terms of the core variables to do with population, territory and wealth (see Figures 11.1, 11.2 and 11.3).

Moreover, Irish policy-makers regard Ireland as a small state and this has implications for how Ireland positions itself in the Union, its approach to the institutional and constitutional developments, how it manages EU affairs, and how it contributes to the EU. Domestically membership of the Union is not presented as a loss of autonomy and sovereignty to Ireland. Speaking on 29 September 2007, the Minister for European Affairs, Dick Roche, argued that

> When we first joined in 1973, there was considerable fear over how membership would impact on our identity and sovereignty. We were and still are a small country and we value greatly our hard won independence. Far from suffering our identity and our sovereignty have both been enhanced by the impact of membership. (Roche, 2007, p. 2)

The official narrative of Ireland's relationship with the Union is that membership enhances the status and capacity to act of this small state. An important shift has, however, occurred since accession in

FIGURE 11.2   EU27 GDP per capita in purchasing power standards, 2007 (EU27 = 100)

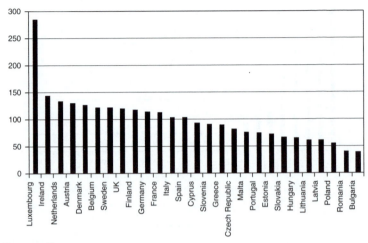

Source: Eurostat.

FIGURE 11.3   EU27 member states by area (square kilometres)

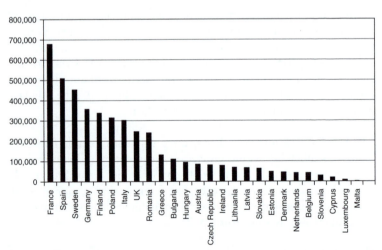

Source: Eurostat.

how Ireland presents itself and how its partners perceive it. Until economic take-off in the 1990s, Ireland was perceived as a small poor state, a taker rather than shaper of the dynamic of integration. In the first decade of the twenty-first century a more confident Ireland, clearly underlined by the Prime Minister's statement that introduces this chapter, is portrayed by its political leaders as a successful member state, a show case of European integration. Ireland's geographical location does however impact on its development of strategic relationships in the Union.

Strategic relationships

It is suggested that one way small states militate against the disadvantages of size is to form coalitions with other states. Coalitions in this sense go beyond *ad hoc* coalition-building to take on the dimensions of a strategic relationship thus enabling small states to enhance their capacity (Archer and Nugent, 2006; Klemenčič, 2007). The most significant small-state strategic relationships in the EU are the Benelux, Nordic cooperation, and more recently the Visegrád group, the Baltic group and the Regional Partnership which includes the countries of East Central Europe and Austria (Klemenčič, 2007). Although the various groupings differ in their objectives and role, all offer the participating member states engagement with a sub-system in the politics of the Union. Geographical proximity increases the incentives to those states to engage formally and informally in dialogue on the European agenda. Ireland's geographic location as an island in North-Western Europe deprives Ireland of the opportunity of engagement in strategic relationships with other small states based on geography; the model of Nordic, Benelux or Visegrad cooperation is not an available option. This has been a cause for concern to Irish policy-makers but, given the dictates of geography, successive Irish governments and officials have had to craft relationships on a different basis. Following the defeat of the first Nice referendum in 2001, the management of Ireland's relationship with the EU was characterized by a focus on developing bilateral relationships with the accession states and in strategically planning visits by senior Irish politicians to the capitals of the new member states. Those responsible for EU policy in Dublin also began to keep in touch with their counterparts in the other member states on a more consistent basis. Coalition-building from an Irish perspective tends to be based on issues and policy domains rather than on the basis of strategic relationships. The former Foreign Minister, Brian Cowen, captured this in 2003 when he suggested that 'We have affinities with countries like Sweden and Finland on security and defence. Our views on the Commission coincide with that of Benelux. We cooperate with the UK on taxation and with France on agriculture' (quoted in *Le Monde*, 4 April 2003).

There is, however, one relationship that has been characterized as a strategic relationship and that is the relationship between Ireland and the United Kingdom. As was clear in Chapter 9, British and Irish governments have cooperated closely in searching for agreement on how to manage the conflict in Northern Ireland, and the intimacy of that relationship and the close ties between the political and official elites has had an impact on their engagement with the EU. Ireland, in the early years of membership, sought to distance itself from the UK in the Union and had a distinctly more *communautaire* profile. The two states do, however, share preferences in a range of areas. Both states favour a liberal rather than a highly regulated Union; both are committed to maintaining autonomy in fiscal policy. The UK's reservations on cooperation in Justice and Home Affairs also led Ireland to remain outside Schengen and to opt-out from the JHA chapter in the Lisbon Treaty (2007). Hence the relationship with the UK is strategic, but neither state sees this relationship as the determining one in relation to engagement with the EU. The UK strategy has been characterized as 'promiscuous bilateralism', which refers to the UK strategy of forging informal strategic relationships with like-minded states in the Union (Klemenčič, 2007, p. 6). Ireland is only one like-minded state, and then only in relation to a number of specific policy areas. The affinity with the Nordic states in security is underpinned by engagement by Ireland in the Nordic Battle Group.

Attitude towards the institutional and constitutional developments

From the outset, Ireland together with other small states was attentive to questions of voice and representation in the EU and to the balance between the large and small states. This was characterized by considerable commitment to the retention of one Commissioner per state. The Commission was regarded as Ireland's 'best friend' (Laffan, 2000), and for successive Irish Governments the presence of a Commissioner in the College was regarded as important to ensure that Ireland had access to information about developments in Commission thinking, had opportunities to influence policy development, and had someone with the authority and presence to assist with difficult bilateral dossiers between Ireland and the Commission. On sensitive issues the presence of an Irish Commissioner and cabinet was deployed informally by successive Irish governments and officials to smooth the relationship with the Commission. On all major dossiers the Irish Commissioners' cabinet is deployed as a source of intelligence and a voice within the College. The commitment to one Commissioner per state was a key principle of Ireland's European policy until Nice, at which point Ireland reluctantly accepted changes to the composition of the Commission as part of the agreement. The justification from the then Irish Foreign Minister highlights the reason behind the change:

> Having ensured an outcome based on the absolute equality of Member States – that Ireland would be treated on exactly the same basis as France, Germany, or any other Member – the Taoiseach and I had no hesitation in supporting the decision. To do otherwise would not only have left us isolated from the other small or medium-sized countries which were ready to accept the outcome. (Cowen, 2000)

Ireland, although conservative on the question of the composition of the Commission, was not prepared to prevent a successful conclusion of the IGC. Re-adjustments to qualified majority voting were considered by the Irish as linked to the commitment by the larger states to reduce their representation in the Commission. Ireland's voting power in the Council is limited by virtue of the size of the state, and hence 'the reality of Council business is that our influence depends far more on our capacity to form alliances with like-minded states, large and small, than on minor variations in statistical voting weight' (Cowen, 2000, p. 2). Put simply, Irish negotiators never placed undue emphasis on Ireland's voting power in the Council as central to the projection of influence. Size did, however, have an impact on attitudes towards the powers of the European Parliament in successive rounds of treaty negotiations. Given the number of MEPs elected by Ireland to the European Parliament, there was traditionally a preference for promoting and protecting Irish preferences in the Council of Ministers rather than the European Parliament where there were few MEPs. That said, when the case for increased powers for the EP became part of the dynamic of successive IGCs, Irish representatives gradually came to accept this as part of any agreed outcome. Hence although conservative on institutional reform, the Irish became increasingly comfortable with the growing powers of the EP.

Balances between large and small states emerged as a significant issue in the Convention in 2002–03 (Magnette and Nicolaidis, 2003). A number of proposals emerging from the large states, particularly France and Germany, caused considerable disquiet among the small states. The idea of a permanent President of the European Council, in contrast to the system of rotating Presidencies, received considerable support from the larger states and became one of the most contentious issues that divided the large and small states at the Convention. The small states were concerned that a permanent Presidency may become a de facto *directoire* of the larger states. Ireland, together with a significant number of small states, became part of a group known as 'the friends of the community method'. Ireland's representative at the Convention, the Minister for European Affairs, Dick Roche, was a very active in drafting the paper submitted to the Convention by 16 smaller states in March 2003 (Norman, 2003, pp. 183–5). Ireland was also part of the small state group that met in September 2003 prior to the opening of the IGC on the Convention text, although its role in this group was subsequently reduced given Presidency responsibilities in the first half of 2004.

Contribution to the EU

In exploring Ireland's contribution to the EU, both size and level of economic development are relevant to any assessment. From the outset, successive Irish Governments were conscious of the importance of EU membership to Ireland's development and hence the need not to appear in the role of *demandeur* at all times. The rotating Presidency provided the Irish administration with an institutional opportunity to make a substantial contribution to the EU on a periodic basis. From the first Presidency in 1975, this opportunity was taken very seriously by the Irish governmental system. Successive Irish Presidencies were based on extensive and careful planning, the deployment of all administrative and public-sector resources and the informality that characterizes Irish culture. The 1975 Presidency signalled Ireland's arrival as a member state and the experience of that Presidency marked the end of Ireland's apprenticeship in the system.

The then Foreign Minister, Garrett FitzGerald, seized the opportunities offered by the Presidency; the conclusion of the first negotiations on the Lomé Convention and the signing of the agreement, discussions with the USA on their 'Year of Europe', and the Euro–Arab dialogue were key highlights of that Presidency.

The 1990 Presidency was confronted by the rapidly developing situation in East Central Europe and in Germany, a major member state. There was a keen appreciation within the Irish administration that German contributions to the EU budget had benefited Ireland, and the then Prime Minister, Charles Haughey, was determined to facilitate in any way the German Government as it responded to developments in the former DDR. A special European Council in 1990 signalled the EU's commitment to and support for German Unification, which in turn facilitated agreement on the Treaty on European Union and the euro. Following the European Council, the Irish insisted on a break with protocol to allow Chancellor Helmut Kohl to host the first press conference, rather than President Mitterrand who would normally expect preference given his status as Head of State.

Ireland was responsible twice during its Presidencies for chairing Intergovernmental Conferences (IGCs) – including the Treaty of Amsterdam in 1997 and the Constitutional Treaty in 2004. Ireland was responsible for the conclusions of the negotiations on the Constitutional Treaty during the 2004 Presidency. It was not a task that could have been anticipated a year before the Presidency, but the failure to conclude negotiations under the 2003 Italian Presidency placed Irish negotiators in the pivotal position. Ireland's status as a small state had an impact on how the negotiations were managed and conducted in Dublin. The Prime Minister, Bertie Ahern, saw the Presidency as an opportunity for Ireland to make an EU contribution, particularly in the light of the 2001/02 Nice referendums. Although the mandate received by the Presidency in December 2003 was to 'listen, assess and report' back to a March European Council, the Prime Minister told his officials in January 2004 that the conclusion of the IGC was a priority for him and that Ireland should do everything that the Presidency could do to conclude the negotiations by June 2004.

The experience of representing a small state in EU negotiations influenced how Ireland handled the negotiations. The Irish negotiating team paid considerable attention to ensuring that all member states, large, medium and small, were listened to and that their concerns were heard. Hence there was a very intensive set of bilateral meetings at both political and official levels with all member states, and in the lead-up to the June European Council the Prime Minister reinstated the tour of capitals, all capitals of the other 24 member states. The Presidency worked closely with the Council Secretariat, a factor also during the Amsterdam Treaty IGC. The Council Secretariat provided the Presidency with its deep knowledge about thinking in the member state representations in Brussels, its skill at drafting text and its institutional memory of previous IGCs. The Presidency papers that were prepared in the lead-up to the June European Council provide insights into the kind of EU that Ireland prefers. The documents are replete with references to 'overall and balanced agreement' (Presidency Paper CIG, 84/91, 1) and to 'balance among all Member States' (Presidency Paper CIG 82/04, 2). For Irish policy-makers, the preferred EU is an EU that is characterized by equilibrium between different forces rather than a hegemonic power structure. The Irish IGC team was very small, consisting of three key officials (augmented when necessary), and the Prime Minister. The Foreign Minister was involved but was not the key political player. The level of trust between political and administrative levels in Ireland and the high level of inter-ministerial trust enabled a small team to get on with the task of concluding the negotiations without having to engage in extensive domestic discussion.

Management of EU affairs

Size has had an important impact on how Ireland manages its engagement with the European Union. Ireland has a relatively small administrative system in comparative terms, and hence has fewer people to devote to EU affairs than many other member states. Irish delegations to EU meetings tend to be small, often only one official, and officials are subject to less formalized processes of coordination domestically. Irish officials tend to adopt a checklist approach to EU negotiations by identifying the five or six problematic areas for Ireland in any set of negotiations and then working to ensure that Ireland's concerns are met in the negotiating process. This has been likened to 'shooting ducks in an arcade'. Irish delegations will tend not to intervene in discussions unless there is a need to and tend to try to get changes to the text of a proposal by working with the Presidency. The key is to ensure that Ireland can live with the outcome of any negotiations. There is a desire not to be isolated in negotiations and to try to go along with the emerging consensus if possible. The prevailing ethos is pragmatic rather than ideological with the careful deployment of Ireland's limited influence in the negotiating process. There is a keen sense that Ireland is a small state and should not oppose for the sake of it.

On issues that are accorded high salience in the domestic system, Irish negotiators devote considerable time and energy to ensuring that the outcome is favourable from an Irish perspective. The negotiations of successive rounds of structural funds underline how the Irish system responds to the 'big issues'. The system creates what are in effect taskforces of highly skilled and experienced officials from a number of Ministries who work closely with the key political players to manage the negotiations from inception to conclusion, usually at the level of the European Council. The taxation dossier also receives careful and sustained attention across the governmental system. Ireland's differential system of corporate tax was deemed discriminatory by the Commission which led to very significant bilateral negotiations between the Commission and the Irish Government. The negotiations were largely managed by two senior civil servants who succeeded in getting the Commission's agreement to a level of corporation tax of 12.5 per cent for all companies. Successive Irish Governments have closely monitored and opposed proposals to move taxation from requiring unanimity to QMV. The Commission and a significant number of member states have attempted on a number of occasions to alter the rules on taxation, particularly during treaty negotiations. Ireland has implacably opposed such moves, together with the UK and a number of the new member states. Taxation is regarded as a red-line issue by the Irish administration; it is seen as a key instrument of economic policy in the context of EMU. The Irish are willing to discuss and negotiate on taxation but only within the shadow of a veto rather than a vote.

Just how Europeanized?

The European Union, although not a state, is a powerful institution, not wholly international or domestic in character but with characteristics of both traditional statehood and international organizations. It is powerful as a market, economic and social regulator, a source of solidarity among the member states, as international actor and as an idea and ideal of interstate relations. It is also an arena of contestation about state/market relations, domestic and European competencies, regulation, styles of governance, boundaries of the Union, the Union's constitutional architecture, social and political identities and global governance. That contestation takes place not just at the European level but is part of the domestic discourse on integration. The European Union has played a powerful role in the transformation of Ireland since the bid for membership in the 1960s but how has that power manifested itself? How significant or influential has the EU been? Put simply, how does the EU impact on its member states, in this case Ireland, and just how Europeanized is Ireland? Recent sociological and historical explorations of the transformation of Ireland have identified various impacts of the EU on Ireland but what is striking is just how few references are made to the EU and Europe. In three major volumes running to a thousand pages, there are a total of 50 references to Europe and the EU in marked contrast to the statement above (Inglis, 2008; Foster, 2007; O'Sullivan, 2007). How do we account for the disjuncture between the degree of significance of the EU identified in all three volumes and the manner in which the EU looms small? The answer depends on the lens that is adopted and on how we understand the EU as a political, economic and social order. The manner in which the EU enters the domestic, is entangled with the domestic, and influences the domestic lies at the heart of this puzzle. Our discussion now turns to the question of Europeanization and to an exploration of the differential impact of Europeanization on Ireland's political economy, polity, legal architecture, governmental institutions and political parties.

The EU as political economy and market has been fundamental to the transformation of the Irish economy from one dominated by agriculture and the British market to one of the most globalized economies in the world. The existence of the large European market, particularly following the Single European Act, enabled Ireland to surf the waves of globalization. The Irish debate about the relative balance between European and US influences on the Irish political economy tends to juxtapose 'Neo-liberal' America versus 'Social' Europe (Foster, 2007, pp. 32–3). This perspective does not sufficiently take account of the strong liberal and liberalizing aspects of market creation in the EU, however. The EU as polity has had significant but varied effects on the Irish political and legal system; the constitutional and legal architecture of the state was altered by the centrality of law to the European Union, and indivisible sovereignty was traded for divisible sovereignty and the Union's corpus of law and regulation. The entanglement between the Irish and European legal orders and the implications of European law for Ireland's common-law tradition has been questioned by lawyers, including a former Minister for Justice, Michael McDowell. The impact of the Union on the core norms of Ireland's political and governmental institutions has, however, been limited. The core executive and the Oireachtas adapted to EU membership but were not transformed by it. The EU did, however, have important effects on the growth of regulatory agencies and new styles of governance in regulation, partnership and programming. Membership altered the opportunity structure for domestic actors, particularly voluntary associations, by adding the Brussels arena to the policy game, but it has not had a major impact on the Irish party system or on the stuff of politics in Ireland. Nor has it altered the domestic political culture.

The impact of the EU on Irish society is multidimensional and complex. EU policy paradigms and laws concerning gender and other forms of equality were and remain part of the national discourse and dynamic. Those groups in Irish society seeking to secure or enhance rights, such as women or the disabled have deployed EU policies and laws to support their case domestically. There was an important co-evolution between the emergence of feminism in Ireland, EU membership and European laws concerning gender equality. The dynamic of EU social policy and legislation has favoured progressive rather than conservative elements within the society. EU student exchange networks have altered Irish universities and supported their internationalization. EU membership offered an additional layer of identity to those Irish who are comfortable with being Irish first but European as well. From 1992 to 2004 the Eurobarometer asked if respondents felt 'Irish only' or 'Irish and European', and the responses suggest that 'Irish only' still predominates although Irish and European increased somewhat. The figures for 'Irish only' in 1992 were 52 per cent and for 'Irish and European', 38 per cent. By 2004, the figures were 49 per cent for nationality only and 44 per cent for 'Irish and European'. The figures for the EU as a whole in 2004 were 41 per cent for nationality only and 46 per cent for nationality and European (Eurobarometer, 2004). For many Irish people, being Irish, whatever that means in the rapidly changing Ireland, is sufficient and additional layers of identity are not sought.

Growing affluence and increased travel have brought continental European foods and tastes to Irish homes and restaurants. The major cities and towns have continental-style cafes that vie with the traditional communal outlet, the pub. Ryan Air, Europe's most successful low-cost airline, brought travel and home-ownership abroad within the grasp of the affluent middle class (Inglis, 2008, p. 105). The most profound impact on Irish society, discussed below, has however been the influx of people from the new member states in search of jobs. There are daily flights between Irish cities and Budapest, Krakow, Prague, Poznan, Riga, Vilnius and Warsaw. These cities did not feature as part of Irish mental maps prior to the collapse of communism, and immigration since 2004, which is not restricted to Irish cities, has altered the aural, cultural and material texture of Irish society. A relatively benign economic environment has facilitated this transformation without a major reaction from Irish society, although racism exists and the integration of the 'New Irish' is a major challenge to Irish public policy and Irish society.

What this 'Union' has meant to Ireland

This section seeks to explore just how significant the EU has been for Ireland. It is difficult to capture the complex interaction between Ireland and the EU in the almost 50 years since membership was first mooted, although the argument above is that the EU had its most pronounced influence on the Irish economy. Its influence on Irish society was largely indirect until the influx of large numbers of Europeans to Ireland post-2004. It is, however, difficult to isolate 'EU' effects in a definitive manner. The Catholic, rural, conservative and relatively poor society of the late 1950s would have changed with or without EU membership; the insularity and isolation was unlikely to survive the global dynamics of the 1960s. Youth culture, the protest movements, the spirit of 'May '68' and the growth of urban Ireland would have altered the societal dynamics of the 1950s without the prospect of EU membership. Ireland's later experience of membership, particularly from the mid-1980s onwards, was bound up with an intensification of globalization in the world economy; in the case of Ireland, Europeanization and globalization are intertwined in complex ways. Membership does, however, matter, and the remainder of the chapter explores the myriad ways in which developments in Ireland were bound up with the EU and the structural impact of the EU on the Irish state, society and economy.

The EU advancing modernization

Membership of the EU was a project for Ireland's future, and the prospect of membership acted as a catalyst for change in the 1960s. Lemass, modern Ireland's first European, deployed the EU as a motor of modernization and industrialization; he used the rhetoric of traditional Irish nationalism to build a bridge between Ireland's past and its future. Long before membership, the EU was instrumental in the domestic project of economic modernization. The Common Agricultural Policy, a legacy of the importance of agriculture in postwar Europe, smoothed economic change, and market access and the increase in farm incomes in the years following membership facilitated the transition from a conservative rural society to one more comfortable with modernity. O'Toole argues that EU membership meant that the conflict between tradition and modernity in Ireland was 'resolved in favour of modernity' (O'Toole, 2003, p. 19). The CAP, according to O'Toole, bought off the 'conservative heartlands of rural Ireland' (*ibid.*, p. 20). It was modernity in the first instance bought by 'green pounds, mechanised milking parlours, beef and butter mountains and headage payments' (*ibid.*); it brought prosperity to the countryside, the villages and small towns and hence made possible the growth of an urban society without deep societal strain.

Europe as framework and scaffolding

One of the most important roles Europe plays for Ireland, a small state, is its role as geo-political framework for the Irish state. Membership of the European Union provides Ireland with a secure rule-bound international position in the world, and the EU as a significant economic and political power in the world enables Ireland to mediate with powerful global forces. Membership of a regional bloc brings advantages to small states. Protecting and promoting interests within the WTO are easier as a member state, and the slender human resources of the Irish state are augmented by the resources of European institutions and other member states. The EU is a partnership of states and being a member state is a badge of state identity and inclusion. Membership has also enabled Ireland to position itself geopolitically in Europe and in its relations with the United Kingdom and the United States, and Europeanization in this sense has not been a zero-sum game for the Irish state.

The discussion of political economy in the previous chapter under-lines the way in which Ireland straddled the European, US and UK dimensions in evolving an approach to mediating globalization and its external environment. The pragmatic adaptable approach of the Irish state elite proved very strategic in mediating core relations. Europe therefore remains fundamental to Ireland's future as scaffold-ing. The centrality of the EU to Ireland is embedded in Irish official discourse, particularly following the critical juncture of the first Nice referendum. The programme for government for the new Irish Government (June 2007) acknowledges the importance of Euro-pean Union membership. The EU does not, however, diminish the importance of relations with the USA, the importance of American capital in Ireland and the role of the USA in encouraging a settlement within Northern Ireland. EU membership also facilitated improve-ments in that other strategic relationship, Ireland's relationship with the United Kingdom. As a small state, Ireland loomed 'small' rather than large in the horizons of the EU, the USA and the UK. Small states have to work harder at developing and embedding priority relations than large states, and the Irish state elite adopted a strategic approach to these three critical relationships.

Europe as arena

The EU is an additional arena of politics and public policy for domes-tic actors. Irish ministers, civil servants, representatives of interest groups, *fonctionnaires* in EU institutions, and office holders and MEPs have multiple opportunities to participate in the governance structures of the Union. Ireland has run six successful Presidencies of the Union. Irish civil servants also have opportunities to serve as officers in European institutions; two Irish officials have served as Secretary General of the Commission, including the first female Secretary General, and Irish politicians have the opportunity to ply their trade as Commissioners and MEPs, including Pat Cox who was President of the European Parliament from 2002 to 2004. Inter-est groups and cause groups are involved in the multilevel politics of the Union seeking to influence European policy and to enhance their position in domestic public policy. Environmental groups, women's groups and others have effectively used Europe to pressurise domestic governments, their two important interlocutors being the Commission and the European Court of Justice. European elections provide an additional electoral contest and serve as mid-term tests for successive governments. An additional layer of policy-making disturbs but does not transform territorial or core executive politics in Ireland.

Europe as policy

The most significant and visible impact of the EU on Ireland is in the realm of public policy. EU policies and positive integration have had a major impact on a range of public policy, notably agriculture, social and environmental regulation, gender policies and market regulation. Ireland was originally a taker rather than shaper of many regulatory policies because of the underdevelopment of policies and regulatory institutions in Ireland. As the Irish economy developed, it would have had to develop a stronger regulatory regime and regulatory policies with or without the EU, but membership enabled Ireland to avail of the policy competence and resources of European institutions and other member states. A range of regulatory agencies such as the Health and Safety Authority and the Environmental Protection Agency (EPA) were established and became part of a wider European regulatory regime. The European budget provided incentives to adopt new governance practices such as evaluation and programming in the management of the structural funds. The EU was not just a source of policy; European law and the euro prohibited certain practices at domestic level and removed certain policy instruments from the Irish government, and European policies on public procurement and state aids had a major impact on all Irish public bodies. The 'thou shall not' aspect of EU membership, negative integration, was as significant as policy integration; it was both constraint and shield for successive Irish governments. It limited the policy options of governments but also shielded governments from demands for subsidization from declining industries.

Europe as polity

The European Union is not a static entity. Since Ireland's membership of the Union in 1973, the future development of the Union has been a constant in Ireland's European policy. The Tindemans Report in 1975 introduced Ireland to the institutional and constitutional politics of the Union, and this was followed by negotiations on direct elections to the European Parliament and the iterative process of Treaty change that began with the Single European Act in 1986.

Ireland's approach to the institutional and constitutional development of the EU follows a well-established path. The fact that Ireland
is a referendum country has a major impact on the attitudes and
strategies of Irish negotiators; how to sell agreements reached among
the member states to the Irish electorate is an important factor in
their calculations and negotiating strategies. Ireland's position as a
small state in a Union of larger states is also important, and ensuring that there is adequate voice and representation for small states
in the Union is a constant in Irish European policy. Until Nice, one
Commissioner per member state was a central plank of policy, but
there was a growing realization, however, that enlargement and scale
altered the institutional dynamics of the Union and required a change
in that policy. Attention has been paid to voting weights but no Irish
minister wants to rely on votes to protect and promote Irish interests. Ireland was never a strong supporter of increased powers for
the Parliament, favouring the Council as the preferred arena for
negotiations. That said, Ireland recognized that enhanced powers
for the Parliament was part of the evolving bargain on European
institutions.

The European in the national

Because membership of the EU was not a major source of conflict
and contestation, European symbols, notably the European flag and
the euro, have become part of Ireland's symbolic universe. Being a
member state forms a core part of Irish official nationalism and has
become an integral part of the official Irish narrative. The extent
of financial transfers from the EU budget meant that the Irish were
reminded of European largesse by the pervasive signs reading, 'This
project has been part funded by the European Regional Development
Fund', and similarly the blue flag on beaches serves as a reminder
that the EU was essential to environmental regulation in Ireland.
European commissioners and officials became part of the official
domestic landscape. In the 1970s, 1980s and 1990s individual Commission officials responsible for the regional and social funds played
a critical role in Irish development. They brought with them ideas,
innovative methodologies and a new voice to the domestic system of
policy-making, providing an external perspective on domestic deliberations and choices. Peer review became part of the repertoire of
Irish governance. Many Commission officials were very committed

to the development of Ireland and saw Ireland as a test case for the role of the EU in economic modernization.

Europeans in Ireland

The first decade of the twenty-first century saw a transformation of the historical pattern of emigration. Whereas traditionally Europeans came to Ireland as tourists, following enlargement to the East, the nationals of other member states began to come to Ireland in significant numbers as workers and potential future citizens. The 2006 census indicates that 10 per cent of the population in Ireland is non-national, a very significant proportion of which originate from the new member states, particularly Poland and the Baltic states. There has also been a notable increase in migration from the UK to Ireland. EU nationals have extensive rights in other member states and are more likely to opt to remain in Ireland on a long-term basis. The political, economic and social consequences of the shift from emigration to immigration and the challenge posed to all facets of public policy is high on the public policy agenda. How Irish society navigates the challenges posed by large-scale immigration and the presence of a significant number of 'New Irish' will have a major impact on the cohesion and quality of Irish life in the first half of the twenty-first century.

Beyond Europe

The centrality of EU membership to Ireland is embedded in official discourse and in the international positioning of the Irish state. Shifts in the global political economy and the impact of globalization underlined the need for Ireland to look beyond Europe and the European market. In 2000, the Prime Minister asked the public service to develop an Asia Strategy that would chart how Irish state agencies and companies should respond to the emergence of China and India as major economic powers. Given the ease of access to the European markets, the focus now is on the opportunities offered by economic growth in Asia for Irish companies. The European and American markets remain important but a slice of Asian growth is necessary for continuing Irish prosperity. Economic prosperity and the benign state of the Irish public finances also allowed Ireland to make a commitment to the quadrupling of aid to less developed states by 2012; Irish Aid will have significantly more financial resources at its disposal to spend on development in Africa and beyond. Ireland has an important contribution to make given its own experience of economic development and the strength of its domestic development agencies. A distinctive Irish signature is being forged in development cooperation. The re-establishment of the Good Friday institutions in May 2007 and the end of that 700-year quarrel between Britain and Ireland may also lead to the emergence of an Irish signature in conflict-resolution and mediation; the Irish Department of Foreign Affairs has established a conflict-resolution unit its own budget. Economic wealth and the peaceful management of the conflict in Northern Ireland heralds the emergence of an Irish presence in the world that is embedded in Europe, but one that goes beyond Europe and that is characterized by a distinctive Irish signature.

Beyond Lisbon

The negative outcome of the referendum on the Lisbon Treaty in June 2008 was a major shock to the incumbent government and the main opposition parties, all of whom favoured ratification. Its impact on Ireland's relations with the EU and the other member states will be played out over the coming years. The EU has experienced a significant number of No votes in domestic referendums, beginning with the Danish No to Maastricht in 1992. Domestic referendums, particularly those that are negative, bring the tensions between the domestic politics of the individual member states and collective EU politics sharply into focus. The outcome of a domestic referendum has implications for the other member states and the system as a whole. There is a discernible pattern whereby, following a period of reflection and assessment, a solution is found to enable the EU to proceed with ratification. In the case of Denmark (Maastricht) and Ireland (Nice), the two states proposed solutions to the other member states that were agreed and emerged as protocols and declarations. The referendums were then re-run. Following the French and Dutch rejection of the Constitutional treaty in 2005, the EU entered a period of reflection which ended with agreement of the Lisbon Treaty. This plan 'B' was rejected by the Irish electorate in June 2008. The immediate response of the other member states was to proceed with ratification of the Treaty. This leaves Ireland in a minority of one. The choice facing Ireland and the EU is either to abandon the Lisbon Treaty or to find way of enabling the member states to make the Lisbon Treaty part of the 'living constitution' of the Union. This will happen in one of two ways. First, the Irish Government, having secured clarifications and declarations, returns to the Irish electorate with a different question. Second, if scenario one is not possible, the other member states would proceed with a 26 + 1 solution, a form of two-tier Union. If scenario two emerges, Ireland would find itself in the kind of Union that it sought to avoid throughout its membership. The national consensus on membership is over.

What the Irish experience tells us about the EU

Ireland's experience of EU membership has taken place in the context of a changing and evolving Union, one that expanded its borders and membership in a dramatic fashion, altered its treaty architecture, and its ambition as market, regulator, and international actor. An exploration of the Irish experience in the Union draws our attention to two important facets of the Union. First, Europeanization is not an all-pervasive and powerful process that squeezes member-state institutions, national identities and domestic choice of all meaning. The obligations of membership, the ties that bind, are thick enough to enfold the member states, but thin enough to allow for considerable domestic choice and latitude. It is precisely this balance between the strength of EU obligations and the need for the EU to go with the grain of the national that enables it to manage, not without strain, the deep diversity that Europe represents. Second, the Irish experience tells us that the manner in which a member state and its society deploys the domestic headroom that is part of the EU has a major impact on how that member state and society engage with and benefit from the opportunities of membership. It took Irish policy-makers and key societal actors until the end of the 1980s to learn to live with an internationalizing political economy. The lessons were learnt following a deep economic recession with consequent social costs. Third, Ireland's referendum experience, particularly Nice and Lisbon, tells us that notwithstanding tangible benefits in terms of economic development, financial transfers and geopolitical positioning, the EU remains a distant and little understood entity for the majority of people. The Brussels insiders, notably the senior politicians, civil servants, representatives of the key lobby groups, MEPs and the EU correspondents of the print and electronic media, act as 'boundary managers' or translators between the national and the European. Deep knowledge about the EU, either in terms of specific policy areas or the dynamics of its legal order and institutional system, is not spread throughout the political system or society. European issues have low salience most of the time. Faced then with a referendum on a European treaty, the electorate is badly prepared to understand and judge the arguments and counter-arguments of those who advocate a Yes or No. In a process akin to cramming for exams, the electorate is inundated with information that it may or may not understand and absorb during a short referendum campaign. This makes the outcome of any EU referendum highly uncertain.

The outcome of the Lisbon referendum in June 2008 leaves Ireland's European policy and its position in the EU loose of its moorings. The old narrative on the EU as a source of modernization and financial transfers is no longer relevant. It has not been replaced by a new narrative of Ireland's place in the EU in the 21st century. Moreover, a prosperous country is beginning to forget the benefits that Ireland has gained from membership. The Prime Minister, Jack Lynch, who signed Ireland's Treaty of Accession in January 1972, suggested to the Irish people that the EU represented 'opportunity'. Availing itself of the opportunities that accompanied membership was neither smooth nor the benefits inevitable. Above all, the EU offered an external environment that was far more benign than colonialism or autarchy. It is not in Ireland's interests to find itself in a two-tier Europe as it navigates the cross-cutting domestic, European and global dynamics that characterize the increasingly fragmented but also connected world of the 21st century.

Further Reading

Details of the process of Irish accession to the EEC are found in Maher (1986) and FitzGerald (2000). A full discussion of Ireland's economic transformation is to be found in Garvin (2004) and an alternative view in Kirby (2003). For an account of the first ten years of Irish membership of the European Union see Coombes (1983) and Drudy and McAleese (1984). Keatinge (1991), O'Donnell (2000), Holmes (2005) and Laffan and Tonra (2005) analyse the impact of the EU on Ireland in more recent times.

Bulmer and Burch (1998, 2000) offer a conceptual framework for analysing the Europeanization of core executives, in particular of the United Kingdom. Laffan (2001, 2006) and Laffan and O'Mahony (2007) investigate the role of small member state core executives in managing EU business.

For full evaluations of European Parliament elections and the second-order election phenomenon see Hix and Marsh (2007), Marsh (1996) and Reif and Schmitt (1980). Taggart (1998) and Taggart and Szczerbiak (2004) are key readings on Euroscepticism in European political parties, while Irish party positions are analysed in Gilland (2004).

Gabel (2001) and McLaren (2006) are good introductions to the study of public attitudes to European integration. Gilland (1999), Sinnott (1995), Garry, Marsh and Sinnott (2005) and Kennedy and Sinnott (2007) investigate Irish attitudes towards European integration through referendums and public opinion polls and the role of EU referendums.

For succinct explications of multilevel governance see Marks et al. (1986) and Marks and Hooghe (2001). Callanan and Keogan (2003) provides the most up-to-date analysis of local government in Ireland. Hayward (2006) explores the reconfiguration of Irish national territory as a result of cross-border cooperation.

For a broad account of the Europeanization of Irish public policy and policy-making see McGowan and Murphy (2003). Further analysis of the impact of the EU on Irish agriculture is found in Crowley (2003) and Daly (2002). Flynn (2007) and Taylor (2001) chart the evolution of environmental policy in Ireland, including the effects of EU membership. Honohan (2000), Honohan and Walsh (2002) and Honohan and Leddin (2004) analyse Irish participation in the EU's macro-economic structures.

For the fullest accounts of the Europeanization of Irish foreign policy since accession in 1973 see Keatinge (1978, 1984a, 1991 and 1998) and Tonra (2001, 2002 and 2006).

Bew and Meehan (1994), Ruane and Todd (1996), Teague (1996) and Laffan and Payne (2001) explore the relationsip between the European Union, the Republic of Ireland and Northern Ireland. Frampton (2005) provides a very interesting survey on Sinn Féin attitudes to the EU.

For accounts of Ireland's underdevelopment until the era of the Celtic Tiger see Lee (1989), O'Hearn (1998) and Garvin (2004). For alternative perspectives of the genesis and impact of Ireland's economic success see Allen (2000), O'Toole (2003), Barry (2005), Fahey *et al.* (2007) and O'Sullivan (ed.) (2007).

Finally, Ingebritsen *et al.* (2006), Archer and Nugent (2006) and Thorhallsson (2006) explore the relationship between small states and the European Union.

Bibliography

Adshead, M. (1996) 'Beyond Clientelism: Agricultural Networks in Ireland and the EU', *West European Politics*, 19(3), pp. 583–608.

Adshead, M. (2005) 'Europeanization and Changing Patterns of Governance in Ireland', *Public Administration*, 83(1), pp. 159–78.

Adshead, M. and I. Bache (2000) 'Developing European Regions? Unity and Diversity in the New Europe', Paper presented to the Political Studies Association of Ireland Annual Conference, University College Cork, 13–14 October.

Ahern, B. (2007) Address to Joint Houses of Parliament Westminster, 15 May. www.taoiseach.gov.ie/index.asp?locID=558&docID=3427 [accessed 8 October 2007].

—— (2005) Speech to Seanad Éireann, 13 October. www.taoiseach.gov.ie. [accessed 20 December 2005].

—— (2003) Radio Telefís Éireann, Radio 1, Thomas Davis Lecture, 27 January.

—— (2002) Speech to Dáil Éireann on 26th Amendment to the Constitution, 10 September.

—— (2002) Speech to Institute of European Affairs, Dublin, 10 September.

Allen, K. (2000) *The Celtic Tiger: The Myth of Social Partnership in Ireland* (Manchester: Manchester University Press).

—— (2007) 'Globalisation, the State and Ireland's Miracle Economy', in S. O'Sullivan (ed.), *Contemporary Ireland. A Sociological Map* (Dublin: University College Dublin Press), pp. 231–47.

Antola, E. (2001) 'Small States in the EU: Experiences and Challenges', Address to Chamber of Deputies, Parliament of the Czech Republic, Prague, 12 June.

Archer, C. and N. Nugent (2006) 'Introduction: Does the Size of Member States Matter in the European Union?', *Journal of European Integration*, 28(1), pp. 3–6.

Arter, D. (2000) 'Small State Influence Within the EU: The Case of Finland's Northern Dimension Initiative', *Journal of Common Market Studies*, 38(5), 677–97.

Bache, I. and A. Jordan (eds) (2006) *The Europeanization of British Politics* (Basingstoke: Palgrave).

Baker, T., J. FitzGerald and P. Honohan (1996) *Economic Implications for Ireland of EMU*. PRS Paper no. 28 (Dublin: The Economic and Social Research Institute).

Barrington, D. (1991) *Local Government Reorganisation and Reform. Report of Expert Advisory Committee* (Dublin: Stationery Office).

—— (1999) 'The Impact of the EU on the Irish Constitution', in J. Dooge and R. Barrington (eds), *A Vital National Interest: Ireland in Europe 1973–1998* (Dublin: Institute of Public Administration), pp. 31–42.

Barry, F. (2003) 'Irish Economic Development over Three Decades of EU Membership', University College Dublin School of Economics Working Paper.

—— (2005) 'Third Level Education, Foreign Direct Investment and Economic Boom in Ireland', Working Paper 05/09, Centre for Economic Research (Dublin: University College Dublin), p. 22.

Barry, F. and J. FitzGerald (2001) 'Irish Fiscal Policy in EMU and the Brussels–Dublin Controversy', in *Fiscal Policy in EMU: Report of the Swedish Committee on Stabilisation Policy in EMU* (Stockholm: Statens Offentliga Utredningar).

Barry, F., J. Bradley and A. Hannan (2001) 'The Single Market, the Structural Funds and Ireland's Recent Economic Growth', *Journal of Common Market Studies*, 39(3), pp. 537–52.

Bartlett, C. and S. Ghoshal (1989) *Managing Across Borders: The Transnational Solution* (London: Hutchinson Business Books).

Bergin, A., J. FitzGerald and D. McCoy (2004) 'How Has Economic Management Evolved Within EMU?', Economic and Social Research Institute Paper, www.esri.ie/pdf/Economic_Wkshop_Oct04.pdf.

Bew P. and E. Meehan (1994) 'Regions and Borders: Controversies in Northern Ireland about the European Union', *European Journal of Public Policy*, 1(1), pp. 95–113.

Binzer Hobolt, S. (2003) 'Europe in Question: Referendum Behaviour in Denmark and Ireland', Paper presented at the 33rd Annual UACES conference, University of Newcastle upon Tyne, 2–4 September.

Blackwell, J. and E. O'Malley (1984) 'The Impact of EEC Membership on Irish Industry', in P.J. Drudy and D. McAleese (eds), *Ireland and the European Community* (Cambridge: Cambridge University Press), pp. 107–44.

Börzel, T. (2000) 'Improving Compliance through Domestic Mobilisation? New Instruments and the Effectiveness of Implementation in Spain', in C. Knill and A. Lenschow (eds), *Implementing EU Environmental Policy: New Approaches to an Old Problem* (Manchester: Manchester University Press), pp. 221–50.

Börzel, T. and T. Risse (2000) 'When Europe Hits Home: Europeanisation and Domestic Change', *European Integration Online Papers* (*EiOP*), 4(15), eiop.or.at/eiop/texte/d000-015a.htm.

—— and —— (2006) 'Europeanisation: The Domestic Impact of European Union Politics', in K.E. Jorgensen, M.A. Pollack and B. Rosamond (eds), *Handbook of European Union Politics* (London: Sage), pp. 483–504.

Bradley, J. (2002) 'The Irish Economy in International Perspective', in W. Crotty and D. E. Schmitt (eds), *Ireland on the World Stage* (Harlow: Pearson), pp. 46–65.

Brady, H. and K. Barysch (2007) *The Centre for European Reform Guide to the Reform Treaty. Briefing Note.* 17 October.

Brown, Tony (2004) 'Ireland's National Forum on Europe'. Federal Trust European Essay No.33, www.fedtrust.co.uk/default.asp?groupid=8 [accessed 24 September 2007].

Browne, Terence (1985) *Ireland. A Social and Cultural History. 1922–1985* (London: Fontana).

Brunt, B. (1988) *The Republic of Ireland* (London: Chapman).

Bulmer, S. and M. Burch (1998) 'Organizing for Europe: Whitehall, the British State and the European Union', *Public Administration*, 76(4), pp. 601–28.

—— and —— (2000) 'The Europeanization of British Central Government', in R.A.W. Rhodes (ed.), *Transforming British Government Vol. 1* (London: Macmillan).

—— and —— (2001) 'The Europeanization of Central Government: The UK and Germany in Historical Institutionalist Perspective', in M.D. Aspinwall and G. Schneider (eds), *The Rules of Integration* (Manchester: Manchester University Press).

Bulmer, S. and C. Lequesne (2005) 'The European Union and its Member States: An Overview', in S. Bulmer and C. Lequesne (eds), *The Member States of the European Union* (Oxford: Oxford University Press), pp. 1–24.

Bulmer, S. and C. Radaelli (2005) 'The Europeanisation of National Policy', in S. Bulmer and C. Lequesne (eds), *The Member States of the European Union* (Oxford: Oxford University Press), pp. 338–59.

Caherty, T. *et al.* (eds) (1992) *Is Ireland a Third World Country?* (Dublin: Beyond The Pale Publications).

Callanan, M. and J. F. Keogan (eds) (2003) *Local Government in Ireland: inside out* (Dublin: Institute of Public Administration).

Callanan, M. (2003) 'Local Government and the European Union', in Callanan, M. and J. F. Keogan (eds), *Local Government in Ireland: inside out* (Dublin: Institute of Public Administration), pp. 404–28.

Capoccia, G. and R. D. Keleman (2007) 'The Study of Critical Junctures. Theory, Narrative and Counterfactuals in Historical Institutionalism', *World Politics*, 59, pp. 341–69.

Carey, S. and M. Lebo (2000) 'In Europe, but not Europeans: The Impact of National Identity on Public Support for the European Union', Paper presented at ECPR Joint Sessions, Grenoble.

Cassells, P. (2000) 'Recasting the European Social Model', in R. O'Donnell (ed.), *Europe: the Irish Experience* (Dublin: Institute of European Affairs), pp. 69–78.

Cech, Z. (2006) 'Ireland: no place like (my own) home?' *ECFIN Country Focus*, 3(13), pp. 1–6.

Christian Solidarity Party (2005) Submission to National Forum on Europe.

Clancy, P. (1996) 'Pathways to Mass Higher Education in the Republic of Ireland', *European Journal of Education*, 31(3), pp. 355–70.

Clerkin, S. (2000) 'Current Needs for Policy to Incorporate Biodiversity Considerations', A Short Communication. An Taisce/ESAI Biodiversity Conference. November.

Coakley, J. and M. Gallagher (eds) (1999) *Politics in the Republic of Ireland*. Third Edition (London: Routledge).

Collier, R.B. and D. Collier (1991) *Shaping the Political Arena: Critical Junctures, the Labor Movement, and Regime Dynamics in Latin America* (Princeton: Princeton University Press).

Collins, N. (1993) 'Still Recognisably Pluralist? State-Farmer Relations in Ireland', in R. J. Hill and M. Marsh (eds), *Modern Irish Democracy: Essays in Honour of Basil Chubb* (Dublin: Irish Academic Press), pp. 104–22.

Connaughton, B. (2005) 'EU Environmental Policy and Ireland', in M. Holmes (ed.), *Ireland and the European Union. Nice, Enlargement and the Future of Europe* (Manchester: Manchester University Press), pp. 36–51.

Coombes, D. (ed.) (1983) *Ireland and the European Communities: Ten Years of Membership* (Dublin: Gill & Macmillan).

Conroy, N. (2000) 'Police Cooperation and Europol', in E. Regan (ed.), *The New Third Pillar. Cooperation Against Crime in the European Union* (Dublin: Institute of European Affairs).

Conway, A. (1991) 'Agricultural Policy', in P. Keatinge (ed.), *Ireland and EC Membership Evaluated* (London: Pinter), pp. 42–59.

Conway, G. (2005) 'Judicial Interpretation and the Third Pillar. Ireland's Acceptance of the Euroepan Arrest Warrant and the Gozutok and Brugge case', *European Journal of Crime, Criminal Law and Criminal Justice*, 13(2), pp. 255–283.

Cortell, A.P. and S. Peterson (1999) 'Altered States: Explaining Domestic Institutional Change', *British Journal of Political Science*, 29, pp. 177–203.

Coughlan, A. (1970) *The Common Market: Why Ireland should not join* (Dublin: Common Market Study Group).

——— (1998) 'Treaty would give Brussels Huge New Powers Over Rights', *The Irish Times*, 11 May.

——— (2002) 'Why the Euro is a Mistake for Ireland', *Irish Democrat*, February. www.irishdemocrat.co.uk/window-on-the-eu/euro-mistake/ [accessed 31 October 2007].

—— (2005) 'Sounding the Death Knell for EU Federation', *The Irish Times*, 31 May.

—— (2007) 'Revised EU Agreement has Radical Implications', *The Irish Times*, 28 June.

Cowen, B. (2000) *State of the Union Address* (Dublin: Institute of European Affairs).

—— (2008) 'Taoiseach Says Ireland Must Not Be Isolated', *The Irish Times*, 16 June.

Coyle, C. and R. Sinnott (1992) 'Europe and the Regions in Ireland: a View from Below', *CEEPA Working Paper No.2.* (Dublin: University College Dublin).

Coyle, C. (1994) 'Administrative capacity and the Implementation of EU Environmental Policy in Ireland', in S. Baker, K. Milton and S. Yearly (eds), *Protecting the Periphery. Environmental Policy in Peripheral Regions of the European Union* (Ilford: Frank Cass).

—— (1997) 'European Integration: A Lifeline for Irish Local Authorities?' in M.J.F. Goldsmith and K.K. Klausen (eds), *European Integration and Local Government* (Cheltenham: Edward Elgar).

Cox, P.G. and B. Kearney (1983) 'The Impact of the Common Agricultural Policy', in D. Coombes (ed.), *Ireland and the European Communities: Ten Years of Membership* (Dublin: Gill & Macmillan), pp. 158–182.

Crotty, v. An Taoiseach (1986) *IEHC 3*, (24 December 1986).

—— (1986) *Ireland in Crisis: A Study of Capitalist Colonial Underdevelopment.* (Dingle: Brandon).

—— (1988) *A Radical's Response* (Dublin: Poolbeg).

—— (1992) *Maastricht: Time to Say No* (Dublin: National Platform for Employment, Democracy and Neutrality).

Crowley, E. (2003) 'The Evolution of the Common Agricultural Policy and Social Differentiation in Rural Ireland', *Economic and Social Review*, 34(1), pp. 65–85.

Dáil Debates Vol. 247, 23 June 1970.

Daly, M. (2002) *The First Department – A History of the Department of Agriculture* (Dublin: Institute of Public Administration).

—— (2006) *The Slow Failure: Population Decline and Independent Ireland 1920–1973* (Wisconsin: University of Wisconsin Press).

De Búrca, D. (2005) 'Institutional Reform and the European Constitution', pana.ie/idn/190405.html.

—— (2007) 'Greens must be Clear on Role in EU', *The Irish Times*, 15 October.

Devine, K.M. (2006) 'The Myth of the 'Myth of Irish Neutrality': Deconstructing Concepts of Irish Neutrality using International Relations Theories', *Irish Studies in International Affairs*, 17, pp. 115–139.

Department of Agriculture and Food. (2004) *A Guide to Irish Agriculture and Food.* www.agriculture.gov.ie [accessed 20 September 2007].

Department of Agriculture and Food. (2005) *Action Plan for Agriculture and Agri-Business.* www.agriculture.gov.ie [accessed 20 September 2007].

Department of the Environment and Local Government. (2002) *Attitudes and Actions. A National Survey on the Environment*, Prepared by Drury Research Ltd.

De Vreese, C., S.A. Banducci, H.A. Semetko and H. Boomgaarden (2006) 'The News Coverage of the 2004 European Parliamentary Election Campaign in 25 Countries', *European Union Politics*, 7(4), pp. 477–504.

Dinan, D. (2005) *Ever Closer Union*, 3rd edn (Basingstoke: Palgrave MacMillan).

Doherty, R. (2000) 'Partnership for Peace: The *Sine Qua Non* for Irish Participation in Regional Peacekeeping', *International Peacekeeping*, 7(2), pp. 63–82.

——— (2002) *Ireland, Neutrality and European Security Integration* (Aldershot: Ashgate).

Dornbusch, R. (1989) 'Credibility, Debt and Unemployment: Ireland's Failed Stabilization', *Economic Policy*, 4(8), pp. 72–209.

Dorr, N. (1996) 'Ireland at the UN: 40 Years On', *Irish Studies in International Affairs*, 7, pp. 41–62.

Doyle, A. (2003) 'Environmental Law: Integrated Control of Pollution?' in M.C. Lucey and C. Keville (eds), *Irish Perspectives on EC Law* (Dublin: Round Hall Ltd).

Drudy, P.J. and D. McAleese (eds) (1984) *Ireland and the European Community* (Cambridge: Cambridge University Press).

Dunleavy, P. and R.A.W. Rhodes (1990) 'Prime Minister, Cabinet and Core Executive – Introduction', *Public Administration*, 68(1), pp. 1–10.

English, R. (2006) *Irish Freedom: The History of Nationalism in Ireland* (London: Macmillan), pp. 625

Environmental Protection Agency (2000) *Ireland's Environment. A Millennium Report.* www.epa.ie/soe/soemain.html [accessed 15 August 2003].

Environmental Protection Agency (2005) *National Waste Report 2004* (Wexford: Environmental Protection Agency).

Eur-lex (1978) Case 88/77. eur-lex.europa.eu/Lexllriserv/Lexllriserv.do?uri=CELEX:61977J0088:EN:HTML

Eurobarometer 57 (2002), 58 (2002), 59 (2003), 63.4 (2004), 63 (2005), 64 (2005), 66 (2006), 67 (2007) 68 (2008): http://ec.europa.eu/public_opinion/standard_en.htm.

European Commission (2004) Communication from the Commission to the Council, the European Parliament, the Economic and Social Committee and the Committee of the Regions. European Electronic Communications Regulation and Markets 2004 (10th Report). Annex I. COM (2004) 759 final.

European Commission (2006) Communication from the Commission to the Council, the European Parliament, the Economic and Social Committee and the Committee of the Regions. European Electronic Communications Regulation and Markets 2005 (11th Report). Annex I. COM (2006) 68 final.

Fahey, E. (2007) 'Reflecting on the Scope of the European Union (Scrutiny) Act, 2002 and Parliamentary Scrutiny in the Draft Constitutional Treaty as to European Integration and the Irish Legal Order', *European Public Law*, 13(1), pp. 85–96.

Fahey, T., H. Russell and C.T. Whelan (eds) (2007) *Best of Times? The Social Impact of the Celtic Tiger* (Dublin: Institute of Public Administration).

Fahey, T. (2007) 'Population', in S. O'Sullivan, *Contemporary Ireland: A Sociological Map* (Dublin: UCD Academic Press), pp. 13–29.

Falkner, G. *et al.* (2004) 'Non-Compliance with EU Directives in the Member States: Opposition through the Backdoor?' *West European Politics*, 27(3), pp. 452–473.

Fanning, R. (ed.) (2002) *Documents an Irish Foreign Policy, Vol. III*, 1926–32 (Dublin: Royal Irish Academy).

Farrell, B. (1971) *Chairman or Chief? The Role of Taoiseach in Irish Government.* Studies in Irish Political Culture 1 (Dublin: Gill & Macmillan).

———— (1983) *Sean Lemass* (Dublin: Gill & Macmillan).

Faughnan, P. and B. McCabe (1998) *Irish Citizen Attitudes and the Environment. A Cross National Study of Environmental Attitudes, Perceptions and Behaviours* (Wexford: Environmental Protection Agency).

Featherstone, K. (2003) 'Introduction: In the Name of 'Europe', in K. Featherstone and C. Radaelli (eds), *The Politics of Europeanisation* (Oxford: Oxford University Press), pp. 3–26.

Ferriter, D. (2004) *The Transformation of Ireland 1900–2000* (London: Profile Books).

Fingleton, J. (2000) 'Privatisation: the Irish Context. Discussion', *Journal of the Statistical and Sociological Inquiry Society of Ireland*, xxix.

Finlay, F. (1998) *Snakes and Ladders* (Dublin: New Island Books).

Fisk, R. (1983) *In Time of War: Ireland, Ulster and the Price of Neutrality 1939–1945* (London: André Deutsch).

FitzGerald, G. (1973) Irish Foreign Policy Statement. Dáil Debates, Vol.265, 9 May.

———— (1991) *All in a Life* (Dublin: Gill & Macmillan).

———— (2007) 'What Caused the Celtic Tiger Phenomenon?' *The Irish Times*, 21 July.

FitzGerald, J. (1998) *An Irish Perspective on the Structural Funds* (Dublin: Economic and Social Research Institute).

———— (2000) 'The Story of Ireland's Failure – and Belated Success', in B. Nolan, P.J. O'Connell and C.T. Whelan (eds), *Bust to Boom? The Irish Experience of Growth and Inequality* (Dublin: Institute of Public Administration).

———— (2001) 'Managing an Economy Under EMU: The Case of Ireland', *The World Economy*, 24(10), pp. 1353–1371.

Bibliography

—— (2004) 'Lessons from 20 Years of Cohesion', *ESRI Working Paper* No.159.

Fitzgerald, M. (2000) *Protectionism to Liberalisation. Ireland and the EEC 1957–1966* (Aldershot: Ashgate).

—— (2001) 'Ireland's Relations With the EEC: From the Treaties of Rome to Membership', *Journal of European Integration History*, 7(1), pp. 11–24.

Fitzgibbon, J. (2007) 'The triumph of strategy over ideology? Euroscepticism in the Irish party system', Paper presented at *Europopulisme* conference, July, Paris.

Flash Eurobarometer 245 (2008) Post Referendum-Survey in Ireland. June.

Flinter, D. (2005) 'The transformation of the Irish Economy', CIT Working Paper, 052112. (Athens: Clemson University Center for International Trade), 21 December.

Flynn, B. (2003) 'Much Talk but Little Action? 'New' Environmental Policy Instruments in Ireland', in A. Jordan, R. Wurzel and A. Zito (eds), *'New' Instruments of Environmental Governance? National Experiences and Prospects* (London: Frank Cass).

—— (2007) *The Blame Game. Rethinking Ireland's Sustainable Development and Environmental Performance* (Dublin: Irish Academic Press).

Forfás. (2007) Forfás Statement on Outward Direct Investment (Dublin: Forfás), www.forfas.ie. September.

Foster, R. (2007) *Luck and the Irish. A Brief History of Change 1970–2000* (London: Allen Lane).

Frampton, M. (2005) 'Sinn Féin and the European Arena: 'Ourselves Alone' or 'Critical Engagement'? *Irish Studies in International Affairs*, 16, pp. 235–253.

Franklin, M., C. van der Eijk and M. Marsh (1995) 'Referendum Outcomes and Trust in Government: Public Support for Europe in the Wake of Maastricht', *West European Politics*, 18(3), pp. 101–17.

Gabel, M. (1998) 'Public Support for European Integration: An empirical Test of Five Theories', *Journal of Politics*, 60(2), pp. 333–354.

—— (2001) 'European Integration, Voters and National Politics', in K. Goetz and S. Hix (eds), *Europeanised Politics? European Integration and National Political Systems* (London: Frank Cass).

Gallagher, M. (1988) 'The Single European Act Referendum', *Irish Political Studies*, 3, pp. 77–82.

—— (2003) 'Referendum Campaigns in Ireland'. Paper Presented at the 8th International EISE Conference on 'Le Campagne Elettorali', Venice, 18–20 December.

Gallagher, M., M. Laver and P. Mair (2001) *Representative Government in Modern Europe*. Third Edition (Boston: McGraw Hill).

Galligan, Y. (2005) 'Women in Politics', in J. Coakley and M. Gallagher (eds), *Politics in the Republic of Ireland*, Fourth Edition (London: Routledge).

Garry, J., M. Marsh and R. Sinnott (2005) '"Second-order" versus "Issue-voting"' Effects in EU Referendums. Evidence from the Irish Nice Treaty Referendums', *European Union Politics*, 6(2), p. 201

Garvin, T. (1992) 'Democracy in Ireland: Collective Somnambulance and Public Policy', *Administration*, 39(1), pp. 42–54.

———— (2000) 'The French are on the Sea', in O'Donnell (ed.), *Europe: The Irish Experience* (Dublin: IEA), pp. 35–43.

———— (2004) *Preventing the Future: why was Ireland so poor for so long?* (Dublin: Gill & Macmillan).

Genschel, P. (2001) 'Comment: The Europeanization of Central Government', in M.D. Aspinwall and G. Schneider (eds), *The Rules of Integration* (Manchester: Manchester University Press).

Gilland, K. (1999) 'Referenda in the Republic of Ireland', *Electoral Studies*, 18(3), pp. 430–8.

———— (2000) 'The 1999 European Parliament Election in the Republic of Ireland', *Irish Political Studies*, 15, pp. 127–133.

———— (2002a) 'Ireland's (First) Referendum on the Treaty of Nice', *Journal of Common Market Studies*, 40(3), pp. 527–35.

———— (2002b) 'Europe and the Irish General Election of May 2002', Royal Institute of International Affairs/Opposing Europe Research Network Election Briefing No.2. www.sussex.ac.uk/sei/documents/paper2irish.pdf. [accessed 22 May 2006].

———— (2003). 'Ireland at the Polls: Thirty Years of European-Related Referendums 1972–2002', York Referendum Forum February 15, www.iri-europe.org/reports/York-KarinGilland.ppt [accessed 21 May 2006].

———— (2004) 'Irish Euroscepticism', *European Studies*, 20, pp. 171–191.

Gillespie, P. (1996) 'Ireland in the New World Order: Interests and Values in the Irish Government's White Paper on Foreign Policy', *Irish Studies in International Affairs*, 7, pp. 143–156.

Goetz, K.H. (2001) 'Making Sense of Post-Communist Central Administration: Modernisation, Europeanization or Latinisation', *Journal of European Public Policy*, 8(6), pp. 1032–51.

Goetz, K.H. and S. Hix (2001) *Europeanized Politics? European Integration and National Political Systems* (London: Frank Cass).

Gormley, J. (2000) 'Greens' Warning on Cost of Euro Ignored', *The Irish Times*, 21 September.

———— (2002) 'EU Declarations do not Guarantee Ireland's Neutrality', *The Irish Times*, 16 October.

———— (2003) 'Should we Back a Pledge to Defend Others if they Come Under Attack?' *The Irish Times*, 3 April.

Government of Ireland (1970) *Membership of the European Communities-Implications for Ireland* (Dublin: Stationery Office).

Government of Ireland (1972) *The Accession of Ireland to the European Communities* (Dublin: Stationery Office).

Government of Ireland (1996) *Challenges and Opportunities Abroad: White Paper on Foreign Policy* (Dublin: Stationery Office).

Graziano, P. and M.P. Vink (2006) *Europeanization. New Research Agendas* (Palgrave: Basingstoke).

Grist, B. (1997) 'Wildlife Legislation – The Rocky Road to Special Areas of Conservation Surveyed', *Irish Planning and Environmental Law Journal*, 4(3).

Haagerup, N.J. (1984) 'Report Drawn up on Behalf of the Political Affairs Committee on the Situation in Northern Ireland', *European Parliament Working Document*, 1-1526/83, 9 March.

Hainsworth, P. (1981) 'Northern Ireland: A European Role?' *Journal of Common Market Studies*, 20(1), pp. 1–15.

Hall, P.A. and R.C.R. Taylor (1996) 'Political Science and the Three New Institutionalisms', *Political Studies*, XLIV/44, pp. 936–957.

Handoll, J. (1995) *Free Movement of Persons in the EU* (Chichester: Wiley).

Harmsen, R. (1999) 'The Europeanization of National Administrations: A Comparative Study of France and the Netherlands', *Governance*, 12, pp. 82–113.

Harney, M. (2000) Tánaiste, Address to a Meeting of the American Bar Association, Dublin, 21 July.

Hart, J. and B. Laffan (1983) 'Consequences of the Community's Regional and Social Policies', in D. Coombes (ed.), *Ireland and the European Communities: Ten Years of Membership* (Dublin: Gill & Macmillan), pp. 133–157.

Hastings, T., B. Sheehan and P. Yeates (2007) *Saving the Future: How Social Partnership Shaped Ireland's Economic Success* (Dublin: Blackhall Publishing).

Haughey, C. (1989) Address to the Irish Council of the European Movement, Dublin, 2 October.

Hayward, K. (2002) 'Not a Nice Surprise: An Analysis of the Debate Surrounding the 2001 Referendum on the Treaty of Nice in the Republic of Ireland', *Irish Studies in International Affairs*, 13, pp. 167–186.

——— (2003) 'If at First you don't Succeed ...': The Second Referendum on the Treaty of Nice, 2002', *Irish Political Studies*, 18(1), pp. 120–32.

——— (2006) 'National Territory in European Space: Reconfiguring the Island of Ireland', *European Journal of Political Research*, 45(6), pp. 897–920.

Hederman, M. (1983) *The Road to Europe: Irish Attitudes 1948–61* (Dublin: Institute of Public Administration).

Héritier, A. *et al.* (2001). *Differential Europe. The European Union Impact on National Policymaking* (Lanham, MD: Rowman & Littlefield).

Higher Education Authority (2005) Press Release. 14 September, www.hea.ie.

Hillery, P. (1999) 'Negotiating Ireland's Entry', in J. Dooge and R. Barrington (eds), *A Vital National Interest: Ireland in Europe 1973–1998* (Dublin: Institute of Public Administration), pp. 18–30.

Hix, S. (2005) *The Political System of the European Union*. Second Edition (Basingstoke: Palgrave).

Hix, S. and M. Marsh (2007) 'Punishment or Protest? Understanding European Parliament Elections', *Journal of Politics*, 69(2), pp. 495–510.

Holmes, M. (1990) 'The 1989 Election to the European Parliament in the Republic of Ireland', *Irish Political Studies*, 5, pp. 85–91.

—— (1993) 'The Maastricht Treaty Referendum of June 1992', *Irish Political Studies*, 8, pp. 105–10.

Holmes, M., N. Rees and B. Whelan (1993) *The Poor Relation. Irish Foreign Policy and the Third World* (Dublin: Gill & Macmillan).

Holmes, M. (1996) 'Irish Political Parties and the European Union', in J. Gaffney (ed.), *Political Parties and the European Union* (London: Routledge), pp. 192–204.

Holmes, M. (ed.) (2005) *Ireland and the European Union. Nice, Enlargement and the Future of Europe* (Manchester University Press: Manchester).

Holmes, M. (2007) 'Europe and the General Election in the Republic of Ireland, 24 May 2007', *Election Briefing No.35*, European Parties Elections and Referendums Network.

Honohan, P. (2000) 'Ireland in EMU: Straightjacket or Skateboard?' *Irish Banking Review*, Winter.

Honohan, P. and B. Walsh (2002) 'Catching Up with the Leaders: The Irish Hare', *Brookings Papers on Economic Activity*, Vol. 1.

Honohan P. and A. J. Leddin (2006) 'Ireland in EMU: More Shocks, Less Insulation?' *Economic and Social Review*, 37(2), pp. 263–294.

House, J.D. and K. McGrath (2004) 'Innovative Governance and Development in the New Ireland: Social Partnership and the Integrated Approach', *Governance*, 17(1), pp. 29–57.

Hug, S. and P. Sciarini (2000) 'Referendums on European Integration. Do Institutions Matter in the Voter's Decision?' *Comparative Political Studies*, 33(1), pp. 3–36.

Humphreys, P. (1997) *The Fifth Irish Presidency of the European Union: Some Management Lessons* (Dublin: Institute of Public Administration).

Hussey, G. (1993) *Ireland Today. Anatomy of a Changing State* (London: Penguin).

Ikenberry, G. J. (1988) 'Conclusion: An Institutional Approach to American Foreign Economic Policy', in G.J. Ikenberry, D.A. Lake and M. Mastanduno (eds), *The State and American Foreign Economic Policy*, (Ithaca NY: Cornell University Press).

Irish Council of the European Movement (ICEM) (1972) *Opportunity: Ireland and Europe*, Dublin, p. 48.

Ingebritsen, C., I. Neumann, S. Gstohl and J. Beyer (2006) *Small States in International Relations* (Seattle: University of Washington/University of Iceland).

Inglis, T. (1998) *Moral Monopoly: The Rise and Fall of the Catholic Church in Modern Ireland* (Dublin: UCD Press).

—— (2008) *Global Ireland* (London: Routledge).

Ishizuka, K. (1999) 'Ireland and the Partnership for Peace', *Irish Studies in International Affairs*, 10, pp. 185–200.

—— (2004) *Ireland and International Peacekeeping Opertions 1960–2000. A Study of Irish Motivation* (London: Frank Cass).

Joint Committee on European Affairs Sub-Committee on European Scrutiny (2007) *Fourth Annual Report on the Operation of the European Union (Scrutiny) Act 2002: 1 January 2006 to 31 December 2006* (Dublin: Stationery Office).

Kassim, H. (ed.) (2001) *The National Coordination of EU Policy: the European Level* (Oxford: Oxford University Press).

Kassim, H. (2003) 'Meeting the Demands of EU Membership: The Europeanization of National Administrative Systems', in K. Featherstone and C. Radaelli (eds), *The Politics of Europeanization* (Oxford: Oxford University Press), pp. 83–111.

Kearney, R. (ed.) (1988) *Across the Frontiers: Ireland in the 1990s – Cultural – Political – Economic* (Dublin: Wolfhound Press).

Keatinge, P. (1978) *A Place Among the Nations. Issues of Irish Foreign Policy* (Dublin: Institute of Public Administration).

—— (1984a) *A Singular Stance. Irish Neutrality in the 1980s* (Dublin: Institute of Public Administration).

—— (1984b) 'The Europeanisation of Irish Foreign Policy', in P.J. Drudy, and D. McAleese (eds), *Ireland and the European Community* (Cambridge: Cambridge University Press), pp. 33–56.

Keatinge, P. (ed.) (1991) *Ireland and EC Membership Evaluated* (London: Pinter).

Keatinge, P. (1995) 'The Irish Foreign Service: an Observer's View', *Seminar on the Irish Foreign Service*, Trinity College, 2 March.

—— (1998) 'Ireland and European Security: Continuity and Change', *Irish Studies in International Affairs*, 9, pp. 31–37.

Keatinge, P. and M. Marsh (1990) 'The European Parliament Election', in M. Gallagher and R. Sinnott (eds), *How Ireland Voted 1989* (Galway: The Centre for the Study of Irish Elections).

Kennedy, K.A. (2001) 'Reflections on the Process of Irish Economic Growth', *Journal of the Statistical and Social Inquiry Society of Ireland*, xxx, pp. 123–139.

Kennedy, L. (1994) *People and Population Change: A Comparative Study of Population Change in Northern Ireland and the Republic of Ireland* (Dublin/Belfast: Cooperation North).

——— (1996) *Colonialism, Religion and Nationalism in Ireland* (Belfast: Institute of Irish Studies, Queens University).

Kennedy, F. and R. Sinnott (2007) 'Irish Public Opinion toward European Integration', *Irish Political Studies*, 22(1), pp. 61–80.

Kennedy, M. and J.M. Skelly (eds) (2000). *Irish Foreign Policy 1919–1966: From Independence to Internationalism* (Dublin: Four Courts).

Kenny, L. (2003) 'Local Government and Politics', in M. Callanan and J.F. Keogan (eds), *Local Government in Ireland: Inside Out* (Dublin: Institute of Public Administration), pp. 103–122.

Keogh, D. (1990) *Ireland and Europe 1919–1989: A Diplomatic and Political History* (Cork and Dublin: Hibernian University Press).

——— (1994) *Twentieth-Century Ireland: Nation and State* (Dublin: Gill & Macmillan).

Keohane, D. (2001). 'Realigning Neutrality? Irish Defence Policy and the EU'. Institute for Security Studies of the WEU, Occasional Paper 24.

Kirby, P. (2002) *The Celtic Tiger in Distress: Growth and Inequality in Ireland* (Basingstoke: Palgrave).

Kirby P., D. Jacobson and D. Ó Broin (eds) (2006) *Taming the Tiger: Social Exclusion in a Globalised Ireland* (Dublin: New Island Books).

Klemenčič, M. (2007) 'Strategic Relationships of Small States in the European Union', Paper presented at the Conference on Small States, University of Birmingham, 4–5 April.

Knill, C. (1998) 'Implementing European Policies: The impact of National Administrative Traditions', *Journal of Public Policy*, 18(1), pp. 1–28.

——— (2001) *The Europeanization of National Administrations* (Cambridge: Cambridge University Press).

Knill, C. and A. Lenschow (eds) (2000) *Implementing EU Environmental Policy: New Approaches to an Old Problem* (Manchester: Manchester University Press).

Ladrech, R. (1994) 'Europeanization of Domestic Politics and Institutions: The Case of France', *Journal of Common Market Studies*, 32(1), pp. 69–88.

——— (2002) 'Europeanization and Political Parties. Toward a Framework for Analysis', *Party Politics*, 8(4), pp. 389–403.

Laffan, B. (1991) 'Women', in Keatinge (ed.), *Ireland and EC Membership Evaluated* (London: Pinter).

——— (1991) 'The Political Process', in P. Keatinge *et al.*, Ireland *and EC Membership Evaluated*, pp. 197–208.

——— (1996) 'Ireland', in D. Rometsch and W. Wessels (eds), *The EU and Member States: Towards Institutional Fusion?* (Manchester and New York: Manchester University Press), pp. 291–312.

——— (1997) *The Finances of the European Union* (Basingstoke: Macmillan).

——— (2000) 'Rapid Adaptation and Light Co-ordination' in R. O'Donnell (ed.), *Europe. The Irish Experience* (Dublin: Institute of European Affairs), pp. 125–147.

——— (2001) *Organising for a Changing Europe: Irish Central Government and the European Union* (Trinity College Dublin: Policy Institute).

——— (2002) 'Irish Politics and European Politics', Radio Telefís Éireann Radio 1, Thomas Davis Lecture, November.

——— (2006) 'Managing Europe from Home in Dublin, Athens and Helsinki: A Comparative Analysis', *West European Politics*, 29(4), pp. 687–708.

Laffan, B. and R. O'Donnell (1999) 'Ireland and the Growth of International Governance', in W. Crotty and D. E. Schmitt (eds), *Ireland and the Politics of Change* (London: Longman).

Laffan, B., R. O'Donnell and M. Smith (1999) *Europe's Experimental Union: Rethinking Integration* (London: Routledge).

Laffan, B. and G. Falkner (2005) 'The Europeanisation of Austria and Ireland: Small can be Difficult?' in S. Bulmer and C. Lequesne, *The Member States of the European Union* (Oxford: Oxford University Press).

Laffan, B. and D. Payne (2001) *Creating Living Institutions: EU Cross-Border Cooperation After the Good Friday Agreement* (Armagh: Centre for Cross Border Studies).

Laffan, B. and B. Tonra (2005) 'Europe and the International Dimension', in M. Gallagher and J. Coakley (eds), *Politics in the Republic of Ireland*, Fourth Edition (London: Routledge (in association with PSAI Press)).

Laffan, B. and J. O'Mahony (2004) 'Misfit, Politicisation and Europeanisation. The Implementation of the Habitats Directive', OEUE Occasional Paper, Dublin European Institute, www.oeue.net [accessed 1 February 2007].

——— and ——— (2007) 'Managing Europe from an Irish Perspective: Critical Junctures and the Increasing Formalisation of the Core Executive in Ireland', *Public Administration*, 85(1), pp. 167–188.

——— and ——— (2008) 'Bringing Politics Back In': Domestic Conflict and the Negotiated Implementation of Nature Conservation Legislation in Ireland', *Journal of Environmental Policy and Planning*, 10(2), pp. 175–97.

Laffan, M. (1999) *The Resurrection of Ireland: The Sinn Féin Party, 1916–1923* (Cambridge: Cambridge University Press).

Laver, M. (2005) 'Voting Behaviour', in J. Coakley and M. Gallagher (eds), *Politics in the Republic of Ireland*, Fourth Edition (London: Routledge (in association with PSAI Press)).

Leddin, A.J. and B.M. Walsh (2003) *The Macroeconomy of the Eurozone. An Irish Perspective* (Dublin: Gill & Macmillan).

Lee M. (2004) 'The Small State Enlargement of the EU: Dangers and Benefits', *Perspectives on European Politics and Society*, 5(2), 331–55.

Lee, J.J. (1989) *Ireland 1912–1985: Politics and Society* (Cambridge: Cambridge University Press).

Lenschow, A. (2005) 'Europeanisation of Public Policy', in J. Richardson (ed.) *European Union. Power and Policy Making*, Third Edition (London: Routledge), pp. 55–69.

Loyal, S. (2007) 'Immigration', in S. O'Sullivan (ed.) *Contemporary Ireland: A Sociological Map*, (Dublin: UCD Academic Press), pp. 30–47.

Ludlow, P. (1997) *A View from Brussels – A Quarterly Commentary on the EU*, No. 4 (Brussels: Centre for European Policy Studies).

MacCoille, C. and D. McCoy (2002) 'Economic Adjustment Within EMU: Ireland's Experience', *Economic and Social Review*, 33(2), pp. 179–193.

MacGinty, R. (1995) 'Almost Like Talking Dirty: Irish Security Policy in Post-Cold War Europe', *Irish Studies in International Affairs* 6, pp. 127–143.

MacKernan, P. (1984) 'Ireland and European Political Co-operation'. *Irish Studies in International Affairs*, 1(4), p. 177.

MacSharry, R. and P.A. White (2000) *The Making of the Celtic Tiger: the Inside Story of Ireland's Boom Economy* (Cork: Mercier Press).

Magnette, P. and K. Nicolaidis (2003) 'Large and Small Member States in the European Union' (Paris: Notre Europe), No. 25 Research and European Issues.

Maher, D. (1986) *The Tortuous Path: The Course of Ireland's Entry into the EEC 1948–1973* (Dublin: Institute of Public Administration).

Mair, P. (2001) 'The Limited Impact of Europe on National Party Systems', in K. Goetz and S. Hix (eds) *Europeanised Politics? European Integration and National Political Systems* (London: Frank Cass).

—— (2006) 'Political Parties and Party Systems', in Graziano and Vink (eds), *Europeanization: New Research Agendas* (Basingstoke: Palgrave Macmillan).

Mair, P. and L. Weeks (2005) 'The Party System', in J. Coakley and M. Gallagher (eds), *Politics in the Republic of Ireland*, Fourth Edition (London: Routledge (in association with PSAI Press)).

Manners, I. and R. Whitman (eds) (2000) *The Foreign Policies of European Union Member States* (Manchester: Manchester University Press).

Mansergh, L. (1999) 'Two Referendums and the Referendum Commission: the 1998 Experience', *Irish Political Studies*, 14, pp. 123–131.

March, J. and J. Olsen (1984) 'The New Institutionalism: Organizational Factors in Political Life', *American Journal of Political Research*, 78(3), pp. 734–749.

Marks, G. *et al.* (1996) *Governance in the European Union* (London: Sage).

Marks, G. and L. Hooghe (2001) 'Types of Multilevel Governance', *European Integration online Papers (EIoP)*, 5(11).

Marsh, M. (1995) 'The 1994 European Parliament Election in the Republic of Ireland', *Irish Political Studies*, 10, pp. 209–215.

—— (1996) 'Ireland: An Electorate with its Mind on Lower Things', in C. Van der Eijk and M. Franklin (eds), *Choosing Europe* (Ann Arbor: University of Michigan Press), pp. 166–185.

—— (1998) 'Testing the Second-Order Election Model after Four European Elections', *British Journal of Political Science*, 28, pp. 591–607.

—— (2006) 'Party Identification in Ireland: An Insecure Anchor for a Floating Party System', *Electoral Studies*, 25(3), pp. 489–508.

Massey, P. and T. Shortall (1999) 'Competition and Regulation in Public Utility Industries', *Competition Authority Discussion Paper No.7*, July.

Massey, P. (2000) 'Privatisation: The Irish Context. Discussion', *Journal of the Statistical and Sociological Inquiry Society of Ireland*, Vol. xxix.

Matthews, A. (1983) 'The Economic Consequences of EEC Membership for Ireland', in D. Coombes (ed.) *Ireland and the European Communities: Ten Years of Membership* (Dublin: Gill and Macmillan), pp. 110–132.

—— (2005) 'Agriculture, Rural Development and Food Safety', in J. O'Hagan and C. Newman (eds), *The Economy of Ireland* (Dublin: Gill & Macmillan).

McAleese, D. (1984) 'Ireland and the European Community: The Changing Pattern of Trade', in Drudy, P.J. and D. McAleese (eds), *Ireland and the European Community* (Cambridge: Cambridge University Press), pp. 145–172.

—— (2000) 'Twenty-five Years a Growing', in R. O'Donnell (ed.), *Europe. The Irish Experience* (Dublin: Institute of European Affairs).

McCabe, I. (1991) *A Diplomatic History of Ireland 1948–49: The Republic, The Commonwealth and NATO* (Dublin: Irish Academic Press).

McCutcheon, P. (1991) 'The Legal System', in Keatinge *et al.*, *Ireland and EC Membership Evaluated* (London: Pinter), pp. 209–229.

McDonald, M.-L. (2005) *Address at Conference organised by European United Left/Nordic Green Left Group in the European Parliament* (Dublin) 28 May.

McDonagh, B. (1998) *Original Sin in a Brave New World: An Account of the Negotiation of the Treaty of Amsterdam* (Dublin: Institute of European Affairs).

McGowan, L. (1999) 'Environmental Policy', in N. Collins (ed.), *Political Issues in Ireland Today*, Second Edition (Manchester: Manchester University Press).

McGowan, L. and M. Murphy (2003) 'Europeanisation and the Irish Experience', in M. Adshead and M. Millar (eds), *Public Administration and Public Policy in Ireland* (London: Routledge), pp. 182–200.

McIntyre, O. (2002) 'Irish Implementation of EC Nature Conservation Law', *Irish Planning and Environmental Law Journal*, 9(3).

McLaren, L. (2006) *Identity, Interests and Attitudes to European Integration* (Basingstoke: Palgrave).

Moxon-Browne, E. (1996) 'Republic of Ireland', in J. Lodge (ed.), *The 1994 Elections to the European Parliament* (London: Pinter), pp. 122–133.

—— (2001) 'Ireland', in J. Lodge (ed.), *The 1999 Elections to the European Parliament* (Basingstoke: Palgrave), pp. 139–148.

—— (2005) 'Ireland', in J. Lodge (ed.), *The 2004 Elections to the European Parliament* (Basingstoke: Palgrave), pp. 146–154.

Mullally, G. and A. Quinlivan. (2004) 'Environmental Policy: Managing the Waste Problem', in Collins and Cradden (eds), *Political Issues in Ireland Today*, Fourth Edition (Manchester: Manchester University Press).

Murphy A. (2000) '*The Celtic Tiger-An Analysis of Ireland's Economic Growth Performance*', *EUI Working Papers, RSC No. 2000/16*, 1–37.

Murphy G. (1997) 'Government, Interest Groups and the Irish Move to Europe: 1957–63', *Irish Studies in International Affairs*, 8, pp. 57–68.

—— (2005) 'Interest Groups in the Policy Making Process', in J. Coakley and M. Gallagher (eds), *Politics in the Republic of Ireland*, Fourth Edition (London: Routledge, in Association with PSAI Press).

Murphy, R. (2002) 'Ireland, Peacekeeping and Defence Policy: Challenges and Opportunities', in B. Tonra and E. Ward (eds), *Ireland in International Affairs. Interests, Institutions and Identities. Essays in Honour of Professor N.P. Keatinge* (Dublin: Institute of Public Administration), pp. 13–45.

National Forum on Europe (2002) *Second Chairman's Report* (Dublin: Stationery Office).

National Forum on Europe (2005) *The Fifth Phase of Work of the National Forum on Europe on the European Constitution July 2004 to June 2005 Chairman's Report* (Dublin: Stationery Office).

National Economic and Social Council (1981) *The Socio-Economic Position of Ireland within the European Economic Community* (Dublin: Government Publications), No. 58, Prl. 9562.

National Economic and Social Council (1989) *Ireland in the European Community: Performance, Prospects and Strategy*, Report No.88 (Dublin: National Economic and Social Council).

National Economic and Social Council (2003) *A Strategy for Quality: Services, Inclusion and Enterprise. Overview, Conclusions and Recommendations*, Report No.110 (Dublin: National Economic and Social Council).

National Platform (EU Research and Information Centre) (2006) *A Europe of Cooperating Independent Democratic Nation States. Our Vision for the Future of Europe*, Submission to the National Forum on Europe.

Nolan, B. and B. Maitre (2007) 'Economic Growth and Income Inequality: Setting the Context', in T. Fahey, H. Russell and C.T. Whelan (eds), *Best of Times? The Social Impact of the Celtic Tiger* (Dublin: Institute of Public Administration).

Norman, P. (2003) *The Accidental Constitution: The Story of the European Convention* (Brussels: EuroComment).

O'Brennan, J. (2003) 'Ireland's Return to "Normal" Voting Patterns on EU Issues: The 2002 Nice Treaty Referendum', www.essex.ac.uk/ECPR/publications/eps/onlineissues/spring2003/feature.htm. Spring, Vol.2, No.2 [accessed 5 April 2006].

O'Brennan, J. (2004) 'Ireland's National Forum on Europe: Elite Deliberation Meets Popular Participation', *European Integration*, 26(2), pp. 171–189.

Ó Cinneide, S. (ed.) (1993) *EC Social Policy and Ireland* (Dublin: Institute of European Affairs).

O' Cleireacain, S. (1983) 'Northern Ireland and Irish Integration: The Role of the European Communities', *Journal of Common Market Studies*, 22(2), pp. 107–24.

Organisation for European Co-operation and Development (2003) (Economic Surveys: Ireland 2003/9-July).

O'Donnell, R. (1991) 'Competition Policy', in P. Keatinge (ed.), *Ireland and EC Membership Evaluated* (London: Pinter), pp. 90–96.

O'Donnell, R. and C. O'Reardon (1996) 'The Irish Experiment. The 'Social Partnership' has yielded Economic Growth together with Social Progress', *New Economy*, 3(1), pp. 33–38.

O'Donnell, R. (1998) *Ireland's Economic Transformation: Industrial Policy, European Integration and Social Partnership*, WP 2, *Centre for West European Studies: EU Center* University of Pittsburgh pp. 26 www.pitt.edu/~westnews

O'Donnell, R. (ed.) (2000) *Europe, The Irish Experience* (Dublin: Institute of European Affairs).

O'Donnell, R. (2001) 'To Be a Member State: The Experience of Ireland', Public Lecture (Dublin European Institute) University College Dublin: 26 September.

O'Donnell, R. and B. Moss (2004) 'Ireland'. Paper Presented at Workshop 'Opening *the Open Method of Coordination*', Joint Saltsa, Observatoire Social Europeen, University of Wisconsin-Madison (Project European University Institute: Florence) 4–5 July.

O'Halpin, E. (1996) 'Irish Parliamentary Culture and the EU: Formalities to be Observed', in P. Norton (ed.), *National Parliaments and the European Union* (London: Frank Cass).

O'Hearn, D. (1998) *Inside the Celtic Tiger: The Irish Economy and the Asian Model* (London: Pluto Press).

O'Mahony, J. (1998) 'The Irish Referendum Experience', *Representation*, 35(4).

——— (2001) '"Not So Nice": The Treaty of Nice, the International Criminal Court, the Abolition of the Death Penalty – the 2001 Referendum Experience', *Irish Political Studies*, 16, pp. 201–13.

——— (2004) 'Ireland and the European Union: A Less Certain Relationship?' in N. Collins and ? Cradden (eds), *Political Issues in Ireland Today*, Third Edition (Manchester: Manchester University Press).

——— (2007) ' 'Europeanisation as Implementation': The Impact of the EU on Irish Environmental Policy-Making', *Irish Political Studies*, 22(3), pp. 245–265.

O'Mahony, P. (2000) 'The Impact of the Third Pillar on Irish Civil Liberties', in E. Regan (ed.), *The New Third Pillar. Cooperation Against Crime in the European Union* (Dublin: Institute of European Affairs).

O'Sullivan, S. (2007) *Contemporary Ireland: A Sociological Map* (Dublin: UCD Academic Press).

O'Riain, S. (2000) 'The Flexible Developmental State: Globalization, Information Technology and the "Celtic Tiger"', *Politics and Society*, 28(2), pp. 157–93.

O'Toole, F. (1994) *Black Hole, Green Card: The Disappearance of Ireland* (Dublin: New Island Books).

—— (2003) *After the Ball* (Dublin: Tasc at New Ireland).

OECD. (2001) *Regulatory Reform in Ireland. OECD Reviews of Regulatory Reform.* April.

Olsen, J. (2002) 'The Many Faces of Europeanization', *Journal of Common Market Studies*, 40(5), pp. 921–52.

Page, E.C. and L. Wouters (1995) 'The Europeanization of National Bureaucracies', in J. Pierre (ed.), *Bureaucracy in the Modern State* (Cheltenham: Edward Elgar).

Patten, Chris. (2005) *Not Quite the Diplomat. Home Truths about World Affairs* (London: Allen Lane/Penguin).

Paus, E.A. (2005) *Foreign Investment, Development and Globalisation. Can Costa Rica Become Ireland?* (New York: Palgrave).

Peace and Neutrality Alliance (PANA) (2005) *Yes to Europe, No to Superstate*, www.pana.ie.

Peers, S. (2006) *EU Justice and Home Affairs Law*, Second Edition (Oxford: Oxford University Press).

Peter, J., E. Lauf and H.A. Semetko (2004) 'Television Coverage of the 1999 European Parliamentary Elections', *Political Communication*, 21, pp. 415–433.

Pierson, P. (2000a) 'The Limits of Design: Explaining Institutional Origins and Change', *Governance*, 13(4), pp. 475–499.

—— (2000b) 'Increasing Returns, Path Dependence, and the Study of Politics', *American Political Science Review*, 94(2), pp. 251–267.

Quinlivan, A. and E. Schön-Quinlivan (2004) 'The 2004 European Parliament Election in the Republic of Ireland', *Irish Political Studies*, 19(2), pp. 85–95.

Radaelli, C.M. (2000) 'Whither Europeanization? Concept Stretching and Substantive Change', *EiOP online papers*, 4(8).

—— (2003) 'The Europeanization of Public Policy', in F. Featherstone and R. Radaelli (eds), *The Politics of Europeanization* (Oxford: Oxford University Press).

Rees, N. (2005a) 'The Irish Presidency: A Diplomatic Triumph', *Journal of Common Market Studies*, 43 Annual Review, 55–8.

—— (2005b) 'Europe and Ireland's Changing Security Policy', in M. Holmes (ed.), *Ireland and the European Union. Nice, Enlargement and the Future of Europe* (Manchester: Manchester University Press), pp. 55–74.

—— (2006) 'Ireland's Foreign Relations in 2005', *Irish Studies in International Affairs*, 17, pp. 151–182.

Referendum Commission (2008) 'Referendum Commission Outlines Public Information Campaign Details as Research Shows Low Public Knowledge of Lisbon Treaty', Press Release, 28 April.

Reif, R. and H. Schmitt (1980) 'Nine Second Order National Elections: A Conceptual Framework for the Analysis of European Election Results', *European Journal of Political Research*, 8, pp. 3–44.

Reinhardt N. (1996) 'Public Attitudes Towards the European Union', in M. Browne and D. Kennedy (eds), *The Dynamics of Conflict in Northern Ireland* (Cambridge: Cambridge University Press).

Rhodes, R.A.W. (ed.) (2000) *Transforming British Government. Volume 1 Changing Institutions* (Basingstoke: Macmillan).

—— (ed.) (2000) *Transforming British Government. Volume 2 Changing Roles and Relationships* (Basingstoke: Macmillan).

Roche, D. (2007) 'Ireland's Vision of European Integration', Address Delivered at NUI Galway, 29 September.

Roche, W.K. (2007) 'Social Partnership in Ireland and New Social Pacts', *Industrial Relations*, 46(3), pp. 395–425.

Ruane, J. and J. Todd. (1996) *The Dynamics of Conflict in Northern Ireland: Power, Conflict and Emancipation* (Cambridge: Cambridge University Press).

Sabel, C.F. (1996) *Ireland: Local Partnerships and Social Innovation* (Paris: OECD).

Salmon, T. C. (1989) *Unneutral Ireland: An Ambivalent and Unique Security Policy* (Oxford: Clarendon Press).

Sargent, T. (2002) 'Vote No to Save Green Vision of a Free Europe of Equals', *Irish Times*, 7 October.

Sbragia, A. (2003) 'Key Policies', in E. Bomberg and A. Stubb (eds), *The European Union: How Does it Work* (Oxford: Oxford University Press).

Scannell, Y. *et al.* (1999) *The Habitats Directive in Ireland* (Trinity College Dublin: Centre for Environmental Law and Policy).

Schmitt, H. (2005) 'The European Parliament Elections of June 2004: Still Second-Order?' *West European Politics*, 28(3), pp. 650–679.

Scott, D. (1994) *Ireland's Contribution to the European Union* (Dublin: Institute of European Affairs Occasional Paper 4).

Scott, R. W. (2001) *Institutions and Organizations*, Second Edition (Thousand Oaks: Sage).

Sheehy, S.J. (1984) 'The Common Agricultural Policy and Ireland', in Drudy, P.J. and D. McAleese (eds), *Ireland and the European Community* (Cambridge: Cambridge University Press), pp. 77–106.

Sinn Féin. (2001) *Treaty of Nice Manifesto*, www.sinnfein.ie.

―――― (2004) *An Ireland of Equals in a Europe of Equals. Sinn Féin EU Election Manifesto 2004*, www.sinnfein.ie.

Sinnott, R. (1995a) *Irish Voters Decide. Voting Behaviour in Elections and Referendums Since 1918* (Manchester: Manchester University Press).

―――― (1995b) *Knowledge of the European Union in Irish Public Opinion: Sources and Implications* (Dublin: Institute for European Affairs).

―――― (2001) *Attitudes and Behaviour of the Irish Electorate in the Referendum on the Treaty of Nice*. Dublin: European Commission Representation in Ireland; also available www.ucd.ie/dempart/workingpapers/ nice1.pdf [accessed 15 December 2005].

―――― (2002) 'Cleavages, Parties and Referendums: Relationships Between Representative and Direct Democracy in the Republic of Ireland', *European Journal of Political Research*, 41, 811–826.

―――― (2003) *Attitudes and Behaviour of the Irish Electorate in the Second Referendum on the Treaty of Nice*, Results of a Survey of Public Opinion Carried out for the European Commission Representation in Ireland, Dublin.

―――― (2007) 'EU Referenda: Selective Veto or Inclusive Consultation?' in *Challenge Europe. Europe @50: Back to the Future* (Brussels: European Policy Centre).

Skelly, J.M. (1997) *Irish Diplomacy at the United Nations, 1945–1965: National Interests and the International Order* (Dublin: Irish Academic Press).

Smith, M.J. (2000) 'Prime Ministers, Ministers and Civil Servants in the Core Executive', in R.A.W. Rhodes (ed.), *Transforming British Government Vol.1* (London: Macmillan), pp. 25–45.

Smith, N.J. (2002) 'The Irish Republic – A '"Showpiece of Globalisation"?' Politics, 22(3), pp. 125–134.

―――― (2005) *Showcasing Globalisation?: The Political Economy of the Irish Republic* (Manchester: Manchester University Press).

Storey, A. (2001) *The Treaty of Nice, NATO and A European Army: Implications for Ireland*, Afri (Action from Ireland): www.afri.ie.

Svensson, P. (2002) 'Five Danish Referendums on the European Community and Union: A Critical Assessment of the Franklin Thesis', *European Journal of Political Research*, 41(6), pp. 733–50.

Taggart, P. (1998) 'A Touchstone of Dissent: Euroscepticism in Contemporary Western European Party Systems', *European Journal of Political Research*, 33, pp. 363–388.

Taggart, P. and A. Szczerbiak (2004) 'Contemporary Euroscepticism in the Party Systems of the European Union Candidate States of Central and Eastern Europe', *European Journal of Political Research*, 43, pp. 1–27.

Taylor, G. (2001) *Conserving the Emerald Tiger: The Politics of Environmental Regulation in Ireland* (Galway: Arlen House).

——— (2002) 'Looking Back (but not in Anger): Policy Transfer and the Role of Institutional Memory in the Construction of the Irish Environmental Protection Agency', *Irish Studies in International Affairs*, 13, pp. 187–200.

——— (2005) *Negotiated Governance and Public Policy in Ireland* (Manchester: Manchester University Press).

Taylor, G. and C. Murphy (2002) 'Environmental Policy in Ireland', in G. Taylor (ed.), *Issues in Irish Public Policy* (Dublin: Irish Academic Press).

Teague, P. (1996) 'The European Union and the Irish Peace Process', *Journal of Common Market Studies*, 34(4), pp. 549–570.

Thelen, K. and S. Steinmo (1992) 'Historical Institutionalism in Comparative Politics', in S. Steinmo, K. Thelen and F. Longstreth (eds), *Structuring Politics: Historical Institutionalism in Comparative Analysis* (Cambridge: Cambridge University Press).

Thelen, K. (1999) 'Historical Institutionalism in Comparative Politics', *Annual Review of Political Science*, 2, pp. 369–404.

Thorhallsson, B. (2006) 'The Size of States in the European Union: Theoretical and Conceptual Perspectives', *Journal of European Integration*, 28(1), pp. 7–31.

Tonra, B. (ed.) (1997) *Amsterdam. What the Treaty Means* (Dublin: Institute of European Affairs).

Tonra, B. (2001) *The Europeanisation of National Foreign Policy. Dutch, Danish and Irish Foreign Policy in the European Union* (Aldershot: Ashgate).

——— (2002) 'Irish foreign policy', in W. Crotty and D.E. Schmitt (eds), *Ireland on the World Stage* (Harlow: Longman), pp. 24–45.

——— (2006) *Global Citizen and European Republic. Irish Foreign Policy in Transition* (Manchester: Manchester University Press).

Tovey, H. (1992) 'Environmentalism in Ireland: Modernisation and Identity', in P. Clancy *et al.* (eds), *Ireland and Poland Comparative Perspectives* (Dublin: University College Dublin, Department of Sociology).

——— (2007) 'Food and Rural Sustainable Development', in S. O'Sullivan, *Contemporary Ireland. A Sociological Map* (Dublin: UCD Press), pp. 283–298.

Tovey, H. and P. Share (2000) *A Sociology of Ireland* (Dublin: Gill & Macmillan).

Traistaru-Siedschlag, I. (2007) 'Macroeconomic Adjustment in Ireland Under the EMU', *ESRI Quarterly Economic Commentary*, pp. 78–92.

Van der Eijk, C. and M. Franklin (1996) *Choosing Europe: The European Electorate and National Politics in the Face of Union* (Ann Arbor: University of Michigan Press).

Walsh, B.M. (1984) 'Ireland's Membership of the European Monetary System: Expectations, Out-turn and Prospects', in P.J. Drudy and D. McAleese (eds), *Ireland and the European Community* (Cambridge: Cambridge University Press), pp. 173–190.

Wessels, W., A. Mauer and J. Mittag. (eds) (2003) *Fifteen into One? The European Union and its Member States* (Manchester: Manchester University Press).

Whitaker, T.K. (1974) 'From Protection to Free Trade – The Irish Experience', *Social Policy and Administration*, 8(2), pp. 95–115.

Wickham, A. (1984) 'Labour Training and Youth Employment: The Role of the European Social Fund', in P.J. Drudy and D. McAleese (eds), *Ireland and the European Community* (Cambridge: Cambridge University Press), pp. 215–242.

Wulf-Mathies M. (1999) Commissioner for Regional Affairs. 'Visit of the Northern Ireland Assembly', Address 4 November.

Index

Note: entries refer to Ireland unless otherwise indicated.

abortion issues 111, 112, 115, 119
abstention in referendums 54, 114
  Nice I 115–16
  Nice II 117, 118
  reasons for 119, 120
adaptation to membership 57–80
  management of EU issues 60–2
Adshead, M. 164, 217
Afghanistan 192
Afri (Action from Ireland) 115, 186, 188
Agenda 2000 75, 144–6, 163
agricultural policy 151, 153
  effect of EU 161–2
agriculture
  1973–2004 EU receipts 161
  and CAP 160–4
  exports 160–1
  and membership 25, 26, 28, 35, 36
  Northern Ireland 204
  subsidies 160, 162
  workforce 161, 162
  see also Common Agricultural Policy
Agriculture and Food, Department of 63, 67, 73, 161, 162
Ahern, Bertie 85, 116, 190, 191, 197, 198–9, 217, 243, 251
  negotiating skills 76
Ahern, Dermot 196, 237
Ahern, Nuala 87, 92
aid, development 182–3, 196, 261–2
Aiken, Frank 13, 179
ALDE (Alliance of Liberals and Democrats for Europe) 92, 94
Allen, K. 225, 234, 239
Alliance Party: Northern Ireland 205, 206, 216
Allister, Jim 204
ambassadorial effect 102–4
Amsterdam Treaty (1997) 34, 52, 88, 89
  electorate knowledge 118
  referendum 48, 106, 108, 112–14; security and defence 186, 187, 188

AnCo 37
Andrews, David 113, 190
Anglo–Irish Agreement (1985) 201, 213
Anglo–Irish Treaty (1921) 6, 9
Annan, Kofi 196
Anti-Discrimination Act (1974) (Ireland) 39
Archer, C. 244, 247
area-based partnerships 143–4
army: overseas operations 192, 193
Asia strategy 261
Attorney General's Office 63, 64, 68, 71, 73
Aylward, Liam 94

Bache, I. 2, 217
Bacik, Ivana 103
Baker, T. 46
Baltic group 247
Banking, Finance and International Services Division (BFID) 66
Bannotti, Mary 93
Barrett, Justin 111, 115
Barrington D./Report (1992) 143
Barrington, Tom 136
Barry, F. 43, 224, 225, 226, 228, 231, 233
Barysch, K. 78
BATNEEC principle 166
battlegroups 177, 193, 194
Beef Tribunal Inquiry 162
begging-bowl mentality 31
Benelux cooperation 247
Bergin, A. 157
Berlusconi, Silvio 91
Better Regulation agenda 78–9
Bew, P. 202, 203, 206
Bilateral Aid Programme 182
Binzer Hobolt, S. 120
Blair, Tony 189, 217
Boel, Mariann Fischer 131
Bonde, Jens Peter 93

Bonn Declaration 20
border controls 171, 172–3
Börzel, T. 2, 166
Bosnia 187, 191
Bradley, J. 43
Brady, H. 78
Brady, Royston 103
Braiden, Olive 102
briefing documents 72–3, 77
British–Irish Council 215, 218
British–Irish relations 197–218
    effect of EU membership 198–201
    see also United Kingdom
Broad Economic Policy Guidelines
    (BEPG) 153, 154–5
Brown, Terence 38
Brown, Tony 130
Brunt, B. 137
Bruton, John 52, 69, 90, 101
Buchanan Report (1969) 138
Budget and Economic Division 66
budget, EU *see* EU budget
Bulmer, S. 2, 56, 57, 58, 72
Burch, M. 56, 57, 58, 72
Burke, Colm 94
Burke, Richard 52, 53
Business and Employers' Confederation
    115
Byrne, David 53

Cabinet, Irish 68, 70–1
    sub-committees 70, 71
Caherty, T. 219
Callanan, M. 136, 143, 147, 149
Capoccia, G. 59
Cassells, P. 39, 40
catch-up *see* development; economic
Catholic Church 23
Catholic values 89
    EU as threat 111, 115
Cech, Z. 157
Celtic Tiger economy 31, 33, 220
    emergence of 42–8
    as model 220, 221
    reasons for 43
Chambers of Commerce of Ireland 115
Chirac, Jacques 41, 189
Christian Solidarity Party 89
Clancy, P. 226
Coakley, J. 99
coalition building 247–8
cohesion policy, EU 148, 149, 152,
    153
cold war 11–12

Cole, Roger 111, 113
Coleman, S. 239
Collier, D. 59
Collier, R.B. 59
Collins, N. 164
Commissioners 248–9
Committee on Industrial Organization
    22
Committee of the Regions 148
Committee of Secretaries 60
committee system 68–71
    and chairs 69
Common Agricultural Policy (CAP) 28,
    30, 35, 152, 257
    and Irish agriculture 160–4
    negotiations 74–5
    and Northern Ireland 207
    receipts from 138
    reforms of 163–4
common fisheries policy 25, 36–7
Common Foreign and Security Policy
    (CFSP) 88, 152, 153, 175, 195
    High Representative 187, 194
    and Ireland 33, 185–8, 196
Common Market Defence Group 26,
    110
Common Market Study Group 27, 107
Commonwealth, engagement with 10
communautaire approach 25, 62, 85
Communicating Europe initiative 131
Communications Regulation Act
    (2002) 159
community initiatives 142, 143–4,
    148–9, 150
Community Workers Co-operative 142
competition: telecoms 159–60
Competition Authority, Irish 44
competition policy 151
competitiveness 43, 45, 157, 238
ComReg 44
Concordia project 203
conflict resolution: as model 236–7,
    262
conflict resolution unit 196, 262
Connaughton, B. 164
Constitutional Treaty (2004) 52, 194–5
    and Irish presidency 40, 41, 80
    negotiations 62
    public attitudes to 127–8
    Sinn Fein attitude to 89
contribution to EU, Irish 250–2
Conway, A. 160
Coombes, D. 31, 35, 41
coordination and consultation 74–5

COPS (Political and Security Committee) 191
core executive 56, 58, 62–4, 80
  adaptation to membership 57–80
  agents 58–9
  components of 57–8
  coordination 74–5
  executive–parliamentary relations 76–9
  horizontal structures 68–72
  information pathways 73–6
  inner core and outer circle 67–8
  institutionalist perspective 56–7
  managing EU issues 60–2
  processes 72–3
  structural component 58
COREPER 71, 72
Coreu link 181, 184
Cortell, A.P. 59
Cosgrave, Liam 39
Coughlan, Anthony 47, 108–9, 110, 112, 115
Coulter, C. 239
Council of Europe 12
Council of Ministers 152
  Irish voting power 249
  rotating Presidency issue 250
County Enterprise Boards 143, 144
county managers 135–6
Cowen, Brian 48, 105, 221, 248, 249
Cox, Pat 32, 36, 52, 92, 101, 103, 258
Coyle, C. 135, 165
crisis, economic 222–4
crisis management, EU 184, 186, 190, 191
  Headline Goal 2010 193
  Irish participation 195, 196
cross-border cooperation 207, 215, 217
Crotty, Raymond 27, 47–8, 107–9, 110, 223
Crowley, Brian 92, 94
Crowley, E. 160

Daly, M. 7, 36, 162, 164
Day, Catherine 52
De Búrca, D. 87
de Gaulle, Charles 18, 21–2, 181
de Rossa, Prionsas 86, 94, 103
de Valera, Eamon 6–8, 10–11, 14, 23, 55
de Valera, Síle 50
De Villiers, Philippe 93

de-parliamentarization 62
defence
  attitudes to 126, 127
  expenditure 195–6
DEHLG 168
Delors, Jacques/packages 42, 61, 111, 139
  I 139–42
  II 142, 144–5
  task force 204
Democratic Left 99
demographic groupings
  attitudes to integration 125–6
  knowledge of EU 128–9
demographic patterns 38
Denmark 21, 28, 198, 237
  globalization level 220
Department of Enterprise, Trade and Employment 63, 64, 67, 70
Department of Environment 61, 63, 64
Department of External Affairs 179–80
Department of Finance 63, 64, 66, 67
  control of EU receipts 138–9, 141
  information sharing 74
Department of Foreign Affairs 61, 63, 70
  EU Coordination Unit 77
  and information pathways 73
  report writing 73
  role of 64–5, 67, 79
  staffing 65
Department of Justice, Equality and Law Reform 61, 63, 64, 67, 70
  information sharing 74
dependence on UK, economic 14–15, 19, 29, 31, 197, 199
  decline in 227
depression 1970s/1980s 222–4
devaluation (1993) 45
development aid 182–3, 196, 261–2
development strategy
  attracting capital 225–6, 227, 229–30, 238, 241–2
  education 225, 226–7, 239, 242
  EU and US influences 234–6
  industrial policy 225–6, 229–30
  investing in education 225, 226–7
  labour market 230–1, 242
  partnership model 228–9
  and single market 231–2, 241
  and structural funds 233
  and taxation 229–30, 232, 242
Devine, K.M. 178
d'Hondt system 211

Dimas, Stavros 168
Dinan, D. 91, 92
Disability Alliance 116
dissolution question 122
Doherty, R. 187
Dooge, Jim 34
Dornbusch, R. 223
Dorr, N. 179
Downing Street Declaration (1993) 213
Doyle, Avril 94, 103
Doyle, Maurice 46
Drudy, P.J. 31, 35, 36
dumping 25, 26
    agriculture 163
Dunleavy, P. 58
DUP: Northern Ireland 204–5, 207, 216

ECOFIN 66
economic dependence on UK 14–15, 19, 29, 31, 197, 199
    decline in 227
economic development 156–7
    catch-up 224–36
    export-led growth 225
    failure 222–4
    and membership 35
    as model 220, 221
    Nordic states' routes 237–8
    societal costs 239–40
    success 42–3, 219–20
Economic Development (Whitaker) 15, 17
economic issues: attitudes to 126
economic policy, EU 153
economic policy, Irish 13–14
    impact of EU on 154–5
    paradigm shift 8, 15, 17, 19, 22
    path to liberalization 14–16
Economic and Social Committee: Irish Border Areas 207
economy
    1970s/1980s performance 222–3
    benefits from membership 43
    governance 154–5
    growth of 42–3, 219–20
    pre-membership 3–4, 219
    and US recession 157
    see also economic development
education 151, 242
    higher 226–7
    impact of EU membership 255
    investment in 225, 226–7
    and labour force skills 43

EFTA 16
Eircom 159–60
elections
    1918 8
    EP and Dáil elections compared 100
    impact of EU on national 83–4
    party share of vote 98
    turnout 95, 96–7, 102
    voting behaviour in EP and national 101
    women candidates 104
    see also EP elections; referendums
Emergency *see* Second World War
emigration 7, 223, 261
Employment Equality Agency 44
employment inequality 38–9
    legislation 39–41
EMS (European Monetary System) 44–5, 200
EMU (Economic and Monetary Union) 33
    impact on Irish economy 154–5, 156–60
    and Irish economic governance 44–5
    reasons for joining 45–6
English language and growth 225
English, R. 8
enlargement
    1970 negotiations 25
    attitudes to 127–8
Enterprise Ireland 238
environment
    EU influences on policy 164–70
    EU policy 68
    impact of NDPs 141
    lobby groups 258
    policy 67–8, 151, 153
environmental legislation, EU 147
    Irish compliance problems 166–8, 169–70
    number of Irish infringements 167, 168
Environmental Protection Agency 44, 165–6, 259
EP elections 258–9
    1979–2004 results by party 99
    ambassadorial effect 102–4
    candidate selection 102–4
    and Dáil elections compared 100
    independent MEPs 101
    and national issues 93, 104
    Northern Ireland 204, 205
    party share of vote 98

EP elections – *continued*
  as second-order elections 4, 81–2, 95–104
  simultaneous contests 96–7
  small party gains 95, 98, 100, 102
  turnout 95, 96–7, 102
episodic change 59
EPP (Christian Democrat European People's Party) 90
EPP–ED (Christian Democrat European People's Party-European Democrats) 90, 91, 92, 94
equality legislation 39–41
  equal pay 39
EU27
  GDP per capita 246
  population 245
  states by area 246
EU budget
  Ireland as net beneficiary 25, 49
  Ireland as net contributor 55, 146, 147
  transfers to Ireland 138–44
EU Scrutiny Act (2002) 77
EU Scrutiny sub-committee 77, 78
  proposals/documents received 79
EUFOR missions 191, 192, 193
EUL/NGL (European United Left/Nordic Green Left) 92–3, 94
Eur-lex 37
euro 154, 156–7
  attitudes to 127
  joining 200
  see also EMU
Eurobarometer surveys 128–9
  attitudes to issues 126–8
  on EU defence policy 188
  EU-25 benefits from membership 122, 123, 124
  identity 255
  Irish support for integration 121–8
  knowledge of EU 47, 54, 106, 128–9
Europe of the Regions 133
European Commission 152
European Communities Committee 61–2
European Court of Human Rights 12
European Court of Justice 152, 258
  and environmental infringements 167
European Defence Agency 195
European Democratic Alliance 91
European Movement 115

European Parliament 249–50
  2004–09 Irish MEPs 94
  and Northern Ireland conflict 209–10
  see also EP elections
European Political Cooperation 41, 42, 175, 180–1
  and Irish presidency 181–2
European Rapid Reaction Force 88, 177, 189, 191, 193
European Regional Development Fund 37, 138, 148
  cross-border cooperation 207, 208–9
European Security and Defence Policy (ESDP) 190–1
European Social Fund 37–8
  engagement with 262–3
  and vocational training 226
European Union
  as arena 258–9
  as framework 257–8
  Ireland's contribution 52, 53, 250–2
  as policy 259
  as polity 259–60
  see also membership
Europeanization 1–2, 256, 262
  definitions 2–3
  institutional adaptation 56–7
  level of 253–6
  as structural change 2–3
Euroscepticism 87–90
  hard and soft 87
  in member states 84, 89–90
  Northern Ireland 206
exchange rates 43, 44
executive–parliamentary relations 76–9
export-led growth 225, 227
exports 227
  changing pattern of 199
  to UK 14–15, 19

Fahey, E. 78
Fahey, T. 225, 239, 241
Falklands crisis and neutrality 183
Falkner, G. 49, 166
Fanning, R. 10
farmers
  advocates of membership 22
  environmental complaints against 169
  incomes 36, 257
  voting at referendums 118
farming lobby 161, 164, 169, 170

Farrell, B. 23
Featherstone, K. 1, 3, 56
Federated Union of Employers 39
Ferriter, D. 39
Fianna Fáil 7, 25, 26
 1932 government 10
 candidate selection 103
 election results 98, 99, 100–1
 and EP party group 90, 91, 92
 opposition to EU 49–50
 support for EU 82, 85, 107
Fianna Fáil–Progressive Democrat
  government 50
finance from Brussels 138–44
Fine Gael 25, 26
 candidate selection 103, 104
 election results 98, 99, 100, 101
 and EPP–ED 90–1
 support for EU 82, 84–5, 107
Fingleton, J. 159
Finland 237
Finlay, F. 142
fiscal policy 46
fishing industry 25, 36
 discriminatory regulation 37
Fisk, R. 11
FitzGerald, Garret 30, 52, 85, 90, 183,
  201, 251
 on economy 42, 43, 44, 230–1
 on EMU 45, 46
 on interdependence 29
FitzGerald, J. 157
Fitzgerald, M. 20, 21
Fitzgibbon, J. 87, 88
Flinter, D. 227, 228, 232, 235
Flynn, B. 165, 166–7, 169, 170
Flynn, Padraig 53
Food Safety Authority 44
foreign direct investment 225–6, 227
 competition for 238
 incentives 16
 increase in 43
 and tax regime 229–30
 US 232, 234, 235
foreign policy 175–96
 and CFSP 185
 and EPC 183–4
 future 195–6
 impact of EU 176–7
 multilateral tradition 9–10
 post-Cold War 184–9
 postwar 12–13
Forfás 238
Forza Europa 91

Foster, R. 7, 221, 234, 239, 254
Framework Document (1995) 213
Frampton, M. 89, 206
Franklin, M. 95, 120, 122
free movement of persons 170–4
Friedman, Thomas 219

Gabel, M. 122, 126
Gallagher, M. 58, 99, 107, 109, 113
Ganley, Declan 110
Garland, Roger 165
Garry, J. 106, 121
Garvin, T. 14, 200, 223, 224
GATT 17, 18
GDP
 EU27 by state 246
 growth 156, 225
gender
 and attitudes to membership 125,
  126
 inequality 38–9, 255
 and knowledge of EU 128
 and voting behaviour 118
Genschel, P. 57
Geoghegan Quinn, Maire 32, 69
geographical location
 impact of 247
 and strategic relationships 247–8
Gilland, K. 50, 84, 87, 89, 113, 116,
  118
Gillis, Alan 103
globalization 224, 234, 235, 256, 258,
  261
 and Europeanization 3
Globalization Index 220
GNP 42–3
Good Friday Agreement (1998) 196,
  198, 204, 211, 213–17
 as conflict-management model 222,
  242
 power-sharing 236, 237
 strand one 213–14
 strand two 214–15
 strand three 215–16
Gormley, J. 88, 167, 176, 186, 188
government
 central–local relations 138, 139,
  149, 150
 impact of EU 260–1
 local 134–8
 multi-level 132–4
 regional 137–8
Graziano, P. 1, 3
Greece 166

Green Party 47, 48, 190
  anti-Nice campaign 115, 116
  attitude to EU 49, 82, 87–8, 90
  election results 99, 100, 101
  EU party alliance 92
  women candidates 104
Green/EFA (Greens/European Free
    Alliance) 92, 94
Greenpeace 165
Guerin, Orla 102, 103

Haagerup, N.J./Report 209–10
Hague Summit (1969) 18, 23, 24
Hain, Peter 237
Hainsworth, P. 202
Handoll, J. 173
Hannan, A. 43
Harkin, Marian 92, 94, 101, 103
Harmsen, R. 57
Harney, M. 86, 113, 234
Hart, J. 35, 37, 38
Haughey, Charles 52, 61–2, 69, 85,
    101, 140, 183, 228
  and German unification 251
Hayes, Maurice 130
Hayward, K. 54, 115, 116, 117, 146
Headline Goal 2010 193
health policy 151
Health and Safety Authority 44, 259
Helsinki summit 190–1
Héritier, A. 2, 152
Higgins, Jim 94
Hillery, Patrick 6, 31, 34, 40, 52, 180,
    182
historical institutionalism 57, 58–9
Hix, S. 83, 95, 126, 152
Holmes, M. 82, 88, 99, 118, 183, 184
Honohan, P. 43, 45–6, 157, 238
Hooghe, L. 132–3
House, J.D. 228, 229
housing market 157
Hume, John 139, 204, 205–6, 211
Humphreys, P. 40
Hussey, G. 31, 32, 47

ICEM (Irish Council of the European
    Movement) 26, 27
identity
  impact of EU 255
  and neutrality 12, 178, 180
Ikenberry, G.J. 59
immigration 222, 240–1, 256, 261
  returning migrants 225, 227, 230

spatial location 240
statistics 240
Independence/Democracy EU group
    93, 94
Industrial Development Agency (IDA)
    137, 232
industrial policy 225, 229–30
industry, indigenous 16, 222, 225, 227
inequality, social 239–40
  gender 38–9
inflation 45, 157
information pathways 73–6
infrastructure, domestic 42
Ingebritsen, C. 179, 244
Inglis, T. 221, 223, 241, 254, 256
institutional development
  critical junctures 59
  episodic and incremental 59
  path-dependence 59
institutionalist perspective 2
  new institutionalism 3
integration
  EU policy 151–2
  Irish support for 121–8; by
    demographic grouping 125–6
Interdepartmental Coordinating
    Committee on EU Affairs 69,
    70
interdependence, route to 29, 199
interest rates and EMU 46
Intergovernmental Conferences
    249–50, 251, 252
internationalism, post-war 11
INTERREG initiative 208–9
investment, inward 43, 227, 229–30,
    238
  attracting 16, 225–6
  from US 232, 234, 235
Irish Alliance for Europe 116
Irish Bishops' Conference 115
Irish Congress of Trade Unions 27,
    107, 109, 115, 116
Irish Creamery and Milk Suppliers
    Association (ICMSA) 164
Irish Farmers Association 115, 116,
    164
  election candidate 103
Irish Free State 8, 9
Irish Regions Office 148
Irish Sovereignty Movement 47
Ishizuka, K. 190
Israel 182
Italy and EU party groupings 91

Joint Oireachtas Committee 77
Jordan, A. 2
Justice and Home Affairs, EU 153–4
  emergency brake 174
  and Ireland 170–4
  and Ireland–UK relationship 248
  opt-outs 172–3, 174
  reforms to 171–2

Kassim, H. 57, 61, 62, 74
Kearney, A.T./globalization index 220
Kearney, B. 36
Kearney, R. 202
Keatinge, P. 11, 179, 187, 189, 198
  on EP elections 97
  on EPC 41
  Europeanization 2
  on foreign policy 64, 175, 176, 178,
    180, 182, 183, 188
  on Presidencies 85
Keleman, R.D. 59
Kennedy, F. 106, 126
Kennedy, L. 10, 199, 209, 210
Kennedy, M. 12
Kenny, L. 137
Keogan, J.F. 136
Keogh, D. 7, 26
Kettle, Thomas 199
KFOR 192, 193
Kirby, P. 225, 239
Kitt, 69
Klemenčič, M. 247, 248
Knill, C. 57
knowledge of EU, public 128–30
  improvement in 129
  and social class 125, 126, 128, 129
Kohl, Helmut 251
Kosovo 187, 189, 192

labour market 43, 230–1, 232, 242
  flexibility 222
  and immigrants 240
Labour party 26, 27, 86
  attitude to EU 82, 84, 86, 107
  candidate selection 103, 104
  election results 99, 100
  and PES 90, 91
Ladrech, R. 2, 83
Laffan, M. 9
Lane, Paddy 103
Laver, M. 58, 164
LEADER programme 143, 149
League of Nations 9, 10, 176, 178, 243

Leddin, A.J. 157, 238
Lee, J.J. 7, 14, 31, 35, 223–4
Lemass, Sean 6–7, 17, 54, 60,
    179–80, 257
  economic policy shift 15–16
  membership application 19, 21,
    22–3
Lenihan, Mary 111
Libertas 110
Lisbon Treaty (2007) 78, 108
  agenda 64, 153, 155–6
  attitudes to 127–8
  and Green Party 88
  JHA chapter 248
  security matters 194–5
local development 143–4, 146
  area-based partnerships 143–4
  enterprise development 143,
    144
local government 134–8
  2001 reorganisation 134, 135
  county managers 135–6
  EU regulation 147
  finance 136–7
  functions of 134–5
Local Government Acts 136, 137
  2001 Act 134, 135, 136
Loftus, Sean 103
Lomé Convention (1975) 183, 251
Loyal, S. 240, 241
Ludlow, P. 40–1
Luxembourg Process 155
Lynch, Jack 6, 8, 34, 101, 180, 199,
    262

Maastricht Treaty (1992) 33, 34, 171
  convergence criteria 155, 156
  electorate knowledge of 118
  media coverage 112
  referendum 108, 109–12
  structural funds 142
Magnette, P. 250
Maher, D. 8, 18, 20, 21, 26
Maher, T.J. 103
Mair, P. 58, 83, 87, 89, 151
Maitre, B. 239
Makenci, Patricia 111
Mallon, Seamus 213
Malone, Bernie 102, 103
management of EU affairs 60–2, 252–3
Mansergh, L. 113
market liberalization 157–60
market-building policies, EU 152, 153

market-correcting policies, EU 152, 153
Marks, G. 132–3
Marsh, M. 81, 85, 86, 95, 96, 97, 100, 101, 102, 120, 121
Marshall Aid 12
Massey, P. 159
Matthews, A. 31, 35, 163
MacCoille, C. 156
MacGinty, R. 178, 186, 188
MacKernan, Padraic 175
Macmillan, Harold 20
MacSharry, Ray 53, 163, 231
McAleese, D. 31, 32, 35, 36, 199
McCabe, I. 11
McCoy, D. 156, 157
McCreevy, Charlie 50, 53, 155
McCutcheon, P. 47, 48, 109
McDaid, Jim 103
McDonald, M.-L. 89, 92, 94
McDowell, Michael 86, 255
McGowan, L. 1, 151, 165, 166
McGrath, K. 228, 229
McGuinness, Mairead 94, 103
McGuinness, Martin 216, 237
McKenna, Patricia 48, 87, 88, 92, 112, 188
McLaren, L. 126
media coverage
    National Forum 131
    referendums 112–13, 115, 117, 118, 119
Meehan, E. 202, 203, 206
membership of EU, Irish
    1973–86 period 32–3, 35–42
    1987–97 period 32, 33, 42–8
    1998–present 32, 48–54
    application for 16, 19–22
    attitudes by demographic groupings 125–6
    and British membership 26–7
    challenges to consensus on 47, 49–52
    criticisms 110–11
    Eurobarometer surveys 121–8
    Europeans in Ireland 261
    impact of 30, 31, 254–6
    Irish concerns 25–6
    and Irish identity 199–200
    Irish impact on EU 254
    key dates 17–18, 34
    legitimizing 26–7
    motivation for 13, 14–17
    and nationalism 200, 260–1

negotiating 23–6
obligations and choice 262
as opportunity 262–3
preparing for 22–3
public perception of benefit 122, 123
referendum on 34
reservations 20–1
significance of 256–62
as small state 244–53
utilitarian perspective 122, 126
White Papers 23–5, 26, 35
MEPs 94
    number of 96
Middle East 182, 192
Milan European Council 201
Millan, Bruce 141
Mitchell, Gay 69, 93, 94
Mitterrand, François 251
model, Ireland as 219, 220, 221
    catch-up 224–36
    conflict resolution 236–7
    as failure 222–4
    reasons for 221–2
modernization 200, 244, 257
    and membership 3–4, 14–15, 28
monetary policy 45, 46, 151
    and EMU 154
Moss, B. 33, 156
Moxon-Browne, E. 81, 98, 101, 103
Mullally, G. 165, 169
multi-level governance 132–4
Murphy, A. 230, 232
Murphy, C. 164
Murphy, G. 15, 22, 164
Murphy, M. 1, 151

National Development Plans 139–42, 145–6, 148
    1999–2006 period 145
    environmental impact 141
    local development 143–4
    NDP II 142–4, 148
    sectoral approach 140, 142, 149
National Forum on Europe 53, 80, 85, 106, 116, 130–1
    impact of 131
    public awareness of 130
National Platform for Employment, Democracy and Neutrality 110–11, 116
National Spatial Strategy (NSS) 145–6, 149
nationalism 8, 200, 260–1

NATO (North Atlantic Treaty
    Organization) 24, 178, 180,
    181, 184, 186
  and Irish EU membership 21
  Partnership for Peace 89, 113, 177,
    179, 189–90, 192; mission
    areas 188
  postwar 11–12
negotiations: Irish policy on 76, 251–3,
    260
neo-liberalism 234, 254
NESC 43, 239
  report 219
  Strategy for Development 224,
    227–8
neutrality 10, 42, 85, 119, 175–6
  and anti-Nice campaign 115
  defining identity 12, 178, 180
  and EPC 181
  EU as threat 206
  and Falklands crisis 183
  and membership 21, 47, 110
  and Second World War 11
  Seville European Council 116
Nice Treaty I referendum 5, 32, 33, 35
  aftermath 53–4, 57, 79–80, 85, 105
  as critical juncture 60, 62, 76
  electorate knowledge 50–1, 80, 114
  EU reaction 51
  and parliamentary scrutiny 72, 77
  results 49, 50–1, 108, 117
  turnout 113, 114, 115–16
  voting behaviour 118, 119
Nice Treaty II referendum 32, 34, 85,
    106
  campaign 116–18
  electorate knowledge 117–18
  results 54, 108, 117
  turnout 117–18
  voting behaviour 120
Nicholson, Jim 204
Nicolaidis, K. 250
Nitrates Directive (EU) 169–70
No to Nice group 111, 115, 116
Nolan, B. 239
Noonan, Joe 111
Nordic battle group 177, 194, 248
Nordic cooperation 247
Norman, P. 250
North–South Ministerial Council 214
Northern Ireland
  assembly elections results 216
  EU involvement 202–12
  EU as model 210–11

EU officials in 211–12
EU policies/reports 207–10
EU as political arena 203–7
Objective One status 208
outbreak of conflict 197, 198
party attitudes to EU 205
peace funds 212
Political Affairs Committee report
    209–10
results of EP elections 204, 205
role of EU in 207–10
Single Programming Document 208,
    212
underrepresentation in EU 203–4
Northern Ireland Centre 203
Northern Ireland conflict 5, 28
  and conflict-resolution unit 196
  effect of EU membership 201–2
  managing 201–2
  US involvement 201
Northern Ireland Partnership Board
    212
Norway 21, 198
Nugent, N. 244, 247
NUTS II regions 145, 149

Ó Cinneide, S. 38
Ó Cuiv, Eamon 50
O Loinsigh, Micheal 27
Ó Neachtain, Sean 93, 94, 103
Objective One status 141, 144–5
  Northern Ireland 208
  NUTS II regions 145, 149
O'Brennan, J. 106, 114, 131
O'Cleireacain, S. 202
O'Dea, Willie 50, 193–4
O'Donnell, R. 31, 33, 43, 44, 45, 156,
    202, 224, 227, 228–9
OECD report 223
  on education 226
OEEC 12, 17, 243
officials 75–6
  training for 75
O'Halpin, E. 77, 178, 190
O'Hanlon, Roderick 115
O'Hearn, D. 223, 224, 239
oil crises 31, 241
Oireachtas 176
  and core executive 76–9
  impact of EU 255
O'Kennedy, Michael 53
Olsen, J. 132
O'Malley, Desmond 103

Open Method of Coordination 156
opposition to membership 47, 49–52
O'Riain, S. 225, 235
O'Rourke, Mary 159
O'Sullivan, David 52
O'Sullivan, S. 221, 254
O'Toole, F. 19, 221, 223, 239, 257

Paisley, Ian 204, 216, 237
parliamentary scrutiny 72, 77, 116
partition 9
partnership model 228–9, 235
  and local governance 143–4, 148,
    149
Partnership for Peace 89, 113, 177,
    179, 188, 189–90, 192
  mission areas 188
path dependency 59
Patten, Chris 41, 76
Payne, D. 215
Peace and Neutrality Alliance 113,
    115, 116, 176
  and EU security issues 186, 188, 190
Peace and Reconciliation fund 204,
    210, 212
peacekeeping activities 179, 185, 187,
    192
  ESCP 191
  opposition to 188, 191
Peers, S. 173
Permanent Representation 59, 65,
    71–2
  local 147–8
  ministries represented 71
  staffing 40, 71
Persson, Goran 51
PES (Party of European Socialists) 90,
    91, 92, 94
Petersburg tasks 185, 186, 187, 195
Peterson, S. 59
Pierson, P. 57, 59
Poland and UEN 91
policies, EU 151–4
  typology 153
policy 2
  domestic; and EU obligations 5
policy, Irish
  paradigm shift 8, 15, 17, 19, 22
policy-making
  impact of EU policy 151, 259
  partnership model 228–9
  selective centralization 74–5
Political Affairs Committee report
    209–10

political impact of membership 41–2
political parties
  attitudes to EU 82, 83–90
  and EP party groupings 90–4
  and referendum voting 118
  and transnational EP groupings
    90–4
political union: attitudes to 126–7
politics, territorial 2
  impact of EU 132, 133–4
  local government 134–7
  regional government 137–8
polity 2, 259–60
polity-building, EU 152, 153
pollution control 165–6
population
  1950s decline 7
  changing patterns 38
  EU27 by state 245
Powell, Enoch 207
PR-STV 96
Presidencies of Council 30, 34, 250–1,
    258
  and adjustment to membership 61
  rotating 250
  success of 40–1, 42, 62, 80
Prodi, Romano 51
Progressive Democrats
  ALDE affiliation 92
  attitude to EU 86–7
  candidate selection 103
  election results 99, 100, 101
protectionism, abandonment of 13, 15
public opinion
  before Nice I 105
  and EU knowledge 106
  see also Eurobarometer

qualified majority voting 253
Quinlivan, A. 81, 97, 103, 104

R&D 233, 238
Radaelli, C. 2, 56
rapid reaction force, EU 88, 177, 189,
    191, 193
REACH Committee 70
Rees, N. 62, 188, 194, 195, 196
Referendum Acts (1994, 1998) 48
Referendum Commission 48, 112, 113,
    117
referendums 4–5, 107–21
  altering Constitution 24, 26, 27, 107
  changing conduct of 112–14

and Crotty injunction 47–8
dissenting voices 110–11
electorate knowledge 50–3, 80, 113,
    116
Euro-critical groups 110–11
funding 112–13
reasons for No votes 118–19
results 114
second-order effects 121
turnout 107, 108, 109, 113, 115–16
voting behaviour 118–21
Yes voting characteristics 119–20
Regional Assemblies 145, 148
regional development 142–3
Regional Development Organizations
    138
regional government 137–8
Regional Partnership (East Central
    Europe/Asia) 247
regional policy, EU 32
Regional Review Committees 141,
    142, 148
regionalism 133, 217
regionalization 217
regulatory impact assessments 78–9
regulatory regime, Irish 43, 44, 259
Reif, R. 81, 82
Reinhardt, N. 205
reporting on negotiations 73
Reynolds, Albert 44, 111, 185
Rhodes, R.A.W. 58
Risse, T. 2
Roche, D. 69, 91, 245, 250
RTE referendum coverage 112
Ruane, J. 202
Rural Environmental Protection
    Scheme 163
Ryan Air 221, 256
Ryan, Eoin 94, 103

Sabel, C.F. 144
Saint Malo summit 189
Salmon, T.C. 11, 178
Sargent, T. 88, 165, 188
Sbragia, A.M. 152
Scallon, Dana Rosemary 101,
    103, 111
Schengen area 67, 154, 171, 172–3,
    174
    and UK opt-out 201, 248
Schmitt, H. 81, 82, 93, 95
Schön-Quinlivan, E. 81, 97, 103, 104
Scotland 203, 204, 215, 218
Scott, D. 32, 44

Scott, R.W. 59
SDLP: Northern Ireland 204–5, 206,
    213, 214, 216
Sea Fisheries regulation 37
Second World War 11, 243
security issues: attitudes to 47, 126,
    127
Senior Officials Group 69,
    70, 71
SEUPB (Special EU Programmes Body)
    214, 215
Seville European Council 116,
    191
SFI (Science Foundation Ireland) 238
Sheehy, S.J. 35, 36
Single European Act (1986) 31, 33, 34,
    47
    ratification injunction 47–8, 107
    referendum 108, 109
Single Programming Document 208,
    212
Sinn Féin 8, 88–9, 190
    anti-Nice campaign 115, 116
    attitude to EU 49, 82, 87, 90
    election results 99, 100, 101
    and EUL/NGL 92–3
    Northern Ireland 204–5, 206, 216
    SEA referendum campaign 109
Sinnott, Kathy 93, 101, 103
Sinnott, R. 84, 107, 109, 126, 135
    abstentions 116
    on candidates 102, 104
    Nice referendums 50, 51, 117–18,
        119–20, 121, 122
    public knowledge of EU 47, 128–9
    public support for EU 106
    results of referendums 114
Skelly, J.M. 12
small states
    representation and voice 248–50,
        260
    strategic relationships 244–8, 249
Smith, M. 58, 202
Smith, N.J. 225
social agenda 30
social class and EU knowledge 125,
    126, 128, 129
social impact of membership 37–41,
    254, 255–6
social partnership 221, 228–9, 235
Socialist Party 89
Socialist Workers' Party 89
Solbes, Pedro 50
Somalia 187

sovereignty 154–5
  concerns 110, 119, 206
  Green Party concerns 88
  Irish Free State 9
  and membership 24, 25, 30, 31, 244
  and neutrality 11
  Sinn Fein on 89
Spain 166
sponger syndrome 31
Spring, Dick 102, 188
Stabenau, Wolfgang 38
Stability and Growth Pact 153, 154–5
staffing in permanent representation 40
Steinmo, S. 58
strategic relationships 247–8
  Ireland–UK 248
  small states 244–8, 249
structural funds 208
  1988 reform 31
  impact on Irish economy 43
  Irish management of 139–44, 233, 253, 259
  and Irish regulatory regime 44
Sutherland, Peter 53
Svensson, P. 120, 121
Sweden 237
Szczerbiak, A. 83, 87

Taggart, P. 83, 84, 87, 89
Taoiseach Department 58, 60
  role in management 61, 66–7, 79
taxation 242
  and FDI 229–30, 232
  negotiations 253
  policy 229–30
Taylor, G. 164, 165, 166, 170
Taylor, John 204
TDs
  as local councillors 137
  women 104
Teague, P. 202
telecoms liberalization 158–60
Thelen, K. 58
Thorhallsson, B. 244
Tindemans Report (1975) 259
Todd, J. 202
Tonra, B. 51, 54, 176, 177, 180, 184, 185, 187, 188, 195
Tovey, H. 144
trade
  changes in composition 227
  impact of membership 35
  with UK 14–15, 19

Trade Agreement, Anglo-Irish 17, 18, 23
trade unions 228, 229
  and equality legislation 38–9
  ICTU 27, 107, 109, 115, 116
training for officials 75
Traistaru-Siedschlag, I. 156, 157
Treaty of Accession
  final negotiations 18
  signing ceremony 6
Treaty on European Union see Maastricht
'triple-lock mechanism' 177, 191, 193, 194, 196
Trojan, Carlo 211
turnout
  in EP elections 95, 96–7; and general 97
  referendums 107, 108, 109; Nice I 113, 114, 115–16; Nice II 117–18

UEN (Union for Europe of the Nations) 91–2, 94
UK Independence Party 93
United Kingdom
  devolved interests 204, 214, 215–16, 217
  and environment 166
  EU membership 19–20, 21–2, 26–7; application 21–2, 197–8; experience 200–1
  Irish access to market 14–15
  Schengen opt-out 172, 173
  see also British–Irish relations
United Nations 186, 244
  Irish membership 12, 13, 176
  in Lebanon 182
  peacekeeping activities 187–8
United States 189
  NATO and Ireland 11–12
  recession 157
  role in Ireland 258
  and WEU 186
urbanization 38
utilitarian perspective on membership 122, 126
UUP: Northern Ireland 204–5, 206–7, 214, 216

van der Eijk, C. 95, 120
Venice Declaration (1980) 182
veto 85

Vink, M.P. 1, 3
Visegrád cooperation 247
vocational training 37–8, 226
    gender equality 40
voting behaviour 118–21
    and gender 118

wage bargaining 43
wage growth 156
wage restraint 228
Wales 203, 204, 215, 218
Walsh, B. 43, 45
war of independence (1919–21) 9
waste disposal: environmental
        infringements 168–9
Weeks, L. 87
welfare system 240
Wessels, W. 59

WEU (Western European Union) 184,
        185, 189
    observer status 186
Whitaker, Ken 14–15, 17
White, P.A. 231
White Papers 23–5, 26, 35
    D for Democracy 131
    foreign policy 188–9, 200
    Irish aid 196
    local government 136
women 258
    election candidates 104
    and employment legislation 39–41
    rights 30, 38–9
Workers' Party 89, 99,
        100, 107
    SEA referendum campaign 109

Wulf-Mathies, M. 212

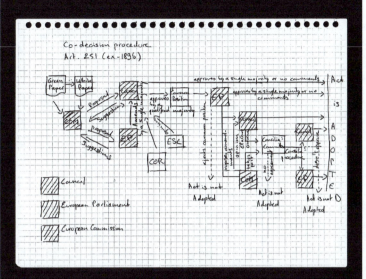